Quick Revision

MIND MAPS *for*

CBSE

Class 12

(Physics, Chemistry, Mathematics & English Core)

• **Corporate Office :** 45, 2nd Floor, Maharishi Dayanand Marg, Corner Market,
Malviya Nagar, New Delhi-110017
Tel. : 011-49842349 / 49842350

DISHA PUBLICATION

For further information about the books from DISHA,
Log on to **www.dishapublication.com** or email to **info@dishapublication.com**

INDEX

Chapterwise Mind Maps Physics (P-1-32)

Chapterwise Mind Maps Chemistry (C-1-32)

Chapterwise Mind Maps Mathematics (M-1-28)

Chapterwise Mind Maps & RTCs English (E-1-68)

FLAMINGO: PROSE (E-2-25)

FLAMINGO: POETRY (E-26-E-43)

VISTAS (E-44-E-68)

CHAPTERWISE
MIND MAPS
PHYSICS

Mind

Surface charge density, $\sigma = \dfrac{\text{charge}}{\text{area}}$

Linear charge density, $\lambda = \dfrac{\text{charge}}{\text{length}}$

Volume charge density, $\rho = \dfrac{\text{charge}}{\text{volume}}$

Distribution of charge

Two similar charged bodies always repel but a charged body may attract a neutral or an oppositely charged body.

Charge density for irregular surface is maximum where radius of curvature is minimum and vice-versa

i.e., $\sigma \propto \dfrac{1}{R}$

Charge-Due to which matter produces and experiences electric and magnetic effects.

Coulomb's Law

$$F = \dfrac{1}{4\pi\epsilon_0}\dfrac{q_1 q_2}{r^2}$$

$$\dfrac{1}{4\pi\epsilon_0} = 9\times 10^9\ Nm^2C^{-2}$$

$\epsilon_0 =$ absolute permittivity of air or free space

$$\epsilon_0 = 8.85\times 10^{-12}\ \dfrac{C^2}{Nm^2}$$

Discrete distribution of change
A system consisting of ultimate individual charges.

Principle of Superposition
If $q_1,\ q_2,\ .....\ q_n$ charges applying force on a charge Q, then $\vec{F}_{net} = \vec{F}_1 + \vec{F}_2 ..... + \vec{F}_n$

$$= K\sum_{i=1}^{n}\dfrac{qq_i}{r_i^2}\hat{r}_i$$

Magnitude of resultant of two electric forces F_1 and F_2 $F_{net} =$

$$\sqrt{F_1^2 + F_2^2 + 2F_1 F_2 \cos\theta}$$

$$\tan\alpha = \dfrac{F_2 \sin\theta}{F_1 + F_2 \cos\theta}$$

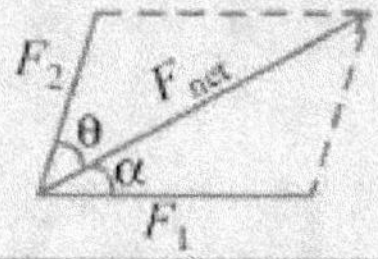

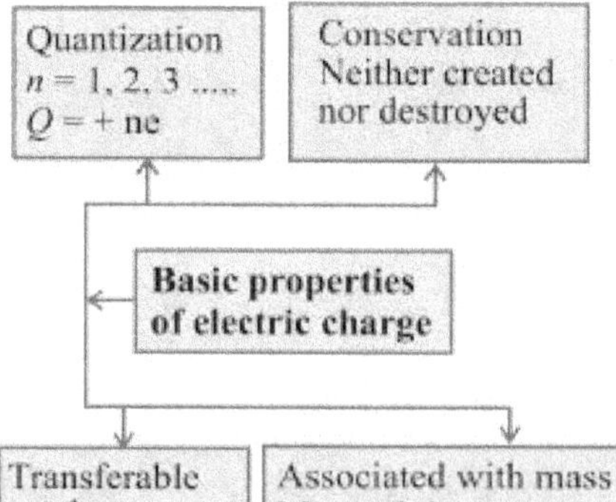

Positive charge
Deficiency of electrons

Negative charge
Excess of electrons
Charge of one electron
$= 1.6\times 10^{-19}\ C$

Neutral No of electrons-no of protons Atoms are electrically neutral

Types of charge

ELECTRIC CHARGES AND FIELDS

When a dielectric medium (K) is completely filled in between charges, then force between them

$$F_{medium} = \dfrac{1}{4\pi\epsilon_0}\dfrac{1}{K}\dfrac{q_1 q_2}{r^2}$$

When a dielectric medium (K) thickness 't' is partially filled between the charges, then force between them

$$F' = \dfrac{1}{4\times\epsilon_0}\dfrac{q_1 q_2}{(r - t + t\sqrt{k})^2}$$

By friction or rubbing
In this method, both +(ve) and –(ve) charges in equal amounts appear simultaneously due to transfer of electrons from one body to the other.

By induction
Induced charge ≤ inducing charge (Q) i.e.,

$$Q' = -Q\left(1 - \dfrac{1}{K}\right)$$

$K =$ dielectric constant or relative permittivity (ϵ_r)

By conduction
Two conductors one is charged and another is uncharged when bring in contact with each other, the conductors will be charged with the same sign.

Methods of charging

Quantization
$n = 1, 2, 3 .....$
$Q = + ne$

Conservation
Neither created nor destroyed

Basic properties of electric charge

Transferable can be transferred from one body to another.

Associated with mass
Mass of electron
$M_e = 9.1\times 10^{-31}\ kg$

Equilibrium of Charged Soap Bubble

For a charged soap bubble of radius R and surface tension T and charge density σ. The pressure due to surface tension $4\dfrac{T}{R}$ and atmospheric pressure P_{out} acts radially inwards and the electrical pressure (P_{el}) acts radially outwards.

The total pressure inside the soap bubble

$$P_{in} = P_{out} + \dfrac{4T}{R} - \dfrac{\sigma^2}{2\epsilon_0}$$

Map-1

Due to descrete distribution of charge
$$\vec{E} = \sum_{i=1}^{n} \vec{E}_i$$

Dipole Two equal and opposite charges separated by a small distance. Dipole moment,
$$\vec{P} = (q \times 2\vec{l})$$

Electric field due to a dipole,

At axial position
$$E = \frac{1}{4\pi\epsilon_0} \frac{2P}{r^3} \hat{r}$$
At equatorial position
$$E = \frac{1}{4\pi\epsilon_0} \frac{-p}{r^3} \hat{r}$$

Electric field Space surrounding a charge in which its electrostatic force can be experienced by any test charge
$$\vec{E} = \frac{\vec{F}}{q} = \frac{1}{4\pi\epsilon_0} \frac{q}{r^2} \hat{r}$$

Torque and potential energy of a dipole

Potential energy
$$U = PE \cos\theta$$
$$U = -\vec{P}.\vec{E}$$

Torque
$$\tau = PE \sin\theta$$
$$\tau = P \times E$$

Electric field due to

(i) Point charge, $E = \dfrac{KQ}{r^2}$

(ii) Line charge
  (a) if point where to find $\vec{E}$ at perpendicular bisector of wire then,
  $$E_x = \frac{2K\lambda}{r} \sin \times \text{ and } E_y = 0$$
  (b) If wire is infinitely long
  $$E_x = \frac{2K\lambda}{r} \text{ and } E_y = 0$$
  (c) If point lies near one end of infinitely long wire $|E_x| = |E_y| = \dfrac{k\lambda}{r}$
  $$E_{net} = \frac{\sqrt{2}K\lambda}{r}$$

(iii) Changed circular ring
$$E = \frac{kQx}{(x^2 + R^2)^{3/2}}, \quad V = \frac{kQ}{\sqrt{x^2 + R^2}}$$
At centre $x = 0$ so $E_{centre} = 0$ and
$$V_{centre} = \frac{kQ}{R}$$
At a point on the axis such that $x >> R$
$$E = \frac{kQ}{x^2}, \quad V = \frac{kQ}{x}$$
If $x = \pm\dfrac{R}{\sqrt{2}}$, $E_{max} = \dfrac{Q}{6\sqrt{3}\pi\varepsilon_0 R^2}$
and $V_{max} = \dfrac{Q}{2\sqrt{6}\pi\varepsilon_0 R}$

Superposition of electric field
Resultant of electric field, due to various charges
$$\vec{E} = \vec{E}_1 + \vec{E}_2 ..... + \vec{E}_n$$

Due to continuous distribution of charge
$$\vec{E} = \frac{1}{4\pi\epsilon_0} \int \frac{dq}{r^3} \vec{r}$$

Electric field lines
Imaginary line along which a positive test charge will move it left free.

Properties of electric field lines

Never intersect each other

Never from closed loops

Charged conducting shpere (or shell of charge)
(a) Outside the sphere: If point P lies outside the sphere
$$E_{out} = \frac{1}{4\pi\varepsilon_0} \cdot \frac{Q}{r^2} = \frac{\sigma R^2}{\varepsilon_0 r^2}$$
(b) At the surface of sphere: At surface $r = R$
$$E_s = \frac{1}{4\pi\varepsilon_0} \cdot \frac{Q}{r^2} = \frac{\sigma}{\varepsilon_0}$$

Electric flux
$$\phi = E.A \cos\theta$$
$$\phi = \vec{E}.\vec{A}$$

Gauss's theorem
Total flux over a closed surface is
$\dfrac{1}{\epsilon_0}$ times the total enclosed charg
$$\phi = \int E.ds = \frac{q_{enclosed}}{\varepsilon_0}$$

Applicaion of Gauss's theorem
(i) Electric Field due to infinitely long straight wire
$$E = \frac{\lambda}{2\pi\varepsilon_0 r}$$
(ii) Infinite plane sheet
$$E = \frac{\sigma}{2\varepsilon_0}$$

Come out of positive charge and go into negative charge

Always normal to conducting surface

Infinite thin plane sheet of charge
$$E = \frac{\sigma}{2\varepsilon_0} (E \propto r^\circ)$$

Mind

Electrostatic Potential And Capacitance

At a point on the surface or inside the spherical shell

$$V = \frac{1}{4\pi\,\epsilon_0}\,\frac{q}{R}\;(r \le R)$$

At a point outside the spherical shell

$$V = \frac{1}{4\pi\,\epsilon_0}\,\frac{q}{r}\;(r > R)$$

At a point on the surface or inside the sphere

$$= \frac{1}{4\pi\,\epsilon_0}\,\frac{q}{R}\;(r \le R)$$

Electrostatic potential due to infinite thin plane sheet of charge

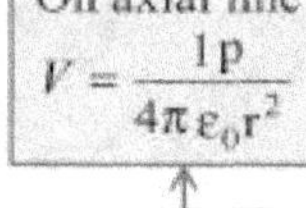

$$V = -\frac{\sigma r}{2\epsilon_0} + C$$

σ = uniform surface charge density

Electric potential due to a charged conducting spherical shell

At a point outside the non-conducting sphere

$$V = \frac{1}{4\pi\,\epsilon_0}\,\frac{q}{r}\;(r > R)$$

Electric potential due to a charged non-conducting sphere

Electric potential due to a dipole

On axial line

$$V = \frac{1p}{4\pi\,\varepsilon_0 r^2}$$

On equatorial line $V = 0$
At general point,

$$V_g = \frac{kP\cos\theta}{r^2}$$

Due to charged circular ring

(i) At a point distance x away from the centre of the ring

$$V = \frac{kQ}{\sqrt{x^2 + k^2}}$$

(ii) At centre,

$$V_{centre} = \frac{kQ}{k}$$

Electrostatic potential (V_0) = $\dfrac{\text{work done } w_\infty}{\text{charge } (q_0)}$
Positive potential due to +(ve) charge and negative potential due to –(ve) charge

Equipotential surface
Imaginary surface joining the points of same potential in an electric field

Electrostatic potential due to a point charge

$$V = K\,\frac{q}{r}$$

Electrostatic potential due to a system of charges

$$V = V_1 + V_2 + V_3 \dots + V_n$$
$$V = K\sum_{i=1}^{n}\frac{q_i}{r_i}$$

- The direction of electric field is perpendicular to the equipotential surface or lines.
- A metallic surface of any shape is an equipotential surface.

Electric potential due to continuous charge distribution

$$V = \int dV = \int \frac{dQ}{4\pi\,\epsilon_0\,r}$$

Relation between electric potential and field,

$$E = -\frac{dV}{dr}$$

Negative of the slope of the v–r graph denotes intensity of electric field, $\tan\theta$

$$\tan\theta = \frac{V}{r} = -E$$

Electrostatic potential energy of a

(i) System of 'n' charges $U = \dfrac{K}{2}\displaystyle\sum_{\substack{i,j \\ i \ne j}}^{n}\dfrac{Q_1 Q_2}{r_{ij}}$

(ii) Uniformly charged sphere, $U = \dfrac{30Q^2}{20\pi\varepsilon_0 R}$

(iii) Uniformly charged thin spherical shell $U = \dfrac{Q^2}{8\pi\varepsilon_0 R}$

(iv) Energy density $U_e = \dfrac{1}{2}\varepsilon_0 \in^2$

Combination of Charged Drops
If n identical drops each having radius r Capacitance, c, Charge, q, Potential, v and energy, u. If these drops are combined to form a big drop of radius, R,
Charge on big drop: $Q = nq$

Potential of big drop: $V = \dfrac{Q}{C} = \dfrac{nq}{n^{1/3}}$ $V = n^{2/3}v$

Map-2

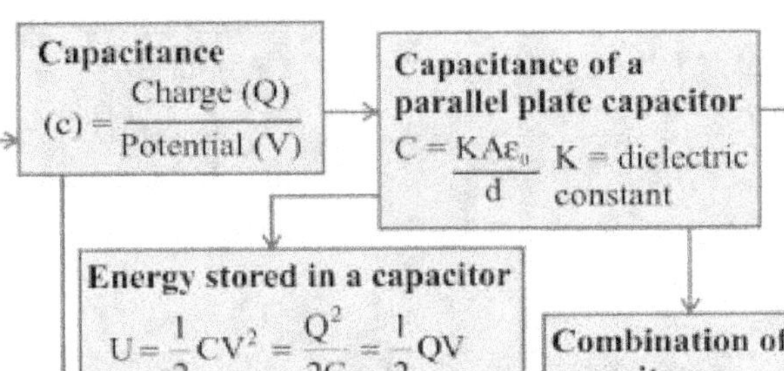

Capacitance
$$(c) = \frac{\text{Charge } (Q)}{\text{Potential } (V)}$$

Capacitance of a parallel plate capacitor
$$C = \frac{KA\varepsilon_0}{d} \quad K = \text{dielectric constant}$$

Energy stored in a capacitor
$$U = \frac{1}{2}CV^2 = \frac{Q^2}{2C} = \frac{1}{2}QV$$

Combination of capacitors

Energy loss when two isolated charged conductors are connected to each other
$$= \frac{1}{2}\frac{C_1 C_2 (V_1 - V_2)^2}{C_1 + C_2}$$

- If a dielectric slab is partially filled between the plates.
$$\Rightarrow C' = \frac{\varepsilon_0 A}{d - t + \dfrac{t}{K}}$$

- If a number of dielectric slabs are inserted between the plate as shown.
$$C' = \frac{\varepsilon_0 A}{d - (t_1 + t_2 + t_3 + ...) + \left(\dfrac{t_1}{K_1} + \dfrac{t_2}{K_2} + \dfrac{t_3}{K_3} + ...\right)}$$

- When a metallic slab is inserted between the plates
$$C' = \frac{\varepsilon_0 A}{(d - t)}$$

Series grouping of capacitors
Equivalent capacitance
$$\frac{1}{C_s} = \frac{1}{C_1} + \frac{1}{C_2} + ... + \frac{1}{C_n}$$

Parallel grouping of capacitors
Equivalent capacitance
$$C_p = C_1 + C_2 + ... C_n$$

Spherical capacitor: It is of two concentric conducting spheres of radii a and b $(a < b)$. Inner sphere is given charge $+Q$, while outer sphere is earthed

Capacitance, $C = 4\pi\varepsilon_0 b \dfrac{ab}{b - a}$.

In the presence of dielectric medium (dielectric constant K) between the spheres
$$C' = 4\pi\varepsilon_0 K \frac{ab}{b - a}$$

If outer sphere is given a charge $+Q$ while inner sphere is earthed

Capacitance $C' = 4\pi\varepsilon_0 \cdot \dfrac{b^2}{b - a}$

This arrangement is not a capacitor. But it's capacitance is equivalent to the sum of capacitance of spherical capacitor and spherical conductor

i.e., $\quad 4\pi\varepsilon_0 \cdot \dfrac{b^2}{b - a}$

$\quad = 4\pi\varepsilon_0 \cdot \dfrac{ab}{b - a} + 4\pi\varepsilon_0 b$

Cylindrical capacitor: It consists of two co-axial cylinders of radii a and b $(a < b)$, inner cylinder is given charge $+Q$ while outer cylinder is earthed. Common length of the cylinders is l

Capacitance, $C = \dfrac{2\pi\varepsilon_0 l}{\log_e\left(\dfrac{b}{a}\right)}$

In series combination potential difference and energy distributes in the reverse ratio of capacitance

i.e., $V \propto \dfrac{1}{C}$ and $U \propto \dfrac{1}{C}$.

If n identical capacitors each having capacitances C are connected
$$C_{eq} = \frac{C}{n}$$

If n identical plates are arranged as shown they constitute $(n - 1)$ capacitors in series. If each capacitor has capacitance
$$\frac{\varepsilon_0 A}{d} \text{ then}$$
$$C_{eq} = \frac{\varepsilon_0 A}{(n - 1)d}$$

$A \qquad B$

In this situation except two extreme plates each plate is common to adjacent capacitors.

Here, effective capacitance C_{eq} is even less than the least of the individual capacitances.

In parallel combination change and energy distributes in the ratio of capacitance i.e., $Q \propto C$ and $U \propto C$

If n identical capacitors are connected in parallel, then Equivalent capacitance $C_{eq} = nC$ and Change on each capacitor $Q' = \dfrac{Q}{n}$

If n identical plates are arranged such that even numbered of plates are connected together and odd numbered plates are connected together, then $(n - 1)$ capacitors will be formed and they will be in parallel grouping.

Equivalent capacitance
$C = (n - 1)C$
where $C = $ capacitance
of a capacitor $= \dfrac{\varepsilon_0 A}{d}$

If C_p is the effective capacity when n identical capacitors are connected in parallel and C_s is their effective capacity when connected in series, then $\dfrac{C_p}{C_s} = n^2$.

Mind

Series grouping of resistances
Equivalent resistance, $R_s = R_1 + R_2 + ... + R_n$
In this case same current flows through each resistance but potential difference distributes in the ratio of resistance

Parallel grouping of resistances
Equivalent resistance,
$$\frac{1}{R_P} = \frac{1}{R_1} + \frac{1}{R_2} + ... + \frac{1}{R_n}$$
In this case same potential across each resistance but current distributes in the reverse ratio of their resistances

After stretching, if length increases by n times then resistance will increase by n^2 times i.e., $R_2 = n^2 R_1$. Similarly if radius be reduced to $\frac{1}{n}$ times then area of cross-section decreases $\frac{1}{n^2}$ times so the resistance becomes n^4 times i.e., $R_2 = n^4 R_1$.
After stretching, if length of a conductor increases by $x\%$, then resistance will increase by $2x\%$ (valid only if $x < 10\%$).

On length (ℓ) and area of cross-section (A)
$$\left.\begin{array}{l} R \propto l \\ \propto \dfrac{1}{A} \end{array}\right\} R = \rho \dfrac{l}{A}$$
ρ = resistivity
Resistivity depends on the material of the conductor only.

Grouping of resistances

Resistance (R) Obstruction offered to flow of electrons

Resistance, $R \propto \dfrac{\ell^2}{m}$
ℓ = length and
m = mass of conducting wire

Dependence of resistance

Ohm's law If the physical conditions remain same, current $I \propto V \Rightarrow V = IR$
R-electric resistance
Substances which obey ohm's law called ohmic and that do not obey called non-ohmic substances.

Colour coding of Resistance
R = AB × C ± D% A, B –
First two significant figures of resistance C-multiplier D-tolerance to remembers the sequence of colour code
B B Roy Great Britain Very Good Wife

On temperature
$R_t = R_0(t + \alpha t)$
α = temperature coefficient of resistance

Current density (J)
Current per unit cross sectional area
(A) $\vec{j} = \dfrac{I}{A} = \dfrac{\vec{E}}{\rho}$

Conductivity (σ)
Reciprocal of resistivity $\sigma = \dfrac{1}{\rho}$
Conductance, $C = \dfrac{1}{\text{resistance}}$

Current Electricity

Electric Current (I) The time rate of flow of charge (Q) through any cross-section
$$I = \frac{Q}{t} ; I = \lim_{\Delta t \to 0} \frac{\Delta Q}{\Delta t} = \frac{dQ}{dt}$$

Drift velocity (V_d)
Average uniform velocity acquired by free electrons $V_d = \dfrac{i}{neA} = \dfrac{J}{ne} = \dfrac{V}{\rho \ell ne}$
$$V_d = \frac{E}{fne}$$
Direction of drift velocity for electrons in a metal is opposite to that of applied electric field.

Mobility (μ)
Drift velocity per unit electric field $\mu = \dfrac{V_d}{E}$

- Using n conductors of equal resistance, the number of possible combinations is 2^{n-1}.
- If the resistances of n conductors are totally different, then the number of possible combinations will be 2^n.
- If n identical resistances are first connected in series and then in parallel, the ratio of the equivalent resistance is given by
$$\frac{R_s}{R_p} = \frac{n^2}{1}.$$
- If a wire of resistance R is cut in n equal parts and then these parts are collected to form a bundle, then equivalent resistance of combination will be $\dfrac{R}{n^2}$.
- If equivalent resistance of R_1 and R_2 in series and parallel be R_s and R_p respectively, then $R_1 = \dfrac{1}{2}\left[R_s + \sqrt{R_s^2 - 4R_s R_p}\right]$ and $R_2 = \dfrac{1}{2}\left[R_s - \sqrt{R_s^2 - 4R_s R_p}\right]$.

Map-3

Electric cell Source of energy that maintains continuous flow of charge in a circuit

Groupings of cells

Electrical energy
$H \propto I^2$
$\propto R$
$\propto t$

Jule's heating law
$H = I^2Rt$; Electrical power $P = \dfrac{V^2}{R}$

Cells in series Current in the circuit, $I = \dfrac{n\varepsilon}{R + nr}$

Cells in parallel Current in the circuit current $I = \dfrac{\varepsilon}{R + \dfrac{r}{m}}$

Cells in series and parallel i.e. mixed Current in the circuit, $I = \dfrac{n\varepsilon}{\dfrac{nr}{m} + R}$

In series combination, power consumed $P_{total} = \dfrac{P}{n}$

Brightness $\propto$ power $\propto V \propto$

$R \propto \dfrac{1}{P_{rated}}$

In parallel combination $P_{total} = nP$

Brightness $\propto$ power $\propto I \propto \dfrac{1}{R}$

Meter bridge Based on Wheatstone bridge
$\dfrac{P}{Q} = \dfrac{R}{S} \Rightarrow \dfrac{l}{100 - l} = \dfrac{R}{S}$

Balanced condition of wheatstone bridge
$\dfrac{P}{Q} = \dfrac{R}{S}$

- **When cell is discharging:** When cell is discharging current inside the cell is from cathode to anode. Current $I = \dfrac{E}{r + R}$

or $E = IR + Ir = V + Ir$ or $V = E - Ir$

When current is drawn from the cell potential difference is less than emf of cell. Greater is the current drawn from the cell smaller is the terminal voltage. When a large current is drawn from a cell its terminal voltage is reduced.

- **When cell is charging:** When cell is charging current inside the cell is from anode to cathode. Current $I = \dfrac{V - E}{r}$ or $V = E + Ir$

During charging terminal potential difference is greater than emf of cell.

When cell is in open circuit: In open circuit $R = \infty$ $\therefore$ $I = \dfrac{E}{R + 1} = 0$ So $V = E$

In open circuit terminal potential difference is equal to emf and is the maximum potential difference which a cell can provide.

Kirchhoff's laws

1st law/Junction law Algebraic sum of all the current meeting at a junction is zero i.e. $\Sigma I = 0$

2nd law/Loop rule Algebraic sum of changes in potential around any closed loop is zero. $\Sigma^E = \Sigma^{IR}$

Potentiometer used to
(i) Compare emfs
$\dfrac{E_1}{E_2} = \dfrac{l_1}{l_2}$

(ii) Find internal resistance of cell
$r = \left(\dfrac{E}{V} - 1\right)S$

- **When cell is short circuited:** In short circuit $R = 0$ so $I = \dfrac{-E}{(R + r)}$ and $V = IR = 0$

In short circuit current from cell is maximum and terminal potential difference is zero.

Power transferred to load by cell:

$P = I^2R = \dfrac{E^2R}{(r + R)^2}$ so, $P = P_{max}$

if $\dfrac{dP}{dR}$ and $P = P_{max}$ if $r = R$

Power transferred by cell to load is maximum when $r = R$ and

$P_{max} = \dfrac{E^2}{4r} = \dfrac{E^2}{4R}$

Potential gradient (x)
Potential difference per unit length of wire $x = \dfrac{V}{L} = \dfrac{volt}{m}$

where $V = iR = \left(\dfrac{e}{R + R_h + r}\right)R$ So,

$x = \dfrac{V}{L} = \dfrac{iR}{L} = \dfrac{i\rho}{A} = \dfrac{e}{(R + R_h + r)} \cdot \dfrac{R}{L}$

(I) Potential gradient directly depends upon
(a) The resistance per unit length (R/L) of potentiometer wire.
(b) The radius of potentiometer wire (i.e., Area of cross-section)
(c) The specific resistance of the material of potentiometer
(d) The current flowing through potentiometer wire (i)
(ii) potential gradient indirectly depends upon
(a) The emf of battery in the primary circuit
(b) The resistance of rheostat in the primary circuit

Sensitivity of potentiometer
A potentiometer is more sensitive, if it measures a small potential difference more accurately.
(i) The sensitivity of potentiometer is assessed by its potential gradient. The sensitivity is inversely proportional to the potential gradient.
(ii) In order to increase the sensitivity of potentiometer.
(a) The resistance in primary circuit will have to be decreased.
(b) The length of potentiometer wire will have to be increased

Mind

⊗ **Cross,** if magnetic field is directed perpendicular and into the plane of the paper
• **Dot,** if magnetic field is directed perpendicular and out of the plane of the paper.

Galvanometer to ammeter conversion : Low resistance or shunt connected in parallel

$$S = \left(\frac{I_g}{1 - I_g}\right) G$$

Reading of ammeter is always less than actual current in the circuit.

Galvanometer to voltmeter conversion : High resistance in series $R = \dfrac{V}{I_g} - G$

Greater the resistance of voltmeter, more accurate its reading.

Magnetic field due to a straight current carrying conductor of infinite lenght $B = \dfrac{\mu_0 I}{2\pi R}$

Biot-Savart's law
Magnetic field due to current carrying element, $dB = \dfrac{\mu_0}{4\pi} \dfrac{I dl \sin\theta_n}{r^2}$
It is an inverse-square law and is the magnetic analogue of coulomb's law

Magnetic field due to a current carrying circular loop

On the axis of circular loop
$$B = \frac{\mu_0 N I a^2}{2(r^2 + a^2)^{3/2}}$$
If $a \gg r$, $B = \ell$
$$\frac{\mu_0}{4\pi} \cdot \frac{2NiA}{a^3}$$

At the centre of circular loop $B = \dfrac{\mu N I}{2R}$
Magnetic field due to circular current carrying are $B = \dfrac{\mu_0 I}{2r}$

Direction of magnetic field- Depends upon the direction of current. **Right hand thumb rule-** Thumb points in the direction of current, curling of fingers represents direction of magnetic field.

Magnetic field space in the surrounding of a magnet or any current carrying conductor in which its magnetic influence can be experienced

Moving Charges And Magnetism

Magnetic field within the solenoid is uniform and parallel to the axis of solenoid.

Amperic law is analogous to Gauss's law $\oint \vec{E} \cdot d\vec{s} = \dfrac{q}{\epsilon_0}$
This law is valid for symmetrical current distributions and is based on the principle of electromagnetism

Magnetic field due to a current carrying wire at a point which lies at a perpendicular distance r from the wire $\quad B = \dfrac{\mu_0}{4\pi} \cdot \dfrac{1}{r}(\sin\phi_1 + \sin\phi_2)$
or, $B = \dfrac{\mu_0}{4\pi} \cdot \dfrac{1}{r}(\cos\alpha - \cos\beta)$
For a wire of finite length Magnetic field at a point which lies on perpendicular bisector of finite length wire $B = \dfrac{\mu_0}{4\pi} \cdot \dfrac{1}{r}(2\sin\phi)$
For a wire of infinite length When the linear conductor is of infinite length and the point lies near the centre of the conductor.
$B = \dfrac{\mu_0}{4\pi} \dfrac{i}{r}(\sin 90° + \sin 90°) = \dfrac{\mu_0 2i}{4\pi r}$
For a wire of semi-infinite length When the linear conductor is of infinite length and the point lies near the end
$B = \dfrac{\mu_0}{4\pi} \cdot \dfrac{i}{r}(\sin 90° + \sin 0°) = \dfrac{\mu_0 i}{4\pi r}$
For axial position of wire When point lies on axial position of current carrying conductor then magnetic field $B = 0$

Magnetic field due to a **solenoid**.
Inside a long solenoid $B = \mu_0 n I$
At a point on one end $B = \dfrac{\mu_0 n I}{2}$
n = number of turns per unit length

Ampere's circuital law
$\oint B dl = \mu_0 \Sigma i$ Absolute permeability of air or vacuum,
$\mu_0 = 4\pi \times 10^{-7} \dfrac{Wb}{Amp - metre}$

Magnetic field due to a **toroid**
$B = \mu_0 n I \; ; \quad n = \dfrac{N}{2\pi r}$

Magnetic field due to a cylindrical wire.
Outside the cylinder Magnetic field $B_{out} = \dfrac{\mu_0 i}{2\pi r}$ and $B_{surface} = \dfrac{\mu_0 i}{2\pi r}$
Inside the hollow cylinder Magnetic field inside the hollow cylinder is zero.

Toroid is like an endless cylindrical solenoid. Number of turns per unit length $n = \dfrac{N}{2\pi r}$

Inside the solid cylinder
Magnetic field $B = \dfrac{\mu_0}{2\pi} \cdot \dfrac{ir}{R^2}$
Inside the thick portion of hollow cylinder:
$$B = \frac{\mu_0 i}{2\pi r} \cdot \frac{(r^2 - R_1^2)}{2\pi r(R_2^2 - R_1^2)}$$

Map-4

Motion of a charged particle in a uniform magnetic field follows a circular path, radius
$$r = \frac{MV\sin\theta}{Bq}$$

Force acting on a charged particle moving in a uniform magnetic field $F = qVB$
$\sin\theta = q(V \times B)$

Zero force i.e., $F = 0$ on a charged particle, if field $\vec{B} = 0$
charge $q = 0$
charge is at rest, $v = 0$
when $\theta = \theta°$ or $180°$

Trajectory of a particle is a straight, line, if the direction of a particle moving with velocity $\vec{v}$ parallel or anti-parallel to $\vec{B}$
i.e., $\theta = 0$ or $\theta = 180°$

Force on a conductor carrying current in a uniform magnetic field,
$F = I\,Bl\sin\theta$
$F = I\,(B \times l)$

Lorentz force
$F = q[\vec{E} + \vec{V} \times \vec{B}]$
Electric force,
$\vec{F_e} = q\vec{E}$
Magnetic force,
$\vec{F_m} = q(\vec{v} \times \vec{B})$

• When $\vec{V}, \vec{E}$ and $\vec{B}$ are all collinear $F_{magnetic} = 0$
$$\vec{F_e} = q\vec{E} \Rightarrow \vec{a} = \frac{\vec{F}}{m} = \frac{q\vec{E}}{m}$$
• When $\vec{V}, \vec{E}$ and $\vec{B}$ are mutually perpendicular
$$\vec{F} = \vec{F_e} \Rightarrow \vec{F_m} = 0$$
$$\Rightarrow a = \frac{\vec{F}}{m} = 0$$

Trajectory of a particle is a circle if particle velocity $\vec{v}$ perpendicular to $\vec{B}$ i.e., $\theta = 90°$ and radius of path,
$$r = \frac{mV}{qB} = \frac{1}{B}\sqrt{\frac{2mV}{q}}$$

Force between two parallel current carrying conductors
$$F = \frac{\mu_0}{4\pi} \cdot \frac{2I_1 I_2}{r} \times l$$

Direction of force If two conductors carry current in same direction, force between them is attractive and if carry currents in opposite direction force between them is repulsive

Trajectory of a particle is helical if a charged particle is moving at an angle to the field other than $0°$, $90°$, $180°$ and radius of path $r = \dfrac{m(V\sin\theta)}{qB}$

If two charges q_1, q_2 are moving with velocities v_1 and v_2 and at any instant distance between then is 'r'
$$F_{magnetic} = \frac{\mu_0}{4\pi}\frac{q_1 q_2 v_1 v_2}{r^2}$$
For charges moving with same velocity
$F_{magnetic} < F_{electrostatic}$

Torque experienced by a current carrying loop in a uniform magnetic field $\vec{T} = MB\sin\theta\,\hat{n}$
$$= M \times B$$

Cyclotron.
A device used to accelerate positively charged particles like α-particles, deuterons, etc. to acquire sufficient energy to carry out nuclear disintegration.
• Cyclorton frequency $v = \dfrac{qB}{2\pi m}$

Cyclotron frequency also known as magnetic resonance frequency

• Time period, $T = \dfrac{2\pi m}{qB}$

• Maximum energy gained by charged particle
$$E_{max} = \left(\frac{q^2 B^2}{2m}\right)r^2$$

• **Torque** experienced is zero when $\theta = 0$ i.e. plane of the coil is perpendicular to the field.
• **Torque** is maximum when $\theta = 90°$ i.e., plane of the coil is parallel to the field, $T_{max} = NBiA$
• **Work** done, $W = MB(1 - \cos\theta)$

W_{max}, if $\theta = 180°$
$W_{max} = 2MB$

• Potential energy,
$$U = -MB\cos\theta \Rightarrow U = -\vec{M}.\vec{B}$$

Mind

Bar magnet: Consists of two equal and opposite magnetic poles separated by a small distance. Effective length, $Le = \dfrac{5}{6}Lg$, Lg = geometric length

Magnet field due to a bar magnet. Magnetic field is measured in $tesla = \text{Wbm}^{-2}$

Repulsive Like poles always repel one another. It is sure test of magnet

Attractive Unlike poles always attract so 4th pole of a magnet attracts north pole of another magnet and vice-versa

Directive: A freely suspended magnet always points in north south direction

Pole strength of the magnet depends on
• Nature of material of magnet
• Area of cross-section i.e., m ∝ A
• Independent of length of magnet

Pole of a magnet always exist in pair Monopoles do not exist

At a point on axial line $B = \dfrac{\mu_0}{4\pi}\dfrac{2M}{d^3}$

At a point on equatorial line $B = \dfrac{\mu_0}{4\pi}\dfrac{M}{(r^2 + \ell^2)3/2}$

Properties of magnet

Gauss's law in magnetism Net magnetic flux through any closed surface is always zero i.e., $\oint \vec{B}\cdot \vec{ds} = 0$

Magnetism Property of attracting a piece of iron, cobalt, nickel etc.

When a bar magnet is placed in magnetic field
• Torque experienced, $\tau = MB \sin\theta = \vec{M} \times \vec{B}$
• Work done, $W = MB(1 - \cos\theta) = \vec{M}\cdot\vec{B}$
• Potential energy, $U = -MB\cos\theta$ = angle made by bar magnet or dipole with the field.
• When a magnetic dipole moves from unstable equilibrium to stable equilibrium in a magnetic field, then kinetic energy decreases by 2 MB.

Magnetism And Matter

Coulomb's law in magnetism Force between two magnetic poles
$$F = K\frac{m_1 m_2}{r^2} = \frac{\mu_0}{4\pi}\frac{m_1 m_2}{r^2}$$

Bohr magneton $\mu_B = \dfrac{eh}{4\pi m} = 9.27 \times 10^{-24} A/m^2$

It is as a natural unit of magnetic moment Magnetic moment of straight current carrying wire = 0 Magnetic moment of toroid = 0

Magnetic permeability Degree extert to which magnetic lines of force can enter a substance.
$\mu = \mu_0 \mu_r$; where μ_0 = absolute permeability of air or free space = $4\pi \times 10^{-7}$ tesla × m/amp. and μ_r = Relative permeability of the medium
$$= \frac{B}{B_0} = \frac{\text{flux density in material}}{\text{flux density in vacuum}}.$$

Intensity of magnetising field $(\vec{H})$
Degree or extent to which a magnetic field can magnetise a substance $H = \dfrac{B}{\mu}$ A/m

Intensity of magnetisation (I)
Degree to which a substance is magnetised when place in a magnetic field.

Magnetic susceptibility (χ_m)
Property of the substance which shows how easily a substance can be magnetised. $\chi_m = \dfrac{1}{H}$

Relation between permeability and susceptibility
$B = B_0 + B_m \Rightarrow B = \mu_0 H + \mu_0 I$
$= \mu_0(H + I) = \mu_0 H(1 + \chi_m)$ or, $\mu_r = (1 + \chi_m)$

Map-5

Earth's magnetic elements

Angle of dip or inclination (δ) Angle made by direction of earth's magnetic field with the horizontal δequator = 0; δpole = 90°

Horizontal component of earth's magnetic field is horizontal only at the magnetic equator Horizontal component $B_v = B \sin\theta$ $B_H = B \cos\theta$

$$B = \sqrt{B_v^2 + B_H^2} \text{ and } tan\,\theta = \frac{B_v}{B_H}$$

Angle of declination Angle between magnetic meridian and geographic meridian At a place it is expressed as $\theta°$ East or $\theta°$ west

Magnetic field lines
Imaginary lines in a magnetic field which continuously represent the direction of magnetic field

Form continuous closed loop Start from N-pole end S-pole outside the magnet and its opposite inside the magnet

Properties of magneticfield lines

Tangent to the field line at a given point represents the direction of the net magnetic field

Come out of surface at any angle

Two magnetic field lines do not intersect each other

Deflection magnetometer
Works on the principle of tangent law.
Tan A position: In this position the magnetometer is set perpendicular to magnetic meridian.

$$B_H \tan\theta = \frac{\mu_0}{4\pi} \cdot \frac{2Mr}{(r^2 - l^2)^2} \text{ or } B_H \tan\theta = \frac{\mu_0}{4\pi} \cdot \frac{2M}{r^3}$$

Tan B position: The arms of magnetometer are set in magnetic meridian, so that the magnetic field due to magnet is at equatorial position.

$$B_H \tan\theta = \frac{\mu_0}{4\pi} \cdot \frac{M}{(r^2 + l^2)^{3/2}} \quad \tan\theta = \frac{\mu_0}{4\pi} \cdot \frac{M}{r^3}$$

Comparison of magnetic moments
$$\frac{M_1}{M_2} = \frac{\tan\theta_1}{\tan\theta_2}$$

According to null deflection method
$$\frac{M_1}{M_2} = \left(\frac{d_1}{d_2}\right)^3$$

Vibration Magnetometer
Vibration Magnetometer is used for comparison of magnetic moment and magnetic fields.
Comparison of horizontal components of earth's magnetic field at two places

$$T = 2\pi\sqrt{\frac{I}{MB_H}} \text{ since I and M of the magnet are constant,}$$

$$T^2 \propto \frac{I}{B_H} \Rightarrow \frac{(B_H)_1}{(B_H)_2} = \frac{T_2^2}{T_1^2}$$

In a uniform magnetic field time period of oscillation of a freely suspended magnet $T = 2\pi\sqrt{\dfrac{I}{MB}}$

Magnetic Materials

Ferromagnetics Strongly magnetised in the direction of magnetic field e.g., Fe, Co, Ni μ_r, I, $\chi_m \gg 1$

Paramagnetics Magnetised in the direction of magnetic field e.g., Al, Mn ; etc, μ_r, I, $\chi_m > 1$ positive

Diamagnetics Magnetised in a direction opposite to the direction of magnetic field e.g., Bi, Cu, Hg etc. μ_r, I and χ_m are negative

Hysteresis Curve
Hysteresis is the lack of retracibility as shown in figure and the curve is hysteresis loop.

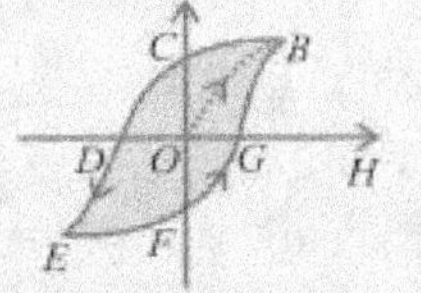

Tangent galvanometer
$$B = B_H \tan\theta \text{ where } B = \frac{\mu_0 ni}{2r}$$
$$\Rightarrow \frac{\mu_0 Ni}{2r} = B_H \tan\theta \Rightarrow i = k$$
$$\tan\theta \text{ where } k = \frac{2rB_H}{\mu_0 N}$$
reduction factor.

Curie Law
$$\chi \propto \frac{1}{T} \Rightarrow \chi = \frac{C}{T};$$
where C = Curie constant, T = absolute temperature. On increasing temperature, the magnetic suscepibility of paramagnetic materials decreases and vice versa but magnetic susceptibility of ferromagnetic substance does not change.
Curie temperature (T_c)
Temperature above which a ferromagnetic material behave like a paramagnetic material. At this temperature the ferromagnetism of the substances suddenly vanishes.
Curie-weiss law: At temperature above Curie temperature the magnetic suscepptibility of ferromagnetic materials is inversely proportional to $(T - T_c)$

Mind

Direction of induced current
Fleming's Right Hand Rule
Thumb, forefinger, central finger of right hand stretched perpendicular to each other then if thumb $\rightarrow$ direction of motion; forefinger $\rightarrow$ direction of magnetic field then central finger $\rightarrow$ induced current

1st law When magnetic flux linked with the circuit changes an emf is induced in the circuit
• Induced emf persists as long as change or cutting of flux

2nd law Induced emf $\propto$ rate of change of magnetic flux $e = \dfrac{d\phi}{dt}$

For 'N' turns $e = -\dfrac{Nd\phi}{dt}$

–(ve) sign indicates 'e' opposes $d\phi$

Magnetic flux, Total number of magnetic lines of force passing normally through an area placed in a magnetic field $\phi_B = \vec{B}.A = BA \cos \theta$

The emf is induced by changing magnetic flux. Flux can be changed by changing
(i) the magnitude of magnetic field at the site of the loop $\left[|\text{emf}| = A\dfrac{dB}{dt} \right]$
(ii) the area of the loop
$\left[|\text{emf}| = B\dfrac{dA}{dt} = Bl\dfrac{dx}{dt} = B/V \right]$
(iii) Angle between $\vec{B}$ and area A

Lenz's law Direction of induced emf or current is always in such a way that it opposes cause due to which it is produced. It is in accordance with conservation of energy

Motional emf $e = -\dfrac{d\phi}{dt} = -Blv$

In vector form, $e = (\vec{V} \times \vec{B}) \cdot l$

Across the end of rod $e = \dfrac{1}{2} B\omega l^2$

$e_{net} = \dfrac{1}{2} B\omega l^2$, $\omega = 2\pi v$ $e_{net} \propto N^\circ$, i.e., total emf does not depends on number of spokes 'N'.

Induced current in a coil rotated in uniform magnetic field

$$I = \frac{NBA\,\omega\sin\omega t}{R} = \frac{e}{R} = -\frac{N}{R}\cdot\frac{d\phi}{dt}$$ Induced charge $dq = i\,dt = -\frac{N}{R}\cdot d\phi$

i.e, independent of time. Induced power $P = \dfrac{e^2}{R} = \dfrac{N^2}{R}\left(\dfrac{d\phi}{dt}\right)^2$
Depends on time and resistance

Faraday's laws of electromagnetic Induction

ELECTROMAGNETIC INDUCTION (EMI)

Motional EMI due to Translatory motion
• When a conducting rod, length l moving with uniform velocity $\vec{v}$ perpendicular to a uniform magnetic field $\vec{B}$ directed into the plane of paper, then $e = Bvl$
If rod is moving by making an angle θ with the direction of magnetic field or length, induced emf $e = Bvl \sin \theta$
• **Motion of conducting rod on an inclined plane**
Induced emf across the ends of the conductor $e = Bv \sin (90° - \theta)l$
$= Bvl \cos \theta$

Induced current $i = \dfrac{Bvl\cos\theta}{R}$

Motional EMI in Loop by Generated Area
• If conducting rod moves on two parallel conducting rails.
Induced emf $|e| = \dfrac{d\phi}{dt} = Bvl$

(i) **Induced current:** $i = \dfrac{e}{R} = \dfrac{Bvl}{R}$

(ii) **Magnetic force:** $F_m = Bil = B\left(\dfrac{Bvl}{R}\right)l = \dfrac{B^2vl^2}{R}$

(iii) **Power dissipated in moving conductor**

$$P_{ext} = \frac{dW}{dt} = F_{ext}.v = \frac{B^2vl^2}{R} \times v = \frac{B^2v^2l^2}{R}$$

(iv) **Electrical power**
$$P_{thermal} = \frac{H}{t} = i^2R = \left(\frac{Bvl}{R}\right)^2 \cdot R; P_{thermal} = \frac{B^2v^2l^2}{R}$$

Motion of conducting rod in a vertical plane: If conducting rod is released from rest (at $t = 0$) then with rise in its speed (v), induced emf (e), induced current (I), magnetic force (F_m), increases but it's weight remains constant.
Rod will achieve a constant maximum (terminal) velocity v, if $F_m = mg$
$or \dfrac{B^2v_T l^2}{R} = mg \Rightarrow v_T = \dfrac{mgR}{B^2l^2}$

Motional EMI due to Rotational Motion
• Emf induce across the ends of the rod, $e = BAv$, $e = \dfrac{1}{2}Bl^2\omega = Bl^2\pi v$
$= \dfrac{Bl^2\pi}{T}$ where v = frequency (revolution).
• **Cycle wheel:** Each spoke of length l is rotating with angular velocity ω in a given magnetic field.
Due to flux cutting each metal spoke becomes identical cell of emf e.

Map-6

Eddy current Induced, when magnetic flux linked with the conductor changes

Applications of eddy currents

→ Electromagnetic damping
→ Induction furnace
→ Magnetic braking
→ Electric power meter

The induced e.m.f. is produced in the inductance due to rate of current through it.

$$e = -L \frac{dI}{dt}$$

The induced e.m.f. in the inductor opposes the e.m.f.

$$\frac{d\phi}{dt}$$

Instantaneous induced e.m.f. produced in a coil
$e = e_s \sin \omega t = nBA\,\omega \sin \omega t$

(i) when $\omega t = 0, \pi$ i.e., coil is vertical, e.m.f. $e = 0$

(ii) when $\omega t = \pi/2$ i.e., coil is horizontal, e.m.f. $e = +$(ve) maximum.

(iii) when $\omega t = \frac{3}{2}\pi$ i.e., coil is horizontal, e.m.f. e $= -$(ve) minimum.

Inductance is analogous to inertia opposes any change of current in the circuit
• It is inherent property of electrical circuit.

Coefficient of self inductance

$$L = \frac{N\phi}{i} \qquad e = -L \frac{di}{dt}$$

L is measured in Wb/amp or henery.

Self inductance of a long solenoid

$$L = \frac{\mu_0 N^2 A}{l}$$

Self inductance for
• Circular coil, $L = \mu_0 \pi N^2 r$

• Toroid, $L = \dfrac{\mu_0 N^2 r}{2}$

• Square coil, $L = \dfrac{\sqrt[2]{2}\,\mu_0 N^2 r}{\pi}$

• Coaxial cylinders, $L = \dfrac{\mu_0}{2\pi} log_e \dfrac{r_2}{r_1}$

Self inductance depends on-
• Number of turns (N)
• Area of cross-section (A)
• Permeability of medium (μ_0)
And not depends on-
Change in current flowing

Magnetic potential energy of inductor

$$\mu = \frac{1}{2} Li^2 = \frac{N\phi i}{2}$$

Mutual Inductance Induced emf in a circuit due to change in magnetic flux in its neighbouring circuit. Coefficients of mutual inductance

$M = \dfrac{\phi}{I}$; If N = number of turns

$N\phi = MI$

Coefficient of mutual inductance between two long solenoids

$$M = \frac{\mu_0 N_1 N_2 A}{l}$$

Mutual Inductance depends on
• Number of turns of both coils (N_1 & N_2)
• Coefficient of self inductance of both coils (L_1 & L_2)
• Area of cross-section of coils
• Magnetic permeability of medium between the coils (μ_r)
• Distance between two coils ($M \propto d$)
• Orientation between primary and secondary coil.
• Coupling factor

$$\left(K = \frac{\text{magnetic flux linked in secondary}}{\text{magnetic flux linked in primary}} \right)$$

between primary and secondary coil. $0 \le K \le 1$

AC Generator or Dynamo Produces electrical energy from mechanical energy. It works on EMI principle.

Mind

RMS value of alternating current and voltage

$$I_{rms} = \sqrt{\dfrac{I_1^2 + I_2^2 + \dots}{n}}$$

$$\sqrt{\overline{I^2}} = \sqrt{\dfrac{\int_0^T I^2 dt}{\int_0^T dt}} = \dfrac{I_0}{\sqrt{2}}$$

$$I_{rms} = \dfrac{I_0}{\sqrt{2}} \qquad V_{rms} = \dfrac{V_0}{\sqrt{2}}$$

Mean or average value of alternating current and voltage

$$\overline{I^2} = \dfrac{1}{T}\int_0^T I^2 dt = \dfrac{I_0^2}{2}$$

i.e., Average of square of instantaneous values in one cycle

$$I_{mean} = \dfrac{2I_0}{\pi} \qquad V_{mean} = \dfrac{2V_0}{\pi}$$

Peak current (I_0) and voltage (V_0): The maximum value of current and voltage

$$\text{Peak factor} = \dfrac{\text{Peak value of ac}}{\text{rms value of ac}}$$

$$\text{Form factor} = \dfrac{\text{rms value of ac}}{\text{average value during half cycle}}$$

$$I_0 = \sqrt{2}\, I_{rms} \qquad V_0 = \sqrt{2}\, V_{rms}$$

Impedance (Z) Opposition offered by ac circuits to the flow of ac through it.
Admittance (Y) Reciprocal of impedance

$$\left(Y = \dfrac{1}{Z}\right), Z = \dfrac{V_0}{i_0} = \dfrac{V_{rms}}{i_{rms}}$$

Susceptance (S): Reciprocal of reactance $\left(S = \dfrac{1}{X}\right)$.
(i) inductive susceptance,
$$S_L = \dfrac{1}{X_L} = \dfrac{1}{2\pi\nu L}$$
(ii) Capacitive susceptance,
$$S_c = \dfrac{1}{X_c} = \omega C = 2\pi\nu C.$$

Reactance (X) Opposition offered by inductor or capacitor or both to the flow of ac through it.
(i) Inductive reactance (X_L) Opposition offered by inductive circuit $X_L = \omega L = 2\pi\nu L$; $v_{dc} = 0$
$\therefore$ for dc, $X_L = 0$.
(ii) Capacitive reactance (X_c): Opposition offered by capacitive circuit
$$X_c = \dfrac{1}{\omega C} = \dfrac{1}{2\pi\nu C} \therefore \text{ for dc } X_c = \infty.$$

- All ac meters read rms value
- All ac meters are based on heating effect of current
- In hot wire meters deflection, $\theta \propto i_{rms}^2$
- Frequency of ac in India is 50 Hz

ALTERNATING CURRENT

Direction of current Changes alternatively and its magnitude changes continuously

Alternating current(I) and alternating voltage (V)
$I = I_0 \sin\omega t$; $V = V_0\sin\omega t$
Phase is the physical quantity which represents both the instantaneous value and direction of alternating quantity at any instant.

RC Circuit
Current: $I = I_0\sin(\omega t + \phi)$
Voltage: $V = \sqrt{V_R^2 + V_C^2}$
Impedance: $Z = \sqrt{R^2 + X_C^2}$
Phase difference: $\tan^{-1}\dfrac{1}{\omega CR}$
Power factor: $\cos\phi = \dfrac{R}{\sqrt{R^2 + X_C^2}}$
Leading quantity: Current

LC Circuit
Current: $I = I_0\sin\left(\omega t \pm \dfrac{\pi}{2}\right)$
Voltage: $V = V_L - V_C$
Impedance: $Z = X_L - X_C$
Phase difference: $\phi = 90°$
Power factor: $\cos\phi = 0$
Leading quantity: Either voltage or current

LR Circuit
Current: $I = I_0\sin(\omega t + \phi)$
Voltage: $V = \sqrt{V_R^2 + V_L^2}$
Impedance: $Z = \sqrt{R^2 + X_L^2}$
Phase difference: $\phi = \tan^{-1}\dfrac{\omega L}{R}$
Power factor: $\cos\phi = \dfrac{R}{\sqrt{R^2 + X_L^2}}$
Leading quantity: voltage

Map-7

Inductive (L) Circuit

Current : $I = I_0 \sin\left(\omega t - \dfrac{\pi}{2}\right)$

Phase difference between V and I : $\phi = 90°$ or $\pi/2$
Power factor : $\cos\phi = 0$
Power : $P = 0$
Phasor : Voltage leads the current by $\pi/2$

Capacitive (C) Circuit

Current : $I = I_0 \sin(\omega t + \pi/2)$
Phase difference between V and I : $\phi = 90°$ or $-\pi/2$ Power factor : $\cos\phi = 0$ Power : $P = 0$
Phasor : Current leads the voltage by $\pi/2$

Resistive (R) Circuit

Current : $I = I_0 \sin\omega t$
Phase difference between V and I $\phi = 0°$ Power factor: $\cos\phi = 1$
Power : $P = \dfrac{V_0 I_0}{2}$
Phasor : Current and voltage both in same phase

AC Circuit

Ac is more dangerous than dc Sinusoidal wave form is used as alternating current/voltage

LCR series Circuit

Current : $I = I_0\sin(\omega t \pm \phi)$: Voltage :
$V = \sqrt{R^2 + (V_L - V_C)^2}$
Impedance $Z = \sqrt{R^2 + (X_L - X_C)^2}$;
Phase difference $\dfrac{X_L - X_C}{R}$
At resonance $X_L = X_C \Rightarrow Z_{min} = R$
Band-width: $\Delta\omega = \dfrac{R}{L}$;
Quality factor $Q = \dfrac{1}{R}\sqrt{\dfrac{L}{C}}$

Power in ac circuit

$P = V i \cos\phi$: V and I are $r.m.s$ values of voltage and current.
Instantaneous power: If in a circuit $V = V_0 \sin\omega t$ and $i = i_0 \sin(\omega t + \phi)$ then $P_{instantaneous} = Vi = V_0 i_0 \sin(\omega t + \phi)$
Average power or True power
Average of instantaneous power in an ac circuit over a full cycle.
$P_{av} = V_{rms} i_{rms} \cos\phi = \dfrac{V_0}{\sqrt{2}} \cdot \dfrac{i_0}{\sqrt{2}} \cos\phi$
$= \dfrac{1}{2} V_0 i_0 \cos\phi = i_{rms}^2 R = \dfrac{V_{rms}^2 R}{Z^2}$
Apparent or virtual power: Product of apparent voltage and apparent current in an electric circuit
$P_{app} = V_{rms} i_{rms} = \dfrac{V_0 i_0}{2}$;

Efficiency of transformer

$\eta\% = \dfrac{P_{output}}{P_{input}} \times 100$
$= \dfrac{V_s I_s}{V_p I_p} \times 100$
- In practical,
$P_{input} = P_{output} + P_{losses}$
Power losses in transformer is due to
- heating effect• flux leakage
- eddy currents
- hysteresis and humming

Uses of Transformer
- In the transmission of ac over long distance
- In voltage regulators for computer, TV etc
- For welding purposes in step-down transformer

Half power frequencies
Frequencies at which the power in the circuit is half of the maximum power i.e., power at resonance
The current in the circuit at half power frequencies (HPF) is $\dfrac{1}{\sqrt{2}}$ or 0.707 or 70.7% of maximum current
(a) $\omega_1 \rightarrow$ lower half power frequency. At this frequency the circuit is capacitive.
(b) $\omega_2 \rightarrow$ upper half power frequency., It is greater than ω_0.

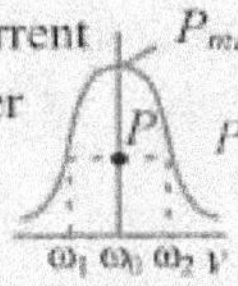

P_{max}
$P = \dfrac{P_{max}}{2}$
$\omega_1\ \omega_0\ \omega_2\ v$

Power Factor
It is the *cosine* of the angle of lag or lead i.e. $\cos\phi$ Also ratio of resistance and impedance i.e. $\dfrac{R}{Z}$
$\dfrac{True\ power}{Apparent\ power} = \dfrac{W}{VA} = \dfrac{kW}{kVA} = \cos\phi.$

Transformer
Device Changes a low voltage of high current into a high voltage of low current and vice-versa
- Transformer works on ac only
- can increase or decrease either voltage or current but not both simultaneously
- Effective resistance between primary and secondary winding is infinite

Step-up transformer
$K > 1$ $K = \dfrac{N_s}{N_p} = \dfrac{E_s}{E_p} = \dfrac{I_p}{I_s}$
$N_s > N_p$; $I_s < I_p$
$V_s > V_p$; $E_s > E_p$
$R_s > R_p$

Step-down transformer
$K < 1$ $K = \dfrac{N_p}{N_s} = \dfrac{E_p}{E_s} = \dfrac{I_s}{I_p}$
$N_s < N_p$; $I_s > I_p$
$V_s < V_p$; $E_s < E_p$
$R_s < R_p$

Mind

Conduction current
Arises due to flow of electrons in a definite closed path

Displacement current (I_D)
Due to time varying electric field
$$I_D = \varepsilon_0 \frac{d\phi_E}{dt}$$

Intensity of Wave
Time average rate per unit area at which energy is transported
$$I = \frac{1}{2}\varepsilon_0 E_0^2 C$$

ELECTROMAGNETIC WAVES
Constituted by mutually perpendicular time varying electric and magnetic fields $E = E_0 \sin(kx - \omega t)$ and $B = B_0 \sin(kx - \omega t)$

Different types of electromagnetic waves

Radio waves
Wavelength > 0.1 m
Uses: in telecommunication and RADAR

Microwave
Wavelength 0.1 m to 1 mm Uses : in microwave oven

Infra -red
Wavelength 1 mm to 700 mm Uses : treat muscular strain

Visible Wavelength : 700 nm to 400 nm
Uses : to see objects

Ultra-violet
Wavelength 400 nm to 1nm
Uses : Preserve food and purifying water

X-ays
Wavelength: 1 nm to 10 nm
Uses : Medical diagnosis

γ-rays
Wavelength : < 10nm
Uses : in medical science & to get information on nuclear structure

Electromagnetic wave with pointing vector $\vec{S}$, incident on a perfectly absorbing surface then,
$$P = \frac{S}{C}$$
If incident on a perfectly reflecting surface then,
$$P = \frac{2S}{C}$$

Maxwell discovered that all the basic principles of electromagnetism can be formulated in terms of four fundamental equations, called **Maxwell's equations**. These are:
(i) Gauss's law for electricity
$$\oint \vec{E} \cdot \vec{dA} = \frac{q}{\epsilon_0}.$$
(ii) Gauss's law for magnetism
$$\oint \vec{B} \cdot \vec{dA} = 0.$$
(iii) Faraday's law of induction
$$\oint \vec{E} \cdot \vec{dl} = \frac{-d\phi_B}{dt}$$
(iv) Ampere's law
$$\oint \vec{B} \cdot \vec{dl} = \mu_0 \left(i_C + \epsilon_0 \frac{-d\phi_E}{dt} \right)$$

Radiation pressure exerted by an electromagnetic wave
$$P = \frac{\text{energy associated with em waves (u)}}{\text{speed of light in vacuum(c)}}$$

Energy associated with an electromagnetic wave
$$U = \frac{1}{2}\varepsilon_0 E^2 + \frac{1}{2}\frac{B^2}{\mu_0}$$

Rate per unit area at which energy is transported via an electromagnetic wave is given by **pointing vector**
$$\vec{S} = \frac{\vec{E} \times \vec{B}}{M_0}$$

Map-8

Characteristics of electromagnetic waves

Do not require any material medium for propagation and form a set of orthogonal vectors

Produced by accelerated charge

Travels with speed of light in free space

$$C = \frac{1}{\sqrt{\mu_0 \varepsilon_0}} = 3 \times 10^8 \text{ m/s}$$

In free space; magnitude of electric field (E) magnetic field (B) = C (speed of light in vacuum)

Transverse in nature $\vec{E}$ and $\vec{B}$ are perpendicular to each other

Oscillating electric and magnetic fields are in phase and their magnitudes bear constant ratio

$$C = \frac{E_0}{B_0}$$

EM Spectrum
The array obtained on arranging all the electromagnetic waves in an order on the basis of their walvelengths

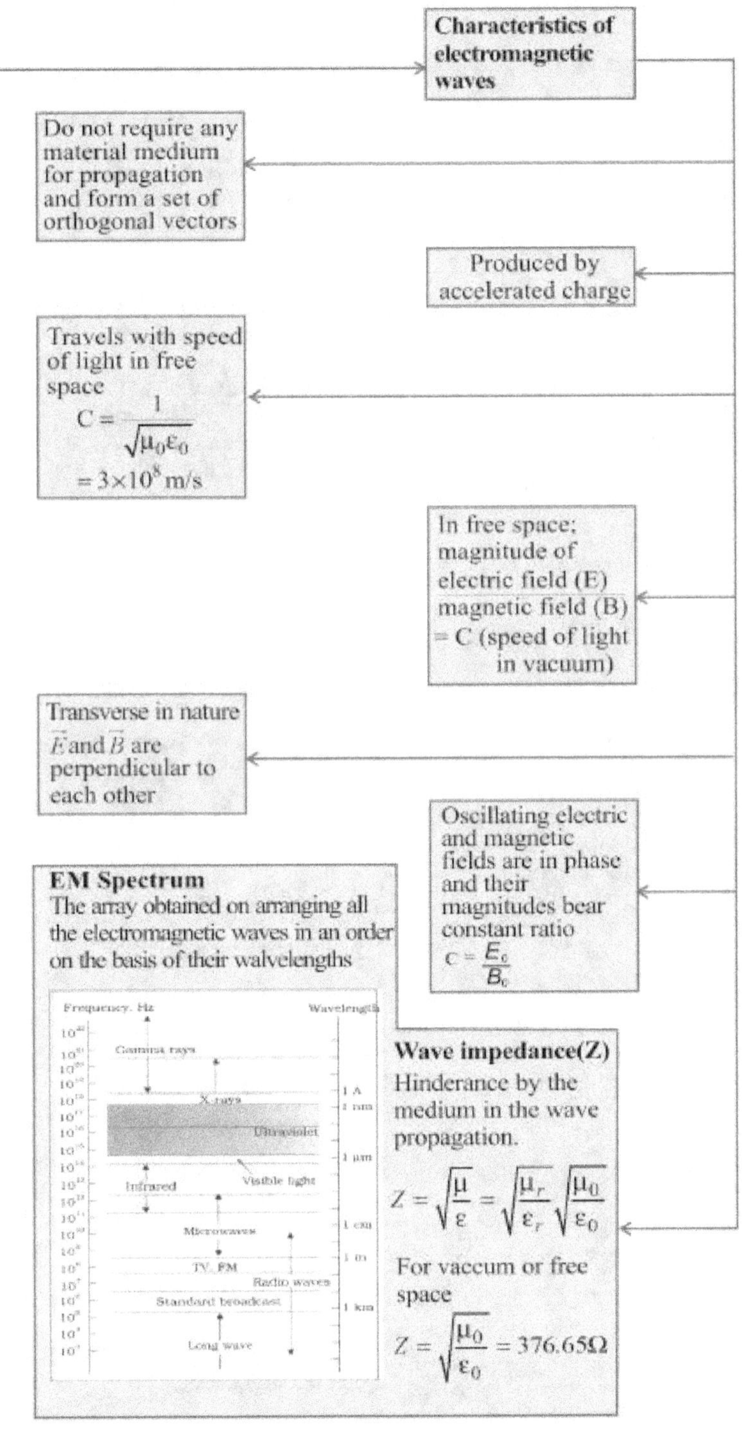

Wave impedance(Z)
Hinderance by the medium in the wave propagation.

$$Z = \sqrt{\frac{\mu}{\varepsilon}} = \sqrt{\frac{\mu_r}{\varepsilon_r}} \sqrt{\frac{\mu_0}{\varepsilon_0}}$$

For vaccum or free space

$$Z = \sqrt{\frac{\mu_0}{\varepsilon_0}} = 376.65\,\Omega$$

Mind

Snell's law $\mu = \dfrac{\sin i}{\sin r}$

For two media

$$_1\mu_2 = \dfrac{\mu_2}{\mu_1} = \dfrac{\sin i}{\sin r}$$

Necessary conditions for TIR
(i) ray of light must travel from denser to rarer medium
(ii) $\angle i > \angle c$ for two media
Critical angle (c) Angle i in denser medium for which angle of refraction in rarer medium is $90°$ $\mu = \dfrac{1}{\sin C}$

Laws of reflection
- The incident ray the normal and the reflected ray all lie in the same plane
- The angle of incidence (I)is always equal to angle of reflection (r) i.e., $\angle i = \angle r$

Mirror formula $\dfrac{1}{f} = \dfrac{1}{u} + \dfrac{1}{v}$
When two plane mirrors are held at an angle θ with their reflecting surfaces facing each other and an object is placed between them, images are formed by successive reflections.
$\qquad f_{concave}$ = negative
$\qquad f_{convex}$ = positive
and $f_{plane} = \infty$

Relation between focal length (f) and radius of curvature, R
$$f = \dfrac{R}{2}$$

Magnification
$$m = \dfrac{v}{u} = \dfrac{\text{height of image}}{\text{height of object}}$$
$$m = \dfrac{f}{f-u} = \dfrac{f-v}{f}$$

The incident ray, the normal and the refracted ray all lie in the same plane

---

Refractive index,
$$\mu = \dfrac{c}{v} = \dfrac{\text{real depth}}{\text{apparent depth}}$$

Total internal Reflection Ray totally reflected back to denser medium
Phenomena based on TIR
- Mirage - optical illusion in deserts
- Looming - optical illusion in cold countries
- optical fibre
- Brilliance of diamond

Reflection of light Turning back of light in the same medium after striking the reflecting surface or mirror
- After reflection, velocity, frequency and wavelength of light remains same but intensity decreases
- If reflection takes place from denser medium then phase change 'π'

Laws of refraction

Refraction of light Bending of light ray while passing from one medium to another medium
- A ray of light bends towards the normal, while going from rarer to denser medium
- And bends away from the normal while going from denser to rarer medium
- Refraction of light takes place because the speed of light is different in the two media

---

Ray optics
Optics - branch of study of light (EM waves wavelength 400 nm to 750 nm). The path of light (always travel in straight line) is ray of light

---

RAY OPTICS AND OPTICAL INSTRUMENTS

Refraction at a single spherical surface $\dfrac{\mu_2}{v} - \dfrac{\mu_1}{u} = \dfrac{\mu_2 - \mu_1}{R}$

(A) In case, the object (real or virtual) is situated in rarer medium so that the incident ray travels in rarer medium and the refracted ray travels in denser medium, then the relation between u, v, R, μ_1 and μ_2 is
$$-\dfrac{\mu_1}{u} + \dfrac{\mu_2}{v} = \dfrac{\mu_2 - \mu_1}{R}$$

(B) In case, the object (real or virtual) is situated in denser medium, so that the incident ray travels in denser medium and refracted ray travels in rarer medium then the relation between u, v, R, μ_1 and μ_2 is
$$-\dfrac{\mu_2}{u} + \dfrac{\mu_1}{v} = \dfrac{\mu_1 - \mu_2}{R}$$

(C) The factor $\dfrac{\mu_2 - \mu_1}{R}$ is called power of the spherical refracting urface. It gives the measure of the degree to which the refracting surface can converge or diverge the rays of light passing through it.

Map-9

Optical Instruments

Microscope Forms large image of tiny objects

Magnification produced by simple microscope

Telescope provide angular magnification of distant objects magnification by telescope

Magnification by compound microscope

Image formed at near point
$$M = 1 + \frac{D}{f} \quad D = 25 \text{ cm}$$

Image formed at infinity $M = \dfrac{D}{f}$

When final image is formed at infinity
$$M = -\frac{v_0}{u_0} \frac{D}{f_e}$$
Length of the microscope
$$L = |v_0| + f_e$$

When final image is formed at near point
$$M = -\frac{v_0}{u_0}\left(1 + \frac{D}{f_e}\right)$$
Length of the microscope
$$L = |v_0| + |u_e|$$

Dispersion Without Deviation (Direct Vision Spectroscope)
- To produce dispersion without mean deviation we use a combination of two prisms of different materials such that
$$A' = -\left(\frac{\mu - 1}{\mu' - 1}\right)A \text{ or } \frac{A'}{A} = \frac{(\mu - 1)}{(\mu' - 1)}$$
- Net dispersion caused
$$= (\mu_v - \mu_R)A + (\mu'_v - \mu'_R)A'$$
$$= (\mu - 1)A(\omega - \omega') = \delta(\omega - \omega')$$

Deviation Without Dispersion (Achromatic Prism)
- To produce deviation without dispersion we use a combination of two prisms of different materials such that $A' = \left[\dfrac{\mu_V - \mu_R}{\mu_V - \mu_R}\right]A$

When final image is formed at near point
$$M = -\frac{f_0}{f_e}\left(1 + \frac{f_e}{D}\right)$$
Length of the telescope,
$$L = f_0 + |u_e|$$

When final image is formed at infinity
$$M = -\frac{f_0}{f_e}$$
Length of the telescope,
$$L = f_0 + f_e$$

Power of a lens
$$P = \frac{1}{f(\text{in metre})}$$
Unit of power of lens is diopter (D)
$P_{convex} \to$ Positve
$P_{concave} \to$ Negative
and $P_{plane} \to$ Zero

Focal length of lens-**Lens maker's formula**
$$\frac{1}{f} = (\mu - 1)\left(\frac{1}{R_1} - \frac{1}{R_2}\right)$$
When one face of a lens is silvered, it behaves as a concave mirror. If f is the effective focal length of the lens, then $\dfrac{1}{f_e} = \dfrac{2}{f_\ell} + \dfrac{1}{f_m}$ is the focal length of the mirror
(i) Plano-convex lens silvered at plane surface, then
$$f_e = \frac{R}{2(\mu - 1)}$$
(ii) Plano-convex lens silvered at plane surface, then
$$f_e = \frac{R}{2\mu}$$

Dispersive power
$$\omega = \left(\frac{\mu_v - \mu_r}{\mu_y - 1}\right)$$

Angle of deviation $\delta = A(\mu - 1)$
- When prism is thin, then value of A will be small ($\leq 10°$) $\delta_m = (n - 1)A$
- Condition for maximum deviation i_1 or $i_2 = 90°$.

Prism Formula
$$\mu = \frac{\sin\left(\dfrac{A + \delta m}{2}\right)}{\sin A/2}$$

Lens formula $\dfrac{1}{f} = \dfrac{1}{v} - \dfrac{1}{u}$
$f_{concave}$ = negative
f_{convex} = positive
and $f_{plane} = \infty$

Refraction by lens

Refraction through Prism

Mind

Doppler's effect in light
Source of light moves towards the stationary observer

$$v' = v\sqrt{\frac{(1+v/c)}{1-v/c}} \text{ and } \lambda' = \lambda\sqrt{\frac{(1-v/c)}{(1+v/c)}}$$

(For $v \ll c$).
(a) Apparent frequency $v' = v\left(1+\dfrac{v}{c}\right)$ and

(b) Apparent wavelength $\lambda' = \lambda\left(1-\dfrac{v}{c}\right)$

(c) Doppler's shift $\Delta\lambda = \lambda.\dfrac{v}{c}$

Source of light moves away from the stationary observer: In this case $v' < v$ and $\lambda' > \lambda$.

$$v' = v\sqrt{\frac{(1-v/c)}{(1+v/c)}} \text{ and } \lambda' = \lambda\sqrt{\frac{(1+v/c)}{1-v/c}}$$

For $v \ll c$)
(a) Apparent frequency $v' = v\left(1-\dfrac{v}{c}\right)$ and

(b) Apparent wavelength $\lambda' = \lambda\left(1+\dfrac{v}{c}\right)$

(c) Doppler's shift, $\Delta\lambda = \lambda\dfrac{v}{c}$

Wavefront
Locus of all particles vibrating in same phase

Huygens' principle
Each point on the primary wavefront is the source of a secondary wavelets
- The locus of the secondary wavelets in the forward direction gives the position of new wavefront at any subsequent time.
- Direction of wave propagation and wavefront are mutually perpendicular to each other.

Drawbacks of wave theory
- Cannot explain photo electric effect, comptan and Raman effect
- Hypothetical medium in vacuum is not true imagination

Forms of wavefront

Cylindrical wavefront
Linear light source
Effective distance -finite
Intensity $I \propto \dfrac{1}{r}$
Amplitude $A \propto \dfrac{1}{\sqrt{r}}$

Plane wavefront Light source at large distance: Effective distance infinite Intensity and amplitude independent of distance

Spherical wavefront Point light source
Effective distance- finite
Intensity $I \propto \dfrac{1}{r^2}$
Amplitude $A \propto \dfrac{1}{r}$

WAVE OPTICS
Describes the connection between waves and rays of light

Coherent sources of light
Sources of light, emitting light of same wavelength same frequency having a zero or constant phase difference.

Interference of light
Redistribution of energy due to superposition of waves

Constructive interference
Phase diff. $\delta = 2n\pi$
Path difference, $\Delta x = 2n(\lambda/2)$
Time interval between two waves $\Delta t = 2n\dfrac{T}{2}$
Resultant amplitude, $A = a_1 + a_3$
Resultant intensity, $I = \sqrt{\sqrt{I_1} + \sqrt{I_2}}^2$

Destructive interference
Phase diff. $\delta = (2n-1)\pi$; Path diff. $\Delta x = (2n-1)\ \lambda/2$
Time interval between two waves, $\Delta t = (2n-1)T/2$
Resultant amplitude $A = a_1 - a_2$
Resultant intensity $I = (\sqrt{I_1} - \sqrt{I_2})^2$

Superposition of waves.
When two similar waves propagate simultaneously then resultant displacement
$$\vec{y} = \vec{y}_1 + \vec{y}_2$$

For two waves, $y_1 = a_1 \sin\omega t$ and $a_2 \sin(\omega t + \phi)$ meeting at a point, Resultant wave, $y = A\sin(\omega t + \phi)$
Resultant amplitude
$$A = \sqrt{a_1^2 + a_2^2 + 2a_1 a_2 \cos\phi}$$
Resultant intensity,
$I \propto (\text{amplitude})^2$;
$$\tan\theta = \frac{a_2\sin\phi}{a_1 + a_2\cos\phi}$$

Map-10

- **Diffraction of light :** The phenomena of bending of light waves around the sharp edges of opaque obstacles or aperture and their encroachment in the geometrical shadow of obstacle or aperture and their encroachment in the geometrical shadow of obstacle or aperture is defined as diffraction of light.
  Necessary conditions of diffraction of waves : The size of the obstacle (a) must be of the order of the wavelength of the wave (λ). i.e. $\frac{a}{\lambda} \approx 1$

- **Fraunhoffer diffraction at single slit :** Diffraction occurs due to superposition between the wavelets originated from same wavefront. For diffraction, size of aperture is order of wavelength of wave.
  $a \sin\theta = \lambda$, for first order minima
  Width of principal maxima $= 2\theta = 2\sin^{-1}(\lambda/a)$

For secondary maximum
Path diff.
$$= \frac{(2n+1)\lambda}{2}$$
Linear distance
$$= \frac{(2n+1)D\lambda}{2a}$$

For secondary minimum
path difference $= n\lambda$
Linear distance $= \dfrac{nD\lambda}{a}$
$$= \frac{n\lambda f}{2}, f = D \text{ focal}$$
length of converging lens

Angular width of central
maxima $= 2\theta = \dfrac{2\lambda}{a}$
Linear width central
maxima $= 2x = 2D\theta$
$$= \frac{2\lambda D}{a}$$

Law of Malus
$I = I_o\cos^2\theta$
$I =$ intensity of transmitted light from analyser
Also, $A^2 = A_0^2 \cos^2\theta$
$\Rightarrow A = A_0 \cos\theta$
If $\theta = 0°, I = 0, A = 0$
If $\theta = 90°, I = 0, A = 0$

$$I = \frac{I_{unpolarised}}{2} \cos^2\theta$$
i.e., If an unpolarised light into plane polarised light its intensity becomes half.

Polarisation
Restricting the vibration of light in a particular direction perpendicular to the direction of propagation of wave

Brewster's law $\mu = \tan\theta_p$, $\theta_p =$ angle of polarisation
For $i < \theta_p$ or $i > \theta_p$ Both reflected and refrected rays becomes partially polarised.
For glass $\theta_p \approx 57°$ and for water $\theta_p \approx 53°$

Fringe visibility : $V = \dfrac{I_{max} - I_{min}}{I_{max} + I_{min}}$

V_{max}, if $I_1 = I_2 = I$ or $I_{min} = 0$
If widths of slits S_1 and S_2 are unequal the brightness of the bright fringe and the darkness of the dark fringe decreases.
If $I_1 >> I_2$ then $I_{max} = I_{min}$

Distance between central fringe and n^{th} dark fringe
$$X_n = \frac{(2n-1)\lambda D}{2d}$$
$$= \frac{(2n-1)\beta}{2} \quad n = 1, 2, 3$$

Young's double slit experiment (YDSE)

Fringe width (β)

Distance between centres of two consecutive bright or dark fringes $\beta = \dfrac{D}{d}\lambda$

Angular width of fringe, $\alpha D = \beta \Rightarrow \alpha = \dfrac{\beta}{D} = \dfrac{\lambda}{d}$

In YDSE pringe pattern shifting

- Fringe shift $= \dfrac{D}{d}(\mu - 1)t = \dfrac{\beta}{\lambda}(\mu - 1)t$

- Additional path difference $= (\mu - 1)t$

- If sift is equivalent to n fringes then $n = \dfrac{(\mu - 1)t}{\lambda}$ or $t = \dfrac{n\lambda}{(\mu - 1)}$

- Shift is independent of the order of fringe (i.e., shift of zero order maxima = shift of nth order maxima).
- Shift is independent of wavelength.

Distance between central fringe and n^{th} bright fringe
$$X_n = \frac{n\lambda D}{d}$$
$D =$ distance between source and screen ;
$d =$ distance between two slits

Mind

Thermionic emission
Emission of electrons by suitably heating of metal surface. It is used in conventional electron tubes like television picture tubes.

Field emission
Emission of electrons by applying a very strong electric field to a metal. **It is also called cold emission.**

Photoelectric emission
Emission of free electrons from the surface of metals when light radiation of suitable frequency fall on it
• **Threshold frequency** Minimum frequency of incident radiation to eject the electrons (v_0)
No photoelectron emission, if $v < v_0$

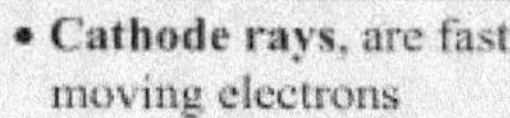

• **Cathode rays,** are fast moving electrons
• They exert mechanical force on the objects they strike
• Produce fluorescence
• Produce heat when they strike a metal surface
• They are deflected by both electric and magnetic field.
• Velocity ranging $\dfrac{1}{30}$ th to $\dfrac{1}{10}$ th to velocity of light.

Methods of electron emission

Electron emission
Emission of electrons from the surface of metal

Work function
Minimum energy required to just escape electron from metal surface $\phi_0 = h v_0 = \dfrac{hc}{\lambda_0}$
In electron volt, $E(ev) = \dfrac{hc}{e\lambda}$
$= \dfrac{12375}{\lambda(\text{Å})} = \dfrac{12400}{\lambda(\text{Å})}$

Einstein's photoelectric equation
$$K_{max} = \frac{1}{2} m v_{max}^2 = h(v - v_0) = hv - hv_0$$
$$= hc\left(\frac{1}{\lambda} - \frac{1}{\lambda_0}\right) \quad hv = hv_0 + K_{max}$$
$$K_{max} = eV_0 \quad v_{max} = \sqrt{\frac{2h(v - v_0)}{m}}$$
$$K_{max} = \frac{1}{2} m v_{max}^2 = eV_0$$
$$= hc\left(\frac{1}{\lambda} - \frac{1}{\lambda_0}\right) = hc\left(\frac{\lambda_0 - \lambda}{\lambda\lambda_0}\right)$$
$$v_{max} = \sqrt{\frac{2hc}{m} \frac{(\lambda_0 - \lambda)}{\lambda\lambda_0}}$$
$$V_0 = \frac{h}{e}(v - v_0) = \frac{hc}{e}\left(\frac{1}{\lambda} - \frac{1}{\lambda_0}\right)$$
$$= 12345\left(\frac{1}{\lambda} - \frac{1}{\lambda_0}\right)$$

Millikan's oil drop experiment
Charge on an oil droplet always an integral multiple of elementary charge 1.602×10^{-19} C
$$q = \frac{6\pi n(v_1 + v_2)d}{v}\left[\frac{9nv_1}{2g(\rho - \sigma)}\right]^{1/2}$$
V_1 = Terminal velocity of drop when no electric field is applied
V_2 = Terminal velocity when electric field applied

Photon Tiny packets of light energy Energy of a photon $E = hv$

Mass of photon Rest mass of the photon is zero. But it's effective mass $E = mc^2 = hv$
$$\Rightarrow m = \frac{E}{c^2} = \frac{hv}{c^2} = \frac{h}{c\lambda}$$
Also, known as kinetic mass of the photon
Momentum of the photon
Momentum $p = m \times c =$
$$\frac{E}{c} = \frac{hv}{c} = \frac{h}{\lambda}$$

Dual Nature of Radiation and Matter
Light has dual nature-wave and particle like nature

Effect of intensity of light on photocurrent for a fixed frequency of incident radiation. Photoelectric current $\propto$ intensity of incident light

Effect of potential on photo-electric current. For a fixed frequency and intensity of incident light photoelectric current increases with increase in the potential

Number of emitted photons: The number of photons emitted per second from a source of monochromatic radiation of wavelength λ and power P
$$(n) = \frac{P}{E} = \frac{P}{hv} = \frac{P\lambda}{hc} \quad E = \text{energy of each photon}$$
Intensity of light (I) $\quad I = \dfrac{E}{At} = \dfrac{P}{A} \quad \left(\dfrac{E}{t} = P = \text{radiation power}\right)$
At a distance r from a point source of power P intensity is given by
$$I = \frac{P}{4\pi r^2} \Rightarrow I \propto \frac{1}{r^2}, \text{ for a line source} \quad I \propto \frac{P}{2\pi l} \Rightarrow I \propto \frac{1}{r}.$$
Number of photons falling per second (n) power of radiation P and E is the energy of a photon then $n = \dfrac{P}{E}$

Map-11

Photocell Converts a change in intensity of illumination into a change in photocurrent It is a technological application of photoelectric effect.

Stopping potential Photoelectric current becomes zero at a particular value of negative potential v_0 called stopping potential or cut-off potential

Stopping potential varies linearly with the frequency of incident radiation for a given photosensitive material

Uses of photocell
- Count the persons entering an auditorium
- Burglar alarm.
- In motion picture and television

X-rays Electromagnetic radiations of very short wavelength, 0.1 Å to 100 Å and high energy which are emitted when fast moving electrons or cathode rays strike a target of high atomic mass.

Types of X-rays
(i) Continuous X-rays
(ii) Characteristic X-rays

Davisson and Germer experiment Confirms the wave nature of electrons

Application of X-rays
- In industry to detect defects in metallic structure
- To determine internal structure of crystal using Bragg's law $n\lambda = 2d \sin \theta$
- In radio therapy
- In medicine and surgery

Absorption of X-Rays
X-rays are absorbed when they are incident on substance.

Intensity of emergent X-rays $I = I_0 e^{-\mu x}$

So intensity of absorbed X-rays $I' = I_0 - I$

$= I_0(1 - e^{-\mu x})$ where x = thickness of absorbing medium, μ = absorption coefficient.

Properties of X-rays
- X-rays are invisible
- They travel in a straight line with speed of light.
- X-rays are measured in Roentgen.
- X-rays carry no charge so they are not deflected in magnetic field and electric field.
- They ionise gases.
- X-rays do not pass through heavy metals and bones.
- They affect photographic plates.
- Long exposure to X-rays is injurious for human body.
- Lead is the best absorber of X-rays.
- For X-ray photography of human body parts, $BaSO_4$ is the best absorber.
- They show all the important properties of light rays like, reflection, interference, diffraction and polarization etc.

Matter Waves (de-Brogile Waves)
Waves associated with moving particle and it propagates in the form of wave packets with group velocity.

- **de-Broglie wavelength**

$$\lambda = \frac{h}{p} = \frac{h}{mv} = \frac{h}{\sqrt{2mE}} \Rightarrow \lambda \propto \frac{1}{p} \propto \frac{1}{v} \propto \frac{1}{\sqrt{E}}$$

- **de-Broglie wavelength associated with the charged particles**

$$\lambda = \frac{h}{p} = \frac{h}{mv} = \frac{h}{\sqrt{2mE}} = \frac{h}{\sqrt{2mqV}}$$

$$\lambda_{Electron} = \frac{12.27}{\sqrt{V}}\,\overset{\circ}{A}, \lambda_{proton} = \frac{0.286}{\sqrt{V}}\,\overset{\circ}{A},$$

$$\lambda_{Deuttron} = \frac{0.202}{\sqrt{V}}\,\overset{\circ}{A}, \lambda_{\alpha-particle} = \frac{0.101}{\sqrt{V}}\,\overset{\circ}{A}$$

- **de-Broglie wavelength associated with uncharged particles:** For Neutron de-Broglie wavelength

$$\lambda_{Neutron} = \frac{0.286 \times 10^{-10}}{\sqrt{E(\text{in } eV)}}\,m = \frac{0.286}{\sqrt{E(\text{in } eV)}}\,\overset{\circ}{A}$$

Energy of thermal neutrons at ordinary temperature

$\because E = kT \Rightarrow \lambda = \dfrac{h}{\sqrt{3mkT}}$; where T = Absolute temperature,

k = Boltzmann's constant = 1.38×10^{-23} Joule/kelvin,

- **Ratio of wavelength of photon and electron**

$$\frac{\lambda_{ph}}{\lambda_e} = \frac{c}{E}\sqrt{2mK} = \sqrt{\frac{2mc^2 K}{E^2}}$$

Characteristics of Matter waves
- Matter waves are not electromagneticin nature.
- de-Broglie or matter wave is independent of the charge on the material particle.
- Electron microscope works on the phenomena of de-Broglie waves.
- The phase velocity of the matter waves can be greater than the speed of the light.
- Matter waves can propagate in vacuum, hence not mechanical waves.
- de-Broglie's matter-wave concept is analogous to the Bohr's hypothesis.

$$2\pi r = n\lambda, \text{ where } \lambda = \frac{h}{mv}$$

$$\Rightarrow 2\pi r = n\frac{h}{mv} \text{ or, } mvr = \frac{nh}{2\pi}$$

Mind

Bohr model of Hydrogen atom

Electron can revolve only in those orbits in which angular momentum about the nucleus is an integral multiple

of $\dfrac{h}{2\pi}$ i.e., $mvr = \dfrac{nh}{2\pi}$

- The radiation of energy occurs only when an electron jumps from one permitted orbit to another.

J.J Thomson model of atom

First model of atom Plum pudding model-positive charge is uniformly distributed and negatively charged electrons are embedded in it like seeds in a watermelon

Rutherford nuclear model

Entire positive charge and most of the mass of the atom is concentrated in nucleus and electrons revolving around the nucleus

Model of atom

Atoms

Consists of elementary particles electrons, protons and neutrons

Drawbacks of Bohr model

- Unable to explain the fine structure of spectral lines
- Valid only for single electron system
- Orbits taken as circular but according to Sommerfield these are elliptical.
- Intensity of spectral lines could not be explained.
- Nucleus was taken as stationary but it also rotates on its own axis.
- It does not explain the Zeeman effect and Stark effect.
- It does not explain the doublets in the spectrum of some of the atoms like sodium (5890 Å and 5896 Å).

Drawbacks of Rutherford's Model

- It could not explain stability of atom
- According to this model the spectrum of atom must be continuous where as practically it is a line spectrum.
- Unable to explain the distribution of electrons outside the nucleus.

Rutherford α- particle scattering experiment

- Most of the α-particles passed through the gold foil i.e., atom has lot of empty space
- Only about 0.14% of the α-particles scatter by more than 1° and one α-particle in every 8000 α-particles deflected by $> 90°$
- Positively charged particles protons confined to core called nucleus, size about 10^{-15} to 10^{-14} m

Some other quantities for revolution of electron in n^{th} orbit

Quantity	Formula
Angular speed	$\omega_n = \dfrac{v_0}{r_n} = \dfrac{\pi m z^2 e^4}{2\varepsilon_0^2 n^3 h^3}$
Frequency	$v_n = \dfrac{w_n}{2\pi} = \dfrac{m z^2 e^4}{4\varepsilon_0^2 n^3 h^3}$
Time period	$T_n = \dfrac{1}{v_n} = \dfrac{4\varepsilon_0^2 n^3 h^3}{m z^2 e^4}$
Angular momentums	$L_n = m v_n r_n = n\left(\dfrac{h}{2\pi}\right)$
Magnetic field	$B = \dfrac{\mu_0 i_n}{2 r_n} = \dfrac{\pi n^2 z^3 e^7 \mu_0}{8\varepsilon_3^0 n^5 h^5}$

Various parameters

Radius of n-th orbit

$r_n = \dfrac{n^2 h^2}{4\pi^2 K Z e^2 m}$

$= 0.53 \dfrac{n^2}{Z}$ Å

Speed of electron in n-th orbit

$v_n = \dfrac{2\pi K Z e^2}{nh}$

$= 2.2 \times 10^6 \dfrac{Z}{n}$ m/s

Potential energy (U_n) in n-th orbit

$U_n = \dfrac{-K Z e^2}{r_n} = \dfrac{-27.2}{n^2} Z^2 eV$

Kinetic energy $E_k = \dfrac{K Z e^2}{2 r_n} = \dfrac{13.6 Z^2}{n^2}$ ev

- Number of a-particles scattered per unit area

$N(\theta) \propto \dfrac{1}{\sin^4 \theta/2}$

- Impact parameter $b = \dfrac{1}{4\pi \epsilon_0} \dfrac{Ze^2 \cot \dfrac{\theta}{2}}{\dfrac{1}{2} mv^2}$

θ = angle of scattering

Distance of closest approach

Minimum distance from the nucleus upto which α-particle approach

$r_0 = \dfrac{Ze^2}{mv^2 \pi\varepsilon_0} = \dfrac{4kZe^2}{mv^2}$

$k = \dfrac{1}{4\pi\varepsilon_0}$

$= 9 \times 10^9 \, Nm^2 c^{-2}$

ε_0 = permittivity of free space

Map-12

Lyman series
$$v = \frac{1}{\lambda}$$
$$= R\left[\frac{1}{1^2} - \frac{1}{n^2}\right]$$
n = 2, 3, 4..........
in uv-region

Balmer series
$$\bar{v} = \frac{1}{\lambda}$$
$$= R\left[\frac{1}{2^2} - \frac{1}{n^2}\right]$$
n = 3, 4, 5
in visible region

Paschem series
$$\bar{v} = \frac{1}{\lambda}$$
$$= R\left[\frac{1}{3^2} - \frac{1}{n^2}\right]$$
n = 4, 5, 6, ...
In infra-red ration

Brackett series
$$\bar{v} = \frac{1}{\lambda}$$
$$= R\left[\frac{1}{4^2} - \frac{1}{n^2}\right]$$
n= 5, 6, 7 ......
In infra-red region

P-fund seried
$$\bar{V} = \frac{1}{\lambda} = R\left[\frac{1}{5^2} - \frac{1}{n^2}\right]$$
n= 6, 7, 8, ...
In infra-red region

Various series of line spectra of hydrogen atom

Hydrogen Spectrum and Spectral Series
Spectral lines arising from the transition of electron forms a spectra series.

- According to the Bohr's theory the wavelength of the radiations emitted from hydrogen atom

$$\frac{1}{\lambda}R\left[\frac{1}{n_1^2} - \frac{1}{n_2^2}\right] \Rightarrow \lambda = \frac{n_1^2 n_2^2}{(n_2^2 - n_1^2)R} = \frac{n_1^2}{\left(1 - \frac{n_1^2}{n_2^2}\right)R}$$

where n_2 = outer orbit (electron jumps from this obrit), n_1 = inner orbit (electron falls in this orbit).

- First line of the series is called first member.
  For this line wavelength is maximum (λ_{max})

For maximum wavelength if $n_1 = n$ then $n_2 = n + 1$

- $\lambda_{max} = \dfrac{n^2(n+1)^2}{(2n+1)R}$

- Last line of the series is called series limit.
  For this line wavelength is minimum (λ_{min})

For minimum wavelength $n_2 = \infty$, $n_1 = n$,

so $\lambda_{min} = \dfrac{n^2}{R}$

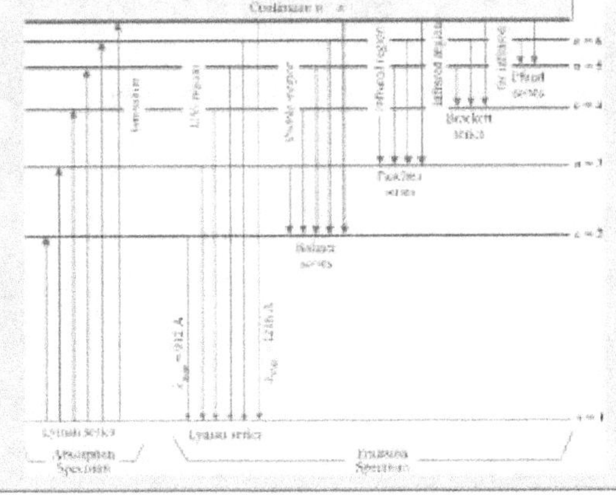

Transition of Electron
When an electron makes transition from higher energy level energy $E_2(n_2)$ to a lower energy level, energy $E_1(n_1)$ then

Energy of emitted radiation

$$\Delta E = E_2 - E_1 = \frac{-RchZ^2}{n_2^2} - \left(\frac{RchZ^2}{n_1^2}\right) = 13.6Z^2\left(\frac{1}{n_1^2} - \frac{1}{n_2^2}\right)$$

Frequency of emitted radiation

$$v = \frac{\Delta E}{h} = \frac{E_2 - E_1}{h} = RcZ^2\left(\frac{1}{n_1^2} - \frac{1}{n_2^2}\right)$$

Wave number/wavelength
Wave number is the number of waves in unit length

$$\bar{v} = \frac{1}{\lambda} = \frac{v}{c} \Rightarrow \frac{1}{\lambda} = RZ^2\left(\frac{1}{n_1^2} - \frac{1}{n_2^2}\right) = \frac{13.6Z^2}{hc}\left(\frac{1}{n_1^2} - \frac{1}{n_2^2}\right)$$

Recoiling of an atom: Due to transition of electron, photon is emitted and the atom is recoiled.
Recoil momentum of atom = momentum of photon

$$= \frac{h}{\lambda} = hRZ^2\left(\frac{1}{n_1^2} - \frac{1}{n_2^2}\right)$$

Also recoil energy $= \dfrac{p^2}{2m} = \dfrac{h^2}{2m\lambda^2}$

Number of spectral lines
If electron falls from orbit n_2 to n_1 then the number of spectral lines emitted $N_E = \dfrac{(n_2 - n_1 + 1)(n_2 - n_1)}{2}$

If electron falls from nth orbit to ground state (i.e., $n_2 = n$ and $n_1 = 1$) then number of spectral lines emitted

$$N_E = \frac{n(n-1)}{2}$$

Mind

Isotopes
Nuclides with same atomic number, Z but different mass number, A or no. of neutrons N

e.g., $_1H^1$, $_1H^2$, $_1H^3$, $_8O^{16}$, $_8O^{17}$, $_8O^{18}$

Isobars
Nuclides with same mass number, A or no. of neutrons N but different atomic number Z

e.g., $_1H^3$, $_2He^3$; $_6H^{14}$, $_7N^{14}$

Isotones
Nuclides with same number of neutrons (N) Atomic number (Z) and mass number (A) are different but (A-Z) same,

e.g., $_{14}Be^9$, $_5Be^{10}$, $_6C^{13}$, $_7N^{14}$

Mirror nuclei
Nuclei having the same mass number, A but number of proton (Z) and number of neutron (A-Z) interchanged. e.g., $_1H^3$ and $_2He^3$, $_3Li^7$ and $_4Be^7$

Nuclide $_Z^A X$
Atomic mass A = Protons + neutrons
Atomic no. Z = no. of protons

Nuclear stability $\left(\dfrac{N}{Z}\,ratio\right)$

- For ligher nuclei-greatest stability when $\dfrac{N}{Z} = 1$
- For heavier nuclei-greater stability only when they have more neutrons than protons.

Atomic mass unit (amu) 1 amu
$= \dfrac{1}{12}$ of mass of $_6C^{12}$ atom

$1\,u = 1.660539 \times 10^{-27}$ kg, 1 amu = 931 Mev

Composition of Nucleus
(Protons + neutrons)

Size of nucleus, radius $R = R_0 A^{1/3}$

$R_0 = 1.1 \times 10^{-15}$ m

Density $\rho = \dfrac{3m}{4\pi R_0^3} = 2.3 \times 10^{17}$ kg/m^3

No. of nucleon (mass of proton + mass of neutron) per unit volume $= 10^{44}$ nucleon/m^3

Mass of proton $m_p = 1.00727u = 1.67 \times 10^{-27}$ kg

Mass of neutron $m_n = 1.00866u = 1.67 \times 10^{-27}$ kg

Mass of electron $m_e = 0.00055u = 9.1 \times 10^{-31}$ kg

Binding energy
$E_b = \Delta m c^2$

Binding energy per necleon
$= \dfrac{Total\ binding\ energy}{Mass\ number}$

$= \dfrac{\Delta m \times 931}{A} = \dfrac{MeV}{Nucleon}$

Binding energy per nucleon $\propto$ stability of nucleons

Mass defect
Sum of masses of nucleons–mass of nucleus $(\Delta m) = M - m$
$= [Zm_p + (A - Z)m_n - m]$

Packing fraction
$f = \dfrac{\Delta m}{A}$

$= \dfrac{Exact\ nuclear\ mass - Mass\ number}{Mass\ number}$

Packing fraction may be +(ve), –(ve) or zero

Binding energy per nucleon current
It is maximum about 8.8 MeV for $F_e^{(56)}$

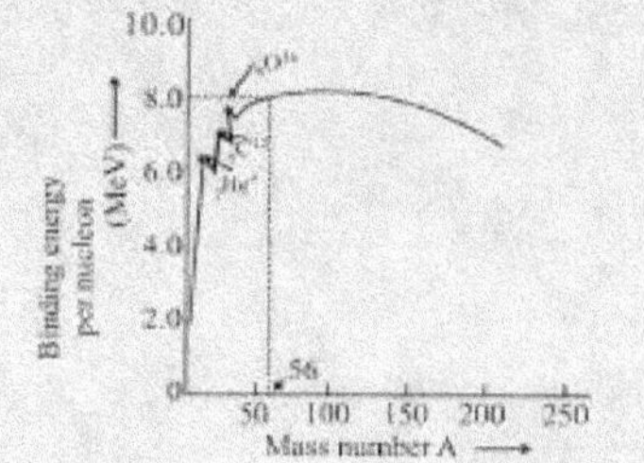

Nuclei
Nuclei consists of protons and neutrons.

- Nuclear forces bound nucleons in the nucleus
- These are attractive forces
- These are short range forces, do not exist at large distance greater than 10^{-15} m
- Nuclear forces are the strongest forces in nature and non-centra
- **Nuclear Force** Acting inside the nucleus or acting between the nucleons due to

Radioactive series

Series	Mass number	Starting isotope	Stable end product	Natural/Artificial
Thorium	4n	$_{90}Th^{232}$	$_{82}Pb^{208}$	Natural
Neptunium	4n+1	$_{93}Np^{237}$	$_{83}Bi^{209}$	Artificial
Uranium	4n+2	$_{92}U^{238}$	$_{82}Pb^{206}$	Natural
Actinium	4n+3	$_{92}U^{235}$	$_{82}Pb^{207}$	Natural

Map-13

Radioactivity
Disintegration of heavy elements into comparatively lighter elements by emission of α, β and γ radiation

Nuclear energy

Nuclear Fission Splitting of a heavy nucleus into two or more lighter nuclei
$$_{92}U^{235} + {}_0n^1 \rightarrow {}_{56}Ba^{141} + {}_{36}Kr^{92} + 3\,{}_0n^1 + \text{energy}$$

Atom bomb
Works on the principle of nuclear fission

Nuclear fusion Combining two lighter nuclei to form one heavy nucleus
$$_1H^2 + {}_1H^2 + {}_1H^2 \rightarrow {}_2He^4 + {}_1H^1 + {}_0n^1 + 21.6\,\text{Mev}$$

Hydrogen bomb
Works on the principle of nuclear fusion

Moderator Slow down fast moving neutrons e.g.: heavy water, graphite

Coolant Remove heat e.g: cold water, liquid oxygen

Control rods Absorb neutrons e.g., boron, cadmium etc.

α-decay i.e., doubly ionised helium ion After emission of one α-particle atomic no. decreases by 2 and mass number by 4

β-decay i.e., fast moving electrons After emission of one β-particle atomic number increases by 1 and mass number remains unchanged

γ-decay
After emission there is no change in atomic number and mass number

Rate of decay law
$$\left(\frac{-dN}{dt}\right) \propto N \Rightarrow -\frac{dN}{dt} = \lambda N$$
No. of undecayed atoms at any instant $N = N_0 e^{-\lambda t}$

Half life $t_{1/2} = \dfrac{0.693}{\lambda}$

Mean life $\tau = \dfrac{1}{\lambda} = \dfrac{1}{0.693}(t_{1/2})$

Time interval, undecayed atom (N) becomes $\dfrac{1}{e}$ times or 0.37 times of original number.

Activity of radioactive element
$$A = \left(-\frac{dN}{dt}\right) = \lambda N = \lambda N_0 e^{-\lambda t}$$
Activity after time, t
$$A = A_0 e^{-\lambda t}$$

Uses of radiaoactive isotope
- In medicine-for cancer Co-60 for testing blood circulation Na-24
- In archaeology-for determining age of archaelogical sample C-14
- In agriculture-as fertilisers P-31

Property	α – rays	β – rays	γ – rays
1. Nature	These are doubly ionized helium atom ${}_2He^4$ Charge $q = +2e = 3.2 \times 10^{-19}C$ Mass $m = 2p + 2n = 4$amu $= 4 \times 1.6 \times 10^{-27}$ kg	These are beams of fast moving electrons $(_{-1}\beta^0)$ and positrons $(_{+1}\beta^0)$ charge $_{-1}\beta^0 = -e = -1.6 \times 10^{-19}C$ $_{+1}\beta^0 = +e = 1.6 \times 10^{-19}C$ $m(_{-1}\beta^0) = m(_{+1}\beta^0) = 9.1 \times 10^{-31}$ kg	These are electromagnetic radiations of high frequency and travel in form of photons. Charge $q = 0$ (chargeless) Rest mass $= 0$ Effective mass $= \dfrac{h\nu}{c^2} = \dfrac{h}{\lambda c}$
2. Speed	Speed ranges between 1.4×10^7 to 2.20×10^7 m/s $v_\alpha \sim 0.05\,c$	Speed ranges from 1% to 90% of velocity of light $v_\beta \sim 0.9c$	Speed equals velocity of light $v_\gamma = c$
3. Ionising power $(\alpha > \beta > \gamma)$	These have maximum ionizing power (10000)	Their ionizing power is less than α particles and more than γ rays (100)	Their ionizing power is least (1)
4. Penetration power $(\alpha < \beta < \gamma)$	The penetration power is smallest. Can only penetrate through 0.01 mm thick Al sheet (1)	Penetration power is about 100 times that of α rays, can penetrate through 1 mm thick Al sheet (100)	Penetration power is very large. 10,000 times that of X - rays. Can penetrate about 30 cm thick Al sheet (10,000)
5. Range	Range is very small (few cms in air)	Range is more than α rays (few meters in air)	Range is very large (many hundreds of meter in air)
6. Nature of spectrum	Line spectrum	Continuous spectrum	Line spectrum
7. Interaction with matter	Produces heat	Produces heat	Produces photoelectric effect, Compton effect and pair production
8. Effect on photographic plate and ZnS	Affects photographic plate and produces fluorescense on ZnS	Affects photographic plate and produces fluorescence on ZnS	Affects photographic plate and produces fluorescence on ZnS
9. Effect of electric and magnetic field	Suffers small deflection	Suffers large deflection	Pass undeflected

Mind

Comparison Between Conductors, Semiconductors and Insulators

Property	Conductors	Semiconductors	Insulators
1. Resistivity range	$10^{-6} - 10^{-8}\ \Omega m$	$10^{5} - 10^{0}\ \Omega m$	$10^{7} - 10^{16}\ \Omega m$
2. Conductivity range	$10^{+6} - 10^{-8}$ mho/m	$10^{-5} - 10^{0}$ mho/m	$10^{-7} - 10^{-16}$ mho/m
3. Temp. coefficient of resistance (α)	Positive	Negative	Negative
4. Flow of current	Due to free electrons	Due to electrons and holes	No current flow
5. Energy band diagram	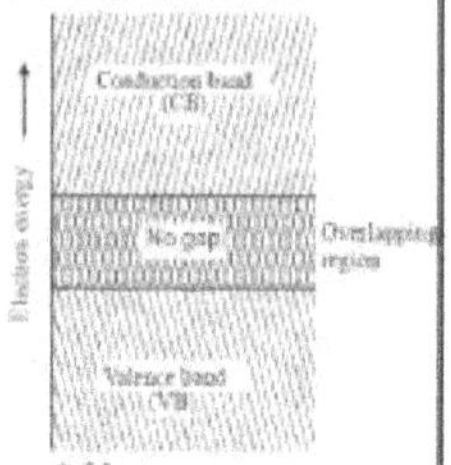 Conduction band (CB) No gap Overlapping region Valence band (VB) Electron energy	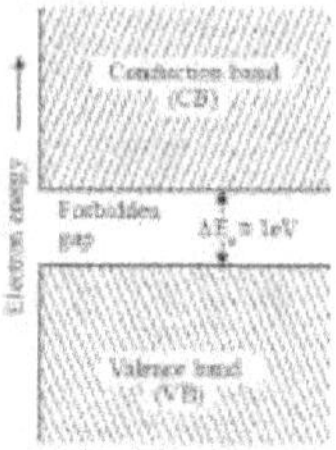 Conduction band (CB) Forbidden gap $\Delta E_g \simeq 1eV$ Valence band (VB) Electron energy	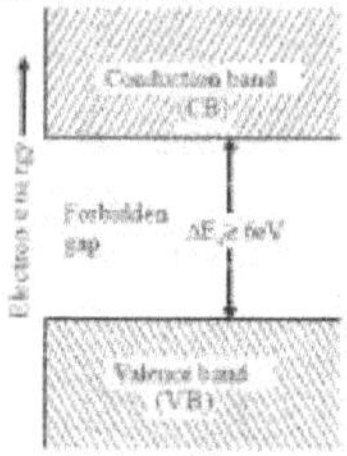 Conduction band (CB) Forbidden gap $\Delta E_g \geq 6eV$ Valence band (VB) Electron energy
6. Forbidden energy gap	$\simeq$ 0eV	$\simeq$ 0.1 – 3eV	$\geq$ 6eV
7. Examples	Pt, Al, Cu, Ag, etc.	Ge(0.67eV), Si(1.14eV), C, Ga, As GaF_2 etc.	Wood, plastic, diamond, mica

Semiconductor

Extrinsic or impure semiconductor
Due to desirable addition of impurity atoms or dopants
This is to improve conductivity

Intrinsic or pure semiconductors
e.g., Si, Ge Intrinsic carrier concentration
$n_i = n_e = n_h$
Total current
$I = n_e + n_h$

N-type semiconductor
Si or Ge doped with pentavalent As, Sb, Bi etc.
Electrons majority and holes minority carriers $n_e >> n_h$

P-type semiconductor
Si or Ge doped with trivalent, B, Al etc.
Electrons minority and holes majority carriers
$n_h >> n_e$

Semiconductor Electronics: Materials, Devices And Simple Circuits

Comparison of Intrinsic, N-type, & P-type and Extrinsic Semiconductor

	Intrinsic semiconductor	N-type (extrinsic semiconductor)	P-type (extrinsic semiconductor)
1.	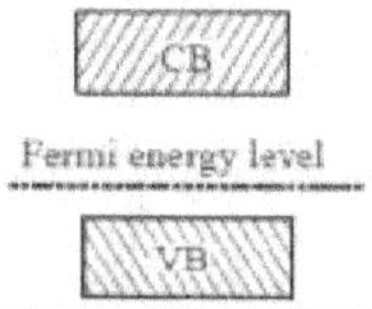 CB Fermi energy level VB	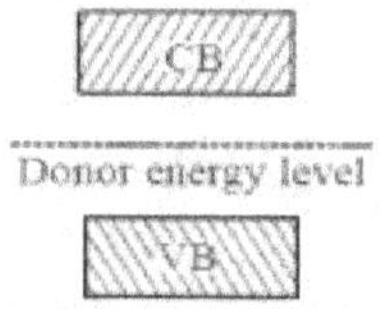 CB Donor energy level VB	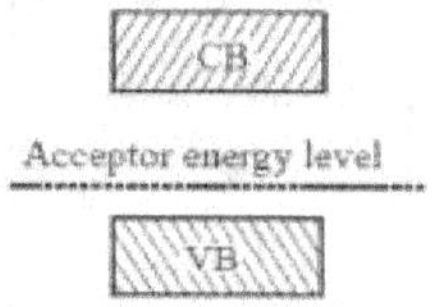 CB Acceptor energy level VB
2.	Current due to both electrons and holes	Current mainly due to electrons	Current mainly due to holes
3.	$n_e = n_h = n_i$	$n_h << n_e$ ($N_D \simeq n_e$)	$n_h >> n_e$ ($N_A \simeq n$)
4.	$I = I_e + I_h$	$I \simeq I_e$	$I \simeq I_h$
5.	Quantity of electrons and holes are equal	Majority carrier - electrons Minority carrier - holes	Majority carrier - holes Minority carrier - electrons
6.	Current density $J = ne\,[v_e + v_h]$	$J \simeq e\,n_h\,v_h$	$J \simeq e\,n_e\,v_e$
7.	Conductance $\sigma = \frac{1}{\rho} = en\,[\mu_e + \mu_h]$	$\sigma = \frac{1}{\rho} \cong e\,n_h\,\mu_h$	$\sigma = \frac{1}{\rho} \cong e\,n_e\,\mu_e$

Map-14

P-N Junction Diode as a Rectifier

Rectifier converts ac to dc. It is of **Half wave rectifier** When the P-N junction diode rectifies half of the ac signal.

Efficiency $\%\eta = \dfrac{P_{out}}{P_{in}} \times 100 = \dfrac{40.6}{1 + \dfrac{r_f}{R_L}}$

Form factor $= \dfrac{I_{rms}}{I_{dc}} = \dfrac{\pi}{2} = 1.57$

Ripple frequency (ω) for half wave rectifier is same as that of ac.

Full wave rectifier: It rectifies both halves of signal.

Difference Between Forward Bias and Reverse Bias

	Forward bias		Reverse bias
1.	Potential barrier reduces.	1.	Potential barrier increases.
2.	Width of depletion layer decreases.	2.	Width of depletion layer increases.
3.	P-N Jn. provide very small resistance.	3.	P-N Jn. provide high resistance.
4.	Forward current flow in circuit.	4.	Very small current flow in circuit.
5.	Order of forward current in milli amp.	5.	Order of current in micro amp.
6.	Mainly majority current flows.	6.	Mainly minority current flows.
7.	Forward characteristic curve	7.	Reverse characteristic curve
8.	Forward resistance $R_f = \dfrac{\Delta V_f}{\Delta I_f} \approx 100\,\Omega$	8.	Reverse resistance $R_r = \dfrac{\Delta V_r}{\Delta I_r} \approx 10^6\,\Omega$
9.	Knee or cut voltage $Ge \to 0.3\,V,\ Si \to 0.7\,V$	9.	Breakdown voltage $Ge \to 25\,V,\ Si \to 35\,V$

Transistor

A three terminal semi-conductor device. n-p-n and p-n-p transistors CE, CC and CB configuration

P-n junction

An arrangement made by a close contact of n-type semiconductor and p-type semiconductor

Logic gates

Digital circuit follows certain logical relationship between the input and output voltage

Inverter

Converts DC to AC

Zener diode

Used as a voltage regulator

OR gate

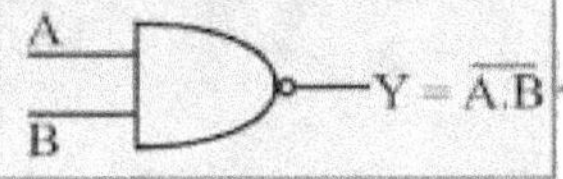

Uses of transistor

Switch

Transistor in cut off or saturation state

Oscillator frequency

$v = \dfrac{1}{2\pi\sqrt{LC}}$

Amplifier

Used for increasing the amplitude of input signal

Forward and Reverse biasing

+(ve) terminal connected to p-side and –(ve) terminal. n-side in forward biasing. In reverse biasing +(ve) terminal connected to n-side and –(ve) terminal connected to P-side of diode

Potential barrier

Potential difference developed across depletion region i.e., region either side of junction free from charge carriers. V_B for silicon $= 0.7\,V$ and for germanium $V_B = 0.3\,V$ Width of depletion region is of the order of 10^{-6} m

AND gate

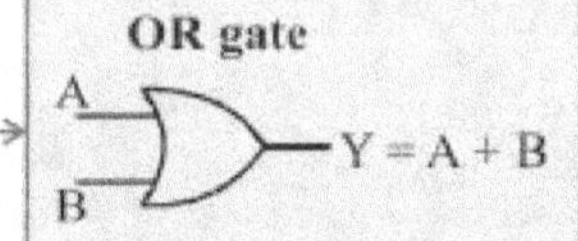

NOT gate

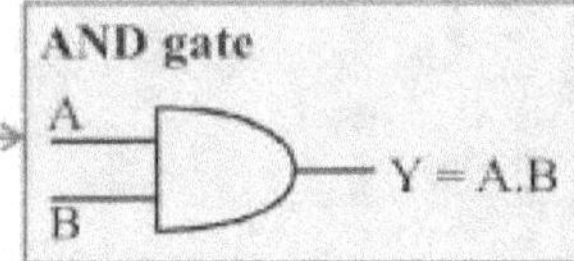

NOR gate

Combination of NOT and OR gate

NAND gate

Combination of NOT and AND gate

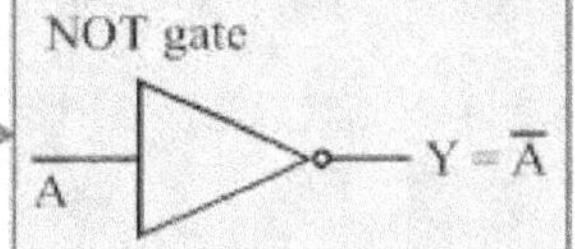

Combination of Basic gates

Comparative study of CB, CE and CC amplifier:

	CB (Common Base)	CE (Common Emitter)	CC (Common Collector)
Input resistance	Low (100Ω)	High (750 Ω)	Very high ~ 750 kΩ
Output resistance	Very high	High	Low
Current gain	$\alpha_{dc} = \dfrac{I_c}{I_e} < 1$; $\alpha_{ac} = \dfrac{\Delta I_c}{\Delta I_e}$	$\beta_{dc} = \dfrac{I_c}{I_b} > 1$; $\beta_{ac} = \dfrac{\Delta I_c}{\Delta I_b}$	$\gamma = \dfrac{I_e}{I_b} > 1$
Voltage gain	$A_V = \dfrac{V_o}{V_i} = \dfrac{I_c R_L}{I_e R_i}$; $A_V = \alpha \dfrac{R_L}{R_i} = 150$	$A_V = \dfrac{V_o}{V_i} = \dfrac{I_c R_L}{I_b R_i}$; $A_V = \beta \dfrac{R_L}{R_i} = 500$	$A_V = \dfrac{V_o}{V_i} = \dfrac{I_e R_L}{I_b R_i}$; $A_V = \gamma \dfrac{R_L}{R_i}$ (less than 1)
Power gain	$A_p = \dfrac{P_o}{P_i}$; $A_p = \alpha^2 \dfrac{R_L}{R_i}$	$A_p = \dfrac{P_o}{P_i}$; $A_p = \beta^2 \dfrac{R_L}{R_i}$	$A_p = \dfrac{P_o}{P_i}$; $A_p = \gamma^2 \dfrac{R_L}{R_i}$
Phase difference (between output and input)	Same phase	Opposite phase	Same phase
Application	For high frequency	For audiocable frequency	For impedance matching

Relation between α, β and γ

α, β	β, γ	α, γ
$I_e = I_b + I_c$	$I_e = I_b + I_c$	$I_c = I_b + I_c$
divide by I_c	divide by I_b	divide by I_c
$\dfrac{I_e}{I_c} = \dfrac{I_b}{I_c} + 1$	$\dfrac{I_e}{I_b} = 1 + \dfrac{I_c}{I_b}$	$\dfrac{I_e}{I_c} = \dfrac{I_b}{I_c} + \dfrac{I_c}{I_c}$
$\alpha = \dfrac{\beta}{1 + \beta}$	$\gamma = 1 + \beta$	$\gamma = 1 + \dfrac{\alpha}{1 - \alpha}$
$\beta = \dfrac{\alpha}{1 - \alpha}$	$\gamma = \dfrac{1}{1 - \alpha}$	

Mind

Transmitter
Process and encode the information and make suitable for transmission

Communication channel
Medium through information propagate from transmitter to receiver

Receiver
Receives and decode the signal received at the channel output

Transmitter consists of Transducer, modulator, amplifier and antenna.

Elements of a communication system

Receiver consists of Pickup antenna, demodulator, amplifier and transducer

Block diagram of communication system

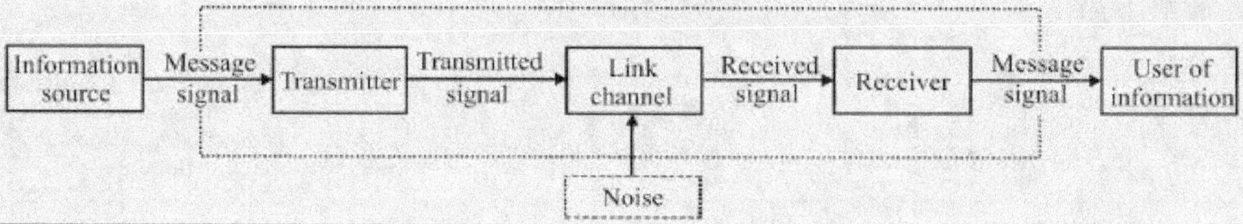

Information source → Message signal → Transmitter → Transmitted signal → Link channel → Received signal → Receiver → Message signal → User of information

Noise

Analog signal
Continuous variation of current or, voltage e.g., sound and picture signal in TV, voice signal in telephony

- Frequency of analog signal varies over a range 20 Hz to 20 kHz
- Complex analog signal consists of two or more waves of different frequencies

Communication Systems
Communication-act of transmission of information

Basic modes of communication

Point-to-point mode
Between a single transmitter and a receiver e.g., telephony

Broadcast mode
Large number of receivers corresponding to a single transmitter e.g., radio and television

- Transducer- Converts one form of energy into another form e.g., microphone, photodetector etc.
- Modulator- Mixing audio electricsignal with high frequency radio waves
- Demodulator- To separate audio signal from modulated signal
- Amplifier- Boosting power of modulated signal
- Antenna- To pick and radiate the signal

Signal
Information converted in electrical form and suitable for transmission

Digital signal
Which take only descrete stepwise values. 0 corresponds to low level 1 corresponds to high level of voltage or current

MODULATION

Continuous wave modulation

Pulse Amplitude modulation PAM

Pulse wave modulation

Amplitude modulation AM

Frequency modulation FM

Phase modulation PM

Pulse time modulation PTM

Pulse code modulation PCM

Map-15

Amplitude modulation
- Modulation index

Process of changing amplitude of a carrier wave in accordance with the amplitude of audio frequency signal.

$$m_a = \frac{kE_m}{E_C}$$

AM wave contains three frequencies
f_c, $(f_c + f_m)$ USB frequency
$(f_c - f_m)$ LSB frequency

Limitation of amplitude modulation
(i) Noisy reception
(ii) Low efficiency
(iii) Small operating range
(iv) Power audio quality

Frequency Modulation (FM)
Process of changing frequency of a carrier wave in accordance with the audio frequency. In FM overall amplitude of FM wave remains constant at all times. In FM total transmitted power remains constant.

Frequency deviation: Maximum change in frequency from mean value (ν_c)

$$\delta = (f_{max} - f_c) = f_c - f_{min} = k_f \cdot \frac{E_m}{2\pi}$$

Carrier swing (CS): Total variation in frequency from the lowest to the highest.

$$CS = 2 \times \Delta f = (f_{max} - f_{min})$$

Frequency modulation Index (m_f): Ratio of maximum frequency deviation to the modulating frequency.

$$m_f = \frac{\delta}{f_m} = \frac{f_{max} - f_c}{f_m} = \frac{f_c - f_{min}}{f_m} = \frac{k_f E_m}{f_m}$$

Frequency spectrum:
$(f_c \pm f_m)$, $(f_c \pm 2f_m)$, $(f_c \pm 3f_m)$.......
The number of side bands depends on the modulation index m_f.
Bandwidth = $2n \times f_m$; where n = number of significant side band pairs

Bandwidth
Frequency range or portion of spectrum occupied by signal
- FM broadcast 88 – 108 MHZ
- Satellite communication 5.925 – 6.425 GHz Uplink 3.7 – 4.2 GHz Downlink
- Television 54 – 72 Hz – VHF 76 – 88 Hz – TV; 174 – 216 MHZ UHF; 420 – 890 Hz – TV
- Cellular mobile and radio 896 – 901 MHz Mobile to base station 840 – 935 MHz Base station to mobile

Power in AM waves-carrier power, $\dfrac{\left(\dfrac{E_c}{2}\right)^2}{R} = \dfrac{E_c^2}{2R}$

- Total power of side bands $P_{sb} = \dfrac{\left(\dfrac{m_a E_c}{2\sqrt{2}}\right)^2}{R} + \dfrac{\left(\dfrac{m_a E_c}{2\sqrt{2}}\right)^2}{R} = \dfrac{m_a^2 E_c^2}{3R}$

- Total power of AM wave $P_{Total} = P_c + P_{sb} = \dfrac{E_c^2}{2R}\left(1 + \dfrac{m_a^2}{2}\right)$

$$\frac{P_t}{P_c} = \left(1 + \frac{m_a^2}{2}\right) \quad \text{and} \quad \frac{P_{sb}}{P_t} = \frac{m_a^2/2}{\left(1 + \dfrac{m_a^2}{2}\right)}$$

- Maximum power in the AM (without distortion) when $m_a = 1$, i.e., $P_t = 1.5$, $P_c = 3\,P_{sb}$

- If I_c = Unmodulated current and I_t = total or modulated current

$$\frac{P_t}{P_c} = \frac{I_t^2}{I_c^2} \Rightarrow \frac{I_t}{I_c} = \sqrt{\left(1 + \frac{m_a^2}{2}\right)}$$

Propagation of Em waves

Space wave: Suitable for frequency 30 – 300 MHz
Maximum (LOS) distance

$$dm = \sqrt{2Rh_T} + \sqrt{2Rh_R}$$

R = Radius of earth
h_t = Height of transmitting antenna
h_R = Height of receiving antenna

Sky wave: Suitable for frequency 2 – 30 MHz

$$V_{critical} = 9(N_{max})^{1/2}$$

N_{max} = Maximum electron density of ionosphere per m^3

Ground wave for local broadcast frequency upto 20MHz

S. No.	Transmission medium	Frequency band	Remarks
1.	Wire (most common)	750 MHz (Bandwidth) (coaxial cable)	Normally operated below 18 GHz
2.	Free space (radio waves)	540 kHz–4.2 GHz	
	(i) Standard AM broadcast	540–108 kHz	
	(ii) FM	88–108 kHz	
	(iii) Television	54–72 MHz	VHF (very high frequencies) TV
		76–88 MHz	
		174–216 MHz	UHF (ultra
		420–890 MHz	high frequency) TV
	(iv) Cellular mobile, radio	896–901 MHz	Mobile to base station
		840–935 MHz	Base station to mobile
	(v) Satellite communication	5.925–6.425 GHz	Uplink
		3.7–4.2 GHz	Downlink
3.	Optical communication using fibres	101 GHz–1000 GHz (microwaves, ultra-violet)	One single optical fibre offers bandwidth > 100 GHz

CHAPTERWISE MIND MAPS CHEMISTRY

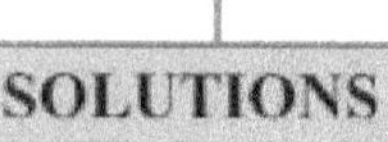

- **Relative Lowering of v.p** : In terms of molecular weight of solute

$$= \frac{P^o - P_s}{P^o} = \chi_A = \frac{n_A}{n_A + n_B} \qquad M_A = \frac{W_A \times M_B}{W_B \left[\frac{P^o - P_s}{P^o} \right]}$$

Where, P^o & P_s = vapour pressure of pure solvent and solution
n_A, n_B = moles of solute & solvent
W_A, W_B & M_A, M_B = W_A, W_B are the masses and M_A, M_B are the molar masses of the solute and solvent respectively.

- **Elevation in b.p.** $\Delta T_b = K_b m$

K_b = boiling point elevation constant or molal elevation constant (**ebullioscopic constant**) having unit K kg mol^{-1}

m = molality $[m = \dfrac{W_A}{M_A \times W_B} \times 1000]$; $\Delta T_b = \dfrac{K_b W_A}{M_A \times W_B} \times 1000$

$$\Delta T_b = T_s - T_b$$

T_s & T_b are the boiling point of solution and pure solvent.

- **Depression in f.p.** $\Delta T_f = K_f m$

K_f = freezing point depression constant or molal depression constant or **cryorcopic constant.**

$$\Delta T_f = \frac{K_f W_A}{M_A \times W_A} \times 1000 \quad ; \quad \Delta T_f = T_f - T_s$$

T_s & T_f are the freezing point of solution and pure solvent.
The values of K_f and K_b, which depend upon nature of the solvent can be determined from the following relations.

$$K_f = \frac{M_B R T_f^2}{1000 \, \Delta_{fus} H} \quad : \quad K_b = \frac{M_B R T_b^2}{1000 \, \Delta_{vap} H}$$

Here, R & M_B stand for the gas constant and molar mass of solvent in $g \cdot mol^{-1}$, T_f & T_b = freezing point and the boiling point. $\Delta_{fus} H$ & $\Delta_{vap} H$ = enthalpies for the fusion and vaporisation of the solvent, respectively.

Colligative properties :
These properties of a solution depend on the total concentration of all solute particles, regardless of their ionic or molecular nature, charge, or size.

$\propto$ No. of particles
$\propto$ No. of molecules (In the solution of non-electrolytes)
$\propto$ No. of ions (In the solution of electrolytes)
$\propto$ No. of moles of solute $\propto$ Mole fraction of solute

SOLUTIONS

Osmotic Pressure (π) :
- Osmotic pressure is the hydrostatic pressure produced when a solution is separated from the solvent by a semipermeable membrane.
- Osmotic pressure may be defined as the excess pressure which must be applied to a solution in order to prevent flow of solvent into the solution through the semipermeable membrane.

Osmotic pressure $(\pi) = \dfrac{n}{V} RT = CRT$

For dilute solutions, osmotic pressure is found to follow the equation $(\pi) = \dfrac{n}{V} RT = CRT$
(Gay-Lussac-van't Hoff law)

when w g of solute are dissolved in V litre of solutions and M is the molar mass of the solute, then

$$(\pi) = \frac{wRT}{MV} \left[\because n = \frac{w}{M} \right]$$

| | Non-ideal solutions | |
Ideal solution	Positive deviation from Raoult's law	Negative deviation from Raoult's law
(i) Obey Raoult's law at every range of concentration.	(i) Do not obey Raoult's law.	(i) Do not obey Raoult's law.
(ii) $\Delta V_{mix} = 0$; total volume of solution is equal to the sum of volumes of the components.	(ii) $\Delta V_{mix} > 0$. Volume is increased after dissolution.	(ii) $\Delta V_{mix} < 0$. Volume is decreased during dissolution.
(iii) $\Delta H_{mix} = 0$; neither heat is evolved nor absorbed during dissolution.	(iii) $\Delta H_{mix} > 0$. Endothermic dissolution; heat is absorbed.	(iii) $\Delta H_{mix} < 0$. Exothermic dissolution; heat is evolved.
(iv) A – A, A – B, B – B molecular interactions present in the two liquids should be same, i.e., A and B are identical in shape, size and character.	(iv) A–B force of attraction are less than A – A and B – B attractive forces. A and B have different shape, size	(iv) A – B force of attraction are greater than A – A and B – B attractive forces. A and B also have different shape, size and character.
(v) $P_{Total} = p_A + p_B = p_A^o x_A + p_B^o x_B$ i.e., $p_A = p_A^o x_A$; $p_B = p_B^o x_B$	(v) $p_A > p_A^o x_A$; $p_B > p_B^o x_B$ $\therefore P_{Total} > p_A^o x_A + p_B^o x_B$	(v) $p_A < p_A^o x_A$; $p_B < p_B^o x_B$ $\therefore P_{Total} < p_A^o x_A + p_B^o x_B$
(vi) Escaping tendency of A and B is same in pure liquids as well as in the solution	(vi) Escaping tendency of A and B is very high (showing higher vapour pressure than expected)	(iv) Due to lower escaping tendency it shows lower vapour pressure than expected
Examples Dilute solutions Ethyl bromide + Ethyl iodide n-Butyl chloride + n-Butyl bromide	**Examples** Acetone + Ethanol CCl_4 + $CHCl_3$	**Examples** Acetone + Aniline Chloroform + Diethyl ether

MAP-1

van't Hoff Factor (i)

Certain solutes which undergo dissociation or association in solutions are found to show abnormal molecular mass. Thus, in order to know about the extent of association or dissociation of solutes in solution van't Hoff in 1886 introduced a factor (i). It is defined as the ratio of the normal mass to the observed molecular mass of the solute i.e.

$$i = \frac{\text{Normal molar mass}}{\text{Observed molar mass}} \quad ; \quad \text{since, molecular mass} \propto \frac{1}{\text{Colligative property}}$$

$$i = \frac{\text{Observed colligative property}}{\text{Normal colligative property}} \quad \therefore i = \frac{\text{Total number of particles after association/dissociation}}{\text{No. of particles before association/dissociation}}$$

The value of i depends upon the state of solute in the solution. Following cases may become possible.

- when $i = 1$, then the solute remains unaffected (i.e., normal) in solution.
- when $i > 1$, then the solute undergoes dissociation in solution.
- when, $i < 1$, then the solute undergoes association in solution.

Modified equation for colligative properties.

$$\frac{P^\circ - P_S}{P^\circ} = i\chi_A = \frac{n_A}{n_A + n_B}; \ \Delta T_b = iK_b m; \ \Delta T_f = iK_f m; \ \pi = i\frac{n}{V}RT$$

Solubility : Maximum amount of a substance that can be dissolved in a specified amount of solvent at a specified temperature it depends upon
- Nature of solute • Nature of solvent • Temperature • Pressure

Solubility of a solid in liquid	Solubility of a gas in liquid
• Effect of nature of solute and solvent ⇒ like dissolves like • Effect of temp ⇒ Exothermic process - increase with rise in temp. • Endothermic process - decrease with rise in temp. • Effect of pressure ⇒ No effect	• Effect of temp. ⇒ Follow same order as in case of solid. • Effect of pressure ⇒ Henry's law states that the partial pressure of the gas in vapour phase (p) is proportional to the mole fraction of the gas (x) in the solution" $p = K_H x$ K_H ⇒ Henry's law constant solubility $\propto \frac{1}{K_H}$

Raoult's Law

$(P_s = P_A^o + (P_B^o - P_A^o)\, x_B$

$P_s = P_A^o + (P_B^o + P_A^o) x_B$ where P_s = Total pressure, P_A^o & P_B^o = vapour pressure in pure state of two constituents A and B in solution

---

Types of solution

Classification based on physical state:

- Gas in gas (Air)
- Gas in liquid (Soda water)
- Gas in solid (Hydrogen in Pd)
- Liquid in gas (Fog)
- Liquid in liquid (Alcohol in water)
- Liquid in solid (Amalgams)
- Solid in gas (Smog)
- Solid in liquid (Sugar in water)
- Solid in solid (Alloys)

Classification based on concentration

- Dilute solutions
- Concentrated solutions
- Saturated solutions
- Supersaturated solutions

Concentration of solutions

- Mass percentage (w/W) = $\dfrac{\text{Mass of solute}}{\text{Total mass of solution}} \times 100$

- Molarity (M) = $\dfrac{\text{No. of moles of solute}}{\text{Volume of solution (L)}}$

- Molality (m) = $\dfrac{\text{No. of moles of solute}}{\text{Weight of the solvent in kg}}$

- Normality (N) = $\dfrac{\text{No. of grams equivalent of solute}}{\text{Volume of solution (L)}}$

- Mole fraction (x) = $\dfrac{\text{No. of moles of solute}}{\text{Total moles in solution}}$

- Volume percentage (v/V) = $\dfrac{\text{Volume of solute}}{\text{Total volume of solution}} \times 100$

- ppm = $\dfrac{\text{No. of parts of solute}}{\text{Total no. of parts of all components of solution}} \times 10^6$

- Mass by volume percentage (w/V) = $\dfrac{\text{mass of solute}}{\text{Total volume of solution (mL)}} \times 100$

• Mass %, ppm, mole fraction and molality are independent of temperature.

In corrosion, a metal is oxidised by loss of electrons to oxygen and forms metal oxide. Corrosion of iron (which is commonly known as rusting) occurs in presence of water and oxygen (air).

Rusting of Iron : According to electrochemical theory, rusting can be represented as :

Oxidation at Anode: $Fe \rightarrow Fe^{2+} + 2e^-$; $E^o_{oxi} = -0.44$ V

Reduction at Cathode : $CO_2 + H_2O \rightarrow H^+ + HCO_3^-$

$$2H^+(aq) + 2e^- \rightarrow 2H$$

$$2H + \frac{1}{2}O_2 \rightarrow H_2O$$

$$\overline{2H^+ + \frac{1}{2}O_2 + 2e \rightarrow H_2O \; ; E^o_{red} = 1.23V}$$

Overall reaction of corrosion cell :

$$Fe + 2H^+ + \frac{1}{2}O_2 \rightarrow Fe^{2+} + H_2O \; ; \; E^o_{cell} = 1.67 \text{ V}$$

The ferrous ions so formed move through water and come at the surface of iron object where these are further oxidised to ferric state by atmospheric oxygen and constitute rust which is hydrated iron (III) oxide.

$$2Fe^{2+} + \frac{1}{2}O_2 + 2H_2O \rightarrow Fe_2O_3 + 4H^+$$

$$Fe_2O_3 + xH_2O \rightarrow Fe_2O_3 . xH_2O$$
Rust

Prevention of Corrosion

- The metal surface is coated with paint which keeps it out of contact with air, moisture etc.
- By applying film of oil and grease on the surface of the iron tools and machinery
- The iron surface is coated with non-corroding metals such as nickel, chromium, aluminium, etc.

Faraday's First Law: When an electric current is passed through an electrolyte, the amount of substance deposited or liberated at an electrode is proportional to the quantity of electric charge passed through the electrolyte.

If W be the mass of the substance deposited by passing Q coulomb of charge, then according to the law, we have the relation. $\qquad W \propto Q$

A coulomb is the quantity of charge when a current of one ampere is passed for one second.

$$Q = \text{current in amperes} \times \text{time in seconds} = I \times t$$
$$W \propto I \times t$$
$$W = Z \times I \times t$$

where Z is a constant, known as electro-chemical equivalent, and is characteristic of the substance deposited.

Electro-chemical equivalent $(Z) =$

$$\frac{\text{equivalent wt. of element}}{96500}$$

Regardless whether a cell is a voltaic or an electrolytic-cell,
— The anode is the electrode at which oxidation occurs
— The cathode is the electrode at which reduction occurs

	Voltaic cell	Electrolytic-cell
Anode	Oxidation, Negative (–) terminal	Oxidation positive (+) terminal
Cathode	Reduction Positive (+) terminal	Reduction negative (–) terminal

- Electrode potential

$$E_{cell} = E^o_{right} - E^o_{left}$$

For SHE, $E^o_{cell} = 0$

- Nernst equation :

For reaction, $M^{n+} + ne^- \rightarrow M(s)$

$$E = E^o - \frac{2.303RT}{nF} \log \frac{1}{[M^{n+}]}$$

- **For reaction :**

$$aA + bB \rightarrow cC + dD$$

$$Ec_{cell} = E^o_{cell} - \frac{2.303RT}{nF} \log \frac{[C]^c[D]^d}{[A]^a[B]^b}$$

At equilibrium $E_{cell} = 0$

$$E^o_{cell} = \frac{2.303RT}{nF} \log K_c$$

$$\Delta_r G = -nFE_{cell} \text{ or } \Delta_r G = -n F E^o_{cell}$$

or $\Delta_r G^o = -RT \ln K = -2.303 RT \log K$

- **Electrochemical series:** Arrangement of elements in order of increasing value of E^o red. Reducing nature decreases form top to bottom in the series.

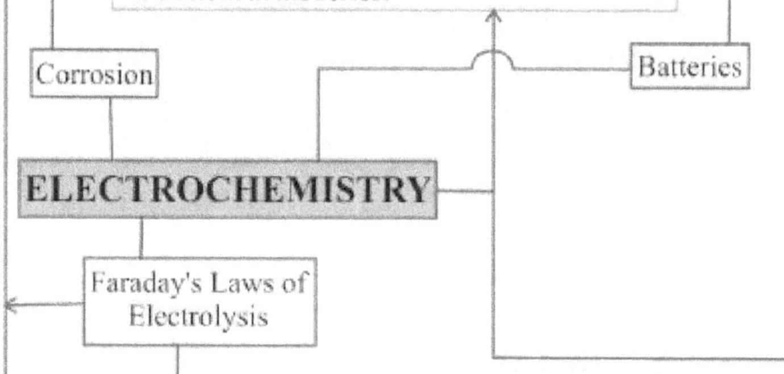

Faraday's Second Law: It states that when same quantity of electricity is passed through different electrolytes, then the quantity of deposit is directly proportional to respective equivalent weight. (Equivalent wt. of electrolytes).

$$W \propto E$$

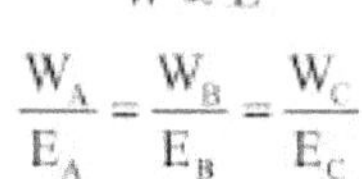
$$\frac{W_A}{E_A} = \frac{W_B}{E_B} = \frac{W_C}{E_C}$$

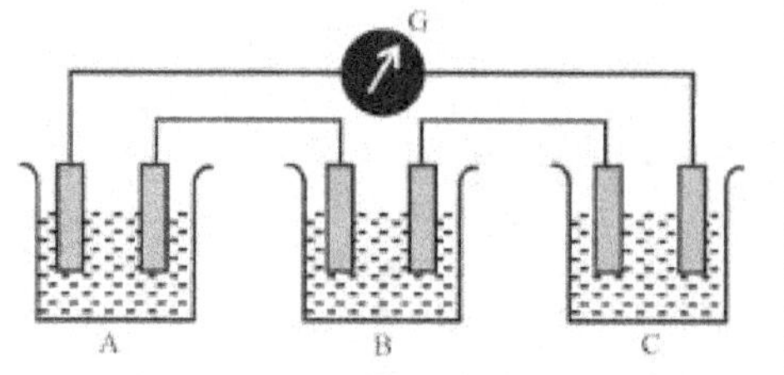

MAP-2

Name of cell/Battery	Anode (−)	Cathode (+)	Electrolyte	Reactions at electrodes	E_{cell}
• Dry cell (primary cell)	Zn container	Graphite rod	Powdered MnO_2 +C +Paste of NH_4Cl + $ZnCl_2$	**Anode:** $Zn(s) \rightarrow Zn^{2+}(aq) + 2e$ **Cathode:** NH_3 forms complex with Zn^{2+} to give $[Zn(NH_3)_4]^{2+}$ $MnO_2 + 2NH_4^+ + e \rightarrow MnO(OH) + NH_3$. NH_3 Forms Complex with Zn^{2+} to give $[Zn(NH_3)_4]^{2+}$	1.25 to 1.5 V
• Mercury cell (primary cell)	Zn-Hg amalgam	Paste of HgO and C	Paste of KOH + ZnO	**Anode:** $Zn(Hg) + 2OH^- \rightarrow ZnO + H_2O + 2e$ **Cathode:** $HgO + H_2O + 2e^- \rightarrow Hg(l) + 2OH^-$	1.35 V
• Lead storage Battery (secondary cell)	Pb	Pb + PbO_2	38% by mass H_2SO_4 (d=1.30 g cm^{-3})	**Anode:** $Pb(s) + SO_4^{2-}(aq) \rightarrow PbSO_4(s) + 2e^-$ **Cathode :** $PbO_2(s) + SO_4^{2-}(aq) + 4H^+(aq) + 2e^- \rightarrow PbSO_4(s) + 2H_2O(l)$ On applying a potential slightly greater than the potential of battery, battery can be recharged.	12 V consists of 6 cell each producing 2 V
• Ni-Cd Secondary cell Or Ni-Cd cell (Rechargeable)	Cd	NiO_2	Moist KOH	**Anode:** $Cd(s) + 2OH^-(aq) \rightarrow Cd(OH)_2(s) + 2e$ **Cathode :** $NiO_2(s) + 2H_2O + 2e \rightarrow Ni(OH)_2(s) + 2OH^-(aq)$	1.4 V
• Fuel cell (H_2-O_2)	Porous carbon containing catalyst (finely divided Pt and Pd)	Porous carbon containing catalyst (finely divided Pt and Pd)	Concentrated NaOH solution	**Anode:** $2H_2(g) + 4OH^-(aq) \rightarrow 4H_2O(l) + 4e^-$ Cathode : $O_2(g) + 2H_2O(l) + 4e \rightarrow 4OH^-(aq)$	0.09 V

Conductance of Electrolytic Solutions:

- Conductance $(G) = \dfrac{1}{Resistance}$

  Unit : ohm^{-1} or Siemens
- Specific conductivity $(\kappa) = G\dfrac{l}{a}\left(\dfrac{l}{a} = \text{cell constant}\right)$

  Unit = ohm^{-1} cm^{-1} or S cm^{-1}
- Molar conductance $(\Lambda_m) = \dfrac{1000 \times \kappa}{M}$

  Unit = S cm^2 mol^{-1}
- Equivalent conductance $(\Lambda_{eq}) = \dfrac{1000 \times \kappa}{N}$

  Unit = cm^2 ohm^{-1} g-eq^{-1}

  Conductance (G), molar conductance (Λ_m) and equivalent conductance (Λ_{eq}) increase with dilution where as specific conductance (κ) decrease with dilution

  Effect of concentration on Λ_m:
- **For strong electrolytes,** Λ_m increases slowly with dilution and can be represented by the equation : $\Lambda_m = \Lambda^\circ_m - AC^{1/2}$

  (Debye–Huckel Onsager equation)

Plot of Λ_m against $C^{1/2}$ is a straight line with intercept equal to Λ°_m and slope equal to '$-A$.'

Thus, Λ_m decreases linearly with $\sqrt{C}$, when $C = 0$, $\Lambda_m = \Lambda^\circ_m$ and Λ°_m can be determined experimentally.

- **For weak electrolytes,** Λ_m increases as C decreases but does not reach a constant value even at infinite dilution. Hence, there Λ°_m cannot be determined experimentally.
- **Kohlrausch's Law :**

  $\Lambda^\circ_{eq} = \lambda^\circ_+ + \lambda^\circ_-$

  Where λ°_+ is the limiting equivalent conductivity of the cation and λ°_- is the limiting equivalent conductivity of the anion. These contributions are called limiting equivalent conductances at infinite dilution. The above equation is, however, correct only for binary electrolyte like NaCl, $MgSO_4$ etc.

Applications of Kohlrausch's Law:

- **Calculation of Molar Conductivity at Infinite Dilution for Weak Electrolytes :**

  In order to calculate Λ°_m or Λ°_m of a weak electrolyte say CH_3COOH, we determine permentally Λ_m values of the strong electrol

  $\Lambda^\circ_{m(CH_3COOH)} = \lambda^\circ_{CH_3COO^-} + \lambda^\circ_{H^+}$ ....(i)

  for strong electrolytes :

  $\Lambda^\circ_{m(CH_3COOK)} = \lambda^\circ_{CH_3COO^-} + \lambda^\circ_{K^+}$ ......(ii)

  $\Lambda^\circ_{m(HCl)} = \lambda^\circ_{H^+} + \lambda^\circ_{Cl^-}$ ......(iii)

  $\Lambda^\circ_{m(KCl)} = \lambda^\circ_{K^+} + \lambda^\circ_{Cl^-}$ ......(iv)

  $\therefore$ eqn (ii) + eqn. (iii) − eqn (iv) = eqn (i)

  i.e., $\Lambda^\circ_{m(CH_3COOK)} + \Lambda^\circ_{m(HCl)} - \Lambda^\circ_{m(KCl)} = \Lambda^\circ_{m(CH_3COOH)}$

- **Calculation of the Degree of Dissociation :**

  Λ^c_m is the molar conductivity of a solution at any concentration C and Λ°_m the molar conductivity at infinite dilution (i.e., zero concentration), we will have $\alpha = \dfrac{\text{no.of dissociat edions}}{\text{no.of totalions present}}$; Degree of dissociation $(\alpha) = \dfrac{\Lambda^c_m}{\Lambda^\circ_m}$

- **Calculation of Dissociation Constant of a Weak Electrolyte :**

  $$K_c = \dfrac{C\alpha^2}{1-\alpha}$$

MIND

CHEMICAL KINETICS

Instantaneous rate :
The rate of reaction at any particular instant during the course of reaction is called as instantaneous rate of reaction. Mathematically, instantaneous rate = (Average rate)$_{\Delta t \to 0}$

Average rate (denoted by r_{av})
$$r_{av} = -\frac{\Delta R}{\Delta t} = -\frac{[R_2]-[R_1]}{(t_2-t_1)}$$
- Average rate depends upon the change in conc. of reactants or products and the time taken for the change to occur.

Rate of reaction a chemical

Integrated Rate Equations

Collision Theory of chemical reactions :
The important points of this theory are :
- If two molecules are to react together they must collide together.
- **Threshold Energy (Energy Barrier):** The minimum energy which the molecules should possess so that their mutual collision result in chemical reaction is called threshold energy.
- **Effective Collisions:** Only those collisions which result in the formation of product are called effective collisions.
- **Collision Frequency:** The number of collisions that take place per second per unit volume of the reaction mixture is called collision frequency.

For a bimolecular elementary reaction $A + B \to$ Products
rate of reaction can be expressed as $\text{Rate} = Z_{AB}e^{-E_a/RT}$
where Z_{AB} represents the collision frequency of reactants, A and B and $e^{-E_a/RT}$ represents the fraction of molecules with energies equal to or greater than E_a.

To account for effective collisions, another factor P, called the probability or steric factor is introduced. It takes into account the fact that in a collision, molecules must be properly oriented i.e., $\text{Rate} = PZ_{AB}e^{-E_a/RT}$

Thus, in collision theory activation energy and proper orientation of the molecules together determine the criteria for an effective collision and hence the rate of a chemical reaction.

Temperature Dependence of Rate of Reaction
For a chemical reaction with rise in temp. by $10°C$, the rate constant is nearly doubled.

Integrated rate law and linear plots for reactions of different orders.

Reaction type	Order	Differential rate law	Integrated rate law	Linear plots	Half life
$R \to P$	0	$d[R]/dt = -k$	$kt = [R]_o - [R]$	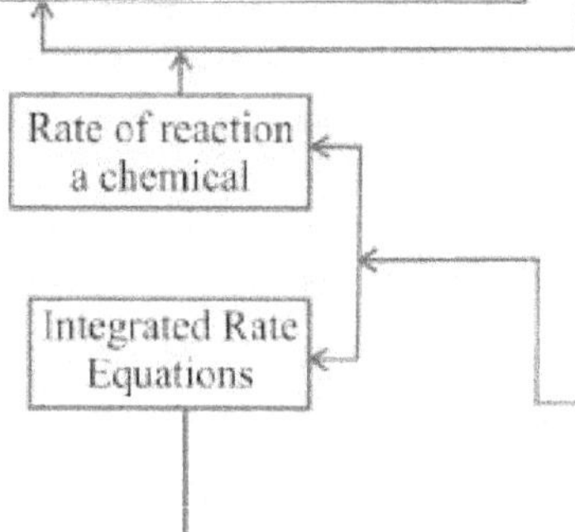	$[R]_o/2k$
$R \to P$	1	$\dfrac{d[R]}{dt} = -k[R]$	$kt = \ln\dfrac{[R]_o}{[R]}$		$0.693/k$

- Rate constant for zero order reaction $k = \dfrac{[R]_o - [R]}{t}$
- Rate constant for 1st order reaction $k = \dfrac{2.303}{t}\log\dfrac{[R]_o}{[R]}$
- Rate constant for 1st order reaction $k = \dfrac{2.303}{t}\log\dfrac{P_i}{(2P_i - P_t)}$ (for gas phase reaction)

(where P_i = initial pressure, P_t = total pressure at time 't')

Arrhenius Equation :
$$k = Ae^{-E_a/RT}$$
$$\ln k = \ln A - \frac{E_a}{RT}$$
$$\log k = \log A - \frac{E_a}{2.303RT}$$

At two different temperatures
$$\log\frac{k_2}{k_1} = \frac{E_a}{2.303}\left(\frac{T_2-T_1}{T_2T_1}\right)$$

where k_1, k_2 are the values of rate constant at temp, T_1 and T_2 respectively. The plot of $\log k$ vs $1/T$ gives a straight line with slope $= \dfrac{-E_a}{2.303R}$ and intercept $= \log A$

MAP-3

Rate expression and rate constant :

The mathematical expression, which practically relates the rate of a chemical reaction and concentration of reactants is called rate law equation e.g. for a hypothetical reaction.

$aA + bB \rightleftharpoons cC + dD$ (Where a, b, c and d are the stoichiometric coefficients)

$$Rate \propto [A]^a [B]^b.$$

$$Rate \propto [A]^x [B]^y \qquad \text{.... (i)}$$

$$Rate = k [A]^x [B]^y \qquad \text{.... (ii)}$$

$$\frac{-d[R]}{dt} = k [A]^x [B]^y \qquad \text{.... (iii)}$$

(Where x and y may or may not be equal to the a and b)

where k is a proportionality constant called rate constant.

Molecularity of reaction :

"The minimum number of molecules, atoms or ions of reactants required for an elementary reaction to occur which is indicated by the sum of the stoichiometric coefficients of the reactant(s) in the chemical equation, is known as molecularity of the reaction".

Thus for an elementary reaction represented by the general chemical equation.

$$aA + bB \rightarrow products$$
$$molecularity = a + b$$

Ex. Reactions	Molecularity
$PCl_5 \rightleftharpoons PCl_3 + Cl_2$	1
$H_2 + I_2 \rightleftharpoons 2HI$	2

Factors Influencing Rate of a reaction :

- **Concentration of the Reactants:** Greater the concentrations of the reactants, faster is the reaction.
- **Temperature:** The rate of reaction increases with increase of temperature.
- **Presence of Catalyst:** A catalyst generally increases the speed of a reaction without itself being consumed in the reaction.

Order of reaction :

Order of reaction is defined as the sum of the powers of the concentration terms appearing in experimentally observed rate law.

In general , let a reaction be represented by the chemical equation:

$$aA + bB \rightarrow Products$$

obeys the following rate law.

$$Rate \propto [A]^m [B]^n, \text{ or } Rate = k[A]^m [B]^n$$

Pseudo First order Reaction :

A bimolecular reaction conforms to the first-order when one of the reactants is taken in large excess and the reaction is said to be pseudo unimolecular or pseudo first order.

An example of this is the hydrolysis of ester by dil. acid i.e.

$$CH_3COOC_2H_5 + H_2O \xrightarrow{H^+} CH_3COOH + C_2H_5OH$$

The reaction is originally obeying the second-order kinetics.

$$Rate = k [CH_3COOC_2H_5] [H_2O]$$

But the reaction is usually carried out taking dilute aqueous solution of ester and acid (HCl) such that in the reaction mixture water exists in large excess as compared to ester

Hence reactions obeys the following 1st order kinetics.

$$Rate = k [CH_3COOC_2H_5]$$

Thus , the molecularity of the above reaction is 'two' but its order is 'one'.

Units of rate constant :

S.No.	Reaction	Order	Units of rate constant
(i)	Zero order reaction	0	$\dfrac{(molL^{-1})}{s} \times \dfrac{1}{(molL^{-1})^0} = molL^{-1} \ s^{-1}$
(ii)	First order reaction	1	$\dfrac{(molL^{-1})}{s} \times \dfrac{1}{(molL^{-1})^1} = s^{-1}$
(iii)	second order reaction	2	$\dfrac{(molL^{-1})}{s} \times \dfrac{1}{(molL^{-1})^2} = mol^{-1} \ Ls^{-1}$
(iv)	nth order reaction	n	$\dfrac{(molL^{-1})}{s} \times \dfrac{1}{(molL^{-1})^n} = mol/L^{1-n} \ s^{-1}$

Effect of Catalyst on Rate of Reaction

- A catalyst is a foreign substance which influence the rate of a reaction without itself undergoing any chemical change.
- It provides an alternate pathway by reducing the activation energy and hence lowering the potential energy barrier as shown in figure.
- It does not alter Gibbs energy, ΔG and ΔH of a reaction.
- It catalyses the spontaneous reactions but does not catalyse non-spontaneous reactions.
- It catalyses the forward as well as the backward reaction to the same extent so that the equilibriun state remains same.

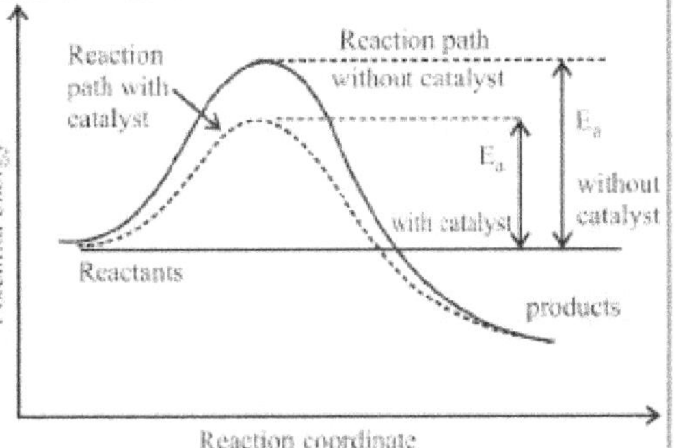

Effect of catalyst on activation energy

MIND

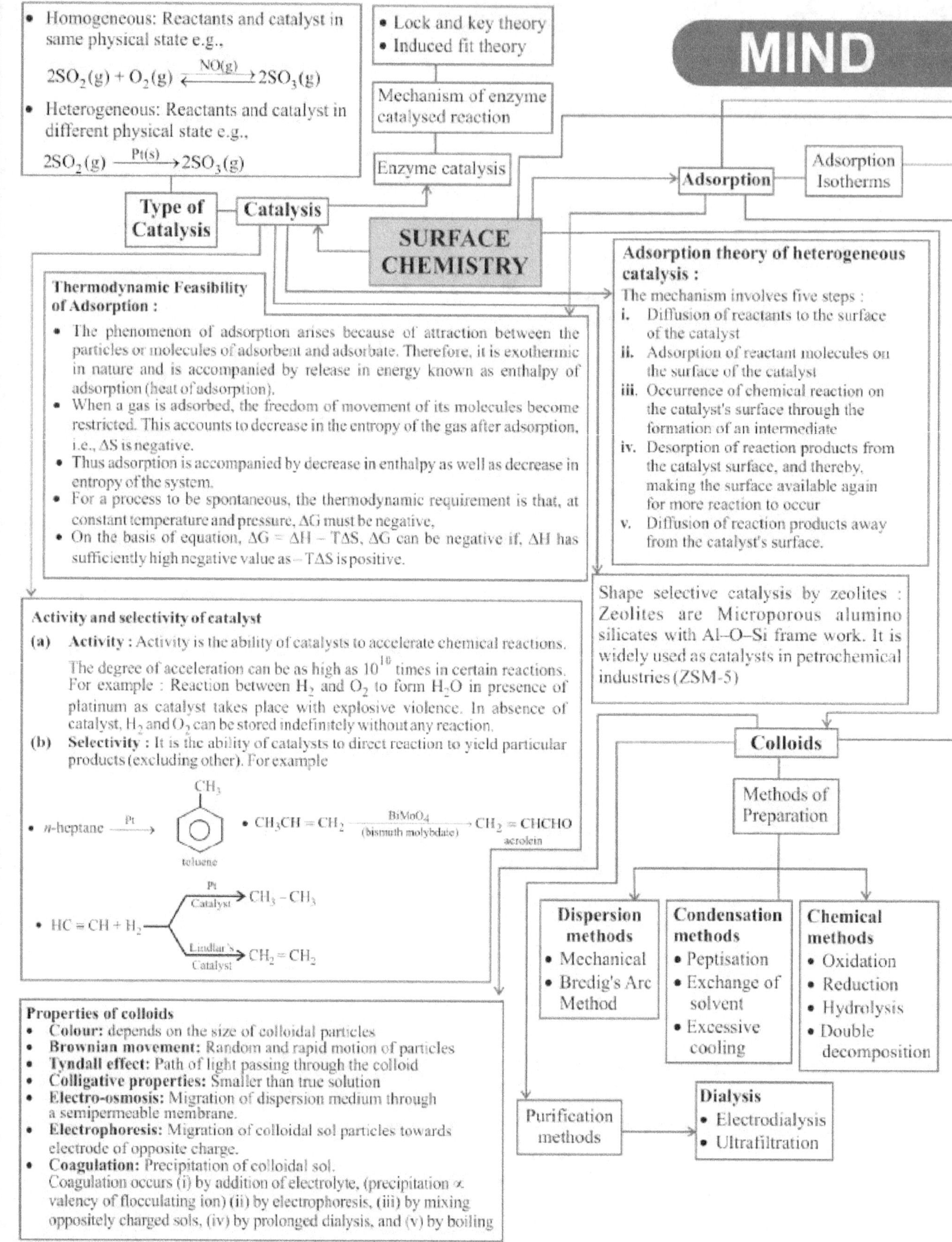
SURFACE CHEMISTRY

Type of Catalysis
Catalysis

Homogeneous: Reactants and catalyst in same physical state e.g.,
$2SO_2(g) + O_2(g) \xrightarrow{NO(g)} 2SO_3(g)$
Heterogeneous: Reactants and catalyst in different physical state e.g.,
$2SO_2(g) \xrightarrow{Pt(s)} 2SO_3(g)$

Lock and key theory
Induced fit theory
Mechanism of enzyme catalysed reaction
Enzyme catalysis

Adsorption
Adsorption Isotherms

Thermodynamic Feasibility of Adsorption :
The phenomenon of adsorption arises because of attraction between the particles or molecules of adsorbent and adsorbate. Therefore, it is exothermic in nature and is accompanied by release in energy known as enthalpy of adsorption (heat of adsorption).
When a gas is adsorbed, the freedom of movement of its molecules become restricted. This accounts to decrease in the entropy of the gas after adsorption, i.e., ΔS is negative.
Thus adsorption is accompanied by decrease in enthalpy as well as decrease in entropy of the system.
For a process to be spontaneous, the thermodynamic requirement is that, at constant temperature and pressure, ΔG must be negative.
On the basis of equation, $\Delta G = \Delta H - T\Delta S$, ΔG can be negative if, ΔH has sufficiently high negative value as $-T\Delta S$ is positive.

Adsorption theory of heterogeneous catalysis :
The mechanism involves five steps :
i. Diffusion of reactants to the surface of the catalyst
ii. Adsorption of reactant molecules on the surface of the catalyst
iii. Occurrence of chemical reaction on the catalyst's surface through the formation of an intermediate
iv. Desorption of reaction products from the catalyst surface, and thereby, making the surface available again for more reaction to occur
v. Diffusion of reaction products away from the catalyst's surface.

Shape selective catalysis by zeolites : Zeolites are Microporous alumino silicates with Al–O–Si frame work. It is widely used as catalysts in petrochemical industries (ZSM-5)

Activity and selectivity of catalyst
(a) Activity : Activity is the ability of catalysts to accelerate chemical reactions.
The degree of acceleration can be as high as 10^{10} times in certain reactions. For example : Reaction between H_2 and O_2 to form H_2O in presence of platinum as catalyst takes place with explosive violence. In absence of catalyst, H_2 and O_2 can be stored indefinitely without any reaction.
(b) Selectivity : It is the ability of catalysts to direct reaction to yield particular products (excluding other). For example

n-heptane $\xrightarrow{Pt}$ toluene

$CH_3CH = CH_2 \xrightarrow[\text{(bismuth molybdate)}]{BiMoO_4} CH_2 = CHCHO$ acrolein

$HC \equiv CH + H_2 \xrightarrow[\text{Catalyst}]{Pt} CH_3 - CH_3$
$HC \equiv CH + H_2 \xrightarrow[\text{Catalyst}]{Lindlar's} CH_2 = CH_2$

Colloids

Methods of Preparation

Dispersion methods
Mechanical
Bredig's Arc Method

Condensation methods
Peptisation
Exchange of solvent
Excessive cooling

Chemical methods
Oxidation
Reduction
Hydrolysis
Double decomposition

Purification methods

Dialysis
Electrodialysis
Ultrafiltration

Properties of colloids
Colour: depends on the size of colloidal particles
Brownian movement: Random and rapid motion of particles
Tyndall effect: Path of light passing through the colloid
Colligative properties: Smaller than true solution
Electro-osmosis: Migration of dispersion medium through a semipermeable membrane.
Electrophoresis: Migration of colloidal sol particles towards electrode of opposite charge.
Coagulation: Precipitation of colloidal sol.
Coagulation occurs (i) by addition of electrolyte, (precipitation $\propto$ valency of flocculating ion) (ii) by electrophoresis, (iii) by mixing oppositely charged sols, (iv) by prolonged dialysis, and (v) by boiling

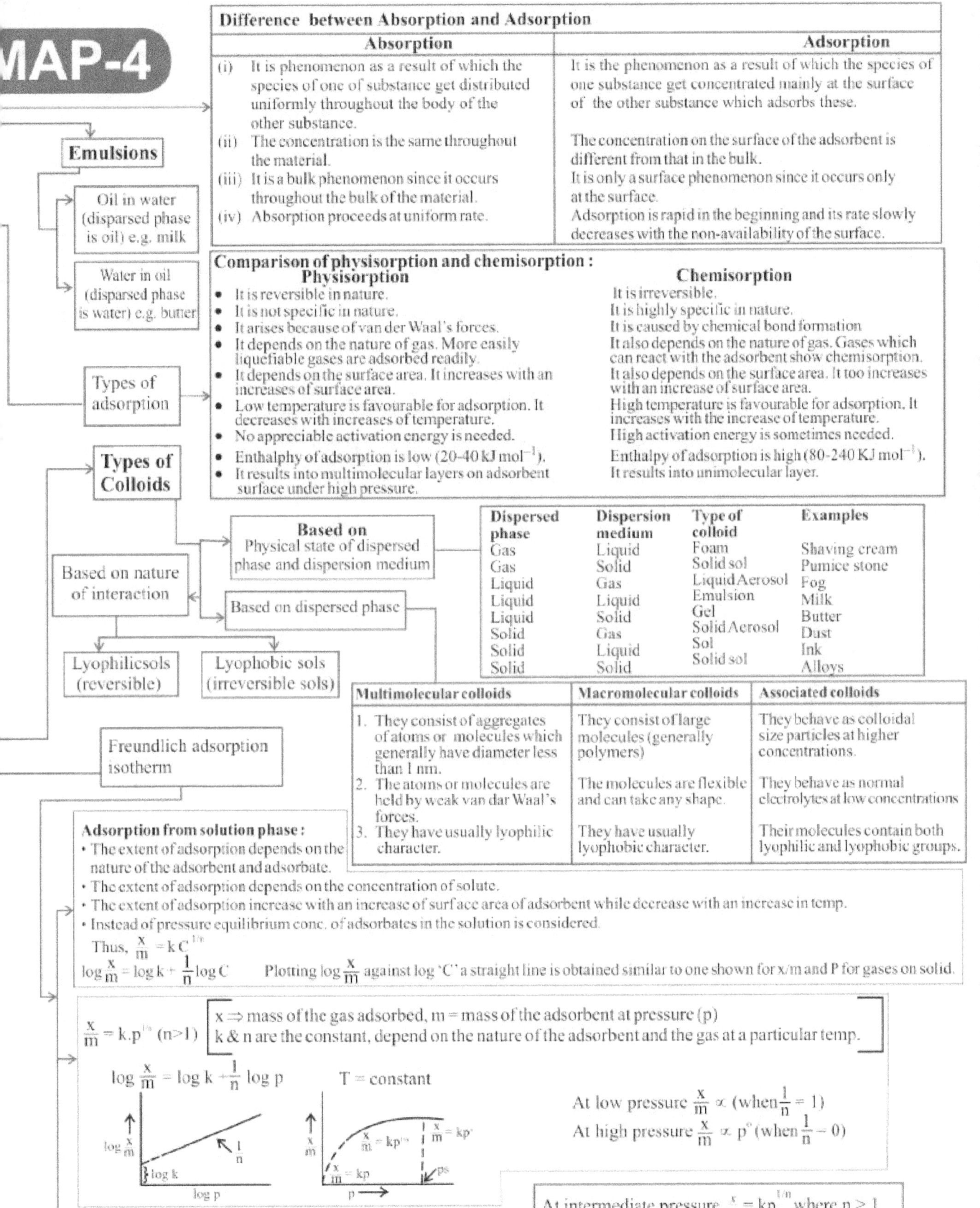

Emulsions

- Oil in water (disparsed phase is oil) e.g. milk
- Water in oil (disparsed phase is water) e.g. butter

Types of adsorption

Types of Colloids

Based on nature of interaction

Based on
Physical state of dispersed phase and dispersion medium

Based on dispersed phase

Lyophilicsols (reversible)

Lyophobic sols (irreversible sols)

Freundlich adsorption isotherm

Difference between Absorption and Adsorption

Absorption	Adsorption
(i) It is phenomenon as a result of which the species of one of substance get distributed uniformly throughout the body of the other substance.	It is the phenomenon as a result of which the species of one substance get concentrated mainly at the surface of the other substance which adsorbs these.
(ii) The concentration is the same throughout the material.	The concentration on the surface of the adsorbent is different from that in the bulk.
(iii) It is a bulk phenomenon since it occurs throughout the bulk of the material.	It is only a surface phenomenon since it occurs only at the surface.
(iv) Absorption proceeds at uniform rate.	Adsorption is rapid in the beginning and its rate slowly decreases with the non-availability of the surface.

Comparison of physisorption and chemisorption :

Physisorption	Chemisorption
• It is reversible in nature.	It is irreversible.
• It is not specific in nature.	It is highly specific in nature.
• It arises because of van der Waal's forces.	It is caused by chemical bond formation
• It depends on the nature of gas. More easily liquefiable gases are adsorbed readily.	It also depends on the nature of gas. Gases which can react with the adsorbent show chemisorption.
• It depends on the surface area. It increases with an increases of surface area.	It also depends on the surface area. It too increases with an increase of surface area.
• Low temperature is favourable for adsorption. It decreases with increases of temperature.	High temperature is favourable for adsorption. It increases with the increase of temperature.
• No appreciable activation energy is needed.	High activation energy is sometimes needed.
• Enthalphy of adsorption is low (20–40 kJ mol^{-1}).	Enthalpy of adsorption is high (80-240 KJ mol^{-1}).
• It results into multimolecular layers on adsorbent surface under high pressure.	It results into unimolecular layer.

Dispersed phase	Dispersion medium	Type of colloid	Examples
Gas	Liquid	Foam	Shaving cream
Gas	Solid	Solid sol	Pumice stone
Liquid	Gas	Liquid Aerosol	Fog
Liquid	Liquid	Emulsion	Milk
Liquid	Solid	Gel	Butter
Solid	Gas	Solid Aerosol	Dust
Solid	Liquid	Sol	Ink
Solid	Solid	Solid sol	Alloys

Multimolecular colloids	Macromolecular colloids	Associated colloids
1. They consist of aggregates of atoms or molecules which generally have diameter less than 1 nm.	They consist of large molecules (generally polymers)	They behave as colloidal size particles at higher concentrations.
2. The atoms or molecules are held by weak van dar Waal's forces.	The molecules are flexible and can take any shape.	They behave as normal electrolytes at low concentrations
3. They have usually lyophilic character.	They have usually lyophobic character.	Their molecules contain both lyophilic and lyophobic groups.

Adsorption from solution phase :
- The extent of adsorption depends on the nature of the adsorbent and adsorbate.
- The extent of adsorption depends on the concentration of solute.
- The extent of adsorption increase with an increase of surface area of adsorbent while decrease with an increase in temp.
- Instead of pressure equilibrium conc. of adsorbates in the solution is considered.

Thus, $\dfrac{x}{m} = k\,C^{1/n}$

$\log\dfrac{x}{m} = \log k + \dfrac{1}{n}\log C$ Plotting $\log\dfrac{x}{m}$ against log 'C' a straight line is obtained similar to one shown for x/m and P for gases on solid.

$\dfrac{x}{m} = k.p^{1/n}\ (n>1)$ $x \Rightarrow$ mass of the gas adsorbed, m = mass of the adsorbent at pressure (p)
k & n are the constant, depend on the nature of the adsorbent and the gas at a particular temp.

$\log\dfrac{x}{m} = \log k + \dfrac{1}{n}\log p$ T = constant

At low pressure $\dfrac{x}{m} \propto$ (when $\dfrac{1}{n} = 1$)

At high pressure $\dfrac{x}{m} \propto p^{\circ}$ (when $\dfrac{1}{n} = 0$)

At intermediate pressure $\dfrac{x}{m} = kp^{1/n}$ where n > 1

MIND

Electrochemical principles of metallurgy:

- Highly reactive metals cannot be obtained from their compounds (or ores) by carbon reduction method. This is because these metals have more affinity for oxygen than carbon has. Such highly electropositive metals can be obtained by electrolytic reduction method.
- For an electrochemical reaction, $\Delta G° = -nFE°$
  where n is the number of electrons involved in the reactions, $E°$ is the standard electrode potential of the redox pair.
- For a reaction to become spontaneous, $E°$ should be positive. For more reactive metals, $E°$ are highly negative.
- To make the net emf positive, an external emf greater than $E°$ is applied in the direction opposite to that of the cell.
- The ions in the solution or melt can be reduced by applying external emf, that is, by electrolysis, (or by electrolytic reduction method). In electrolytic reduction, the ions of the metal get reduced to the corresponding metal at the cathode, (negative electrode).

GENERAL PRINCIPLES AND PROCESS OF ISOLATION OF ELEMENTS

Thermodynamic principle of metallurgy
Ellingham diagram :

- Provides a basis for the choice of reducing agent for reduction of a particular metal oxide.
- Temperature is chosen such that the sum of $\Delta G°$ in two combined redox process is negative.
- There is a point in curve below which $\Delta G°$ is negative and above this point metal oxide decompose automatically.

Applications of Ellingham diagram

- Iron oxides ores are reduced by using coke (carbon-reduction method) in a blast furnace.
  The net reaction for the reduction of FeO by carbon is
  $$FeO(s) + C(s) \rightarrow Fe(s) + CO(g)$$
  The change in the free energy for this reaction is given by
  $$\Delta_r G° = \Delta_f G°(C, CO) + \Delta_f G°(FeO, Fe)$$
  The reduction reaction will be feasible if $\Delta_r G°$ is negative.

  From Ellingham diagram $\Delta_f G°(C, CO)$ vs T plot goes downwards, and $\Delta_f G°(Fe, FeO)$ vs T plot goes upwards.

  At temperature above 700 K, the C, CO line falls below Fe, FeO line. Therefore above, 700 K, carbon should be able to reduce FeO to Fe, and itself gets oxidised to CO.

  From the Ellingham plots it can be seen that below 980 K, carbon monoxide (CO) is a better reducing agent and above it, haematite is reduced by carbon.
- From the $\Delta_r G°$ vs T plots the Cu – Cu$_2$O plot is almost at the top. Both C – CO and C – CO$_2$ plots are much lower particularly beyond 500-600 K. Therefore, Cu$_2$O can be easily reduced by heating with coke.
- From the $\Delta_r G°$ vs T plot, it can be seen that the Zn – ZnO curve lies above the C – CO line beyond 1100 K. Therefore ZnO can be easily reduced to Zn by carbon.

Concentration of ore:

- **Hydraulic washing :** Based on difference in specific gravities of the gangue and ore particles. It is mainly used for oxides ores.
- **Electromagnetic separation :** When one of the component either ore or impurities is magnetic in nature e.g., iron ores.
- **Froth floatation method :** This method is generally applied to sulphide ores. It is based on the fact that surface of sulphide ores is preferentially wetted by oils while that of the gangue is preferentially wetted by water.
- **Chemical method (leaching) :** Consists of treating powdered ore with suitable reagent which can selectively dissolve the ore but not the impurity.
  It is used for Al, Ag, Au etc e.g., bauxite $(Al_2O_3.xH_2O)$

Principal ores of some important metals :

Metal	ores
Al	Bauxite
Fe	Haematits, Magnetite, Iron pyrite, Siderite
Cu	Copper pyrite, Malachite Cuprite, Copper glance
Zn	Zinc blende, Calamine, Zincite

MAP-5

Reduction of metal oxide into metal:

• **Carbon reduction :**
Metal oxides are heated with coke.

• **Reduction by Aluminium :**
Used for metals which have high melting points.

• **Self reduction :**
No external reducing agent is used. Metal ore is heated with air.

• **Electrolytic refining :**
Metal is obtained by the electrolysis of fused metal ore.

Conversion of concentrated ore into metal oxide:

• **Calcination :** Heating carbonate ore below its fusion temperature in absence of air. e.g.,

$ZnCO_3(s) \xrightarrow{\Delta} ZnO(s) + CO_2(g)$

• **Roasting:** Heating sulphide ores in presence of air below their fusion temperature. e.g.,

$2ZnS + 3O_2 \rightarrow 2ZnO_2 + 2SO_2$

Refining of metal:

• **Distillation :** The metals with low boiling points can be purified by distillation. The impure metal is evaporated to obtain the pure metal as distillate. Examples – Zn, Cd, Hg etc.

• **Liquation :** This process is used when the impurity is less fusible than the metal itself. The impure metal is placed on the sloping floor of the furnace and heated. The metal melts and drains away leaving behind the impurities. For e.g. tin, lead etc.

• **Oxidation method :** This method is employed when the impurity have greater affinity with oxygen as compared to metal. The impurities are oxidized to form scum. The scum is skimmed off. Sometimes metal oxides are used as oxidizing agents. For example, copper oxide is added to impure copper.

• **Vapour-phase refining :** In this method, the crude metal is free from impurities by first converting it into a suitable volatile compound by heating it with a specific reagent at a lower temperature and then decomposing the volatile compound at some higher temperature to give the pure metal. This method is illustrated by two processes :

* **Mond process :** It is used for the refining of Ni. The impure Ni is heated with CO. Nickel carbonyl thus formed is then decomposed to get pure Ni and CO.

$$Ni + 4CO \xrightarrow[\text{Impure}]{330 - 350 \text{ K}} Ni(CO)_4 \xrightarrow{450 - 470 \text{ K}} Ni + 4CO \quad \text{Pure nickel}$$

* **van Arkel method :** The crude metal is converted into volatile compound, while impurities remain unaffected during compound formation. The resulting compound is then decomposed to get pure metal. The method is used for refining of Ti and Zr.

$$Ti(s) + 2I_2(s) \xrightarrow{523 \text{ K}} TiI_4(g) \xrightarrow{1700 \text{ K}} Ti(s) + 2I_2(g)$$

$$Zr(s) + 2I_2(g) \xrightarrow{870 \text{ K}} ZrI_4(g) \xrightarrow[\text{Tungsten filament}]{2075 \text{ K}} Zr(s) + 2I_2(g)$$

• **Electrolytic refining :** Most of the metals like Ag, Au, Pb, Ni, Sn, Zn, etc., are refined by this method.

• **Zone refining method :** The method is based upon the principle that the impurities are more soluble in the molten state (melt) than in the solid state of the metal. It is employed for obtaining metals in ultrapure state.

• **Chromatographic methods :** This method is based on the principle that different components of a mixture are differently adsorbed on an adsorbent. The mixture is put in a liquid or gaseous medium which is moved through the adsorbent. Different components are adsorbed at different levels on the column. Later the adsorbed components are removed (eluted) by using suitable solvents (eluant).
This is very useful for purification of the elements which are available in minute quantities and the impurities are not very different in chemical properties from the element to be purified.

MIND

THE *p*-BLOCK ELEMENTS (GROUP 15, 16, 17 AND 18)

Group 18 Elements

Elements: He, Ne, Ar, Kr, Xe and Rn
- **Electronic configuration :** ns^2, np^4 except He ($1s^2$)
- **Physical properties**
- **Atomic radii** increase down the group
* **I.E.** decrease down the group and it is very high due to stable electronic configuration.
* **Electron gain enthalpy** is positive because they have no tendency to accept the electron.
- Least reactive due to stable inert gas configuration and due to high I. E. and more positive electron gain enthalpy.
- Xe Forms 3 binary fluorides XeF_2, XeF_4 and XeF_6

$$Xe(g) + F_2(g) \xrightarrow{673\,K,1bar} XeF_2(s)$$
$$\text{excess}$$
$$Xe(g) + 2F_2(g) \xrightarrow{873\,K,7bar} XeF_4(s)$$
$$\text{(1:5 ratio)}$$
$$Xe(g) + 3F_2(g) \xrightarrow{573\,K,\,60-70\,bar} XeF_6(s)$$
$$\text{(1:20 ratio)}$$

These are powerful fluorinating agents.

$$XeF_2 + PF_5 \rightarrow [XeF]^+ [PF_6]$$
$$XeF_6 + MF \rightarrow M^+ [XeF_7] \quad (M = Na, K, Rb\ or\ (s)$$

* The oxides of Xe are XeO_3, $XeOF_4$ and XeO_2F_2

$$XeF_6 + 3H_2O \rightarrow XeO_3 + 6HF$$
$$XeF_6 + 2H_2O \rightarrow XeO_2F_2 + 4HF$$
$$XeF_6 + H_2O \rightarrow XeOF_4 + 2HF$$

Str. of xenon compounds :

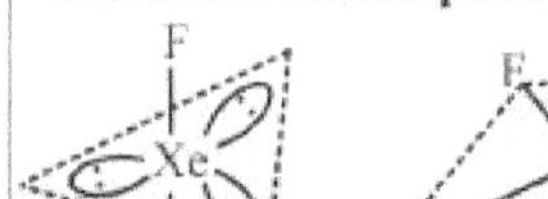

XeF_2 (linear)

XeF_4 (square planar)

XeF_6 (distorted octahedral)

$XeOF_4$ (square pyramidal)

XeO_3 (pyramidal)

Group 15 Elements

- **Elements:** N, P, As, Sb and Bi
- **Electronic configuration:** ns^2np^3
- **Physical properties :**
* Melting point : N < P < Bi < Sb < As (exceptional case)
* Ionization enthalpy is much greater than group 14 elements due to extra stability of half filled *p*-orbitals.
* All elements except Bi show allotropy.
- **Oxidation states:** Common oxidation states are -3, $+3$ and $+5$
- **Hydrides:** Form hydrides of type MH_3

NH_3, PH_3, AsH_3, SbH_3 and BiH_3

Basic character : $NH_3 > PH_3$ (other are not basic)

Melting point : $PH_3 < AsH_3 < SbH_3 < NH_3$

Boiling point : $PH_3 < AsH_3 < NH_3 < SbH_3 < BiH_3$

Reducing character: $NH_3 < PH_3 < AsH_3 < SbH_3 < BiH_3$

- **Oxides :** Form oxides of type M_2O_3, M_2O_4 and M_3O_5. Acidic character of oxides decreases down the group
- **Halides:** Form halides of type EX_3 and EX_5
- In case of nitrogen, only NF_3 is known to be stable. It does not form pentahalides due to non-availability of the *d*-orbitals in its valence shell.
- **Reactivity towards metals:** All form binary compound (such as Ca_3N_2, Ca_3P_2, Na_3As, Zn_3Sb_2, Mg_3Bi_2) exhibiting -3 oxidation state.

Oxoacids of phosphorus :

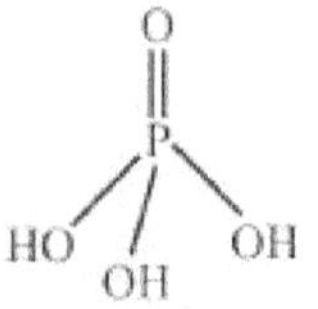

H_3PO_4 — Orthophosphoric acid

$H_4P_2O_7$ — Pyrophosphoric acid

H_3PO_3 — Orthophosphorous acid

H_3PO_2 — Hypophosphorous acid

$(HPO_3)_3$ — Cyclotrimetaphosphoric acid

$(HPO_3)n$ — Polymetaphosphoric acid

MAP-6

Group 16 Elements

Elements: O, S, Se, Te and Po

- **Electronic configuration:** ns^2, np^4
- **Physical properties :**
* **Electron gain enthalpy :** O < S > Se > Te > Po
* M.P & B.P : O < S < Se < Te > Po
* All these elements exhibit allotropy. For ex,
  oxygen $\Rightarrow$ O_2 & O_3
  Sulphur $\Rightarrow$ Rhombic & monoclinic

Chemical properties :

- **Oxidation states :** 'O' $\Rightarrow$ –2, –1, 1, 2
  S, Se, Te $\Rightarrow$ –2, 4, 6; Po $\Rightarrow$ 2, 4
* + 4 and + 6 are more common oxidation state due to inert pair effect. The stability of + 6 decreases down the group while + 4 increases.
- **Hydrides :** Form Hydrides of type H_2E
  Boiling point : $H_2S < H_2Se < H_2Te < H_2O$

  Reducing power : $H_2Te > H_2Se > H_2S > H_2O$
  Acidic character : $H_2O < H_2S < H_2Se < H_2Te$
- **Oxides :** Form oxides of type EO_2, and EO_3
  Both type of oxides are acidic in nature.
  Reducing property decreases from SO_2 to TeO_2.
- **Halides :** Form halides of type EX_6,
  EX_4, EX_2, and E_2X_2
* Stability of halides decreases in order
  $F^- > Cl^- > Br^- > I^-$
  Monohalides exist as dimer.
* Tetra fluorides, such as SF_4 (gas), SeF_4 (l) and TeF_4
  (s) have sp^3d hybridization (see – saw) geometry
- Amongst hexahalides hexafluorides are the only stable halides

Oxo-acids of sulphur :

Sulphur forms a number of oxo-acids. Some of these are unstable and cannot be isolated. They are known only in aqueous solutions or in form of their salts. The structures of some important oxoacids are given as follows :

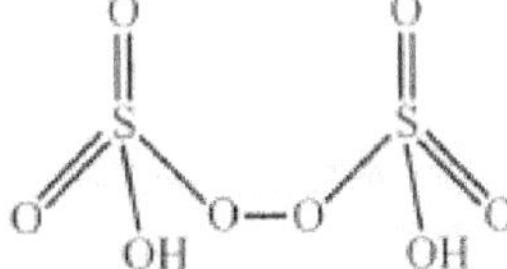

(i) Sulphurous acid (H_2SO_3)

(ii) Sulphuric acid (H_2SO_4)

(iii) Peroxodisulphuric acid or Marshall's acid ($H_2S_2O_8$)

(iv) Pyrosulphuric acid (oleum, $H_2S_2O_7$)

Group 17 Elements

- **Elements:** F, Cl, Br, I, At
- **Electronic configuration:** ns^2, np^4
  Physical properties : Exceptional properties
  Electron gain enthalpy F < Cl > Br > I [small size & inter electronic repulsions of 'F']
  Bond dissociation enthalpy $F_2 < Cl_2 > Br_2 > I_2$ [large repulsions of the lone pairs of F_2]
- **Oxidation states:** Fluorine show –1, +1 (except. case)
  other shows –1, + 1, + 3, + 5 and + 7
  Oxidising power :
* $F_2 > Cl_2 > Br_2 > I_2$
* Relative oxidising power can be illustrated by their reaction with water.

$$2F_2(g) + 2H_2O(l) \rightarrow 4H^+(aq) + 4F^-(aq) + O_2(g)$$
$$X_2(g) + H_2O(l) \rightarrow HX(aq) + HOX(aq)$$
(where X = Cl, Br)
$$4I^-(aq) + 4H^+(aq) + O_2(g) \rightarrow 2I_2(s) + 2H_2O(l)$$

Hydrogen halides :
Boiling point HF > HI > HBr > HCl
Melting point HI > HF > HBr > HCl
Acidic strength HI > HBr > HCl > HF
- **Reaction with metals:**
- Ionic character: MF > MCl > MBr > MI
- **Displacement reaction:**
F replaces Cl, Br and I, Cl replaces Br and I
Oxo-acids of halogens:
* Due to high electronegativity and small size 'F' forms only one oxoacid (HOF, hypofluorous acid) while other hologens form oxoacids of the type
HOX, HXO_2, HXO_3 and HXO_4

Cl	Br	I	
HOCl	HOBr	HOI	Hypohalous acid
$HClO_2$	$HBrO_2$	–	Halous acid
$HClO_3$	$HBrO_3$	HIO_3	Halic acid
$HClO_4$	$HBrO_4$	HIO_4	Perhalic acid

* Acid-character of oxo-acids of same halogen increases with increase in O.S. e.g.,
$HOCl < HClO_2 < HClO_3 < HClO_4$
* **Oxidising power :** HOCl > HOBr > HOI
* **Thermal stability**
$HOCl < HClO_2, < HClO_3 < HClO_4$
Interhalogen compounds:
* Compounds of halogens themselves.
* These are covalent compounds
(XX', XX'_3, XX'_5, XX'_7,)

$X \Rightarrow$ large size halogen, $X' \Rightarrow$ small large size halogen,
* More reactive than halogens except
'F' due to weaker A–X bond than X–X bond.
XX'_3 (ClF_3, BrF_3, IF_3 I_2Cl_6) $\Rightarrow$ Bent T-shaped
XX'_5 (IF_5, BrF_5, ClF_5) $\Rightarrow$ Square pyramidal
XX'_7 (IF_7) $\Rightarrow$ Pentagonal bipyramidal

MIND

KMnO₄:
- Prepared from the mineral pyrolusite

$$2MnO_2 + 4KOH + O_2 \rightarrow 2K_2MnO_4 + 2H_2O$$
$$3MnO_4^{2-} + 4H^+ \rightarrow 2MnO_4^- + MnO_2 + 2H_2O$$

commercial method :

$$MnO_2 \xrightarrow[\text{Oxidised with air or KNO}_3]{\text{Fused with KOH}} MnO_4^{2-}$$

Maganate ion

$$MnO_4^{2-} \xrightarrow[\text{in alkaline solution}]{\text{Electrolytic oxidation}} MnO_4^-$$

Permaganat ion

• Oxidising properties:
In acidic medium:

$$MnO_4^- + 8H^+ + 5e^- \rightarrow Mn^{2+} + 4H_2O$$

It oxidises I^- to I_2, NO_2 to NO_3^-, Fe^{2+} to Fe^{3+}, $C_2O_4^{2-}$ to CO_2

In neutral or faintly alkaline medium,

$$MnO_4^- + 2H_2O + 3e^- \rightarrow MnO_2 + 4H_2O$$

It oxidises $S_2O_3^{2-}$ to SO_4^{2-}, Mn^{2+} to MnO_2, I^- to IO_3^- etc.

K₂Cr₂O₇:
- Prepared from chromite ore ($FeCr_2O_4$)

$$4FeCr_2O_4 + 8Na_2CO_3 + 7O_2 \rightarrow 8Na_2CrO_4 + 2Fe_2O_3 + 8CO_2$$
$$2Na_2CrO_4 + H_2SO_4 \rightarrow Na_2Cr_2O_7 + Na_2SO_4 + H_2O$$
$$Na_2Cr_2O_7 + 2KCl \rightarrow K_2Cr_2O_7 + 2NaCl$$

The chromates and dichromates are interconvertible in aqueous solution depending upon pH of the solution.

$$2CrO_4^{2-} + 2H^+ \rightarrow Cr_2O_7^{2-} + H_2O$$
(orange)
$$Cr_2O_7^{2-} + 2OH^- \rightarrow CrO_4^{2-} + H_2O$$
(yellow)

• Oxidising properties:
Ionic equation :

$$Cr_2O_7^{2-} + 14H^+ + 6e^- \rightarrow 2Cr^{3+} + 7H_2O$$
$$Fe^{2+} \rightarrow Fe^{3+} + e^- \ ; \ 2I^- \rightarrow I_2 + 2e^-$$
$$SO_2 + 2H_2O \rightarrow SO_4^{2-} + 2H^+ + 2e^- \ ; \ C_2O_4^{2-} \rightarrow 2CO_2 + 2e^-$$

The full equation is obtained by adding the half reaction for potassium dichromate to the half reaction for the reducing agent

for e.g. $Cr_2O_7^{2-} + 14H^+ + 6I^- \rightarrow 2Cr^{3+} + 7H_2O + 3I_2$
Green

• Chromly chloride Test :

$$K_2Cr_2O_7 + 4KCl + 6H_2SO_4 \rightarrow 2CrO_2Cl_2 + 6KHSO_4 + 3H_2O$$
(chromyl chloride)

Some important *d*-block elements compound

The *d*- Block elements

THE *d*-& *f*-BLOCK ELEMENTS

The *f*- block Elements

Actinoids
- General E.C: $5f^{1-14} 6d^{0-1} 7s^2$

Ionic Sizes: The general trend in lanthanoids is observable in the actinoids as well. There is a gradual decrease in the size of atoms or M^{3+} ions across the series. This may be referred to as the actinoid contraction (like lanthanoid contraction). The contraction is, however, greater from element to element in this series resulting from poor shielding by $5f$ electrons.

Most stable O.S. is + 3. Also shows O.S like +4, + 5, +6 and +7
- These are mostly radioactive
- Have much greater tendency to form complexes than lanthanides. Their magnetic properties are more complex than those of lanthanoids
- Their IE's are lower than for the early lanthanoids. This is because the $5f$ electrons are more effectively shielded from the nuclear charge than the $4f$ electrons of the corresponding lanthanoids.

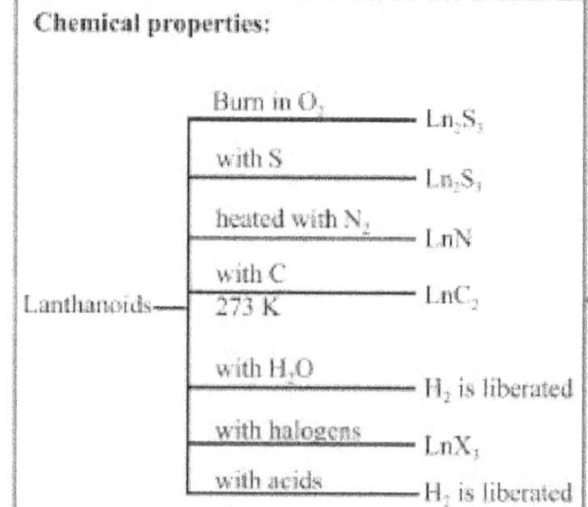

MAP-7

- **Four transition series:**
  - (i) 3d series: From Sc (21) to Zn (30)
  - (ii) 4d series : From Y (39) to Cd (48)
  - (iii) 5d series: La (57), Hf (72) to Hg (80)
  - (iv) 6d series : Ac (89), Rf (104) to Cn (112)
- **Electronic configuration:** $(n-1)d^{1-10}ns^{1-2}$
  - **Atomic Size :** Atomic and ionic radii of d-block elements is smaller than s-block elements. Atomic radii depends on effective nuclear charge (Z_{eff}) and screening effect (SE).

    In 3d series : Sc $\rightarrow$ Cr (Z_{eff} > SE) $\therefore$ radius decreases

    Mn $\rightarrow$ Ni (Z_{eff} = SE) $\therefore$ radius remains constant; Cu $\rightarrow$ Zn (Z_{eff} < SE) $\therefore$ radius increases

    Decrease in the radii with increase in atomic number is not regular. Atomic radii tend to reach minimum near at the middle of the series and increase slightly towards the end of the series.
  - **Melting and boiling points :** M.P. and B.P. of d-block elements is greater than of s-block (the reason is stronger metallic bond and presence of covalent bond formed by unpaired d-electrons.).
  - **Ionisation potentials :** The ionisation potentials of d-block elements increase as we move across each series from left to right, although the increase is not quite regular, e.g., in the first series, the values for Sc, Ti, V and Cr differ very slightly. Similarly the values Fe, Co, Ni and Cu are fairly close to one another. The value for Zn is appreciably higher due to the additional stability associated with completely filled 3d-level in Zn (Zn $\rightarrow$ 3$d^{10}4s^2$).
  - **Standard electrode potential :** $E^{\circ}_{M^{2+}/M}$ values are more negative than $E^{\circ}_{2H^{+}/H_2}$ values (except Cu). These metals (except Cu) evolve $H_2(g)$ and hence are oxidised easily when reacted with acid solutions is $E^{\circ}_{Cu^{2+}/Cu}$ highest (+ 0.34) in first transition series and does not liberate $H_2(g)$ from acids. is highest (+ 0.34) in first transition series and does not liberate $H_2(g)$ from acids.
  - Cr is unreactive although high negative $E^{\circ}_{Cr^{2+}/Cr}$ value due to the formation of non-reactive invisible layer of Cr_2O_3
  - $E^{\circ}_{M^{3+}/M^{2+}}$ of Co and Ni is exceptionally high positive value due to high (negative) hydration enthalpy.
  - **Oxidation state:** Shows variable oxidation states due to involvement of (ns) and ($n-1$)d electrons in bonding.
  - **Magnetic property:** Transition elements and many of their compounds are paramagnetic. The magnetic moment (μ) can be calculated by using $\mu = \sqrt{n(n+2)}$ where 'n' is the number of unpaired electrons in the metal ion
  - **Coloured compounds:** Forms coloured compounds due to d-d transition.
  - **Forms complexes:** Due to small highly charged ions and vacant d-orbitals
  - **Forms interstitial compounds:** As they are able to entrap atoms of elements having small atomic size like H, C, N, B etc.
  - **Oxides:** Oxides in lower oxidation states are basic, whereas those with higher. oxidation state are acidic or amphoteric

Lanthanoids: 14 elements from Ce to Lu General E.C: $6s^2 5d^{0-1} 4f^{1-14}$

Atomic and Ionic Sizes

In the lanthanoid series with increasing atomic number, there is a progressive decrease in the size from lanthanum to lutetium (La^{3+} to Lu^{3+}). This contraction in size is known as lanthanoid contraction. In these elements the added electron enters in the deep seated f-orbitals and therefore experiences considerable pull by the nucleus. Such an electron cannot add to the size of the element and also because the intervening $5s^2 p^6 d^1$ electronic shells, have very little screening effect on the outermost $6s^2$ electrons. Hence with increasing atomic number, the enhanced nuclear charge leads to contraction in the size of atoms and ions.

Oxidation states : All the lanthanoids attains +3 oxidation state and only cerium, praseodymium, terbium, and dysprosium exhibit higher oxidation state (+4).

Oxidation states + 2 and +4 occur particularly when they lead to

(a) A noble gas configuration e.g. Ce^{4+} (f^0)   (b) A half filled 'f' orbital e.g. Eu^{2+}, Tb^{4+}, (f^7)

(c) A completely filled 'f' orbital e.g. Yb^{2+} (f^{14})

Colour : The lanthanoid ions have unpaired electrons in their 4f- orbitals. Thus these ions absorbs visible region of light an undergo f-f transition and hence exhibit colour.
  - They are highly dense metals with high m.pts.
  - **Ionisation Energies** - The first I.E.'s are around 600 kJ mol^{-1} and second about 1200 kJ mol^{-1} which are comparable with those of calcium. The 3rd I.E. is low if it leads to stable empty, half-filled or completely filled configuration. This is the reason for very low 3rd I.E. of La, Gd and Lu.
  - **Electropositive character**- High due to low I.P.
  - Complex formation- Do not have much tendency to form complexes due to low charge density because of their large size.
  - **Reducing Agent** - They readily lose electrons so they act as good reducing agents.

    Due to lanthanide contraction, pairs of elements such as Zr/Hf, Nb/Ta and Mo/W are almost identical in size.

    They are used in the production of alloy steel known as mirsch metal (Ln–95%, Fr–5% traces of S, C, Ca & Al) which is used in making Mg – based alloy to produce bullets, shell and lighter flint.

MIND

Some important terms:

Denticity: The number of ligating (linking) atoms present in ligand is called denticity.

*** Unidentate ligands:** The ligands whose only one donor atom is bonded to metal atom are called unidentate ligands. Examples: H_2O, NH_3, CO, CN

*** Bidentate ligands:** The ligands which contain two donor atoms or ions through which they are bonded to the metal ion.

Examples: Ethylene diamine $H_2NCH_2CH_2NH_2$ has two nitrogen atoms, oxalate ion has two oxygen atoms which can bind with the metal atom.

*** Polydentate ligand:** When several donor atoms are present in a single ligand, the ligand is called polydentate ligand.

Examples: In $N(CH_2CH_2NH_2)_3$, the ligand is said to be polydentate and $EDTA^{4-}$ is an important hexadentate ligand.

*** Chelate:** An inorganic metal complex in which there is a close ring of atoms caused by attachment of a ligand to a metal atom at two points e.g., $[Cu (NH_2(CH_2)_2NH_2)_2]^{2+}$.

*** Ambidentate ligand:** Ligands which can linked through two different atoms present in it are called ambidentate ligand.

Example: NO_2^- and SCN^-. Here, NO_2^- can link through N as well as O while SCN^- can link through S as well as N atom.

Werner's coordination theory:
- The postulates of Werner's theory are:
* Metal shows two different kinds of valences: primary valency and secondary valency.
* The ions/ groups bound by secondary linkages to the metal have characteristic spatial arrangements corresponding to different coordination numbers.
* The most common geometrical shapes in coordination compounds are octahedral, square planar and tetrahedral.
- **Primary valency**
* This valency is normally ionisable.
* It is equal to positive charge on central metal atom.
* These valencies are satisfied by negatively charged ions.
- **Secondary valency**
* This valency is non – ionisable.
* The secondary valency equals the number of ligand atoms coordinated to the metal.
* It is also called coordination number of the metal.
* It is commonly satisfied by neutral and negatively charged, sometimes by positively charged ligands.

COORDINATION COMPOUNDS

Isomerism

Stereoisomerism

Geometrical   Optical

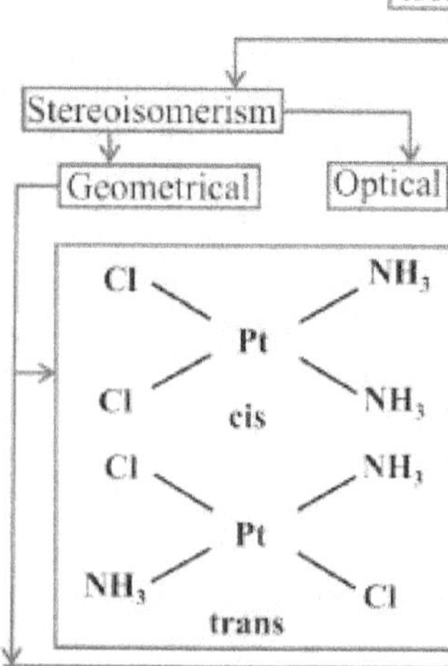

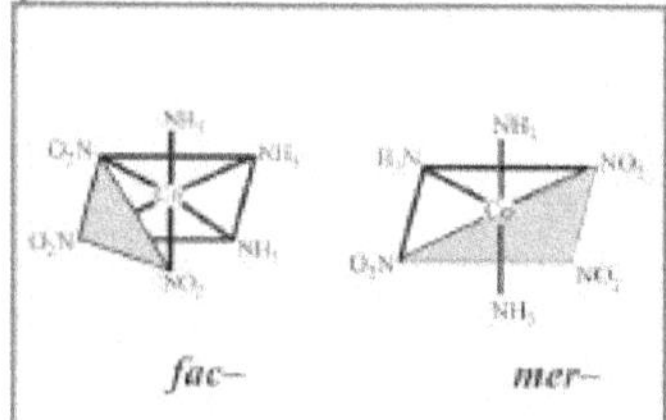

Structural isomerism

- **Linkage isomerism:**
  $[Co (NH_3)_5 (NO_2)] Cl_2$,
  $[Co (NH_3)_5 (ONO)] Cl_2$
  Nitrite ion bound through either oxygen or nitrogen.
- **Coordination isomerism:**
  $[Co (NH_3)_6][Cr (CN)_6]$,
  $[Cr (NH_3)_6][Co (CN)_6]$
  Interchange of ligands between cationic and anionic entities.
- **Ionisation isomerism:**
  $[Co (NH_3)_5(SO_4)]Br$,
  $[Co (NH_3)_5Br]SO_4$
  These give different ion in solution
- **Solvate isomerism:**
  $[Cr(H_2O)_6]Cl_3$
  $[Cr(H_2O)_5Cl]Cl_2.H_2O$

Naming of coordination compounds: The following rules are used for naming coordination compounds:
- The cation is named first in both positively and negatively charged coordination entities.
- The ligands are named in an alphabetical order before the name of the central atom/ion.
- Names of the anionic ligands end in–o, those of neutral and cationic ligands are the same except aqua for H_2O, ammine for NH_3, carbonyl for CO and nitrosyl for NO. While writing the formula of coordination entity, these are enclosed in brackets.
- Prefixes mono, di, tri, etc., are used to indicate the number of the individual ligands in the coordination entity. When the names of the ligands include a numerical prefix, then the terms, bis, tris, tetra, kis are used, the ligand to which they refer being placed in parentheses e.g., $[NiCl_2(PPh_3)_2]$ is named dichloridobis (triphenylphosphine) nickel (II).
- Oxidation state of the metal in cation, anion or neutral coordination entity is indicated by Roman numeral in parenthesis.
- If the complex ion is a cation, the metal is named same as the element. For example, Co in a complex cation is called cobalt and Pt is called platinum. If the complex ion is an anion, the name of the metal ends with the suffix – ate.
- The neutral complex molecule is named similar to that of the complex cation.

MAP-8

Stability of coordination compounds: The stability of complex in solution refers to the degree of association between the two species involved in the state of equilibrium. It is expressed as stability constant (K).

$$M^+ + nL^{x-} \rightleftharpoons [MLn]^{y-} ; K = \frac{[(MLn)^{y-}]}{[M^+][L^{x-}]^n}$$

- The factors on which stability of the complex depends :

* **Charge on the central metal atom:** As the magnitude of charge on metal atom increases, stability of the complex increases.

* **Nature of metal ion:** The stability order is $3d < 4d < 5d$ series.

* **Basic nature of ligands:** Strong field ligands form stable complex.

Colour in coordination compounds: The crystal field theory attributes the colour of the coordination compounds to d-d transition of the electron, i.e., electron jump from t_{2g} level to higher e_g level.
In the absence of ligands, crystal field splitting does not occur and hence the substance is colourless.e.g.,
$[Ti(H_2O)_6]^{3+}$ - Violet in colour
$[Cu(H_2O)_4]^{2+}$ - Blue in colour, etc.

Metal carbonyls: Metal carbonyls are homoleptic complexes in which carbon monoxide (CO) acts as the ligand e.g., $Ni(CO)_4$

- The metal-carbon bond in metal carbonyls possess both s and p character.
- **The M–C σ bond** is formed by the donation of lone pair of electrons from the carbonyl carbon into a vacant orbital of the metal.
- **The M–C π bond** is formed by the donation of a pair of electrons from a filled d orbital of metal into the vacant antibonding π orbital of carbon monoxide.
- The metal to ligand bonding creates a synergic effect which strengthens the bond between CO and the metal.

Crystal field theory (CFT): In this theory, ligands are treated as point charges in case of anions and dipoles in case of neutral molecules.

- The five d-orbitals are classified as
* Three d-orbitals i.e., d_{xy}, d_{yz} and d_{zx} are oriented in between the coordinate axes and are and d_{zx} are oriented in between the coordinate axes and are called t_{2g} – orbitals.
* The other two d-orbitals, i.e., $d_{x^2-y^2}$ and d_{z^2} oriented along the x, y axes are called e_g – orbitals.
- A series in which ligand are arranged in order of increasing magnitude of crystal field splitting, is called **spectrochemical series**.

$$I^- < Br^- < SCN^- < Cl^- < S^{2-} < F^- < OH^- < C_2O_4^{2-} < H_2O$$
$$< NCS^- < EDTA^{4-} < NH_3 < en < CN^- < CO$$

- In case of octahedral complexes, Energy of e_g set of orbitals > energy of t_{2g} set of orbitals.
- The energy of e_g orbitals will increase by $(3/5)\,\Delta_0$ and t_{2g} will decrease by $(2/5)\,\Delta_0$.
- Ligands for which $\Delta_0 < P$ are known as weak field ligands and form high spin complexes.
- If $\Delta_0 > P$, it becomes more energetically favourable for the fourth electron to occupy a t_{2g} orbital which produce this effect are known as strong field ligands and form low spin complexes.
- In tetrahedral complexes, Energy of t_{2g} set of orbitals > Energy of e_g set of orbitals.
- Pairing of electrons is not possible in tetrahedral complexes, so these are high spin complexes.

Valence bond theory (VBT):
The salient features of the theory are :
(i) The central metal ion a number of empty orbitals for accommodating electrons donated by the ligands. The number of empty orbitals is equal to the coordination number of the metal ion for the particular complex.
(ii) The atomic orbitals (s, p or d) of the metal ion hybridize to form hybrid orbitals with definite directional properties. These hybrids orbitals now overlap with the ligand orbitals to form strong chemical bonds.

Number of orbitals and types of hybridisation :

Coordination number	Type of hybridisation	Distribution of hybrid orbitals in space
4	sp^3	Tetrahedral
4	dsp^2	Square planar
5	sp^3d	Trigonal bipyramidal
6	sp^3d^2	Octahedral
6	d^2sp^3	Octahedral

- The d-orbitals involved in the hybridization may be either inner (n-1) d orbitals or outer nd-orbitals. The complexes formed in these two ways are referred to as low spin and high spin complexes, respectively.
- If the complex contains unpaired electrons, it is paramagnetic in nature, while if it does not contain unpaired electron, it is diamagnetic in nature.

MIND

HALOALKANES AND HALOARENES

Haloalkanes

Preparation:

- **From alcohols:**

$$ROH + HX \longrightarrow RX + H_2O$$
$$ROH + PCl_5 \longrightarrow PCl + POCl + HCl$$
$$ROH + SOCl_2 \longrightarrow RCl + SO_2 + HCl$$

From hydrocarbons:

$$CH_2 = CH_2 + HX \longrightarrow CH_3CH_2X$$

Order of reactivity HI > HCl > HF
In case of unsymmetrical alkenes addition occurs according to Markownikoff's rule only in case of Hbr in presence of peroxides addition occures according to anti Markowinkoff's rule

$$CH_2 = CH_2 + Br_2 \xrightarrow{CCl_4}$$
$$BrCH_2CH_2Br$$

$$CH_4 \xrightarrow[hv]{Cl_2} CH_3Cl + CH_2Cl_2 + CHCl_3 + CCl_4$$

From halogen exchange

With NaI **(Finkelstein reaction)**

$$\underset{(X=Cl,Br)}{R-X} + NaI \xrightarrow{Acetone} \underset{Iodoalkane}{R-I} + NaX$$

with AgF **(Swarts reaction)**

$$C_2H_5Cl + AgF \longrightarrow \underset{Fluoroethane}{C_2H_5F} + AgCl$$

Properties:

Physical properties

- Lower alkyl halides are colourless with sweet smell or pleasant oily liquid, except CH_3F, CH_3Cl, CH_3-CH_2-F, CH_3-CH_2-Cl which are gaseous in nature.
- Alkyl halides having 18-carbon or more than it are solid in nature.
- These are completely soluble in organic solvents but insoluble in H_2O
- Reactivity order is RI > RBr > RCl > RF
- For same halide group, reactivity order is 3° (halide) > 2° (halide) > 1° (halide)
- Polarity order is RF > RCl > RBr > RI
- Melting & Boiling points, for same alkyl group the order is RI > RBr > RCl > RF
- Fluorides and chlorides are lighter than water whereas bromides and iodides are heavier than H_2O due to higher density of bromine than oxygen.

Chemical properties:

- **Nucleophilic substitution:**

$$RX + KOH \longrightarrow ROH + KX$$
$$RX + H_2O \longrightarrow ROH + HX$$
$$RX + NaOR \longrightarrow ROR + NaX$$
$$RCl + NaI \xrightarrow{Acetone} RI + NaCl$$
$$RX + LiAlH_4 \longrightarrow RH + LiX + AlX_3$$

- **These reactions** are of two types:
- **S_N1 type** (Unimolecular nucleophilic reactions) proceeds in two steps:

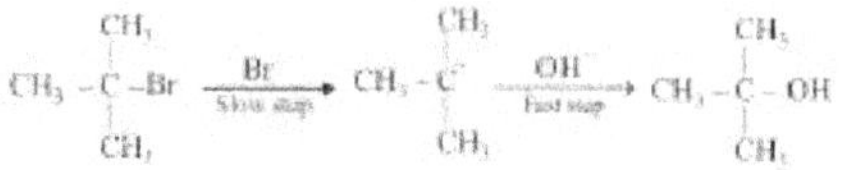

$$CH_3-\overset{\overset{\displaystyle CH_3}{|}}{\underset{\underset{\displaystyle CH_3}{|}}{C}}-Br \xrightarrow[\text{Slow step}]{Br} CH_3-\overset{\overset{\displaystyle CH_3}{|}}{\underset{\underset{\displaystyle CH_3}{|}}{C}} \xrightarrow[\text{Fast step}]{OH} CH_3-\overset{\overset{\displaystyle CH_3}{|}}{\underset{\underset{\displaystyle CH_3}{|}}{C}}-OH$$

* Rate, r = k[RX]. It is a first order reaction.
* Reactivity order of alkyl halide towards S_N1 mechanism 3° > 2° > 1°
* Polar solvents, low concentration of nucleophiles and weak nucleophiles favour S_N1 mechanism.
* In S_N1 reactions, partial racemisation occurs due to the possibility of frontal as well as backside attack on planar carbocation

- **S_N2 type** (Bimolecular nucleophilic substitution), these reactions proceed in one step.
* It is a second order reaction with r = k[RX][Nu].
* During S_N2 reaction, inversion of configuration occurs
* Reactivity of halides towards S_N2 mechanism is 1° > 2° > 3°
* Rate of reaction in S_N2 mechanism depends on the strength of the attacking nucleophile.
* Non-polar solvents, strong nucleophiles and high concentration of nucleophiles favour S_N2 mechanism.

- **Elimination reaction:**

$$CH_2CH_2Br \xrightarrow{OH^-} CH_2CH_2 + H_2O + Br^-$$

- **Reaction with metal:**

$$CH_3CH_2Br + Mg \xrightarrow{Dry\ Ether}$$
$$CH_2CH_2 + MgBr$$

Grignard reagents are highly reactive and react with any source of proton (H_2O, alcohols, amines etc. to give hydrocarbons.)

- **Wurtz reaction:**

$$2RX + 2Na \longrightarrow RR + 2NaX$$

MAP-9

Haloarenes

Preparation:

From arenes:

$$C_6H_6 + Cl_2 \xrightarrow[\text{dark}]{\text{Fe}} C_6H_5Cl$$

From benzene diazonium chloride:

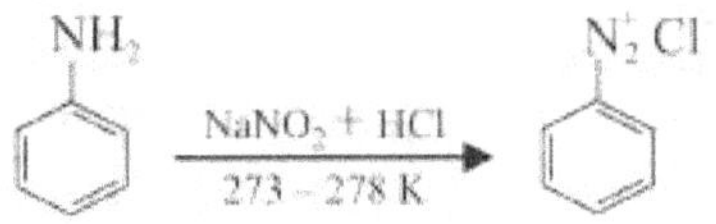

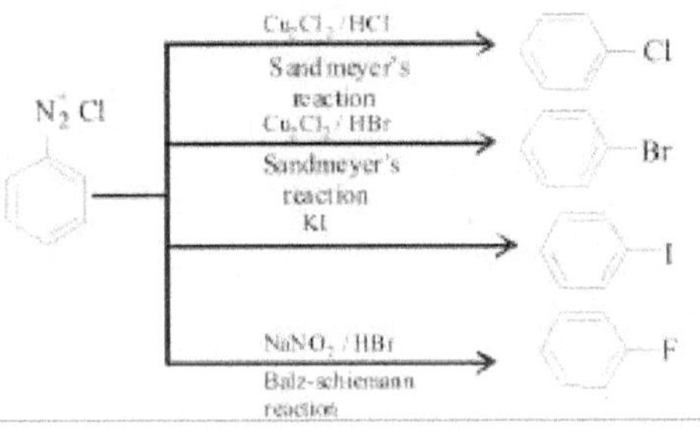

$$NH_2 \xrightarrow[273-278\text{ K}]{NaNO_2 + HCl} N_2^+Cl$$

From N_2^+Cl:

- $\xrightarrow{Cu_2Cl_2/HCl}$ Sandmeyer's reaction → Cl
- $\xrightarrow{Cu_2Cl_2/HBr}$ Sandmeyer's reaction → Br
- $\xrightarrow{KI}$ → I
- $\xrightarrow{NaNO_2/HBF_4}$ Balz-schiemann reaction → F

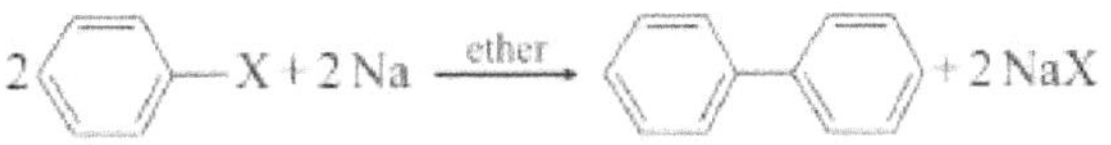

Polyhalogen compound:

- **Dichloromethane (CH_2Cl_2):** It is useful as solvent in industries. Mostly it is used as solvent in the production of chemicals used in removal of colour.

  *It is Harmful to nervous system. If it comes in direct contact with eye it damages the cornea. In addition, if it comes in direct contact with skin, red rashes are formed.

- **Tetrachloromethane (CCl_4):** It is used in the manufacture of refrigerants and propellants for aerosol cans.

  *Used as a cleaning solvent, degreasing agent and as fire extinguisher.

  *It causes permanent damage to nerve cells.

  *In atmosphere, it depletes the ozone layer.

- **Freons:** Chlorofluorocarbon compounds of methane and ethane are collectively known as freons and it is manufactured by **swarts reaction** using tetrachloromethane.
* Freon 12 (CCl_2F_2) is one of the most common freons in industrial use.
* Freon is able to initiate radical chain reactions that can disturb the natural ozone balance.
- **DDT:** It is a powerful insecticide.
* It is a persistent organic pollutant that is readily adsorbed to soils and sediments, which can act both as sinks and as long-term sources of exposure affecting organisms.
* It is not metabolised very rapidly by animals.

Properties:

Physical properties:

* Aryl halides are colourless liquids or colourless solids with characteristic odour.
* Boiling point generally increases with increase in the size of aryl group or halogen atom. Boiling point order
  $$Ar-I > Ar-Br > Ar-Cl > Ar-F$$
* The melting point of p-isomer is more than o- and m-isomer. This is because of more symmetrical nature of p-isomer.
* Due to resonance in chlorobenzene, C-Cl bond is shorter and hence, its dipole moment is less than that of cyclohexyl chloride.

Chemical properties:

• **Nucleophilic substitution reactions:**

Aryl halides are less reactive towards nucleophilic substitution reaction. Their low reactivity is attributed due to the following reasons:

* Due to resonance, C-X bond has partial double bond character.
* Stabilisation of the molecule by delocalisation of electrons.
* Instability of phenyl carbocation.

However, aryl halides having electron withdrawing groups (like $-NO_2$, $-SO_3H$, etc.) at ortho and para positions undergo nucleophilic substitution reaction easily.

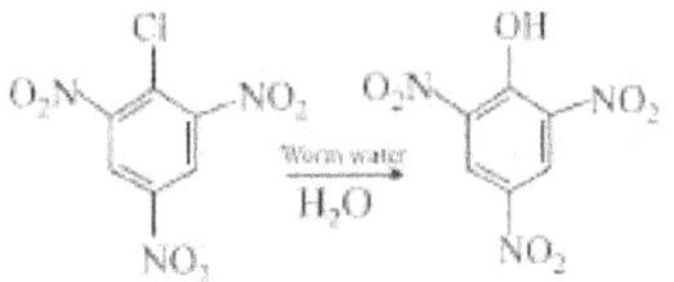

$$\xrightarrow[H_2O]{\text{Warm water}}$$

• **Electrophilic substitution reactions:**

Haloarenes are o, p-directing, due to $+ I$ effect of halogen group electrondensity increases at ortho and para positions e.g., halogenation, nitration, sulphonation, Friedel-crafts reaction etc.

Reaction with metals:

* Wurtz fitting reaction:

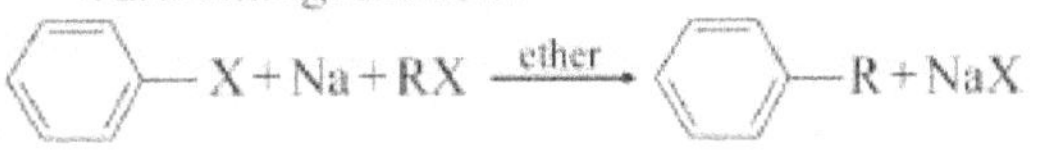

$$\langle \rangle - X + Na + RX \xrightarrow{\text{ether}} \langle \rangle - R + NaX$$

Fitting reaction:

$$2\langle \rangle - X + 2Na \xrightarrow{\text{ether}} \langle \rangle - \langle \rangle + 2NaX$$

MIND

ALCOHOLS, PHENOLS AND ETHERS ← **Alcohols**

Preparation:

- **By acid catalysed hydration**: Alkanes reacts with H_2O in presence of acid (as catalyst).

$$CH_3CH = CH_2 + H_2O \xrightarrow[\text{(markovnikov's addition)}]{H^+} CH_3CH(OH)CH_3$$

- **By Hydroboration-Oxidation:**
  Diborane with alkene gives trialkyl boride which gives alcohol with H_2O_2/OH^-

$$CH_3CH = CH_2 \xrightarrow[\substack{\text{(ii) } H_2O_2, OH^- \\ \text{anti-markovnikov's addition}}]{\text{(i) } B_2H_6/THF} CH_3CH_2CH_2OH$$

- **Reduction of Aldehydes and Ketones**

$$\text{Aldehyde} \xrightarrow{H_2/Pd} 1°\text{Alcohol}$$

$$\text{Ketone} \xrightarrow{NaBH_4} 2°\text{ Alcohol}$$

- **Reduction of carboxylic acids:**

$$RCOOH \xrightarrow[\text{(ii) } H_2O]{\text{(i) } LiAlH_4} RCH_2OH$$

- **From Grignard Reagent:**

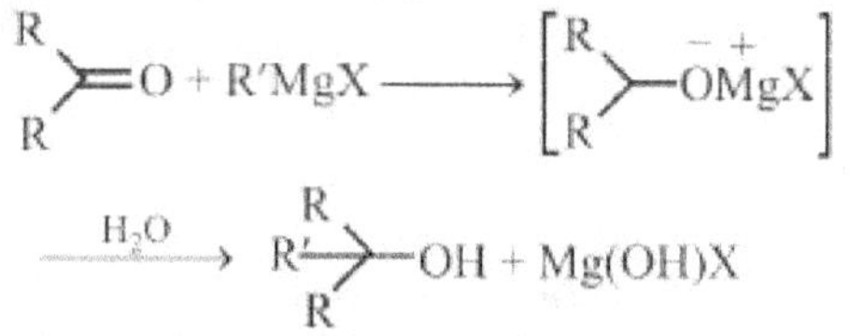

$$\underset{R}{\overset{R}{>}}=O + R'MgX \longrightarrow \left[\underset{R}{\overset{R}{>}}\overset{-\ +}{OMgX}\right]$$

$$\xrightarrow{H_2O} \underset{R}{\overset{R}{R'>}}-OH + Mg(OH)X$$

- **Physical Properties of Alcohols:**
- Alcohols are colourless with characteristic smell (alcoholic).
- They are soluble in water due to H–bonding.
- These are partially soluble in organic solvents.
- They are liquid in nature up to 12–carbon.
- Melting point and boiling point $\propto$ molecular mass $\propto \dfrac{1}{\text{No. of branches}}$
- Boiling point of alcohols are higher than the corresponding ether due to H–bonding.

- **Chemical Properties:**
- $2ROH + 2M \longrightarrow 2R-\overset{-\ +}{O}M + H_2$ (M = Na, K, Cl)
- $RCOOH + H - OR' \longrightarrow RCOOR' + H_2O$
- $RCOCl + H - OR' \longrightarrow RCOOR' + HCl$
- $ROH + R'MgX \longrightarrow R' - H + ROMgX$

Commercially important alcohols:

- **Methanol**: Methanol, CH_3OH, also known as 'wood spirit', was produced by destructive distillation of wood. Methanol is used as a solvent in paints, varnishes and for making formaldehyde.
- **Ethanol**: Ethanol is a colourless liquid with boiling point 351 K. It is used as a solvent in paint industry and in the preparation of a number of carbon compounds. The commercial alcohol is made unfit for drinking by mixing in it some copper sulphate (to give it a colour) and pyridine (a foul smelling liquid). It is known as denaturation of alcohol.

Preparation:
Physical Properties of Ethers

- Dimethyl ether and ethyl methyl ether are gases. All other are colourless liquids with pleasant odour.
- They are sparingly soluble in water but readily soluble in organic solvents. Solubility of ether in water is due to hydrogen bonding between ether and water molecule.

$$\underset{R}{\overset{}{R - O - - - H - O - H}}$$

- Boiling points of ether show a gradual increase with increase in molecular weight. Ethers have low boiling points than isomeric alcohols as there is no association with hydrogen bonding between ether molecules. The boiling points of ethers are close to the boiling points of alkanes.
- They are lighter than water.
- Lower ethers are highly volatile and inflammable.

- $R - OH + HCl \xrightarrow{\text{anh. } ZnCl_2} R - Cl + H_2O$
- $CH_3CH_2OH \xrightarrow{\text{conc. } H_2SO_4} CH_2 = CH_2 + H_2O$
- $RCH_2OH \xrightarrow{[O]} R - \overset{H}{C} = O \xrightarrow{[O]} R - \overset{O}{\overset{\|}{C}} - OH$

MAP-10

Phenols

Ethers

Preparation:

- Chlorobenzene + NaOH $\xrightarrow[\text{(ii) HCl}]{\text{(i) 623 K, 300 atm.}}$ Phenol

- Benzene $\xrightarrow[\text{(ii) NaOH, H}^-]{\text{(i) Oleum}}$ Phenol

- Aniline $\xrightarrow[\text{272–278K}]{\text{NaNO}_2 + \text{HCl}}$ Diazonium salt $\xrightarrow{\text{H}_2\text{O}}$ Phenol

- Cumene $\xrightarrow[\text{(ii) H}^+ / \text{H}_2\text{O}]{\text{(i) O}_2}$ Phenol

Physical properties:

- Phenols are colorless crystalline solid or liquid having characteristic odour.
- Due to hydrogen bonding phenols has higher boiling point and more solubility compared to arene compounds which contains approximately same molecular mass.

Chemical Properties:

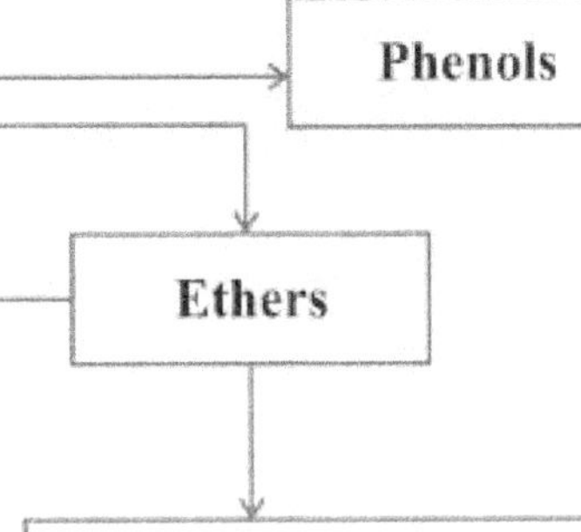

Preparation:

- **Dehydration of alcohol**:

$$2CH_3CH_2OH \xrightarrow[413\ K]{H_2SO_4} C_2H_5OC_2H_5 + H_2O$$

- **Williamson's synthesis**:

  $R - X + R' - ONa \longrightarrow ROR' + NaX$

  Here, alkyl halide should be primary because secondary and tertiary alkyl halides give elimination reaction rather than substitution.

  Thus, the reactivity order is $1^\circ > 2^\circ > 3^\circ$

Chemical Properties:

- Cleavage of C–O bond:

  $ROR + HX \longrightarrow RX + ROH$

  $ROH + HX \longrightarrow RX + H_2O$

  $PhOR + HX \longrightarrow PhOH + RX$

- Reactivity with HX:

  Reactivity order of HX is HI > HBr >> HCl.

$CH_3OCH_2CH_3 \xrightarrow{HI} CH_3I + CH_3CH_2OH$

$CH_3OCH_2CH_3 \xrightarrow[\text{high temp.}]{HI\ (excess)} CH_3I + CH_3CH_2OH \xrightarrow{HI} CH_3CH_2I + H_2O$

$C(CH_3)_3OCH_3 + HI \xrightarrow{S_N1} C(CH_3)_3I$

- **Electrophilic substitution:**

MIND

Preparation of aldehydes and ketones:

- **Oxidation of alcohols:**

$$1° \text{ Alcohol} \xrightarrow{K_2Cr_2O_7 + H_2SO_4} \text{Aldehyde}$$

$$2° \text{ Alcohol} \xrightarrow{K_2Cr_2O_7 + H_2SO_4} \text{Ketone}$$

- **Dehydrogenation of alcohols:**

$$1° \text{ Alcohol} \xrightarrow{Cu, 573 K} \text{Aldehyde}$$

$$2° \text{ Alcohol} \xrightarrow{Cu, 573 K} \text{Ketone}$$

- **Ozonolysis of alkenes:**

$$CH_3CH = CHCH_3 + O_3 \xrightarrow{H_2O, Zn} 2CH_3CHO$$

- **Hydration of alkynes:**

$$CH \equiv CH + H_2O \xrightarrow[HgSO_4]{dil. H_2SO_4} CH_3 - CHO$$

$$CH_3C \equiv CH + H_2O \xrightarrow[HgSO_4]{dil. H_2SO_4} CH_3 - \underset{\underset{O}{\|}}{C} - CH_3$$

- **Preparation of aldehydes only:**

* **Rosenmund reduction:**

$$\text{Acyl chloride} \xrightarrow{H_2Pd-BaSO_4} \text{Aldehyde}$$

* **Stephen reaction:**

$$RCN + SnCl_2 + HCl \xrightarrow{H_3O^+} RCHO$$

* **Etard Reaction:**

$$\text{(toluene)} \xrightarrow[\text{(ii) } H_3O^+]{\text{(i) } CrO_2Cl_2} \text{(benzaldehyde)}$$

* **Side chain chlorination:**

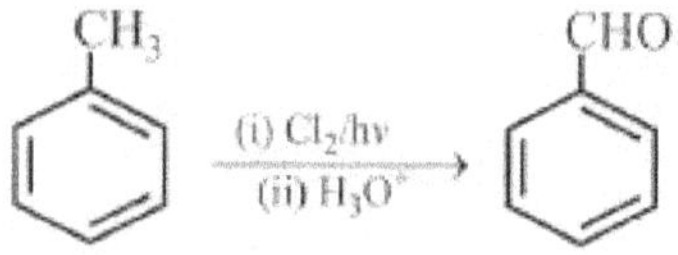

$$\text{(toluene)} \xrightarrow[\text{(ii) } H_3O^+]{\text{(i) } Cl_2/h\nu} \text{(benzaldehyde)}$$

* **Gatterman-Koch reaction:**

$$\text{Benzene} \xrightarrow[\text{anhy. } AlCl_3/CuCl]{CO, HCl} \text{Benzaldehyde}$$

- **Preparation of Ketones only:**

* **Friedel crafts acylation:**

$$C_6H_6 + R - \underset{\underset{}{\overset{\overset{O}{\|}}{C}}} - Cl \xrightarrow{AlCl_3} C_6H_5 - COR$$

* **From nitriles:**

$$C_2H_5CN \xrightarrow[\text{(ii) } H_3O^+]{\text{(i) } CH_3MgBr} C_2H_5COC_6H_5$$

* **From acyl chloride:**

$$2 RMgX + CdCl_2 \longrightarrow R_2Cd + 2 Mg(X)Cl$$

$$2 R'COCl + R_2Cd \longrightarrow 2 R'COR + CdCl_2$$

Carboxylic acids

Preparation:

- $RCH_2OH \xrightarrow[\text{(ii) } H_3O^+]{\text{(i) alk. } KMnO_4} RCOOH$

- $RCN \xrightarrow[H_2O]{H^+/OH^-} R - C(O) - NH_2 \xrightarrow[OH^-]{H^+ \text{ or }} RCOOH$

- $R - Mg - X + CO_2 \xrightarrow[\text{(ii) } H_3O^+]{\text{(i) dry ether}} RCOOH$

- $RCOCl \xrightarrow{H_2O} RCOOH + Cl^-$

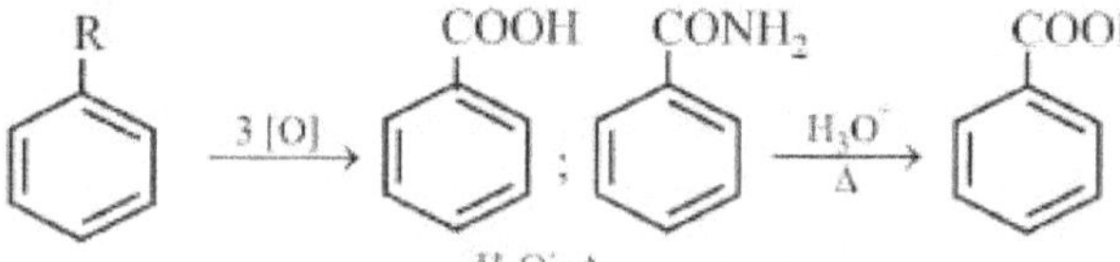

$$\text{(Ar-R)} \xrightarrow{3[O]} \text{(Ar-COOH)} ; \text{(Ar-CONH}_2) \xrightarrow[\Delta]{H_3O^+} \text{(Ar-COOH)}$$

$$RCOOR' \xrightarrow[NaOH, H_3O^-]{H_3O^-, \Delta} RCOOH$$

Properties:

- **Physical State :**
  C_1 to C_3 = Colourless pungent smelling liquids
  C_4 to C_9 = Oily liquids having goat's butter like smell.
  C_{10} + = Colourless and odourless waxy solids.
  These are polar substances and can form H-bonds with each other to form dimer structures.

- **Acidity of Carboxylic Acids :** The acidic character of carboxylic acids is due to resonance in the acidic group which imparts electron deficiency (positive charge) on the oxygen atom of the hydroxyl group.

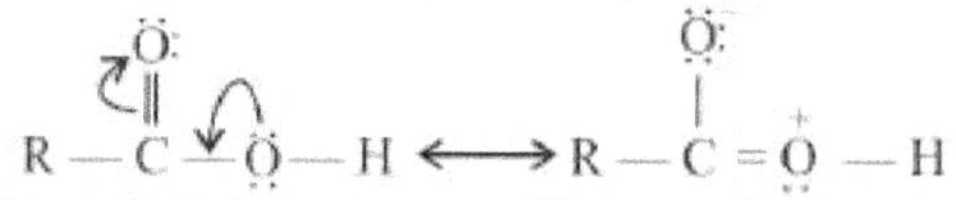

$$R - \underset{}{\overset{\overset{\ddot{O}:}{\|}}{C}} - \ddot{O} - H \longleftrightarrow R - C = \overset{+}{O} - H$$

Non-equivalent structures   (Resonance less important)

- Gives CO_2 with carbonates and $NaHCO_3$

- 2 Ethanoic acid $\xrightarrow{H, \Delta}$ Ethanoic anhydride

- **Esterification** $^{\text{or } P_2O_5, \Delta}$

- $RCOOH + R'OH \rightleftharpoons RCOOR' + H_2O$

- $RCOOH + PCl_5 \longrightarrow RCOCl + PCl_3 + HCl$

- $RCOOH + SOCl_2 \longrightarrow RCOCl + SO_2 + HCl$

- $RCOOH \xrightarrow{NH_3} RCONH_2$

- $RCOOH \xrightarrow[\text{(i) } LiAlH_4]{\Delta, H_2O} RCH_2OH$

- $RCOONa \xrightarrow[NaOH \,\&\, CaO/\Delta]{\text{(ii) } H_3O^-} RH + Na_2CO_3$ (decarboxylation)

- **Hell–Volhard Zelinsky reaction:**

$$RCH_2COH \xrightarrow[\text{(ii) } H_2O]{\text{(i) } X_2/Red P} RCH(X)COOH$$

MAP-11

ALDEHYDES, KETONES AND CARBOXYLIC ACIDS

Aldehydes and Ketones

- **Clemmensen reduction**:

$$\mathrm{C=O} \xrightarrow[\text{HCl}]{\text{Zn–Hg}} \mathrm{CH_2 + H_2O}$$

- **Wolff–kishner reduction**:

$$\mathrm{C=O} \xrightarrow[\text{(ii) KOH/ethylene glycol}]{\text{(i) NH_2 – NH_2}} \mathrm{CH_2 + N_2}$$

- **Oxidation**:

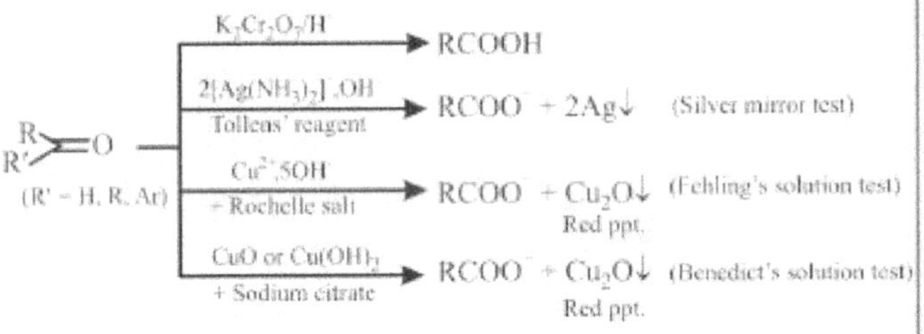

$$R,R' C = O$$
(R' = H, R, Ar)

- $\xrightarrow{K_2Cr_2O_7/H}$ RCOOH
- $\xrightarrow[\text{Tollens' reagent}]{2[Ag(NH_3)_2]^+ .OH}$ RCOO$^-$ + 2Ag↓ (Silver mirror test)
- $\xrightarrow[\text{+ Rochelle salt}]{Cu^{2+},SOH}$ RCOO$^-$ + Cu$_2$O↓ (Fehling's solution test) Red ppt.
- $\xrightarrow[\text{+ Sodium citrate}]{CuO \text{ or } Cu(OH)_2}$ RCOO$^-$ + Cu$_2$O↓ (Benedict's solution test) Red ppt.

- Aldehydes give positive test with Tollen's reagent Benedict's reagent and Fehling solution while ketones do not give such test.

$$\mathrm{RCOCH_3} \xrightarrow{\text{NaOX}} \mathrm{RCOONa + CHX_3} \ (X = Cl, Br, I)$$

- **Aldol condensation**:
  Condensation of aldehydes and ketones having atleast one α–H atom.

$$2\ \mathrm{CH_3CHO} \xrightarrow[\text{Aldol reaction}]{\text{dil. NaOH}}$$
$$\mathrm{CH_3CH(OH)CH_2CHO} \xrightarrow[\text{condensation}]{\Delta \ \text{Aldol}} \mathrm{CH_3CH=CHCHO}$$

- **Cannizzaro reaction**:
  Aldehydes with no α-hydrogen undergoes, self oxidation and reduction.

$$2\ \mathrm{HCHO} \xrightarrow{\text{conc. KOH}} \mathrm{CH_3OH + HCOOK}$$
(No α–hydrogen)

- **Crossed Cannizzaro reaction**:
$$\mathrm{C_6H_5CHO + HCHO} \xrightarrow{\Delta} \mathrm{C_6H_5CH_2OH + HCOONa}$$

Properties of aldehydes and ketones:

- **Physical state**: Formaldehyde (methanal) is a gas. All other aldehydes and ketones upto C_{11} are colourless volatile liquids. Higher members are solids at room temperature.
- **Odour**: Lower aldehydes have an unpleasant odour. Higher aldehydes and ketones have a pleasant odour.
- **Solubility**: Lower carbonyl compounds are soluble in water due to the formation of hydrogen bonds between the solute and water molecules but solubility decreases with increase in molecular weight due to the hydrophobic nature of the bigger alkyl groups in the higher members.
- **Boiling point**: Boiling point and Melting point $\propto$ Molecular weight $\propto 1/$ Branching
  Boiling points of carbonyl compounds are less than the corresponding alcohols of comparable molecular weight but are higher than corresponding alkanes. The relative boiling points of the carbonyl compounds with the same number of carbon atoms follow the order,
  Amides > Carboxylic acids >> Esters ≈ Acyl chlorides ≈ Ketones ≈ Aldehydes
- **Reactivity**: Reactivity depends on the nature of alkyl group attached to it. Smaller the alkyl group, the more reactive is the compound.
  Reactivity $\propto$ Magnitude of (+)ve charge on carbon atom of the carbonyl group.
- 40% aqueous solution of HCHO is called formalin. It is used as a disinfectant and antiseptic. It is also used for preserving biological specimen.
- HCHO + Lactose = Formamint used for throat infection.
- **Chemical Reaction**:
  Aldehydes are more reactive than ketones in nucleophilic addition reactions **due to electric and electronic resonance**. These reactions are following:

$$\mathrm{C=O} + :CN \rightleftharpoons \mathrm{C} \begin{smallmatrix} CN \\ OH \end{smallmatrix}$$

$$\mathrm{C=O} + NaHSO_3 \rightleftharpoons \mathrm{C} \begin{smallmatrix} SO_2Na \\ OH \end{smallmatrix}$$

$$\mathrm{C=O} \xrightarrow[\text{(ii) H_2O/H^+}]{\text{(i) RMgX}} \mathrm{C-OH} + Mg \begin{smallmatrix} OH \\ X \end{smallmatrix}$$
$$|$$
$$R$$

$$\text{Aldehydes + alcohols} \xrightarrow{\text{dry HCl}} \text{Acetal}$$

$$\text{Ketones + alcohols} \xrightarrow{\text{dry HCl}} \text{Ketal}$$

$$\mathrm{C=O + H_2N-Z} \longrightarrow \mathrm{C=N-Z + H_2O}$$

(Z = Alkyl, aryl, –NH$_2$, –OH
–NH–C$_6$H$_5$, –NHCONH$_2$ etc.)

MIND

AMINES

Tests for amines (Hinsberg's test)

$1°$ amine $+ C_6H_5SO_2Cl \rightarrow$ ppt. soluble in NaOH

$2°$ amine $+ C_6H_5SO_2Cl \rightarrow$ ppt soluble in NaOH

$3°$ amine $+ C_6H_5SO_2Cl \rightarrow$ No reaction

Classification of amines: Primary, secondary and tertiary on the basis of hydrogen atom (s) replaced by alkyl or aryl group of NH_3

When alkyl groups are similar they are called simple amines and when alkyl groups different they are called mixed.

Preparations:

- Reduction of nitro compounds:

$$RNO_2 \xrightarrow[\text{or } H_2/Pd \text{ or } LiAlH_4/ether]{Sn/HCl \text{ or } Fe/HCl} RNH_2$$

- Ammonolysis of alkyl halides:

$$R-X \xrightarrow{NH_3} R-\overset{+}{N}H_3X^- \xrightarrow{NaOH}$$
$$R-NH_2 + H_2O + \overset{+}{Na}X^-$$

- Reduction of nitriles:

$$R-C \equiv N \xrightarrow[\text{or } Na(Hg)/C_2H_5OH]{H_2/Ni \text{ or } LiAlH_4} RCH_2NH_2$$

- Reduction of amides

$$RCONH_2 \xrightarrow[(ii)H_2O]{(i)LiAlH_4} R-CH_2NH_2$$

- Gabriel phthalimide synthesis:

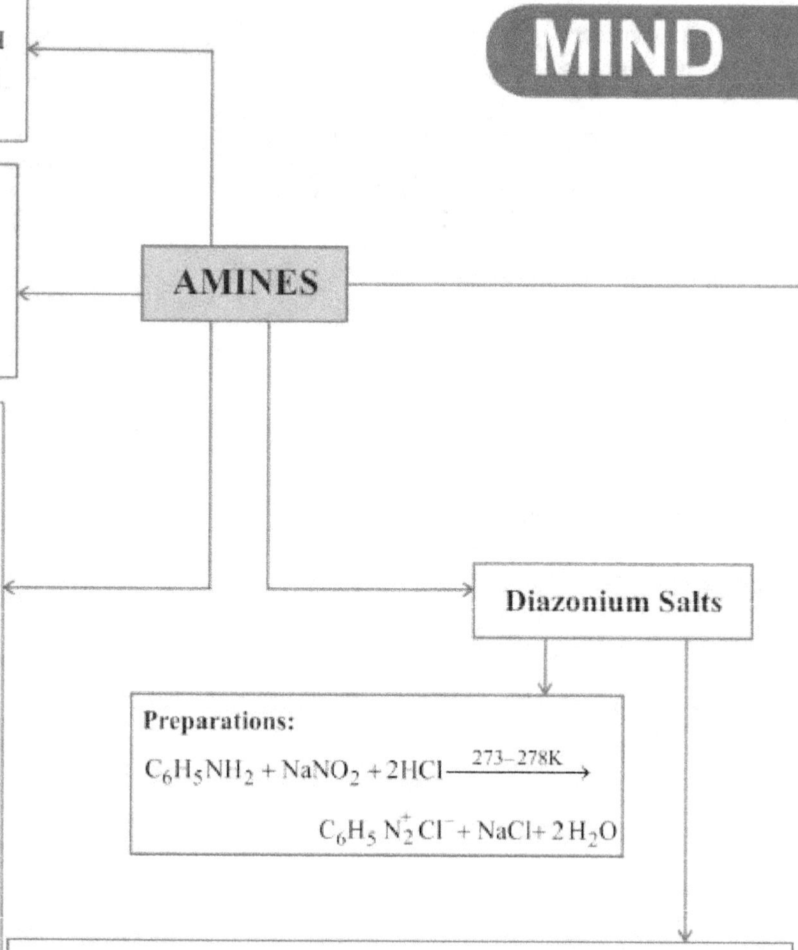

$$\xrightarrow[\substack{(ii)RX, \Delta \\ (iii) H^+ \text{ or } OH^- \\ /H_2O/\Delta}]{(i)KOH (alc.)} RNH_2$$

* Aromatic primary amines cannot be prepared by this method because aryl halides do not undergo nucleophilic substitution with the anion formed by phthalimide.

- Hoffmann bromamide degradation reaction:

$$R-CONH_2 + Br_2 + 4NaOH \longrightarrow R-NH_2 + Na_2CO_3 + 2NaBr + 2H_2O$$

* The amine formed by this reaction contains one carbon less than that present in the amide.

Diazonium Salts

Preparations:

$$C_6H_5NH_2 + NaNO_2 + 2HCl \xrightarrow{273-278K}$$
$$C_6H_5 \overset{+}{N_2} Cl^- + NaCl + 2H_2O$$

Physical Properties: colourless, soluble in water, decompose in dry state, benzene chloride aqueous solution is a good conductor of electricity.

Chemical Properties:

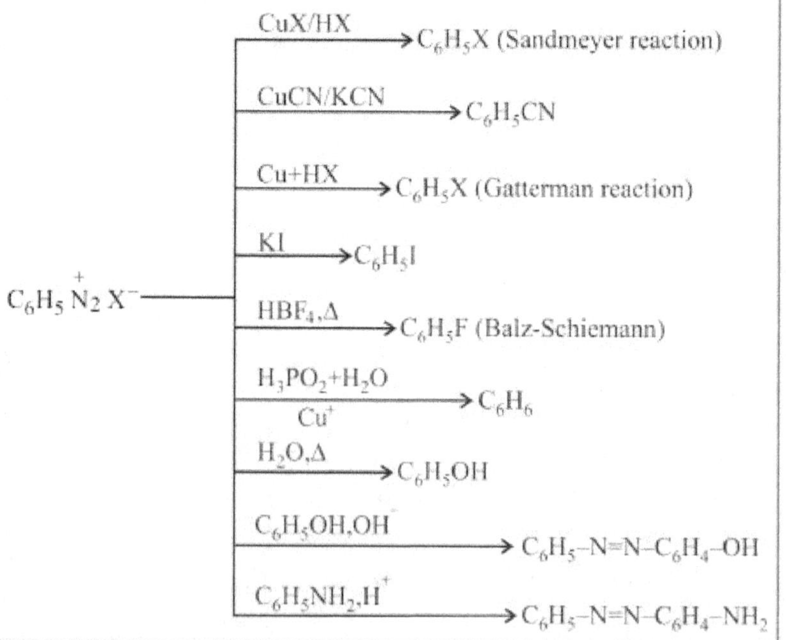

MAP-12

Physical Properties:
• **Physical state**: Lower aliphatic amines are gases, intermediate members are liquids (Fishy odour), while higher members are solids.
• **Solubility**: Lower aliphatic amines (up to C_6) are soluble in water because of H-bonding, while higher amines ($>C_6$) are insoluble in water. In general,

$$\text{Solubility} \propto \frac{1}{\text{Molecular weight}} \longrightarrow$$

• **Boiling point**: (a) b.p. of alcohols and carboxylic acids > b.p. of amines > b.p. of alkanes
             (b) b.p. of 1° amine > 2° amine > 3° amine
* Primary and secondary amines form intermolecular H-bonds, while tertiary amines do not form inter-molecular H-bonds. As a result, 1° & 2° amines show high b.p. than 3°amines.
* H-bonding in amines is through nitrogen atoms while in alcohols and carboxylic acids, it is through oxygen atoms and nitrogen is less electronegative than oxygen. So H-bonding in amines is weaker than that in carboxylic acids and alcohols.
Chemical Properties:
Basic character: All aliphatic amines are strong bases than NH_3 while aromatic amines are weaker bases than NH_3.
• Factors affect the basicity are: (i) Inductive effect (ii) Solvation effect (iii) Steric hindrance

Thus, the order of basicity of amines is

3° amine > 2° amine > 1° amine > NH_3 (In gaseous phase)

$(CH_3)_2NH > CH_3NH_2 > (CH_3)_3N > NH_3$ (In aqueous phase)

$(C_2H_5)_2NH > (C_2H_5)_2N > C_2H_5NH_2 > NH_3$ (In aqueous phase)

$$R-NH_2 \xrightarrow{\quad R'-X \quad} R-NH-R'$$

$$\xrightarrow[\text{Carbylamine reaction}]{CHCl_3+KOH} R-NC \text{ (used as a test of 1° amine)}$$

$$\xrightarrow{\quad HNO_2 \quad} R-OH$$

$$\xrightarrow{\quad R^1-COCl \quad} R-NH-CO-R^1$$

$$\xrightarrow[-HCl]{C_6H_5SO_2Cl} RNHSO_2C_6H_5 \text{ (soluble in NaOH)}$$

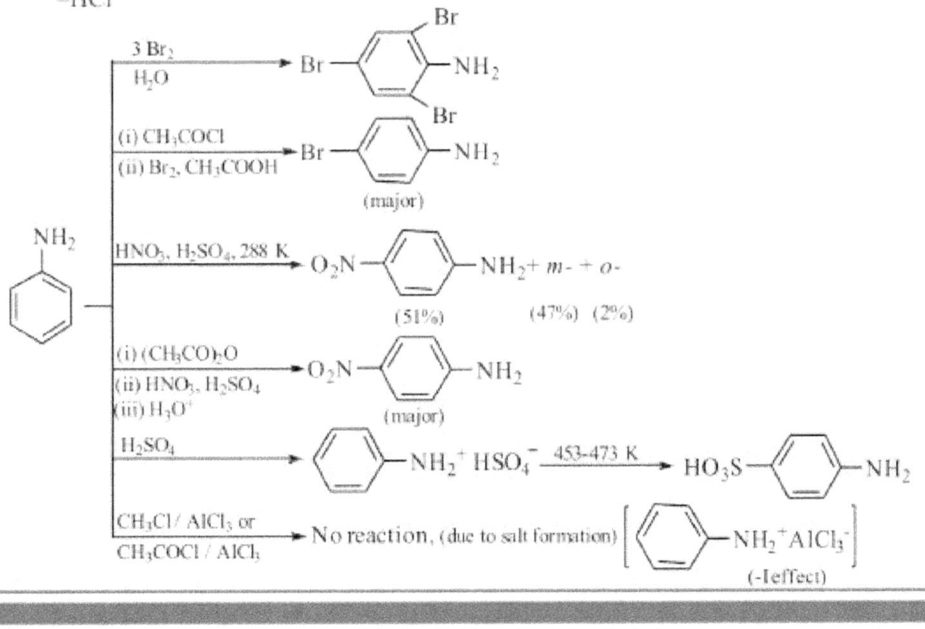

$$\text{(aniline)} \xrightarrow[H_2O]{3\,Br_2} \text{Br}-\!\!\bigcirc\!\!-NH_2 \text{ (with Br at positions)}$$

$$\xrightarrow[\text{(ii) } Br_2,\ CH_3COOH]{\text{(i) } CH_3COCl} \text{Br}-\!\!\bigcirc\!\!-NH_2 \text{ (major)}$$

$$\xrightarrow{HNO_3,\ H_2SO_4,\ 288\ K} O_2N-\!\!\bigcirc\!\!-NH_2 + m- + o- \quad (51\%)\ (47\%)\ (2\%)$$

$$\xrightarrow[\text{(iii) } H_3O^+]{\text{(i) } (CH_3CO)_2O,\ \text{(ii) } HNO_3,\ H_2SO_4} O_2N-\!\!\bigcirc\!\!-NH_2 \text{ (major)}$$

$$\xrightarrow{H_2SO_4} \bigcirc\!\!-NH_2^+\ HSO_4^- \xrightarrow{453-473\ K} HO_3S-\!\!\bigcirc\!\!-NH_2$$

$$\xrightarrow{CH_3Cl/AlCl_3 \text{ or } CH_3COCl/AlCl_3} \text{No reaction, (due to salt formation)} \left[\bigcirc\!\!-NH_2^+AlCl_3^-\right] \text{(-I effect)}$$

BIOMOLECULES

MIND

Carbohydrates

Classification
- **Monosaccharides** : cannot be hydrolysed further.
- **Oligosaccharides** : yield two to ten monosaccharides
- **Polysaccharides** : yield a large number of monosaccharide units

Maltose:
- It is prepared by hydrolysis of starch with the enzyme diastase.
- It is **reducing sugar**.
- It hydrolyses into two α-D-glucose molecules in the presence of enzyme maltase.

Lactose:
- It is found in the milk.
- It is a **reducing sugar**.
- Lactose on hydrolysis gives equimolar quantities of β-D-glucose and β-D-glactose.

Sucrose:
- It is obtained commercially from sugarcane or sugar beets.
- It is **non-reducing sugar**.
- Sucrose on hydrolysis gives equimolar mixture of α-D-glucose or β-D-fructose.

Glucose
- Preparation : Sucrose $\xrightarrow{H^+}$ Glucose + Fructose

  Starch + $nH_2O \xrightarrow{H^+}$ Glucose
- Chemical Properties

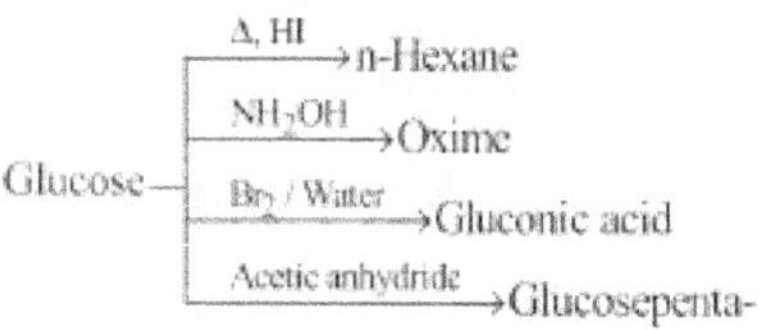

Limitations of the Open Chain Structure:
Glucose penta-acetate does not react with hydroxyl amine thus indicating the absence of free –CHO group.

Cyclic Structure of Glucose:

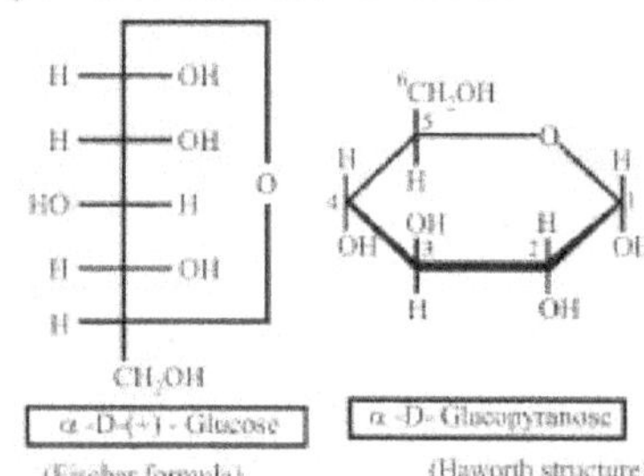

Proteins

Nucleic Acids Properties
- Play important role in replication and protein synthesis polymer of nucleotides
- Nucleotide consist of a sugar unit, nitrogeneous base and a phosphate group.
- During formation of dinucleotide or polynucleotide, nucleotide units are joined by 3' – 5' phosphodiester linkages
- Nucleoside : Sugar + base

Structure of bases :

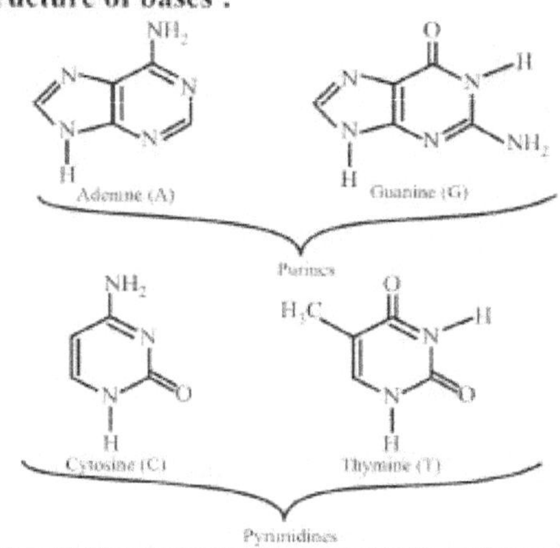

Starch:
- It is found exclusively in plants as stored as food.
- It is a polymer of α-D-glucose and consists of two components, amylose and amylopectin.
- Amylose–water soluble, constitutes about 15–20% of starch.
  * It is a long unbranched chain with 200–1000 glucose units.
  * 1,4-α-glycosidic linkage is present.
- Amylopectin-water insoluble, constitutes about 80-85% of starch.
  * It is a branched chain polymer of glucose units in which main chain is formed by C1–C4 linkage where branching occurs by C1–C6 glycosidic linkage.

Cellulose:
- It is the chief constituents of the cell walls of plant.
- It contains 1-4 glycosidic linkages.
- Cellulose on hydrolysis gives β-D-glucose.

Glycogen:
- It is commonly known as animal starch.
- Its structure is similar to amylopectin.
- It is present in liver, muscles and brain.

Enzymes:
Proteins which are used as catalysts in biochemical reactions are known as biocatalysts (enzymes). Enzymes have following two specific characteristics :

(i) Specificity of Enzymes:
(a) Generally one enzyme can catalyze only one biochemical reaction. (b) It can increase rate of reaction upto 10^{20} times.

(ii) Efficiency of Enzymes:
(a) One molecule of enzyme can convert millions of substrate molecules into product(s) per second.
  eg. Carbonic anhydrase enzyme present in red blood cells has a highest turn over number.

(b) Enzymes are denatured at higher temperature.

(c) Enzymes are very efficient and very specific in nature. The optimum temperature for enzyme activity lies between 40°C to 60°C.

MAP-13

Amino acids Classification

- Essential aminoacids: cannot be synthesised in the body.　　• Non Essential aminoacids : can be synthesised in the body.

(i) Essential amino acids : These are as follows

(a) Leucine	(b) Isoleucine	(c) Lysine	(d) Methionine
(e) Phenylalanine	(f) Threonine	(g) Tryptophan	(h) Valine
(i) Histidine			

Arginine and histidine are **semi-essential** amino acids i.e. they are partly synthesized in tissues.

(ii) Non - essential amino acids : These are as follows

(a) Alanine	(b) Aspargine	(c) Aspartic acid	(d) Cysteine
(e) Glutamic acid	(f) Glutamine	(g) Hydroxyproline	(h) Glycine
(i) Proline	(j) Serine	(k) Tyrosine	(l) Arginine
(m) Cystine			

Properties

- They are **fairly soluble in water,** but insoluble in non-polar solvents like petroleum ether, benzene, or ether.
- Amino acids have much **larger dipole moments** than simple amines and simple acids.

$$H_3N^+ - CH_2 - COO^-$$
Glycine, $\mu = 14D$

$$CH_3CH_2CH_2NH_2$$
Propylamine, $\mu = 1.4D$

$$CH_3CH_2COOH$$
Propanoic acid, $\mu = 1.7D$

- Amino acids are **less acidic than most carboxylic acids and less basic than most amines.** In fact, the acidic part of the amino acid molecule is the $-NH_3^+$ group, not a $-COOH$ group, while the basic part of the amino acid is the $-COO^-$ group, and not a free $-NH_2$ group.

$$R - COOH \qquad R - NH_2 \qquad H_3\overset{+}{N} - \overset{R}{\underset{|}{C}} H - COO^-$$
$$pK_a = 5 \qquad\qquad pK_b = 4 \qquad\qquad pK_a = 10;\ pK_b = 12$$

The above properties point out toward the salt like character (dipolar ion structure) to amino acids. Actually, in the dry state, amino acids exist as **dipolar ions** (also known as **zwitterions** or **inner salts**), a form in which the carboxyl group is present as a carboxylate ion, $-COO^-$, and the amino group as an aminium ion, $-NH_3^+$.

Proteins

- Polymero of α-amino acids
- connected by peptide bond.

Classification

- **Fibrous Protein :** Polypeptide chains run parallel and held together by hydrogen and disulphide bonds e.g kertin, myosin
- **Globular Proteins :** Polypeptide chain is folded, looped and twisted e.g., albumin, haemoglobin.

Structure

- **$1°$ structure :** It is the unique sequence of amino acids in each kind or protein.
- **$2°$ structure :** Exist in two different type α–helix and β- pleated.
- **$3°$ structure :** Overall folding of polypeptide chains
- **$4°$ structure :** Spatial arrangement of subunits (two or more polypetide chain) with respect to each other.

The main forces which stabilise the $2°$ and $3°$ structures of proteins are hydrogen bonds, disulphide linkages, vander waals and electrostatic force of attraction.

Denaturation of proteins :

Native protein $\xrightarrow{\text{change in temp, pH}}$ Hydrogen bonds are disturbed
(Protein looses its biological activity)
The denaturation causes change in $2°$ or $3°$ structures but $1°$ structure remains intact.

Types of nucleic acid

DNA

- Carries genetic information
- Sugar unit is 2- deoxyribose
- Bases are : adenine, thymine, cytosin and guanine
- It has double stranded structure

In both chains, in between A and T, 2 hydrogen bonds are present while in C and G, 3 H-bonds are present. (A = T) (C ≡ G)

RNA

- Control protein synthesis
- Sugar unit is robose
- Bases are adenine, uracil, cytosin and guanine
- It has single stranded structure

On the basis of their function RNAs mainly are of three types. Messenger RNA (m-RNA), Transfer RNA (t-RNA), Ribosomal RNA (r-RNA)

Vitamins

It has been observed that certain organic compounds are required in small amounts in our diet but their deficiency causes specific diseases. These compounds are called vitamins.

Classification of Vitamins

Vitamins are classified into two groups depending upon their solubility in water or fat.

(i) Fat Soluble Vitamins : Vitamins which are soluble in fat and oils but insoluble in water are kept in this group. These are vitamins A, D, E and K. They are stored in liver and adipose (fat storing) tissues.

(ii) Water Soluble Vitamins : B-complex and vitamin C are soluble in water so they are grouped together. Water soluble vitamins must be supplied regularly in diet because they are readily excreted in urine and can not be stored (except vitamin B_{12}) in our body.

MIND

POLYMERS

Important Condensation Polymers

i)　Nylons : Synthetic polyamides are known as nylons

(a) Nylon-6,6 : Copolymer of adipic acid (6C) and hexamethylenediamine (6C).

$$n\,HOOC(CH_2)_4COOH + n\,H_2N(CH_2)_6NH_2 \rightarrow$$

Adipic acid　　　　　　Hexamethylenediamine

$$\{C-(CH_2)_4-C-NH-(CH_2)_6-NH\}_n$$

Nylon–6,6

It has high tenacity and elasticity. It is resistant to abrasion and not affected by sea water. It is used for reinforcement of rubber tyres, manufacture of parachute, safety belts, carpets and fabrics.

(b) Nylon 6 : Homopolymer of caprolactam (6C)

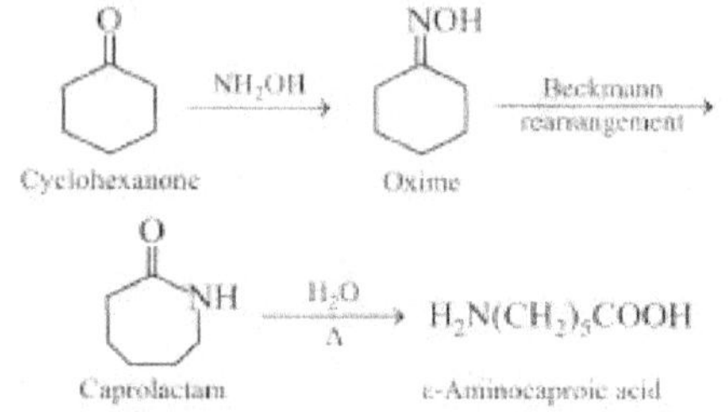

Cyclohexanone $\xrightarrow{NH_2OH}$ Oxime $\xrightarrow[\text{rearrangement}]{\text{Beckmann}}$

Caprolactam $\xrightarrow[\Delta]{H_2O}$ $H_2N(CH_2)_5COOH$ ε-Aminocaproic acid

$\xrightarrow[\text{Polymerisation}]{\Delta}$ $\{NH(CH_2)_5-C-NH-(CH_2)_5-C\}_n$

Nylon-6

(ii) Polyesters : Condensation polymers of a dibasic acid and a diol

(a) Terylene (dacron) / Polyethylene terephthalate (PET)

It is resistant to mineral and organic acids. It is used for blending with wool to provide better crease, in safety helmets and aircraft battery boxes.

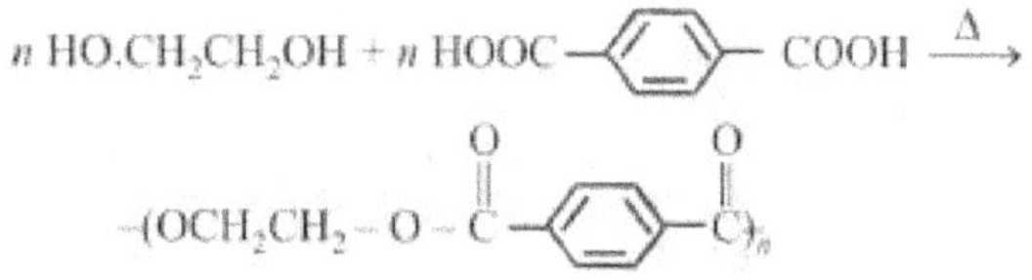

$$n\,HO.CH_2CH_2OH + n\,HOOC-\langle\rangle-COOH \xrightarrow{\Delta}$$

$$-(OCH_2CH_2-O-C-\langle\rangle-C)_n$$

(b) Glyptal or Alkyd resin (general name) **:** Condensation polymers of dibasic acids and polyhydroxy alcohols

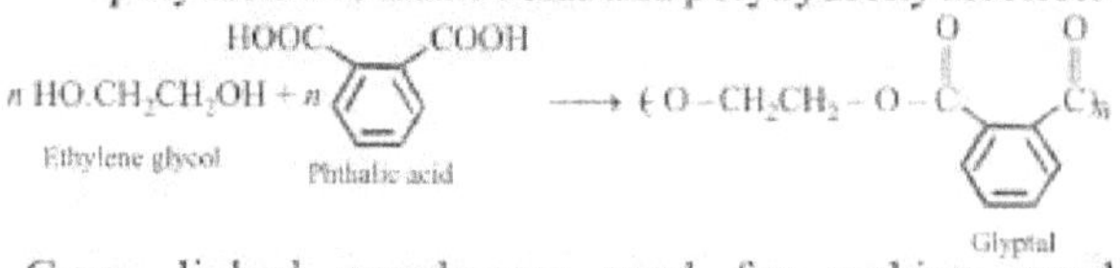

$$n\,HO.CH_2CH_2OH + n\;\text{(HOOC, COOH on benzene)} \rightarrow \{O-CH_2CH_2-O-C-\langle\rangle-C\}_n$$

Ethylene glycol　Phthalic acid　　　　　　　　　Glyptal

Cross linked copolymer; used for making good insulators, sheets, rods, switches, lacquers and adherant paints.

(iii) Thermosetting Resins

(a) Bakelite : Phenol formaldehyde resin

$$n\;\text{(Phenol, OH)} + n\,HCHO \xrightarrow{OH} \text{Bakelite}$$

Phenol　Formaldehyde

Rubber

Natural rubber (manufactured from rubber latex: It is linear polymer of isoprene (2-methyl-1,3-butadiene)

Vulcanisation of rubber :

Raw rubber + Sulphur $\xrightarrow[375-415K]{\Delta}$

stiffened rubber (cross linked)

Synthetic rubber :

(i)　Buna-S or SBR:

It is used for manufacture of tyres, floor tiles, gaskets, cable insulators etc.

$$n\,CH=CH_2 + n\,CH_2=CH-CH=CH_2 \xrightarrow[\Delta]{Na}$$

$|$
C_6H_5
Styrene　　　　　　　　Butadiene

$$\{CH-CH_2-CH_2-CH=CH-CH_2\}_n$$
$|$
C_6H_5
Buna-S

(ii)　Nitrile Rubber (Buna–N):

Excellent resistant to heat and chemicals. It is used for making conveyer belts, printing rollers, automobile parts.

$$n\,CH_2=CH-CH=CH_2 + n\,CH_2=CH\!\!\begin{array}{c}CN\\|\end{array}\longrightarrow$$

Butadiene　　　　　　Acrylonitrile

$$\{CH_2-CH=CH-CH_2-CH_2-CH\}_n$$
$\qquad\qquad\qquad\qquad\qquad\quad|$
$\qquad\qquad\qquad\qquad\qquad CN$

Nitrile rubber

(iii) Neoprene:

$$n\,CH_2=CH-\underset{|}{\overset{Cl}{C}}=CH_2 \xrightarrow{K_2S_2O_8}$$

Chloroprene

$$\{CH_2-CH=\underset{|}{\overset{Cl}{C}}-CH_2\}_n$$

Neoprene

MAP-14

Biodegradable polymers

Non-resistent to environmental degradation
(i) PHBV
(ii) Nylon-2-nylon-6

Polymerisation reaction:

•Addition Polymerisation: Governed by free radical mechanism.
Steps involved:
(a) Chain initiation
(b) Chain Propagating
(c) Chain terminating
• Condensation Polymerisation: involves stepwise intermolecular condensation.

Teflon or
•Polytetrafluoroethylene(PTFE):

$$n\ CF_2 = CF_2 \xrightarrow[\text{Amm. peroxosulphate } (NH_4)_2S_2O_8]{\text{Benzoyl peroxide or}}$$

Tetrafluoroethene

$$\left(C - C \right)_n$$

with F, F above and F, F below

It is extremely tough, resistant to heat and chemicals. It is used for making gaskets, pump parts, coating utensils, high frequency insulators.

**•Polyacrylonitrile (PAN),
Acrilon or Orlon:**

$$n\ CH_2 = CH \longrightarrow (CH_2 - CH)_n$$

with CN above each

Acrylonitrile   Orlon

It is hard used in preparing clothes and carpets.

Classification

• **Based on Source :**
(a) **Natural polymers:** protein, cellulose (b) **Semi-synthetic:** cellulose nitrate (c) **Synthetic:** PVC, nylon-6, 6
• **Based on structure :**
(a) **Linear:** Polymers containing the monomeric units linked together to form long straight chains stacked over one another to give packed structure. Such polymers have high tensile strength, high densities, high m.p. and b.p. Examples - fibres and plastics.
(b) **Brached :** Long chain of monomer units containing side chains of different lengths form branched polymers. The chains are loosely packed, hence polymers have low density, low m.p. and low tensile strength. Examples - amylopectin and glycogen.
(c) **Cross linked:** Such polymers have three dimensional network and are hard, brittle and rigid. Examples - bakelite, melamine.
• **Based on Polymerisation :**
(a) **Addition Polymers:** In addition polymerisation, the unsaturated monomeric molecules undergo repeated addition reactions in the presence of catalysts like O_2, organic peroxides. Some examples of addition polymers are polythene from ethylene, polypropylene from propylene, polyisoprene from isoprene, etc.
(b) **Condensation Polymers:** Condensation polymerisation normally takes place by repeated condensation of monomeric molecules usually with the elimination of small molecules like water, alcohol, CO_2, HCl, etc. For example, terylene is formed by removal of water molecule from ethylene glycol and terephthalic acid molecules.

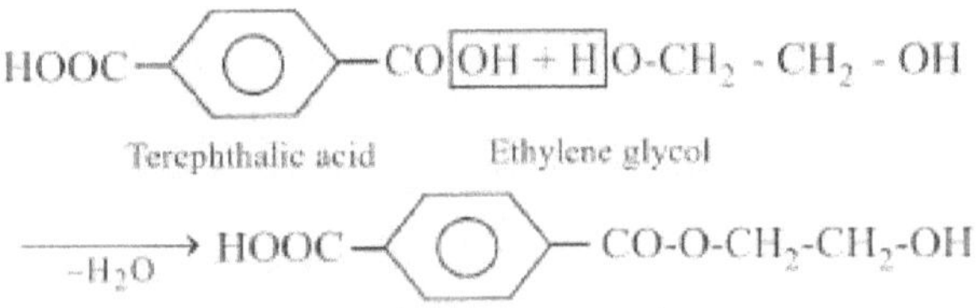

$$HOOC - \langle O \rangle - CO[OH + H]O\text{-}CH_2 \text{ - } CH_2 \text{ - } OH$$

Terephthalic acid   Ethylene glycol

$$\xrightarrow{-H_2O} HOOC - \langle O \rangle - CO\text{-}O\text{-}CH_2\text{-}CH_2\text{-}OH$$

This condensation step goes on repeating to form terylene.

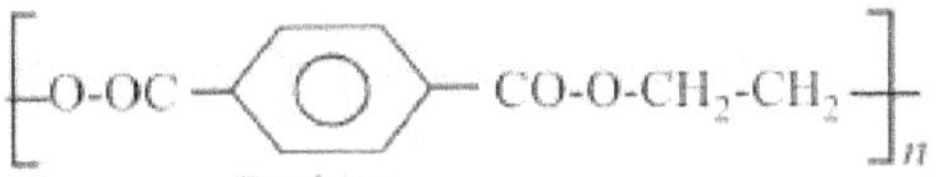

$$\left[O\text{-}OC - \langle O \rangle - CO\text{-}O\text{-}CH_2\text{-}CH_2 \right]_n$$

Terylene

Condensation is also known as *step growth polymerisation.*
• **Based on Molecular force :**
(a) **Elastomers:** Here, the intermolecular forces of attraction between the polymer chains are the weakest. They have high degree of elasticity and consist of randomly called molecular chains of irregular shape having a few cross-links. For ex : natural rubber, vulcanized rubber, etc.
(b) **Fibres:** These polymers have very least stretchability, because the polymeric chains in them are joined together by very strong intermolecular forces like innumerable hydrogen bonds and have sharp melting points. Nylon-6,6 is an important example of this class.
(c) **Thermoplastics:** Thermoplastic polymers readily become soft on heating and thus can be moulded into required shapes. Some important examples of this class of polymers are polyvinyl chloride, polythene, polypropylene, polystyrene etc.
(d) **Thermosetting:** They are semi-fluid substances with low molecular masses which when heated become hard and infusible, because of sufficiently large number of cross links. They acquire a shape of three-dimensional network. Important examples of this class of polymers are bakelite, urea formaldehyde resin, etc.

MIND

CHEMISTRY IN EVERYDAY LIFE

Drug - Target Interaction:

•**Enzyme as drug targets** : Drugs inhibit the attachment of substrate for their attachment on the active sites of enzymes. Some drugs have the capability to bind allosteric site of the enzyme and changing the shape of active site so that substrate cannot recognise it.

•**Receptors as drug targets** : Drugs that bind to the receptor site and inhibit its natural function (antagonists). These are useful when blocking of message is required. Some drugs mimmic the natural messenger by switching on the receptor (agonists). These are useful when there is lack of natural chemical messenger.

Classification of Drugs:

- **Based on pharmacological effect** : This classification is based on pharmacological effect of the drugs. It is useful for doctors.
- **Based on drug action** : Drugs which act on a particular biochemical process are kept under one class.
- **Based on Chemical Structure** : Drugs having common structural features are grouped together in one class
- **Based on molecular target** : It is based on the interaction with biomolecules such as lipids, proteins, carbohydrates and nucleic acid.

Therapeutic Action of Drugs

- **Antacids** : Antacids are the drugs which neutralize excess acid in the gastric juices and give relief from acid indigestion. They remove the excess acid and raise the pH to appropriate level in stomach. There are mainly weak bases. Examples– $Mg(OH)_2$, $KHCO_3$ Omeprazole,Lansoprazole, Histamine, Cimetidine and Ranitidine.
- **Antihistamines** : Antihistamines are the drugs which diminish the main action of histamine(Chemical substance which cause allergic reactions in body) released in the body and thus prevent the allergic reactions. These are also anti-allergic drugs. Examples diphenhydramine hydrochloride (Banadryl) , Pheniramine maleate (Avil) etc.
- **Tranquilizers** : The chemical substances used to cure mental diseases are called **tranquilizers**.These are used to release mental tension and reduce anxiety.These are the constituents of sleeping pills. They act on higher centres of nervous system. e.g. equanil, serotonin, valium etc.
- **Analgesics** : For relieving pain.
- **Non-narcotic analgesics (non-addictive)** : Aspirin and paracetamol
- **Narcotic analgesics (addictive)** : Morphine, heroin, codeine etc.
- **Antibiotics** : (a) Bactericidal destroy microbes e.g. penicilin, ofloxacin etc.
  (b) Bacteriostatic : Inhibit growth of microbes e.g. Chloramphenicol, erythromycin etc.
- **Spectrum** : The complete range of microorganism that can be killed by a particular antibiotic is known as spectrum. These are of following types:
  (i) Narrow spectrum antibiotics : Streptomycin, Chloromycetin.
  (ii) Broad spectrum antibiotics : Chloramphenicol, Tetracycline.
- **Antiseptics** : May kill or stop growth of microbes e.g. dettol.
- **Antifertility** : Control menstrual cycle and ovulation of females e.g., norethindrone, novestrol etc.

MAP-15

Soaps and Detergents

Detergents:

* Sodium salts of alkylbenzene sulphonic acids.
* **Types of detergents :**
  Detergents are of three types :
  (i) Anionic detergents
  (ii) Cationic detergents
  (iii) Non-ionic detergents.
  (i) **Anionic detergents.** These are so called because a large part of their molecules are anions. These are of two types.
      (a) **Sodium alkyl sulphates :**
      Example of this type of detergents is : sodium lauryl sulphate,

  $$C_{11}H_{23}CH_2OSO_3^-Na^+$$

      (b) **Alkyl benzene sulphonates** :
      Example :
      Sodium-4-(1-dodecyl) benzenesulphonate (SDS).

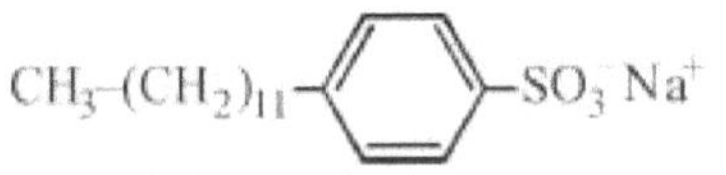

  $$CH_3-(CH_2)_{11}-\!\!\!\bigcirc\!\!\!-SO_3^-Na^+$$

      Sod. 4-(dodecyl)benzenesulphonate

  (ii) **Cationic detergents :**
  e.g., cetyltrimethylammonium bromide.
  (iii) **Non-ionic detergents :**
  Example

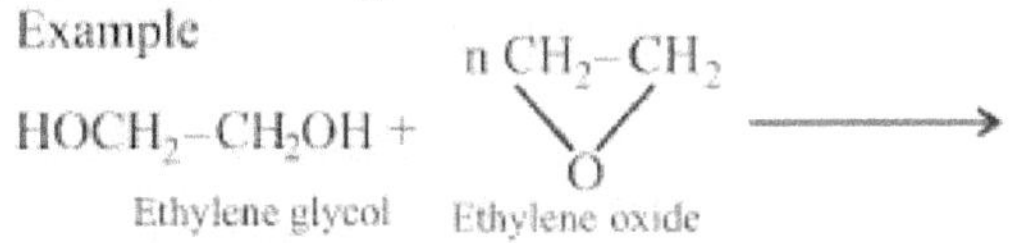

  $$HOCH_2-CH_2OH + \underset{\text{Ethylene oxide}}{\overset{n\,CH_2-CH_2}{\diagdown\;O\;\diagup}} \longrightarrow$$

  Ethylene glycol   Ethylene oxide

  $$HO(CH_2CH_2O)_n CH_2CH_2OH \xrightarrow[-H_2O]{CH_3(CH_2)_{16}COOH}$$

  Polyethylene glycol

  $$CH_3(CH_2)_{16}COO(CH_2CH_2O)_nCH_2CH_2OH$$

  Polyethylene glycol stearate
  (A non-ionic detergent)

* **Cleansing action of detergents:** The cleansing action of detergents are same as that of soaps. For example. A detergents, Sodium lauryl sulphate, $CH_3(CH_2)_{11}CH_2O\text{-}SO_2Na$, contains the polar group $-OSO_3^-$ alongwith the long hydrocarbon chains. It is an anionic detergent in which anions associate together to form an ionic micelle. Similarly, Cationic detergent also forms micelle.

Soaps:

* Sodium salts of long chain fatty acids like stearic acid, oleic acid, palmitic acid etc, are called hard soaps and the potassium salts of these fatty acids are called soft soaps
* **Types of Soaps:**
  (a) Toilet soaps
  (b) Floating soaps
  (c) Medicated soaps
  (d) Transparent soaps
  (e) Shaving soaps
  (f) Laundary soaps

Chemicals in Food:

* **Food Additives:** The chemicals, synthetic or natural substances added to food preparations for different purposes as given below are known as food additives.
  (i) **Nutrients :** To increase the nutritive value of the food e.g., carbohydrates, proteins etc.
  (ii) **Preservatives :** To retard spoilage from bacterial action. e.g., $NaNO_2$ and $NaNO_3$ (in meat), C_6H_5COONa (in tomato katchup, fruit juices), Sodium metabisulphite (in pickles), Citric acid (fruit drinks), Sodium propionate (in bread and cheese) and SO_2 (in wine and juices).
  (iii) **Flavouring agents :** To enhance the flavour or to develop flavour e.g., alkyl alkanoates (esters), mono-sodium glutamate (MSG), vanillin, cinnamaldehyde.
  (iv) **Antioxidants :** To exclude oxygen to retard or prevent spoilage eg. BHT (Butylated hydroxy toluene) and BHA (Bulylated hydroxy anisole).
  (v) **Sweetners :** To add sweet taste e.g., saccharin, aspartame, sucralose.

Artificial sweetener	Sweetness Value
Aspartame	100
Saccharin	550
Sucralose	600
Alitame	2000

  (vi) **Colourants :** To give colour eg. Amaranth, Kesar etc.

CHAPTERWISE MIND MAPS MATHEMATICS

Mind

RELATIONS & FUNCTIONS

Types of Relations

Empty Relation is the relation R in a set A, in which no element of A is related to any element of A, i.e., $R = \phi \subset A \times A$.

Universal Relation is the relation R in a set A, in which each element of A is related to every element of A, i.e., $R = A \times A$. Both the empty relation and the universal relation are some times called trivial relations.

Reflexive Relation : $(a, a) \in R$, for every $a \in A$.

Symmetric Relation : $(a_1, a_2) \in R$ implies that $(a_2, a_1) \in R$, for all $a_1, a_2 \in A$.

Transitive Relation : $(a_1, a_2) \in R$ & $(a_2, a_3) \in R$ implies that $(a_1, a_3) \in R$, for all $a_1, a_2, a_3 \in A$.

Equivalence Relation : A relation R in a set A is said to be an equivalence relation if R is reflexive, symmetric & transitive.

Equivalence class {a} containing $a \in A$ for an equivalence relation R in A is a subset of A containing all elements b related to a.

2

Relation

A relation from a non-empty set A to itself is a subset of cartesian product $A \times A$.

Relation from a set A to set B is a subset of cartesian product $A \times B$.

1

3

Function

For any two non-empty sets X & Y, a function f is a rule or mapping which associates each element of set X to a unique element in set Y.

4

Types of Functions

One-One Function : A function $f : X \rightarrow Y$ is one-one (or injective) if the images of distinct elements of X under f are distinct, i.e.,

$$f(x_1) = f(x_2) \Rightarrow x_1 = x_2 \, \forall x_1, x_2 \in X.$$

Otherwise, f is called many-one.

Onto Function : A function is onto (or surjective) if every element of Y is the image of some element of X under f, i.e., for every $y \in Y$, there exists an element x in X such that $f(x) = y$

Into Function : A function $f : X \rightarrow Y$ is into if there exists atleast one element in Y which has no pre-image in A.

One-One & Onto Function : A function $f : X \rightarrow Y$ is said to be one-one & onto (or bijective) if f is both one-one & onto.

Map-1

Composition of Functions

Let $f : A \to B$ & $g : B \to C$ be two functions. Then the composition of f & g, denoted by gof, is defined as the function $gof : A \to C$ given by
$gof(x) = g(f(x))$, $\forall\, x \in A$

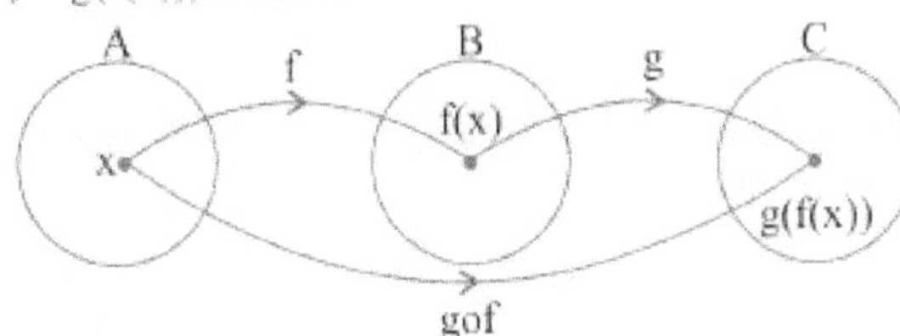

Theorem : If $f : X \to Y$, $g : Y \to Z$ & $h : Z \to S$ are functions, then

$$ho(gof) = (hog)of$$

If gof is one-one $\Rightarrow$ f is one-one
If gof is onto $\Rightarrow$ g is onto.
If $f : X \to Y$ is a function such that there exists a function $g : Y \to X$ such that
$gof = I_x$ & $fog = I_y$,
then f must be one-one and onto.

Invertible Function

A function $f : X \to Y$ is defined to be invertible, if there exists a function $g : Y \to X$ such that $gof = I_x$ & $fog = I_y$.
The function g is called the inverse of f & is denoted by f^{-1}.

Note : A function $f : X \to Y$ is invertible if & only if f is one-one & onto.

Theorem : Let $f : X \to Y$ & $g : Y \to Z$ be two invertible functions. Then gof is also invertible with $(gof)^{-1} = f^{-1}og^{-1}$.

Binary Operations

A binary operation * on a set A is a function * $: A \times A \to A$. We denote *(a, b) by a * b.

Addition, multiplication, subtraction & division are examples of binary operation, as 'binary' means 'two'.

Types of Binary Operations

- A binary operation * on set A is called **commutative** if, a * b = b * a for every a, b $\in$ A.

- A binary operation * $: A \times A \to A$ is **associative** if, (a * b) * c = a * (b * c), $\forall$ a, b, c $\in$ A.

- An element e $\in$ A, if it exists, is called an **identity** element for binary operation

  * $: A \times A \to A$ if, a * e = a = e * a, $\forall$ a $\in$ A.

- An element a $\in$ A is said to be invertible with respect to the operation * $: A \times A \to A$ if there exists an element b in A such that a * b = e = b * a.
  Then, b is called the inverse of a & is denoted by a^{-1}.

Inverse Function	Domain	Principal Value Branch
$y = \sin^{-1} x$	$[-1, 1]$	$\left[\dfrac{-\pi}{2}, \dfrac{\pi}{2}\right]$
$y = \cos^{-1} x$	$[-1, 1]$	$[0, \pi]$
$y = \operatorname{cosec}^{-1} x$	$R - (-1, 1)$	$\left[\dfrac{-\pi}{2}, \dfrac{\pi}{2}\right] - \{0\}$
$y = \sec^{-1} x$	$R - (-1, 1)$	$[0, \pi] - \left\{\dfrac{\pi}{2}\right\}$
$y = \tan^{-1} x$	R	$\left(\dfrac{-\pi}{2}, \dfrac{\pi}{2}\right)$
$y = \cot^{-1} x$	R	$[0, \pi]$

Mind

1

INVERSE TRIGONOMETRIC FUNCTIONS

2

Properties Of Inverse Trigonometric Functions

Property-1

(i) $\sin^{-1}(\sin\theta) = \theta$, if $\dfrac{-\pi}{2} \le \theta \le \dfrac{\pi}{2}$

(ii) $\cos^{-1}(\cos\theta) = \theta$, if $0 \le \theta \le \pi$

(iii) $\tan^{-1}(\tan\theta) = \theta$, if $\dfrac{-\pi}{2} < \theta < \dfrac{\pi}{2}$

(iv) $\cot^{-1}(\cot\theta) = \theta$, if $0 < \theta < \pi$

(v) $\sec^{-1}(\sec\theta) = \theta$, if $0 \le \theta < \dfrac{\pi}{2}$ or $\dfrac{\pi}{2} < \theta \le \pi$

(vi) $\operatorname{cosec}^{-1}(\operatorname{cosec}\theta) = \theta$, if $-\dfrac{\pi}{2} \le \theta < 0$ or $0 < \theta \le \dfrac{\pi}{2}$

Property-2

(i) $\sin(\sin^{-1} x) = x$, if $-1 \le x \le 1$

(ii) $\cos(\cos^{-1} x) = x$, if $-1 \le x \le 1$

(iii) $\tan(\tan^{-1} x) = x$, if $-\infty < x < \infty$

(iv) $\cot(\cot^{-1} x) = x$, if $-\infty < x < \infty$

(v) $\sec(\sec^{-1} x) = x$, if $-\infty < x \le -1$ or $1 \le x < \infty$

(vi) $\operatorname{cosec}(\operatorname{cosec}^{-1} x) = x$, if $-\infty < x \le -1$ or $1 \le x < \infty$

Property-3

(i) $\sin^{-1}(-x) = -\sin^{-1} x$, if $-1 \le x \le 1$

(ii) $\cos^{-1}(-x) = \pi - \cos^{-1} x$, if $-1 \le x \le 1$

(iii) $\tan^{-1}(-x) = -\tan^{-1} x$, if $-\infty < x < \infty$

(iv) $\cot^{-1}(-x) = \pi - \cot^{-1} x$, if $-\infty < x < \infty$

(v) $\sec^{-1}(-x) = \pi - \sec^{-1} x$, if $-\infty < x \le -1$ or $1 \le x < \infty$

(vi) $\operatorname{cosec}^{-1}(-x) = -\operatorname{cosec}^{-1} x$, if $-\infty < x \le -1$ or $1 \le x < \infty$

Property-4

(i) $\sin^{-1} x + \cos^{-1} x = \dfrac{\pi}{2}$, $x \in [-1, 1]$

(ii) $\tan^{-1} x + \cot^{-1} x = \dfrac{\pi}{2}$, $x \in R$

(iii) $\sec^{-1} x + \operatorname{cosec}^{-1} x = \dfrac{\pi}{2}$, $x \in (-\infty, -1] \cup [1, \infty)$

Map-2

Property-5

(i) $\sin^{-1} x = \operatorname{cosec}^{-1}\left(\dfrac{1}{x}\right),\ -1 \le x \le 1$

(ii) $\operatorname{cosec}^{-1} x = \sin^{-1}\left(\dfrac{1}{x}\right),\ x \in R - (-1,1)$

(iii) $\cos^{-1} x = \sec^{-1}\left(\dfrac{1}{x}\right),\ -1 \le x \le 1$

(iv) $\sec^{-1} x = \cos^{-1}\left(\dfrac{1}{x}\right),\ x \in R - (-1,1)$

(v) $\tan^{-1} x = \cot^{-1}\left(\dfrac{1}{x}\right),\ x \in R$

(vi) $\cot^{-1} x = \tan^{-1}\left(\dfrac{1}{x}\right),\ x \in R$

Property-6

(i) $\tan^{-1} x + \tan^{-1} y = \tan^{-1}\left(\dfrac{x+y}{1-xy}\right),\ \text{if } xy < 1$

(ii) $\tan^{-1} x - \tan^{-1} y = \tan^{-1}\left(\dfrac{x-y}{1+xy}\right),\ \text{if } xy > -1$

(iii) $\tan^{-1} x + \tan^{-1} y + \tan^{-1} z$
$$= \tan^{-1}\left[\dfrac{x+y+z-xyz}{1-xy-yz-zx}\right],$$
$$\text{if } x > 0, y > 0, z > 0$$
$$\text{and}\,(xy + yz + zx) < 1$$

Property-7

(i) $\sin^{-1} x + \sin^{-1} y$
$$= \sin^{-1}\{x\sqrt{1-y^2} + y\sqrt{1-x^2}\},$$
$$\text{if } -1 \le x, y \le 1$$
$$\text{and}\, x^2 + y^2 \le 1$$
$$\text{or if } xy < 0\, \text{and}\, x^2 + y^2 > 1$$

(ii) $\sin^{-1} x - \sin^{-1} y$
$$= \sin^{-1}\{x\sqrt{1-y^2} - y\sqrt{1-x^2}\},$$
$$\text{if } -1 \le x, y \le 1$$
$$\text{and}\, x^2 + y^2 \le 1$$
$$\text{or if } xy > 0$$
$$\text{and}\, x^2 + y^2 > 1$$

Property-8

(i) $\cos^{-1} x + \cos^{-1} y = \cos^{-1}\{xy - \sqrt{1-x^2}\,\sqrt{1-y^2}\},$
$$\text{if } -1 \le x,\, y \le 1 \text{ and } x + y \ge 0$$

(ii) $\cos^{-1} x - \cos^{-1} y = \cos^{-1}\{xy + \sqrt{1-x^2}\,\sqrt{1-y^2}\},$
$$\text{if } -1 \le x,\, y \le 1 \text{ and } x \le y$$

Property-9

(i) $2\sin^{-1} x = \sin^{-1}(2x\sqrt{1-x^2}),\ \text{if } \dfrac{-1}{\sqrt{2}} \le x \le \dfrac{1}{\sqrt{2}}$

(ii) $3\sin^{-1} x = \sin^{-1}(3x - 4x^3),\ \text{if } \dfrac{-1}{2} \le x \le \dfrac{1}{2}$

Property-10

(i) $2\cos^{-1} x = \cos^{-1}(2x^2 - 1),\ \text{if } 0 \le x \le 1$

(ii) $3\cos^{-1} x = \cos^{-1}(4x^3 - 3x),\ \text{if } \dfrac{1}{2} \le x \le 1$

Property-11

(i) $2\tan^{-1} x = \tan^{-1}\left(\dfrac{2x}{1-x^2}\right),\ \text{if } -1 < x \le 1$

(ii) $3\tan^{-1} x = \tan^{-1}\left(\dfrac{3x - x^3}{1 - 3x^2}\right),\ \text{if } \dfrac{-1}{\sqrt{3}} < x < \dfrac{1}{\sqrt{3}}$

Property-12

(i) $2\tan^{-1} x = \sin^{-1}\left(\dfrac{2x}{1+x^2}\right),\ \text{if } -1 \le x \le 1$

(ii) $2\tan^{-1} x = \cos^{-1}\left(\dfrac{1-x^2}{1+x^2}\right),\ \text{if } 0 \le x < \infty$

Property-13

(i) $\sin^{-1} x = \cos^{-1}\sqrt{1-x^2} = \tan^{-1}\dfrac{x}{\sqrt{1-x^2}}$
$$= \cot^{-1}\dfrac{\sqrt{1-x^2}}{x} = \sec^{-1}\left(\dfrac{1}{\sqrt{1-x^2}}\right) = \operatorname{cosec}^{-1}\left(\dfrac{1}{x}\right)$$

(ii) $\cos^{-1} x = \sin^{-1}\sqrt{1-x^2} = \tan^{-1}\left(\dfrac{\sqrt{1-x^2}}{x}\right)$
$$= \cot^{-1}\left(\dfrac{x}{\sqrt{1-x^2}}\right) = \sec^{-1}\left(\dfrac{1}{x}\right) = \operatorname{cosec}^{-1}\left(\dfrac{1}{\sqrt{1-x^2}}\right)$$

(iii) $\tan^{-1} x = \sin^{-1}\left(\dfrac{x}{\sqrt{1+x^2}}\right) = \cos^{-1}\left(\dfrac{1}{\sqrt{1+x^2}}\right) = \cot^{-1}\left(\dfrac{1}{x}\right)$
$$= \sec^{-1}\sqrt{1+x^2} = \operatorname{cosec}^{-1}\left(\dfrac{\sqrt{1+x^2}}{x}\right)$$

Mind

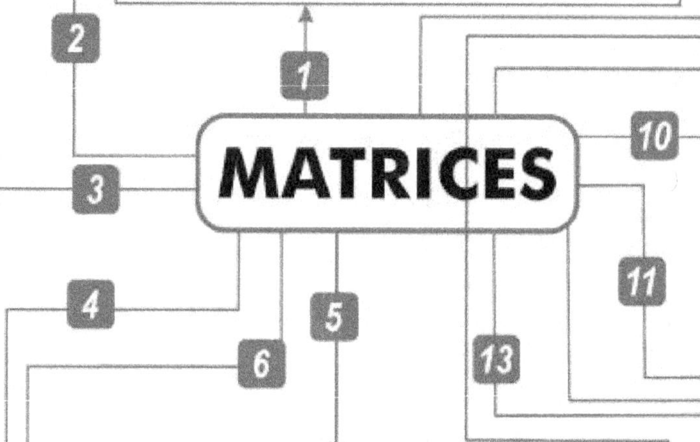

Order of a Matrix

A matrix having m rows and n columns is called a matrix of order m×n or simply m×n matrix.

or $A = [a_{ij}]_{m \times n}, 1 \le i \le m, 1 \le j \le n \ i, j \in N$

a_{ij} is an element lying in the ith row & j^{th} column. The number of elements in m×n matrix will be mn.

Matrix

A matrix is an ordered rectangular array of numbers or functions. The numbers or functions are called the elements of the matrix.

For example $\begin{bmatrix} 1 & 2 & 5 \\ 3 & 4 & 6 \end{bmatrix}$ is a matrix.

The horizontal lines of elements in the above matrix are said to constitute, **rows** of the matrix & vertical lines of elements are said to constitute **columns** of the matrix. Thus above matrix has 2 rows and 3 columns.

Types of Matrix

(i) **Column Matrix :** A matrix is said to be a column matrix if it has only one column, i.e., $A = [a_{ij}]_{m \times 1}$ is a column matrix of order m×1.

(ii) **Row Matrix :** Row matrix has only one row, i.e., $B = [b_{ij}]_{1 \times n}$ is a row matrix of order 1×n.

(iii) **Square Matrix :** Square matrix has equal number of rows and columns, i.e., $A = [a_{ij}]_{m \times m}$ is a square matrix of order m.

(iv) **Diagonal Matrix :** A square matrix is said to be diagonal matrix if all of its non-diagonal elements are zero, i.e., $B = [b_{ij}]_{m \times n}$ is said to be a diagonal matrix if $b_{ij} = 0$, where $i \ne j$.

(v) **Scalar Matrix :** It is a diagonal matrix with all its diagonal elements equal, i.e., $B = [b_{ij}]_{m \times n}$ is a scalar matrix if

$b_{ij} = 0$, where $i \ne j$

$b_{ij} = k$, when $i = j$ & k = constant.

(vi) **Identity Matrix :** It is a diagonal matrix having all its diagonal elements equal to 1, i.e., $A = [a_{ij}]_{m \times n}$ is an identity matrix if

$$a_{ij} = \begin{cases} 1, & \text{if } i = j \\ 0, & \text{if } i \ne j \end{cases}$$

we denoted identity matrix by I_n when order is n.

(vii) **Zero Matrix :** A matrix is said to be zero or null matrix if all its elements are zero. It is denoted by O.

Addition of Matrices

Sum of the two matrices is a matrix obtained by adding the corresponding elements of the given matrices, i.e., $A = [a_{ij}]$ and $B = [b_{ij}]$ are two matrices of same order m×n. Then sum of two matrics A & B is defined as $C = [c_{ij}]$, where $c_{ij} = a_{ij} + b_{ij}$ for all i & j.

Difference of matrices : The difference $A - B$ is defined as $D = [d_{ij}]$, where $d_{ij} = a_{ij} - b_{ij}$ for all i & j. In order words $D = A - B = A + (-B)$, that is the sum of matrices A & (−B).

Properties of matrix Addition

(i) **Commulative Law:** $A + B = B + A$

(ii) **Associative Law:** $(A + B) + C = A + (B + C)$

(iii) **Existance of Additive Identity:** Let $A = [a_{ij}]_{m \times n}$ & O = zero matrix of order m×n, then $A + O = O + A = A$. Here O is the additive identity for matrix addition.

(iv) **Existance of Additive Inverse**
Let $A = [a_{ij}]_{m \times n}$ be any matrix then we have another matrix as $-A = [-a_{ij}]_{m \times n}$ such that $A + (-A) = (-A) + A = O$. Here −A is the additive inverse of A or negative of A.

Equality of Matrices

Two matrices $A = [a_{ij}]$ and $B = [b_{ij}]$ are said to be equal if
(i) they are of the same order
(ii) each element of A is equal to the corresponding element of B, i.e., $a_{ij} = b_{ij}$ for all i & j

Multiplication of a Matrix by a Scalar

Let $A = [a_{ij}]_{m \times n}$ be a matrix & k be a number.
Then, $kA = Ak = [ka_{ij}]_{m \times n}$

Properties
(I) $k(A + B) = kA + kB$ (ii) $(k + t)A = kA + tA$.

Map-3

Multiplication of Matrices

If A & B are any two matrices, then their product AB will be defined only when the number of columns in A is equal to the number of rows in B. If $A = [a_{ij}]_{m \times n}$ and $B = [b_{ij}]_{n \times p}$, then their product $AB = C = [c_{ij}]$, is a matrix of order $m \times p$, where $(ij)^{th}$ element of $AB = C_{ij} = \sum_{r=1}^{n} a_{ir} b_{rj}$

Properties of Matrix Multiplication

(I) Associative Law for Multiplication : If A, B & C are three matrices of order $m \times n$, $n \times p$ & $p \times q$ respectively, then $(AB)C = A(BC)$

(ii) Distributive Law : For three matrices A, B & C
(a) $A(B + C) = AB + AC$
(b) $(A + B)C = AC + BC$, whenever both sides of equality are defined.

(iii) Matrix Multiplication is not commutative in general, i.e., $AB \neq BA$ (in general).

(iv) Existence of Multiplicative Identity : For every square matrix A, there exists an identity matrix I of same order such that $IA = AI = A$.

Transpose of a Matrix

The matrix obtained from a given matrix A by changing its rows into its corresponding columns or columns into its corresponding rows is called transpose of matrix A & it is denoted by A^T or A'. If the order of A is $m \times n$, then order of A^T is $n \times m$. In other words if $A = [a_{ij}]_{m \times n}$ then $A^T = [a_{ji}]_{n \times m}$

Properties of Transpose of the Matrices

For any matrices A & B of suitable orders, we have:
(i) $(A^T)^T = A$
(ii) $(kA)^T = k(A)^T$ (where k is constant)
(iii) $(A \pm B)^T = A^T \pm B^T$
(iv) $(AB)^T = B^T A^T$

Symmetric & Skew Symmetric Matrices

Symmetric Matrix
A square matrix $A = [a_{ij}]$ is called a symmetric matrix, if $a_{ij} = a_{ji}$ for all i, j or $A^T = A$

Skew Symmetric Matrix
A square matrix $A = [a_{ij}]$ is called a skew-symmetric matrix, if $a_{ij} = -a_{ji}$ for all i, j or $A^T = -A$.

Properties of Symmetric & Skew Symmetric Matrices
(I) For any square matrix A with real number entries, $(A + A^T)$ is a symmetric matrix & $(A - A^T)$ is a skew symmetric matrix.
(ii) Any square matrix A can be expressed as the sum of a symmetric & a skew symmetric matrix as

$$A = \left[\frac{1}{2}(A + A^T)\right] + \left[\frac{1}{2}(A - A^T)\right]$$

Invertible Matrix and Inverse Matrix

If A is a square matrix and there exists another square matrix B of the same order such that $AB = BA = I$, then B is called the inverse matrix of A & it is denoted by A^{-1}.
In that case A is said to be invertible matrix.

Properties of Invertible Matrices
(i) Uniqueness of Inverse : Inverse of a square matrix, if it exists, is unique.
(ii) $(AB)^{-1} = B^{-1}A^{-1}$

Inverse of a Matrix by Elementary Operations

If A is a matrix such that A^{-1} exists, then to find A^{-1} using elementary row operations, write $A = IA$ & apply a sequence of row operations on $A = IA$ till we get, $I = BA$. The matrix B will be the inverse of A. Similarly, if we wish to find A^{-1} using column operations, we write $A = AI$ & apply a sequence of column operations on $A = AI$ till we get, $I = AB$.

Elementary Operation (Transformation of a Matrix)

There are six operations on a matrix, three of which are due to rows & three due to columns, called elementary operations or Transformations.

(i) The interchange of any two rows or two columns symbolically, interchange of ith & j^{th} rows is denoted by $R_i \leftrightarrow R_j$ & same will be for columns, i.e., $C_i \leftrightarrow C_j$.

(ii) The multiplication of the elements of any row or column by a non zero number. For rows it is denoted as $R_i \leftrightarrow kR_i$, $k \neq 0$ & for columns: $C_i \leftrightarrow kC_i$.

(iii) The addition to the elements of any row or column, the corresponding elements of any other row or column multiplied by any non-zero number. Symbolically, the addition to the elements of ith row, the corresponding elements of jth row multiplied by k is denoted as: $R_i \leftrightarrow R_i + kR_j (k \neq 0)$

For columns : $C_i \leftrightarrow C_i + kC_j$

Determinant of a Square Matrix of Order Three

Consider $A = [a_{ij}]_{3 \times 3}$

Then, $|A| = \begin{bmatrix} a_{11} & a_{12} & a_{13} \\ a_{21} & a_{22} & a_{23} \\ a_{31} & a_{32} & a_{33} \end{bmatrix}$,

Expansion along first Row (R_1)

$|A| = a_{11}(a_{22}a_{33} - a_{32}a_{23}) - a_{12}(a_{21}a_{33} - a_{31}a_{23}) + a_{13}(a_{21}a_{32} - a_{31}a_{22})$

$\quad = a_{11}a_{22}a_{33} - a_{11}a_{32}a_{23} - a_{12}a_{21}a_{33} + a_{12}a_{31}a_{23} + a_{13}a_{21}a_{32} - a_{13}a_{31}a_{22}$

Determinant

Every square matrix associates to an expression or a number which is known as its determinant. If $A = [a_{ij}]$ is a square matrix of order n, then the determinant of A is denoted by det (A) or $|A|$ or Δ.

Mind

DETERMINANTS

Properties of Determinants

(i) The value of a determinant remains unchanged if its rows and columns are interchanged.

(ii) If any two rows (or columns) of a determinant are interchanged, then sign of determinant changes.

(iii) If any two rows (or columns) of a determinant are identical, then the value of determinant is zero.

(iv) If each element of a row (or a column) of a determinant is multiplied by a constant k, then its value gets multiplied by k.

(v) If some or all the elements of a row or column of a determinant are expressed as a sum of two (or more) terms, then the determinant can be expressed as a sum of two (or more) determinants.

(vi) If the equimultiples of corresponding elements of other row (or column) are added to each element of any row or column of a determinant, then the value of the determinant remains the same.

(vii) $\left|A^T\right| = |A|$, where A^T = transpose of A.

(viii) If $A = [a_{ij}]_{3\times3}$, then $|kA| = k^3|A|$.

(ix) The determinant of the product of matrices is equal to product of their respective determinants, i.e., $|AB| = |A|\,|B|$, where A & B are square matrices of same order

Area of a Triangle

Area of a triangle with vertices (x_1, y_1), (x_2, y_2) and (x_3, y_3) is given by

$$\Delta = \frac{1}{2}\begin{vmatrix} x_1 & y_1 & 1 \\ x_2 & y_2 & 1 \\ x_3 & y_3 & 1 \end{vmatrix}$$

Minor and Cofactor of an Element of a Determinant

Minor: The determinant that is left by cancelling the row and column intersecting at a particular element of a determinant is called the minor of that element of the determinant. Minor of an element a_{ij} of a determinant is denoted by M_{ij}.

Cofactor: The cofactor of an element a_{ij} of a determinant is denoted by A_{ij} (or C_{ij}) and is equal to $(-1)^{i+j} M_{ij}$.

Map-4

Adjoint of a Matrix

If $A = \begin{bmatrix} a_{11} & a_{12} & a_{13} \\ a_{21} & a_{22} & a_{23} \\ a_{31} & a_{32} & a_{33} \end{bmatrix}$, then adj $A = \begin{bmatrix} A_{11} & A_{21} & A_{31} \\ A_{12} & A_{22} & A_{32} \\ A_{13} & A_{23} & A_{33} \end{bmatrix}$,

where A_{ij} is the cofactor of a_{ij}

If A be any given square matrix of order n, then
$A(\text{adj } A) = (\text{adj } A) A = |A| I$
where I is the identity matrix of order n.

Singular and Non-SIngular Matrices

A square matrix A is said to be singular if $|A| = 0$, otherwise it is called non-singular matrix.
If A & B are non-singular matrix of same order, then AB & BA are also non-singular matrices of same order.

7

8

9

Inverse of a Matrix

If A and B are two matrices such that
$AB = I = BA$

then B is called the inverse of A and it is denoted by A^{-1}.

Also, $A^{-1} = \dfrac{\text{adj} A}{|A|}$, if $|A| \neq 0$

Properties of Inverse Matrix
Let A and B are two invertible matrices of the same order, then

(i) $(AB)^{-1} = B^{-1}A^{-1}$

(ii) $(A^T)^{-1} = (A^{-1})^T$

(iii) $\text{adj}(A^{-1}) = (\text{adj } A)^{-1}$

Applications of Determinants and Matrices

Solution of System of Linear Equations using Inverse of a Matrix
Consider the system of equations
$a_1x + b_1y + c_1z = d_1$
$a_2x + b_2y + c_2z = d_2$
$a_3x + b_3y + c_3z = d_3$

Let $A = \begin{bmatrix} a_1 & b_1 & c_1 \\ a_2 & b_2 & c_2 \\ a_3 & b_3 & c_3 \end{bmatrix}$, $X = \begin{bmatrix} x \\ y \\ z \end{bmatrix}$ & $B = \begin{bmatrix} d_1 \\ d_2 \\ d_3 \end{bmatrix}$

Then, we can write, $AX = B$ i.e.,

- Unique solution of the equation $AX = B$ is given by $X = A^{-1}B$, when $|A| \neq 0$
- A system of equations is said to be consistent or inconsistent according as its solution exists or not.
- For a square matrix A in the matrix equation $AX = B$

(i) If $|A| \neq 0$, there exists a unique solution and the system of equations is consistent.

(ii) If $|A| = 0$, and $(\text{adj } A) B \neq 0$, then there exists no solution and the system of equations is inconsistent

(iii) If $|A| = 0$ and $(\text{adj } A) B = 0$, then the system may or may not be consistent according as the system has either infinitely many solutions or no solution.

Mind

CONTINUITY AND DIFFERENTIABILITY

Continuity

Continuity of a Function at a Point

Suppose f is a real function on a subset of the real numbers & let c be a point in the domain of f. Then f is continuous at c if

$$\lim_{x \to c} f(x) = f(c)$$

Continuity of a Function in an Interval

Suppose f is a function defined on a closed interval [a, b], then for f to be continuous, it needs to be continuous at every point in [a, b] including the end points a & b.

Continuity of f at a, $\lim_{x \to a^+} f(x) = f(a)$

Continuity of f at b, $\lim_{x \to b^-} f(x) = f(b)$

A function which is not continuous at point x = c is said to be discontinuous at that point

Algebra of Continuous Functions

Theorem 1: Suppose f & g be two real functions continuous at a real number c, Then
(1) f + g is continuous at x = c
(2) f − g is continuous at x = c
(3) f·g is continuous at x = c
(4) f/g is continuous at x = c, (provided g (c) ≠ 0)

Theorem 2: Suppose f & g are real valued functions such that (fog) is defined at c. If g is continuous at c & if f is continuous at g(c), then (fog) is continuous at c.

Differentiability

A function f is said to be differentiable at a point c in its domain, if its left hand & right hand derivatives exist at c & are equal.

Here at x = c,

Left Hand Derivative,

$$\text{L.H.D.} = \lim_{h \to 0} \frac{f(c-h) - f(c)}{-h} = L f'(c)$$

Right Hand Derivative,

$$\text{R.H.D.} = \lim_{h \to 0} \frac{f(c+h) - f(c)}{h} = R f'(c)$$

Theorem: If a function f is differentiable at a point c, then it is also continuous at that point. Therefore, every differentiable function is continuous, but the converse is not true.

Algebra of Derivatives

Let u, v be the functions of x.
(1) **Sum and Difference Rule**
$(u \pm v)' = u' \pm v'$
(2) **Leibnitz or Product Rule**
$(uv)' = u'v + uv'$
(3) **Quotient Rule**
$$\left(\frac{u}{v}\right)' = \frac{u'v - uv'}{v^2}$$

Chain Rule

If y is a function of u, u is a function of v & v is a function of x.

Then, $\dfrac{dy}{dx} = \dfrac{dy}{du} \times \dfrac{du}{dv} \times \dfrac{dv}{dx}$

Implicit Functions

An equation in the form f(x, y) = 0 in which y is not expressible in terms of x is called an implicit function of x & y.

Derivative of Implicit Functions

Let y = f(x, y), where f(x, y) be an implicit function of x & y.
- Firstly differentiate both sides of equation w.r.t x
- Then take all terms involving $\dfrac{dy}{dx}$ on L.H.S. & remaining terms on R.H.S. to get the required value.

Map-5

Differentiation of Inverse Trigonometric Functions

$f(x)$	$f'(x)$	Domain of f'
$\sin^{-1} x$	$\dfrac{1}{\sqrt{1-x^2}}$	$(-1,1)$
$\cos^{-1} x$	$\dfrac{-1}{\sqrt{1-x^2}}$	$(-1,1)$
$\tan^{-1} x$	$\dfrac{1}{1+x^2}$	R
$\cot^{-1} x$	$\dfrac{-1}{1+x^2}$	R
$\sec^{-1} x$	$\dfrac{1}{|x|\sqrt{x^2-1}}$	$|x|>1$
$\operatorname{cosec}^{-1} x$	$\dfrac{-1}{|x|\sqrt{x^2-1}}$	$|x|>1$

7

Logarithmic Differentiation

Logarithmic Differentiation is a very useful technique to differentiate functions of the form $f(x) = [u(x)]^{v(x)}$, where $f(x)$ & $u(x)$ are positive.

We apply logarithm (to base) on both sides to the above equation & then differentiate by using chain rule, in this way we can find $f'(x)$. This process is called logarithmic

$$\frac{d}{dx}(e^x) = e^x, \quad \frac{d}{dx}(\log x) = \frac{1}{x} \quad \& \quad \frac{d}{dx}a^x = a^x \log a$$

8

Derivatives of Functions in Parametric Form

The set of equations $x = f(t)$, $y = g(t)$ is called the parametric form of an equation.

Here, $\dfrac{dy}{dx} = \dfrac{dy/dt}{dx/dt}$ or $\dfrac{g'(t)}{f'(t)}$

Here, $\dfrac{dy}{dx}$ is expressed in terms of parameter only without directly involving the main variables.

9

10

Second Order Derivative

Let $y = f(x)$, then $\dfrac{dy}{dx} = f'(x)$

If $f'(x)$ is differentiable, then we may differentiate it again w.r.t. x & get the second order derivative represented by:

$$\frac{d}{dx}\left(\frac{dy}{dx}\right) \text{ or } \frac{d^2y}{dx^2} \text{ or } f''(x) \text{ or } D^2y \text{ or } y'' \text{ or } y_2$$

11

Mean Value Theorem

If $f : [a, b] \to R$ is continuous on $[a, b]$ & differentiable on (a, b). Then there exists some c in (a, b) such that

$$f'(c) = \frac{f(b) - f(a)}{b - a}$$

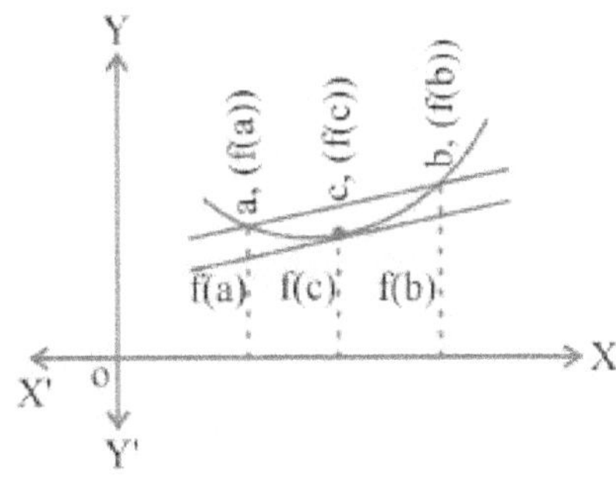

The Mean value Theorem states that there is a point c in (a, b) such that the slope of the tangent at $(c, f(c))$ is same as the slope of the secant between $(a, f(a))$ and $(b, f(b))$ or there is a point c in (a, b) such that the tangent at $(c, f(c)$ is parallel to the secant between $(a, f(a))$ & $(b, f(b))$.

Rolle's Theorem

If $f : [a, b] \to R$ is continuous on $[a, b]$ & differentiable on (a, b) such that $f(a) = f(b)$, then there exists some c in (a, b) such that $f'(c) = 0$

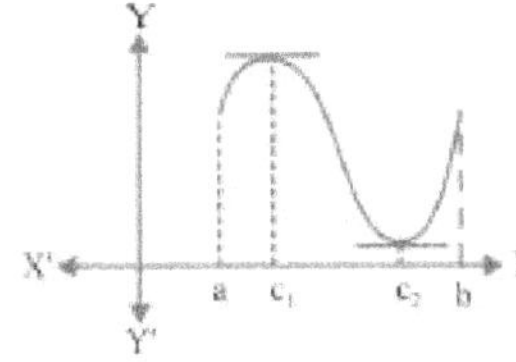

In the above graph, the slope of tangent to the curve at least at one point becomes zero. The slope of tangent at any point on the graph of $y = f(x)$ is nothing but the derivative of $f(x)$ at that point.

Mind

APPLICATION OF DERIVATIVES

Increasing and Decreasing Functions

(1) (I) Let I be an open interval contained in the domain of a real valued function f. Then f is said to be

    (i) increasing on I if $x_1 < x_2$ in I
$$\Rightarrow f(x_1) \le f(x_2) \ \forall \ x_1, x_2 \in I.$$

    (ii) strictly increasing on I if $x_1 < x_2$ in I
$$\Rightarrow f(x_1) < f(x_2) \ \forall \ x_1, x_2 \in I.$$

    (iii) decreasing on I if $x_1 < x_2$ in I
$$\Rightarrow f(x_1) \ge f(x_2) \ \forall \ x_1, x_2 \in I.$$

    (iv) strictly decreasing on I if $x_1 < x_2$ in I
$$\Rightarrow f(x_1) > f(x_2) \ \forall \ x_1, x_2 \in I.$$

    (II) A function f is said to be increasing at x_0 if there exists an interval $I = (x_0 - h, x_0 + h), h > 0$ such that for x_1, x_2
$$x_1 < x_2 \text{ in } I \Rightarrow f(x_1) \le f(x_2)$$

Similarly, the other cases i.e., strictly increasing, decreasing and strictly decreasing can be clarified.

(2) A function $f(x)$ defined in the interval [a,b] will be

Monotonic increasing $\Leftrightarrow f'(x) \ge 0 \ x \in (a, b)$

Monotonic decreasing $\Leftrightarrow f'(x) \le 0 \ x \in (a, b)$

Constant function $\Leftrightarrow f'(x) = 0 \ x \in (a, b)$

Strictly increasing $\Leftrightarrow f'(x) > 0 \ x \in (a, b)$

Strictly decreasing $\Leftrightarrow f'(x) < 0 \ x \in (a, b)$

Properties of Monotonic Functions

(1) If $f(x)$ and $g(x)$ are monotonically (strictly) increasing (decreasing) functions on [a, b], then gof (x) is a monotonically (strictly) increasing function on [a, b].

(2) If one of the two functions f (x) and g(x) is strictly (monotonically) increasing and other is strictly (monotonically) decreasing, then gof (x) is strictly (monotonically) decreasing on [a, b].

Rate of Change of Quantities

The rate of change of y with respect to x at a point $x = x_0$ is given by $\left(\dfrac{dy}{dx}\right)_{x=x_0}$

Note that $\dfrac{dy}{dx}$ is positive if y increases with increase in x and is negative if y decreases with increase in x.

2

1

4

5

7

3

Tangents and Normals

- The equation of the tangent at (x_0, y_0) is given below:

$y - y_0 = m(x - x_0)$,

where m = slope of tangent $= \left(\dfrac{dy}{dx}\right)_{(x_0, y_0)}$ or $f'(x_0)$

- The equation of the normal at (x_0, y_0) is given below:

$y - y_0 = -\dfrac{1}{m}(x - x_0)$,

where m = slope of tangent at (x_0, y_0)

Approximations

Let y = f(x), Δx be a small increment in x & Δy be the increment in y corresponding to the increment in x, i.e., $\Delta y = f(x + \Delta x) - f(x)$. Then approximate value of

$$\Delta y = \left(\dfrac{dy}{dx}\right) \Delta x$$

Map-6

Maxima and Minima

1. Let f be a funciton defined on an interval I. Then
   (a) f is said to have a maximum value in I. if there exists point c in I such that $f(c) \geq f(x)$, for all $x \in I$.
   f(c) is the maximum value and point c is a point of maximum value of f in I.
   (b) f is said to have a minimum value in I. if there exists a point c in I such that $f(c) \leq f(x)$, for all $x \in I$.
   f(c) is the minimum value and point c is a point of minimum value of f in I.
   (c) f is said to have an extreme value in I if there exists a point c in I such that f(c) is either a maximum value or a minimum value of f in I.
   f(c) is an extreme value and point c is called an extreme point.
2. Let f be a real valued function and let c be an interior point in the domain of f. Then
   (a) c is called a point of local maxima if there is an $h > 0$ such that
   $f(c) \geq f(x)$, for all x in $(c - h, c + h)$
   The value f(c) is called the local maximum value of f.
   (b) c is called a point of local minima if there is an $h > 0$ such that
   $f(c) \leq f(x)$, for all x in $(c - h, c + h)$
   The value f(c) is called the local minimum value of f.
3. Let f be a function defined on an open interval I. Suppose $c \in I$ be any point. If f has a local maxima or a local minima at $x = c$, then either $f(c) = 0$ or f is not differentiable at c.

Test of Local Maxima & Minima

First Derivative Test:
Let f(x) be a function differentiable at $x = a$. Then
(a) $x = a$ is a point of local maximum of f(x), if
   (i) $f'(a) = 0$ and
   (ii) f '(x) changes sign from positive to negative as x increases through a
(b) $x = a$ is a point of local minimum of f(x), if
   (i) $f'(a) = 0$ and
   (ii) f '(x) changes sign from negative to positive as x increases through a
(c) If $f'(a) = 0$, but f'(x) does not change sign as x increases through a, that is f'(a) has the same sign in the complete neighourhood of a, then a is neither a point of local maximum nor a point of local minimum. In this case, $x = a$ is a point of inflection.

Second Derivative Test:
Let f be a function defined on an interval I and $c \in I$. Let f be twice differentiable at c. Then
(i) $x = c$ is a point of local maxima if $f'(c) = 0$ and $f''(c) < 0$
   The value f(c) is local maximum value of f.
(ii) $x = c$ is a point of local minima if $f'(c) = 0$ and $f''(c) > 0$
   In this case, f(c) is local minimum value of f.
(iii) The test fails if $f'(c) = 0$ and $f''(c) = 0$
   In this case, we go back to the first derivative test and find whether c is a point of local maxima, local minima or a point of inflection.

Absolute Maxima & Absolute Minima

Let f be a continuous function on an interval I = [a, b]. Then f has the absolute maximum value and f attains it at least once in I. Also, f has the absolute minimum value and attains it at least once in I.
Let f be a differentiable function on a closed interval I and let c be any interior point of I. Then
(i) $f'(c) = 0$ if f attains its absolute maximum value at c.
(ii) $f'(c) = 0$ if f attains its absolute minimum value at c.

Steps for Finding Absolute Maxima and/or Absolute Minima

(i) Find all critical points of f in the interval, i.e., find value of x where either $f'(x) = 0$ or f is not differentiable.
(ii) Take the end points of the interval.
(iii) At all the above points (in step (i) and (ii)) calculate the value of f.
(iv) Identify the maximum and minimum values of f out of the values calculated in step (iii). The maximum value will be the absolute maximum value of f and the minimum value will be the absolute minimum value of f.

INDEFINITE INTEGRAL

Mind

1. Standard Integrals

(i) $\int x^n dx = \dfrac{x^{n+1}}{n+1} + C, n \neq -1$

(ii) $\int \dfrac{1}{x} dx = \log|x| + C$

(iii) $\int e^x dx = e^x + C$

(iv) $\int a^x dx = \dfrac{a^x}{\log a} + C$

(v) $\int \sin x \, dx = -\cos x + C$

(vi) $\int \cos x \, dx = \sin x + C$

(vii) $\int \sec^2 x \, dx = \tan x + C$

(viii) $\int \text{cosec}^2 x \, dx = -\cot x + C$

(ix) $\int \sec x \tan x \, dx = \sec x + C$

(x) $\int \text{cosec } x \cot x \, dx = -\text{cosec } x + C$

(xi) $\int \cot x \, dx = \log|\sin x| + C$

(xii) $\int \tan x \, dx = \log|\sec x| + C$

(xiii) $\int \sec x \, dx = \log|\sec x + \tan x| + C$

(xiv) $\int \text{cosec } x \, dx = \log|\text{cosec } x - \cot x| + C$

(xv) $\int \dfrac{1}{\sqrt{a^2 - x^2}} dx = \sin^{-1}\left(\dfrac{x}{a}\right) + C$

(xvi) $\int -\dfrac{1}{\sqrt{a^2 - x^2}} dx = \cos^{-1}\left(\dfrac{x}{a}\right) + C$

(xvii) $\int \dfrac{1}{a^2 + x^2} dx = \dfrac{1}{a}\tan^{-1}\left(\dfrac{x}{a}\right) + C$

(xviii) $\int -\dfrac{1}{a^2 + x^2} dx = \dfrac{1}{a}\cot^{-1}\left(\dfrac{x}{a}\right) + C$

(xix) $\int \dfrac{1}{x\sqrt{x^2 - a^2}} dx = \dfrac{1}{a}\sec^{-1}\left(\dfrac{x}{a}\right) + C$

(xx) $\int -\dfrac{1}{x\sqrt{x^2 - a^2}} dx = \dfrac{1}{a}\text{cosec}^{-1}\left(\dfrac{x}{a}\right) + C$

2. Methods of Integration

When integration cannot be reduced into some standard form, then integration is performed using following methods :
(i) Integration by Substitution
(ii) Integration using Partial Fractions
(iii) Integration by Parts

3. Integration by Substitution

A change in the variable of integration often reduces an integral to one of the fundamental integrals. The method by which we change the variable of integration to some other variable is known as the method of substitution.

Consider $I = \int f(x) dx$

Put $x = g(t)$, so $\dfrac{dx}{dt} = g'(t)$

i.e., $dx = g'(t)\, dt$

Thus, $I = \int f(x) dx = \int f(g(t)) g'(t) dt$

Some Important Substitutions are:

Function	Substitutions
$\sqrt{a^2 - x^2}$	$x = a \sin\theta$ or $x = a\cos\theta$
$\sqrt{a^2 + x^2}$	$x = a\tan\theta$
$\sqrt{x^2 - a^2}$	$x = a\sec\theta$

4. Integration Using Partial Fractions

Consider a rational function of the form $\dfrac{P(x)}{Q(x)}$

where $P(x)$ & $Q(x)$ are polynomials in x & $Q(x) \neq 0$. If degree of $P(x)$ is greater than the degree of $Q(x)$, then we may divide $P(x)$ by $Q(x)$ such that

$$\dfrac{P(x)}{Q(x)} = T(x) + \dfrac{R(x)}{Q(x)}$$

where, $T(x)$ is a polynomial in x & degree of $R(x)$ is less than the degree of $Q(x)$.
$T(x)$ being a polynomial can be easily integrated.

$\dfrac{R(x)}{Q(x)}$ can be integrated by expressing $\dfrac{R(x)}{Q(x)}$ as the sum of partial fractions of the following types:

(i) $\dfrac{px + q}{(x-a)(x-b)} = \dfrac{A}{x-a} + \dfrac{B}{x-b}, a \neq b$

(ii) $\dfrac{px + q}{(x-a)^2} = \dfrac{A}{x-a} + \dfrac{B}{(x-a)^2}$

(iii) $\dfrac{px^2 + qx + r}{(x-a)(x-b)(x-c)} = \dfrac{A}{x-a} + \dfrac{B}{x-b} + \dfrac{C}{x-c}$

(iv) $\dfrac{px^2 + qx + r}{(x-a)^2(x-b)} = \dfrac{A}{x-a} + \dfrac{B}{(x-a)^2} + \dfrac{C}{x-b}$

(v) $\dfrac{px^2 + qx + r}{(x-a)(x^2 + bx + c)} = \dfrac{A}{x-a} + \dfrac{Bx+C}{x^2 + bx + c}$

where $x^2 + bx + c$ cannot be factorised further.

5. Integration by Parts

$$\int u \cdot v \, dx = u\int v \, dx - \int\left[\dfrac{du}{dx} \cdot \int v \, dx\right] dx$$

Here, u is the first function & v is the second function.
Selection of first function : For applying integration by parts, we choose the first function as the function which comes first in the word **ILATE**, where
I   stands for the inverse trigonometric function
     $(\sin^{-1}x, \cos^{-1}x, \tan^{-1}x$ etc)
L   stands for the logarithmic function
A   stands for the algebraic functions
T   stands for the trigonometric functions
E   stands for the exponential functions

6. Integrals of Some Special Functions

(i) $\int \dfrac{dx}{x^2 - a^2} = \dfrac{1}{2a}\log\left|\dfrac{x-a}{x+a}\right| + C$

(ii) $\int \dfrac{dx}{a^2 - x^2} = \dfrac{1}{2a}\log\left|\dfrac{a+x}{a-x}\right| + C$

(iii) $\int \dfrac{dx}{\sqrt{x^2 - a^2}} = \log\left|x + \sqrt{x^2 - a^2}\right| + C$

(iv) $\int \dfrac{dx}{\sqrt{x^2 + a^2}} = \log\left|x + \sqrt{x^2 + a^2}\right| + C$

7. Two Standard Forms of an Integral

(i) $\int e^x [f(x) + f'(x)] dx = e^x f(x) + C$

(ii) $\int [xf'(x) + f(x)] dx = xf(x) + C$

8. Some Special Types of Integrals

(i) $\int \sqrt{x^2 - a^2}\, dx = \dfrac{x}{2}\sqrt{x^2 - a^2} - \dfrac{a^2}{2}\log\left|x + \sqrt{x^2 - a^2}\right| + C$

(ii) $\int \sqrt{x^2 + a^2}\, dx = \dfrac{x}{2}\sqrt{x^2 + a^2} + \dfrac{a^2}{2}\log\left|x + \sqrt{x^2 + a^2}\right| + C$

(iii) $\int \sqrt{a^2 - x^2}\, dx = \dfrac{x}{2}\sqrt{a^2 - x^2} + \dfrac{a^2}{2}\sin^{-1}\left(\dfrac{x}{a}\right) + C$

(iv) Integrals of the types $\int \dfrac{dx}{ax^2 + bx + c}$ or $\int \dfrac{dx}{\sqrt{ax^2 + bx + c}}$

can be transformed into standard form by expressing

$$ax^2 + bx + c = a\left[x^2 + \dfrac{bx}{a} + \dfrac{c}{a}\right]$$

$$= a\left[\left(x + \dfrac{b}{2a}\right)^2 + \left(\dfrac{c}{a} - \dfrac{b^2}{4a^2}\right)\right]$$

(v) Integrals of the types $\int \dfrac{px + q}{ax^2 + bx + c} dx$

or $\int \dfrac{px + q}{\sqrt{ax^2 + bx + c}} dx$

can be transformed into standard form by

expressing $px + q = A\dfrac{d}{dx}(ax^2 + bx + c) + B$

$= A(2ax + b) + B$ where A & B can be determined by comparing coefficients on both sides.

Map-7

DEFINITE INTEGRAL

① Definite Integral

The definite integral of f(x) between the limits a to b i.e., in the interval [a, b] is denoted by

$$\int_a^b f(x)dx$$ and is defined as follows:

$$\int_a^b f(x)dx = [F(x)]_a^b = F(b) - F(a)$$

where, $\int f(x)dx = F(x)$

The definite integral $\int_a^b f(x)dx$ is also defined as the area bounded by the curve y = f(x), the ordinates x = a, x = b and the x-axis

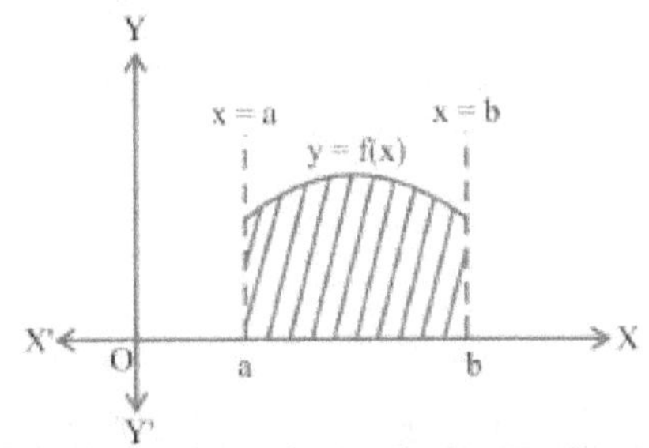

② Definite Integral as the Limit of a Sum

$$\int_a^b f(x)dx = \lim_{h \to 0}[f(a) + f(a+h) + \cdots + f(a+(n-1)h)]$$

or

$$\int_a^b f(x)dx = (b-a) \lim_{n \to \infty} \frac{1}{n}[f(a) + f(a+h) + \cdots + f(a+(n-1)h]$$

where, $h = \dfrac{b-a}{n} \to 0$ as $n \to \infty$

The above expression is known as the definite integral as the limit of a sum.

③ Fundamental Theorem of Calculus

Theorem 1 : Let f be a continuous function on the closed interval [a, b] and let A(x) be area function. Then A'(x) = f(x), $\forall\ x \in$ [a, b]

Theorem 2 : Let f be a continuous function defined on the closed interval [a, b] & F be the anti-derivative of f.

Then $$\int_a^b f(x)dx = [F(x + c)]_a^b = F(b) - F(a)$$

This is called the definite integral of f over the range [a, b], where a & b are called the limits of integration, a being the lower limit & b the upper limit.

④ Evaluations of Definite Integrals by Substitution

Consider a definite integral of the following form

$$\int_a^b f\big(g(x)\big)g'(x)dx$$

To evaluate this integral we proceed as following

Step 1 : Substitute

Step 2 : Find the limits of integration in new system of variable, i.e. the lower limit is g(a) and

the upper limit is g(b), and the integral is now $\displaystyle\int_{g(a)}^{g(b)} f(t)dt$

Step 3 : Evaluate the integral so obtained by usual method.

⑤ Properties of Definite Integrals

(i) $\displaystyle\int_a^b f(x)dx = \int_a^b f(t)dt$

(ii) $\displaystyle\int_a^b f(x)dx = -\int_b^a f(x)dx$, in particular $\displaystyle\int_a^a f(x)dx = 0$

(iii) $\displaystyle\int_a^b f(x)dx = \int_a^c f(x)dx + \int_c^b f(x)dx$ where a < c < b

(iv) $\displaystyle\int_a^b f(x)dx = \int_a^b f(a + b - x)dx$

(v) $\displaystyle\int_0^a f(x)dx = \int_0^a f(a - x)dx$

(vi) $\displaystyle\int_{-a}^a f(x)dx = 2\int_0^a f(x)dx$, if f(x) is an even function i.e., f(–x) = f(x)

$\displaystyle\int_{-a}^a f(x)dx = 0$, if f(x) is an odd function i.e., f(–x) = –f(x)

(vii) $\displaystyle\int_0^{2a} f(x)dx = \int_0^a f(x)dx + \int_0^a f(2a - x)dx$

(viii) $\displaystyle\int_0^{2a} f(x)dx = 2\int_0^a f(x)dx$, if f(2a – x) = f(x)

$\qquad\qquad\quad = 0$, if f(2a – x) = –f(x)

Mind

Area of the region bounded by a Curve $y = f(x)$ & x-axis between the two ordinates

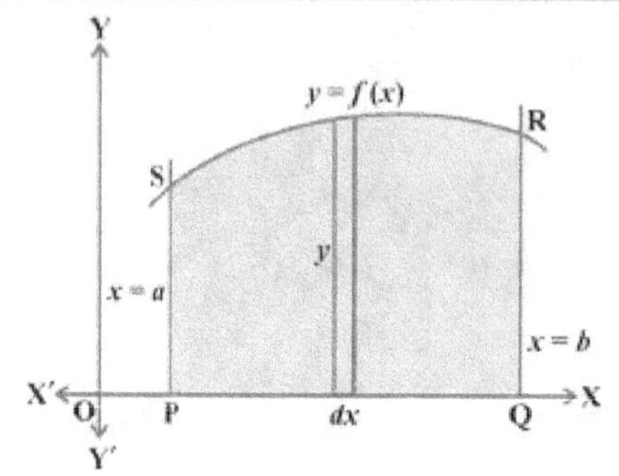

$$\text{Area, } A = \int_a^b dA = \int_a^b y\,dx = \int_a^b f(x)\,dx$$

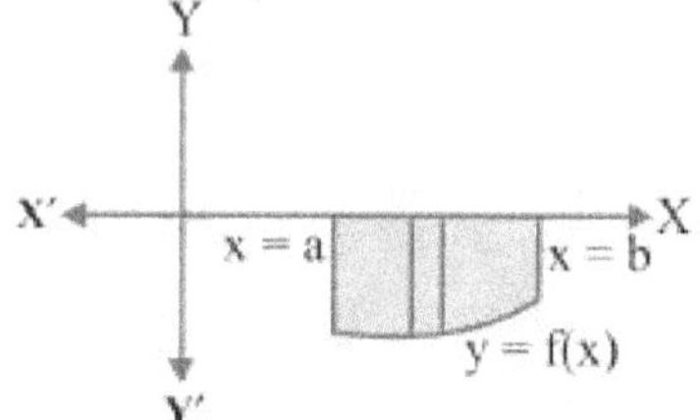

Remark :

If the position of the curve under consideration is below the x-axis. Then, area is negative. So, we take its absolute value, i.e.,

$$\text{Area } (A) = \left| \int_a^b f(x)\,dx \right|$$

Area under simple curves

APPLICATION OF INTEGRALS

1

i

ii

Area of the region bounded by a curve $x = f(y)$ and y-axis between two abscissae.

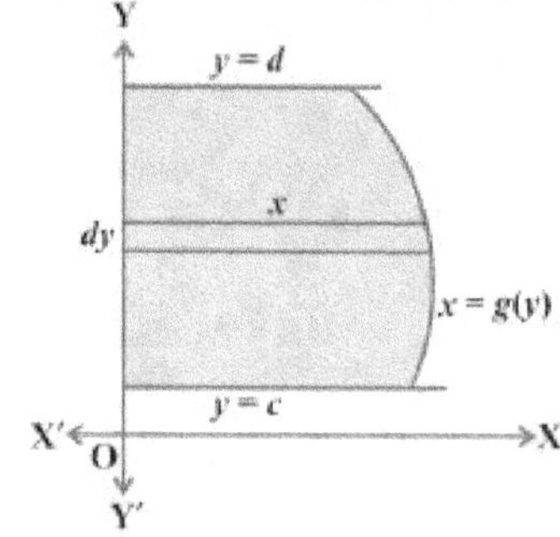

$$\text{Area, } A = \int_c^d x\,dy = \int_c^d g(y)\,dy$$

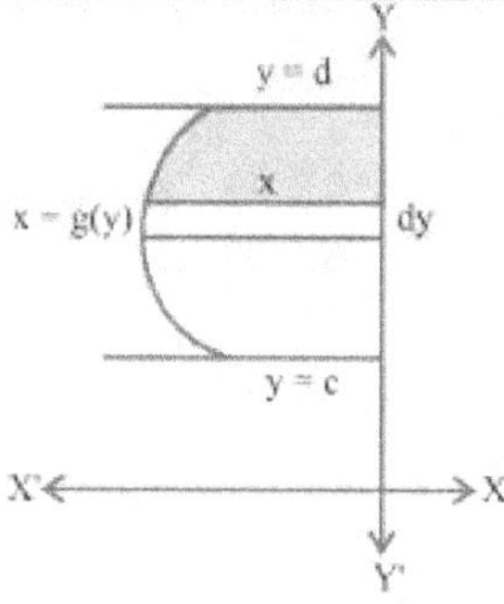

If the position of the curve under consideration is on the left side of y-axis. Then, area is negative. So, we take its absolute value, i.e.,

$$\text{Area } (A) = \left| \int_c^d g(y)\,dy \right|$$

Map-8

Case-I

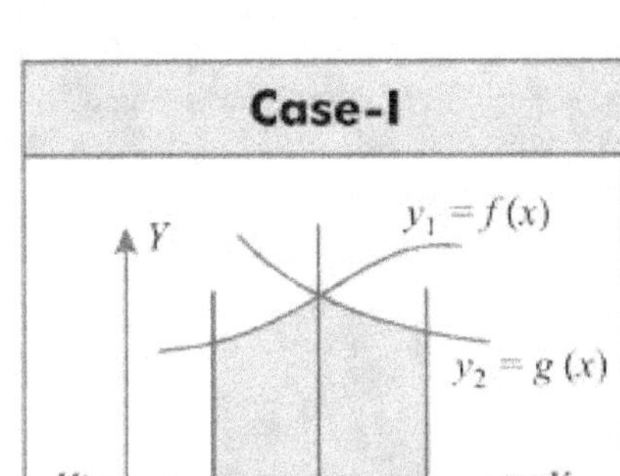

$$A = \int_{a}^{c} f(x)dx + \int_{c}^{b} g(x)dx$$

Case-II

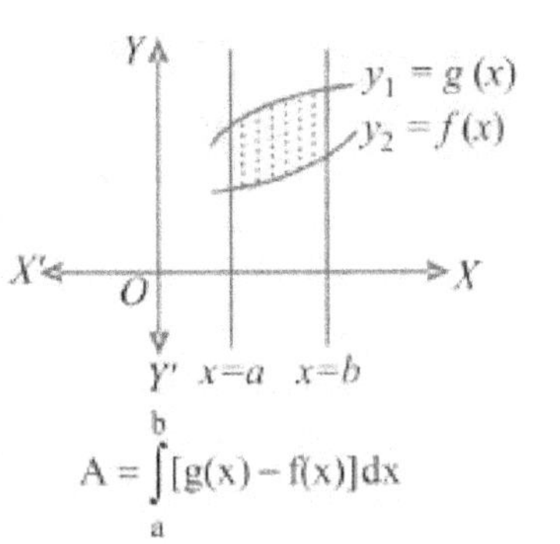

$$A = \int_{a}^{b} [g(x) - f(x)]dx$$

Case-III

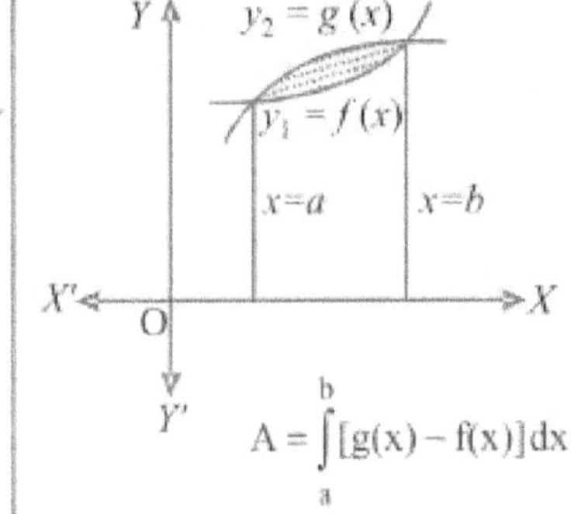

$$A = \int_{a}^{b} [g(x) - f(x)]dx$$

Area between different Curves

i **ii** **iii** **iv** **v**

2

Case-V

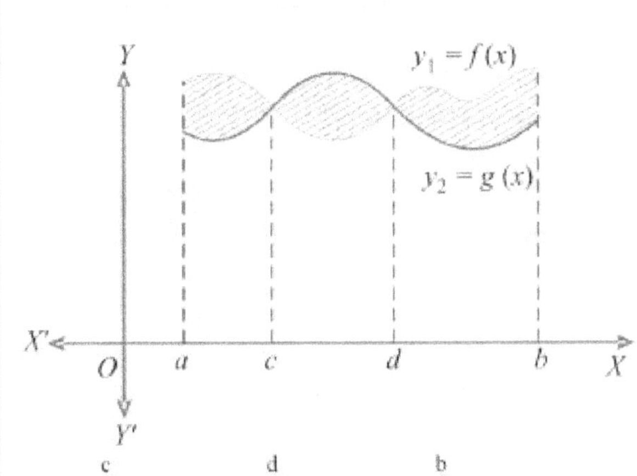

$$A = \int_{a}^{c} (y_1 - y_2)dx + \int_{c}^{d} (y_2 - y_1)dx + \int_{d}^{b} (y_1 - y_2)dx$$

Case-IV

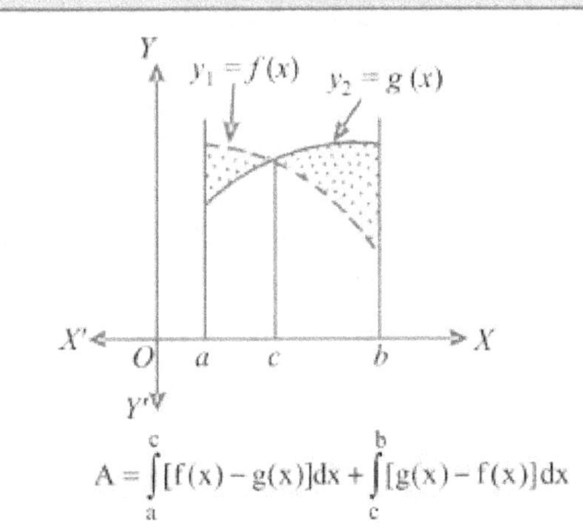

$$A = \int_{a}^{c} [f(x) - g(x)]dx + \int_{c}^{b} [g(x) - f(x)]dx$$

Mind

Order of Differential Equation

The order of a differential equation is the order of the highest derivative occuring in the differential equation.

For example

$\dfrac{d^2y}{dx^2} + y = 0$ is a second order differential equation.

$\left(\dfrac{d^3y}{dx^3}\right) + x^2\left(\dfrac{d^2y}{dx^2}\right)^3 = 0$ is a third order differential equation.

Differential Equation

An equation containing an independent variable, dependent variable & differential coefficients of dependent variable w.r.t. independent variable is called a differential equation.

For example,

(i) $\dfrac{dy}{dx} = \sin x$ (ii) $\dfrac{dy}{dx} + xy = \cot x$ (iii) $\dfrac{d^2y}{dx^2} - \dfrac{5dy}{dx} + 6y = x^2$

A differential equation involving derivatives of the dependent variable w.r.t only one independent variable is called an ordinary differential equation. Above equations are all ordinary differential equations.

Degree of Differential Equation

The degree of a differential equation is the highest degree of the highest derivative occuring in the differential equation when it is a polynomial of the differential coefficients i.e., differential coefficients free from radicals & fractions.

For example

Since, $\dfrac{d^3y}{dx^3} + x^2\left(\dfrac{d^2y}{dx^2}\right)^3 = 0$ as order = 3

$\therefore$ its degree = 1, as $\dfrac{d^3y}{dx^3}$ has power 1.

DIFFERENTIAL EQUATIONS

Solution of Differential Equations

Any relation between the dependent & independent variables (not involving the derivatives) which, when substituted in the differential equation reduces it to an identity is called a 'solution of the differential equation'.

General Solution : The solution which contains a number of independent arbitrary constants equal to the order of the equation is called general solution.

Particular Solution : Solutions obtained from the general solution by giving particular values to independent arbitrary constants are called particular solutions.

Formation of Differential Equation

Formation of a differential equation from a given equation representing a family of curves means finding a differential equation whose solution is the given equation.

The order of a differential equation representing a family of curves is same as the number of arbitrary constants present in the equation corresponding to the family of curves.

Map-9

Differential Equations with Variables Separable

If a first order-first degree equation can be expressed in such a manner that coefficient of dx is f(x) & coefficient of dy is g(y), then we say that variables are separable. A first order-first degree differential equation is of the form $\dfrac{dy}{dx} = F(x,y)$

Above equation can also be written as:

$\dfrac{dy}{dx} = h(y) \cdot g(x)$ [if F(x, y) can be expressed as product of g(x) & h(y)]

Separating the variables, we have $\dfrac{dy}{h(y)} = g(x) \cdot dx$

$\therefore$ Integrate both sides $\displaystyle\int \dfrac{dy}{h(y)} = \int g(x) \cdot dx$

which is the required solution.

6

7

Linear Differential Equations

A differential equation of the form $\dfrac{dy}{dx} + Py = Q$, where P & Q are constants or functions of x only, is known as a First Order Linear Differential Equation.

$\dfrac{dy}{dx} + y = \sin x, \quad \dfrac{dy}{dx} + \left(\dfrac{1}{x}\right)y = e^x$

are some examples of Linear differential equations.

Steps to Solve First Order Linear Differential Equation :

(i)   Write the given differential equation in the form $\dfrac{dy}{dx} + Py = Q$

(ii) Find the Integrating Factor $(I.F) = e^{\int P dx}$

(iii) Write the solution of the given differential equation as

$$y(I.F) = \int (Q \times I.F)dx + c$$

Note that if the first order differential equation is in the form

$\dfrac{dx}{dy} + P'x = Q'$ where P' & Q' are constants or functions of y only.

Then $I.F = e^{\int P dy}$ & the solution of the differential equation is given by

$x(I.F) = \int (Q' \times I.F)dy + c$

Homogeneous Differential Equations

An equation in x & y is said to be homogeneous

if it can be put in the form $\dfrac{dy}{dx} = \dfrac{f(x,y)}{g(x,y)}$ where

f(x, y) & g(x, y) are homogeneous functions of the same degree in x & y.

Here, $(x - y)\dfrac{dy}{dx} = x + 2y$

or $\dfrac{dy}{dx} = \dfrac{x + 2y}{x - y}$ is an example of homogeneous differential equation.

To solve the homogeneous differential equation $\dfrac{dy}{dx} = \dfrac{f(x,y)}{g(x,y)}$,

Substitute $y = vx$ & so $\dfrac{dy}{dx} = v + x\dfrac{dv}{dx}$

Thus $v + \dfrac{x dv}{dx} = F(v) \Rightarrow \dfrac{dx}{x} = \dfrac{dv}{F(v) - v}$

Therefore, solution is $\displaystyle\int \dfrac{dx}{x} = \int \dfrac{dv}{F(v) - v} + c$

Mind

Position Vector

Let O be the origin & P be a point in space having coordinates (x, y, z) with respect to the origin O. Then the vector $\overrightarrow{OP}$ is called the position vector of the point P with respect to O.

$$|\overrightarrow{OP}| = \sqrt{x^2 + y^2 + z^2}$$

The angles made by $\overrightarrow{OP}$ with positive direction of x, y, & z-axes (say α, β & γ respectively) are called its direction angles, and the cosine value of these angles i.e., $\cos\alpha$, $\cos\beta$ & $\cos\gamma$ are called direction cosines of $\overrightarrow{OP}$, denoted by l, m & n respectively.

Vector Quantity

A quantity which has magnitude & also a direction in space is called a vector quantity.

The direct line segment AB is a vector denoted as $\overrightarrow{AB}$ or $\vec{a}$. The point A from where the vector $\overrightarrow{AB}$ starts is called its initial point, & the point B where it ends is called its terminal point. The distance between these two points is called the magnitude of the vector denoted as $|\overrightarrow{AB}|$ or $|\vec{a}|$ or a.

VECTOR ALGEBRA

Types of Vectors

1. **Zero Vector :** A vector whose initial and terminal points coincide, is called a zero vector (or null vector) denoted as $\vec{O}$. It has zero magnitude.
2. **Unit Vector :** A vector whose magnitude is unity (i.e., 1 unit) is called unit vector. The unit vector in the direction of is denoted as .
3. **Coinitial Vectors :** Two or more vectors having the same initial point are called coinitial vectors.
4. **Collinear Vectors :** Two or more vectors are called collinear, if they are parallel to the same line, irrespective of their magnitude.
5. **Equal Vectors :** Two vectors are said to be equal, if they have same magnitude & direction regardless of the position of their initial points.
6. **Negative of a vector :** A vector whose magnitude is the same as that of the given vector, but the direction is opposite to that of it, is called negative of the given vector.

Addition of Vectors

1. Triangle Law of Vector Addition

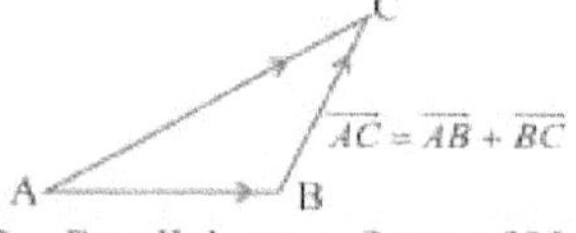

$$\overrightarrow{AC} = \overrightarrow{AB} + \overrightarrow{BC}$$

2. Parallelogram Law of Vector Addition

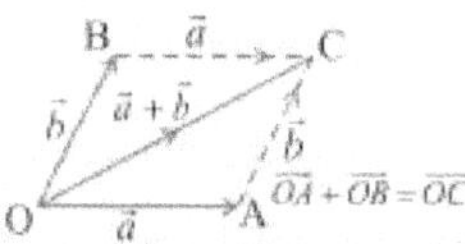

$$\overrightarrow{OA} + \overrightarrow{OB} = \overrightarrow{OC}$$

Properties of Vector Addition :

(i) For any two vectors $\vec{a}$ & $\vec{b}$,
$$\vec{a} + \vec{b} = \vec{b} + \vec{a}$$
(commutative property)

(ii) For any three vectors $\vec{a}, \vec{b}, \& \vec{c}$,
$$(\vec{a} + \vec{b}) + \vec{c} = \vec{a} + (\vec{b} + \vec{c})$$
(Associative property)

Multiplication of a Vector by a Scalar

Multiplication of any vector $\vec{a}$ by a scalar λ is denoted as $\lambda\vec{a}$ & its magnitude is given as:
$$|\lambda\vec{a}| = |\lambda| \, |\vec{a}|.$$

Unit Vector in the Direction of a given vector : A unit vector in the direction of given vector ($\vec{a}$) is given as: $\hat{a} = \dfrac{1}{|\vec{a}|}\vec{a}$.

Component of Vector

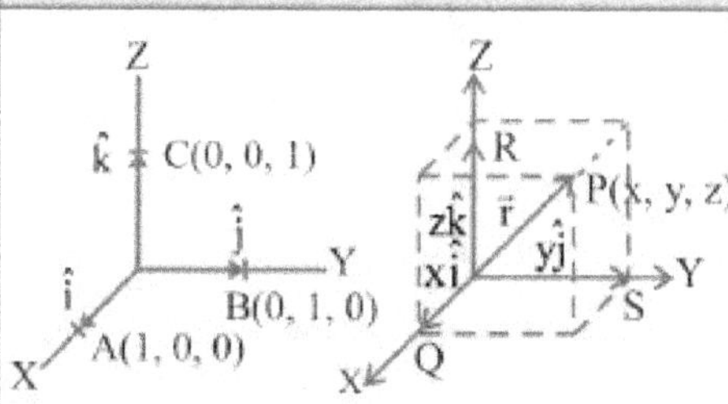

$\overrightarrow{OA}$, $\overrightarrow{OB}$ & $\overrightarrow{OC}$ are unit vectors along x, y & z axes respectively, denoted by $\hat{i}, \hat{j}$ & $\hat{k}$ respectively

Position Vector of P with reference to O is given by:
$$\overrightarrow{OP} (\text{or } \vec{r}) = x\hat{i} + y\hat{j} + z\hat{k}.$$

This form of any vector is called its component form.
Also, $|\overrightarrow{OP}| = |\vec{r}| = \sqrt{x^2 + y^2 + z^2}$
Consider two vectors $\vec{a} = a_1\hat{i} + a_2\hat{j} + a_3\hat{k}$ & $\vec{b} = b_1\hat{i} + b_2\hat{j} + b_3\hat{k}$, then;

(i) $\vec{a} \pm \vec{b} = (a_1 \pm b_1)\hat{i} + (a_2 \pm b_2)\hat{j} + (a_3 \pm b_3)\hat{k}$.

(ii) Vector $\vec{a}$ & $\vec{b}$ are equal if & only if : $a_1 = b_1$, $a_2 = b_2$ & $a_3 = b_3$.

(iii) $\lambda\vec{a} = \lambda a_1\hat{i} + \lambda a_2\hat{j} + \lambda a_3\hat{k}$.

Map-10

Vector Joining Two Points

Let $A(x_1, y_1, z_1)$ & $B(x_2, y_2, z_2)$ be any two points in the space, then $\overrightarrow{OA} = x_1\hat{i} + y_1\hat{j} + z_1\hat{k}$ & $\overrightarrow{OB} = x_2\hat{i} + y_2\hat{j} + z_2\hat{k}$

$\therefore \overrightarrow{AB} = \overrightarrow{OB} - \overrightarrow{OA} = (x_2 - x_1)\hat{i} + (y_2 - y_1)\hat{j} + (z_2 - z_1)\hat{k}$

$\left|\overrightarrow{AB}\right| = \sqrt{(x_2 - x_1)^2 + (y_2 - y_1)^2 + (z_2 - z_1)^2}$

Section Formulae

The position vector of a point R dividing a line segment joining the points P & Q whose position vectors are $\vec{a}$ & $\vec{b}$ respectively, in the ratio $m : n$

(i) internally, is given by $\dfrac{m\vec{b} + n\vec{a}}{m + n}$

(ii) externally, is given by $\dfrac{m\vec{b} - n\vec{a}}{m - n}$

The position vector of the middle point of PQ is given by $\dfrac{1}{2}\left(\vec{a} + \vec{b}\right)$

Scalar (or dot) Product of Two Vectors

Let $\vec{a}$ & $\vec{b}$ be the two non-zero vectors inclined at an angle θ, then scalar product is defined as:

$\vec{a} \cdot \vec{b} = |\vec{a}|\,|\vec{b}|\cos\theta,\ 0 \leq \theta \leq \pi$

Observations:

- $\vec{a} \cdot \vec{b}$ is a real number
- $\vec{a} \cdot \vec{b} = 0 \Rightarrow \vec{a} \perp \vec{b}$
- $\hat{i} \cdot \hat{i} = \hat{j} \cdot \hat{j} = \hat{k} \cdot \hat{k} = 1$ & $\hat{i} \cdot \hat{j} = \hat{j} \cdot \hat{k} = \hat{k} \cdot \hat{i} = 0$
- $\cos\theta = \dfrac{\vec{a} \cdot \vec{b}}{|\vec{a}||\vec{b}|}$ or $\theta = \cos^{-1}\left(\dfrac{\vec{a} \cdot \vec{b}}{|\vec{a}||\vec{b}|}\right)$
- The scalar product is commutative i.e., $\vec{a} \cdot \vec{b} = \vec{b} \cdot \vec{a}$

Projection of Vector Along a Directed Line

Projection of a vector $\vec{a}$ on other vector $\vec{b}$, is given by

$\vec{a} \cdot \hat{b} = \vec{a} \cdot \left(\dfrac{\vec{b}}{|\vec{b}|}\right) = \dfrac{(\vec{a} \cdot \vec{b})}{|\vec{b}|}.$

Vector (or Cross) Product of Two Vectors

Let $\vec{a}$ & $\vec{b}$ be two non-zero vectors inclined at an angle θ. Then, vector product is defined as: $\vec{a} \times \vec{b} = |\vec{a}|\,|\vec{b}|\sin\theta\,\hat{n}$ where, $\hat{n}$ is a unit vector perpendicular to both vectors $\vec{a}$ & $\vec{b}$, such that $\vec{a}, \vec{b}$ & $\hat{n}$ form a right handed system.

Observations:

- $\vec{a} \times \vec{b}$ is a vector
- $\vec{a} \times \vec{b} = \vec{0} \Rightarrow \vec{a} \parallel \vec{b}$
- $\hat{i} \times \hat{i} = \hat{j} \times \hat{j} = \hat{k} \times \hat{k} = \vec{0}$
- $\hat{i} \times \hat{j} = \hat{k}, \hat{j} \times \hat{k} = \hat{i}, \hat{k} \times \hat{i} = \hat{j}$
- $\sin\theta = \dfrac{|\vec{a} \times \vec{b}|}{|\vec{a}||\vec{b}|}$

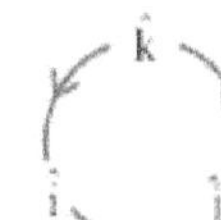

- Vector product is not commutative.
  $\vec{a} \times \vec{b} = -\vec{b} \times \vec{a}$
  $\hat{j} \times \hat{i} = -\hat{k}, \hat{k} \times \hat{j} = -\hat{i}$ & $\hat{i} \times \hat{k} = -\hat{j}$
- If $\vec{a}$ & $\vec{b}$ represent the adjacent sides of a triangle, then its area is given by $\dfrac{1}{2}\left|\vec{a} \times \vec{b}\right|$
- If $\vec{a}$ & $\vec{b}$ represent the adjacent sides of a parallelogram then its area is given by $\left|\vec{a} \times \vec{b}\right|$

Cross Product of Vectors in Component Form

Let $\vec{a} = a_1\hat{i} + a_2\hat{j} + a_3\hat{k}$ & $\vec{b} = b_1\hat{i} + b_2\hat{j} + b_3\hat{k}$, Then

$$\vec{a} \times \vec{b} = \begin{vmatrix} \hat{i} & \hat{j} & \hat{k} \\ a_1 & a_2 & a_3 \\ b_1 & b_2 & b_3 \end{vmatrix}$$

Properties Regarding Scalar and Vector Product

1. **Scalar Product Property:**
   (i) For three vectors $\vec{a}, \vec{b}$ & $\vec{c}$,
   $\vec{a} \cdot (\vec{b} + \vec{c}) = \vec{a} \cdot \vec{b} + \vec{a} \cdot \vec{c}$ (distributive property)
   (ii) For two vector $\vec{a}$ & $\vec{b}$ & any scalar λ,
   $(\lambda\vec{a}) \cdot \vec{b} = \lambda(\vec{a} \cdot \vec{b}) = \vec{a} \cdot (\lambda\vec{b})$

2. **Vector Product Property:**
   (i) For any three vectors $\vec{a}, \vec{b}$ & $\vec{c}$,
   $\vec{a} \times (\vec{b} + \vec{c}) = (\vec{a} \times \vec{b}) + (\vec{a} \times \vec{c})$ (distribution property)
   (ii) For any two vector $\vec{a}$ & $\vec{b}$ and any scalar λ,
   $\lambda(\vec{a} \times \vec{b}) = (\lambda\vec{a}) \times \vec{b} = \vec{a} \times (\lambda\vec{b}).$

Mind

THREE DIMENSIONAL GEOMETRY

② Direction Ratios of a Line (DR's)

Any three numbers a, b and c proportional to the direction cosines l, m and n, respectively are called direction ratios of the line.

- The direction ratios of a line passing through two points $P(x_1, y_1, z_1)$ and $Q(x_2, y_2, z_2)$ are $(x_2 - x_1)$, $(y_2 - y_1)$, $(z_2 - z_1)$

- $\dfrac{l}{a} = \dfrac{m}{b} = \dfrac{n}{c}$

- $l = \pm \dfrac{a}{\sqrt{a^2 + b^2 + c^2}}$, $m = \pm \dfrac{b}{\sqrt{a^2 + b^2 + c^2}}$ and $n = \pm \dfrac{c}{\sqrt{a^2 + b^2 + c^2}}$

① Direction Cosines of a Line (DC's)

The direction cosines are generally denoted by l, m, n.

Hence, $l = \cos \alpha$, $m = \cos \beta$, $n = \cos \gamma$

Note that $l^2 + m^2 + n^2 = 1$

③ Equation of a Line

1. **Equation of a line through a given point with position vector $\vec{a}$ and parallel to a given vector $\vec{b}$:**
   In vector form, $\vec{r} = \vec{a} + \lambda \vec{b}$
   In cartesian form,
   $$\dfrac{x - x_1}{a} = \dfrac{y - y_1}{b} = \dfrac{z - z_1}{c}$$
   where, $\vec{r} = x\hat{i} + y\hat{j} + z\hat{k}$, $\vec{a} = x_1\hat{i} + y_1\hat{j} + z_1\hat{k}$, $\vec{b} = a\hat{i} + b\hat{j} + c\hat{k}$
   Here, a, b, c are also the direction ratios of the line.

2. **Equation of a line passing through two given points with position vectors $\vec{a}$ and $\vec{b}$:**
   In vector form, $\vec{r} = \vec{a} + \lambda(\vec{b} - \vec{a})$
   In cartesian form,
   $$\dfrac{x - x_1}{x_2 - x_1} = \dfrac{y - y_1}{y_2 - y_1} = \dfrac{z - z_1}{z_2 - z_1}$$
   where, $\vec{r} = x\hat{i} + y\hat{j} + z\hat{k}$, $\vec{a} = x_1\hat{i} + y_1\hat{j} + z_1\hat{k}$ & $\vec{b} = x_2\hat{i} + y_2\hat{j} + z_2\hat{k}$

④ Angle Between Two Lines

In vector form,
The angle between two lines
$\vec{r} = \vec{a}_1 + \lambda\vec{b}_1$ & $\vec{r} = \vec{a}_2 + \mu\vec{b}_2$ is given as:

$$\cos \theta = \left| \dfrac{\vec{b}_1 \cdot \vec{b}_2}{|\vec{b}_1||\vec{b}_2|} \right|$$

In cartesian form,
The angle between two lines :
$$\dfrac{x - x_1}{a_1} = \dfrac{y - y_1}{b_1} = \dfrac{z - z_1}{c_1}$$
and $\dfrac{x - x_2}{a_2} = \dfrac{y - y_2}{b_2} = \dfrac{z - z_2}{c_2}$ is :

$$\cos \theta = \left| \dfrac{a_1 a_2 + b_1 b_2 + c_1 c_2}{\sqrt{a_1^2 + b_1^2 + c_1^2}\, \sqrt{a_2^2 + b_2^2 + c_2^2}} \right|$$

$\cos \theta = |l_1 l_2 + m_1 m_2 + n_1 n_2|$

- If two lines are perpendicular, then $\vec{b}_1 \cdot \vec{b}_2 = 0$ or $a_1 a_2 + b_1 b_2 + c_1 c_2 = 0$
- If two lines are parallel, then $\vec{b}_1 = \lambda \vec{b}_2$
  or $\dfrac{a_1}{a_2} = \dfrac{b_1}{b_2} = \dfrac{c_1}{c_2}$

⑤ Shortest Distance Between Two Lines

1. **Distance Between Parallel Lines**
   The shortest distance between parallel lines
   $L_1 : \vec{r} = \vec{a}_1 + \lambda\vec{b}$ and $L_2 : \vec{r} = \vec{a}_2 + \mu\vec{b}$ is
   $$d = \left| \dfrac{\vec{b} \times (\vec{a}_2 - \vec{a}_1)}{|\vec{b}|} \right|$$

2. **Distance Between Two Skew Lines**
   In vector form,
   The distance between two skew lines
   $\vec{r} = \vec{a}_1 + \lambda\vec{b}_1$ & $\vec{r} = \vec{a}_2 + \mu\vec{b}_2$ is given as:
   $$d = \left| \dfrac{(\vec{b}_1 \times \vec{b}_2) \cdot (\vec{a}_2 - \vec{a}_1)}{|\vec{b}_1 \times \vec{b}_2|} \right|$$

   In cartesian form,
   The distance between two skew lines :
   $$\dfrac{x - x_1}{a_1} = \dfrac{y - y_1}{b_1} = \dfrac{z - z_1}{c_1}$$
   and $\dfrac{x - x_2}{a_2} = \dfrac{y - y_2}{b_2} = \dfrac{z - z_2}{c_2}$ is :

   $$d = \dfrac{\begin{vmatrix} x_2 - x_1 & y_2 - y_1 & z_2 - z_1 \\ a_1 & b_1 & c_1 \\ a_2 & b_2 & c_2 \end{vmatrix}}{\sqrt{(b_1 c_2 - b_2 c_1)^2 + (c_1 a_2 - c_2 a_1)^2 + (a_1 b_2 - a_2 b_1)^2}}$$

⑥ Equation of a Plane in Normal Form

Vector Form
$$\vec{r} \cdot \hat{n} = d$$
Here $\vec{r} = x\hat{i} + y\hat{j} + z\hat{k}$
$\hat{n}$ is the unit vector along the normal from origin to the plane.
d is perpendicular distance of the plane from the origin.

Cartesian Form
$lx + my + nz = d$
where l, m, n are the direction cosines of $\hat{n}$ (unit vector along the normal from origin to the plane).

Map-11

(7) Equation of a Plane Perpendicular to a Given Vector and Passing Through a Given Point

Vector Form

Let a plane pass through a point with position vector $\vec{a}$ and perpendicular to the vector $\vec{N}$. Then its equation is given as: $(\vec{r} - \vec{a}) \cdot \vec{N} = 0$

Cartesian Form

Let a plane pass through a point (x_1, y_1, z_1) & the direction ratio of the vector perpendicular to the plane be A, B, C. Then its equation is given as:
$$A(x - x_1) + B(y - y_1) + C(z - z_1) = 0$$

(8) Equation of a Plane Passing Through Three Non-Collinear Points

Vector Form

$$\left[\vec{r}\,\vec{b}\,\vec{c}\right] + \left[\vec{r}\,\vec{a}\,\vec{b}\right] + \left[\vec{r}\,\vec{c}\,\vec{a}\right] = \left[\vec{a}\,\vec{b}\,\vec{c}\right]$$

or $(\vec{r} - \vec{a}) \cdot [(\vec{b} - \vec{a}) \times (\vec{c} - \vec{a})] = 0$

where, $\vec{a}, \vec{b}, \vec{c}$ are the position vector of three given non-collinear points through which the plane passes.

Cartesian Form

The equation of plane passing through three non-collinear points Y with coordinates (x_1, y_1, z_1), (x_2, y_2, z_2) & (x_3, y_3, z_3) is given as:

$$\begin{vmatrix} x - x_1 & y - y_1 & z - z_1 \\ x_2 - x_1 & y_2 - y_1 & z_2 - z_1 \\ x_3 - x_1 & y_3 - y_1 & z_3 - z_1 \end{vmatrix} = 0$$

(9) Intercept Form of the Equation of a Plane

$$\frac{x}{a} + \frac{y}{b} + \frac{z}{c} = 1$$

Where a, b, c are the intercepts made by the plane on x, y & z axes respectively.

(10) Plane Passing Through the Intersection of Two Given Planes

Vector Form

Equation of plane passing through the point of intersection of two planes $\vec{r} \cdot \vec{n}_1 = d_1$ and $\vec{r} \cdot \vec{n}_2 = d_2$ is given as:
$$\vec{r} \cdot (\vec{n}_1 + \lambda \vec{n}_2) = d_1 + \lambda d_2$$

Cartesian Form

Let
$$\vec{n}_1 = A_1\hat{i} + B_1\hat{j} + C_1\hat{k}$$
$$\vec{n}_2 = A_2\hat{i} + B_2\hat{j} + C_2\hat{k}$$
and $\vec{r} = x\hat{i} + y\hat{j} + z\hat{k}$,

therefore its cartesian equation is:
$$(A_1x + B_1y + C_1z - d_1) + \lambda(A_2x + B_2y + C_2z - d_2) = 0$$

(11) Coplanarity of Two Lines

Vector Form

Two lines $\vec{r} = \vec{a}_1 + \lambda \vec{b}_1$ and $\vec{r} = \vec{a}_2 + \mu \vec{b}_2$

are coplanar, if $(\vec{a}_2 - \vec{a}_1) \cdot (\vec{b}_1 \times \vec{b}_2) = 0$

Cartesian Form

Two lines $\dfrac{x - x_1}{a_1} = \dfrac{y - y_1}{b_1} = \dfrac{z - z_1}{c_1}$

and $\dfrac{x - x_2}{a_2} = \dfrac{y - y_2}{b_2} = \dfrac{z - z_2}{c_2}$

are coplanar, if $\begin{vmatrix} x_2 - x_1 & y_2 - y_1 & z_2 - z_1 \\ a_1 & b_1 & c_1 \\ a_2 & b_2 & c_2 \end{vmatrix} = 0$

(14) Angle Between a Line and a Plane

Vector Form

Angle between a line $\vec{r} = \vec{a} + \lambda \vec{b}$ and a plane $\vec{r} \cdot \vec{n} = d$ is
$$\cos\theta = \left|\frac{\vec{b} \cdot \vec{n}}{|\vec{b}||\vec{n}|}\right|$$

Cartesian Form

Angle between a line $\dfrac{x - x_1}{a_1} = \dfrac{y - y_1}{b_1} = \dfrac{z - z_1}{c_1}$ and a plane $a_2x + b_2y + c_2z = d$ is given as:
$$\cos\theta = \left|\frac{a_1a_2 + b_1b_2 + c_1c_2}{\sqrt{a_1^2 + b_1^2 + c_1^2}\,\sqrt{a_2^2 + b_2^2 + c_2^2}}\right|$$

- If line is perpendicular to the plane, then $\vec{n} = \lambda\vec{b}$ or $\dfrac{a_1}{a_2} = \dfrac{b_1}{b_2} = \dfrac{c_1}{c_2}$
- If line is parallel to the plane, then $\vec{n} \cdot \vec{b} = 0$ or $a_1a_2 + b_1b_2 + c_1c_2 = 0$

(13) Distance of a Point from a Plane

Vector Form

Distance of a point with position vector $\vec{a}$ from a plane $\vec{r} \cdot \vec{n} = d$ is given as:
$$\frac{|\vec{a} \cdot \vec{n} - d|}{|\vec{n}|}$$

Cartesian Form

Distance of a point (x_1, y_1, z_1) from a plane : $ax + by + cz = d$ is given as :
$$\frac{|ax_1 + by_1 + cz_1 - d|}{\sqrt{a^2 + b^2 + c^2}}$$

(12) Angle Between Two Planes

Vector Form : The angle between two planes
$$\vec{r} \cdot \vec{n} = d_1 \ \& \ \vec{r} \cdot \vec{n} = d_2 \text{ is given as:}$$

$$\cos\theta = \left|\frac{\vec{n}_1 \cdot \vec{n}_2}{|\vec{n}_1||\vec{n}_2|}\right|$$

Cartesian Form The angle between two planes $a_1x + b_1y + c_1z + d_1 = 0$ and $a_2x + b_2y + c_2z + d_2 = 0$ is given as
$$\cos\theta = \left|\frac{a_1a_2 + b_1b_2 + c_1c_2}{\sqrt{a_1^2 + b_1^2 + c_1^2}\,\sqrt{a_2^2 + b_2^2 + c_2^2}}\right|$$

- If two planes are perpendicular, then $\vec{n}_1 \cdot \vec{n}_2 = 0$ or $a_1a_2 + b_1b_2 + c_1c_2 = 0$
- If two planes are parallel, then $\vec{n}_1 = \lambda\vec{n}_2$ or $\dfrac{a_1}{a_2} = \dfrac{b_1}{b_2} = \dfrac{c_1}{c_2}$

Mathematical form of Linear Programming Problems

The general mathematical form of a linear programming problem may be written as follow.

Objective Function : $Z = C_1 x + C_2 y$

Subject to constraints are:

$a_1 x + b_1 y \le d_1$

$a_2 x + b_2 y \le d_2$ etc

and non-negative restrictions are $x \ge 0, y \ge 0$

(1) **Objective Function :** A linear function $Z = ax + by$, where a & b are constants, which has to be maximized or minimized according to a set of given conditions, is called a linear objective function.

(2) **Decision Variables :** In the objective function $Z = ax + by$, the variables x, y are said to be decision variables.

(3) **Constraints :** The restrictions in the form of inequalities on the variables of a linear programming problem are called constraints. The condition $x \ge 0, y \ge 0$ are known as non-negative restrictions.

In the constraints given in the general form of a LPP there may be anyone of the 3 signs $\le, =, \ge$.

Some Important Terms Related to LPP

1. **Feasible Region :** The common region determined by all the constraints including non-negative constraints $x, y \ge 0$ of linear programming problem is known as feasible region (or solution region). If we shade the region according to the given constraints, then the shaded area is the feasible region which is the common area of the regions drawn under the given constraints.

2. **Feasible Solution :** Each point within & on the boundary of the feasible region represents feasible solution of constraints. Note that in the feasible region there are infinitely many points which satisfy the given condition.

3. **Optimal Solution :** Any point in the feasible region that gives the optimal value (maximum or minimum) of the objective function is called an optimal solution.

Linear Programming Problems

A linear programming problem is concerned with finding the minimum or maximum value of a linear function Z (called objective function) of several variables (say x & y), subject to certain conditions that the variables are non-negative & satisfy a set of linear inequalities (called linear constraints).

LINEAR PROGRAMMING

Mind

Theorems for Solving Linear Programming Problems

Theorem 1

Let R be the feasible region (convex polygon) for a linear programming problem and let $Z = ax + by$ be the objective function. When Z has an optimal value (maximum or minimum), where the variables x and y are subject to constraints described by linear inequalities, the optimal value must occur at a corner point of the feasible region.

Theorem 2

Let R be the feasible region for a linear programming problem, and let $Z = ax + by$ be the objective function. If R is bounded then the objective function Z has both maximum and minimum value on R and each of these occurs at a corner point of R.

Map-12

5

Corner Point Method of Solving LPP

Steps Involved :
(1) Find the feasible region of the LPP & determine its corner points (vertices) either by inspection or by solving the two equations of the lines intersecting at that point.
(2) Evaluate the objective function $Z = ax + by$ at each corner point. Let M & m, respectively be the largest & smallest values of these points.
(3) (i) When the feasible region is bounded, M & m are the maximum & minimum values of Z.
    (ii) In case the feasible region is unbounded, we have:
    (a) M is the maximum value of Z, if the open half plane determined by $ax + by > M$ has no point in common with the feasible region. Otherwise, Z has no maximum value.
    (b) Similarly, m is the minimum value of Z, if the open half plane determined by $ax + by < m$ has no point in common with the feasible region. Otherwise, Z has no minimum value.

6

Types of Linear Programming Problems

(i) Manufacturing Problems
In such problem, we determine the number of units of different products which should be produced and sold by a firm when each product requires a fixed man power, machine hours, labour hour per unit of product, ware house space per unit of the output etc., in order to make maximum profit.

(ii) Diet Problems
We determine the amount of different types of constituents or nutrients which should be included in a diet so as to minimise the cost of the desired diet such that it contains a certain minimum amount of each constituent / nutrients.

(iii) Transportation Problems
In these problems, we determine a transportation schedule in order to find the cheapest way of transporting a product from plants/factories situated at different locations to different markets.

7

Mathematical Formulation of Linear Programming Problems

The following Algorithm will be helpful in the mathematical Formation of L.P.P.
Algorithm
Step-1 In every LPP certain decision are to be made. These decision are represented by decision variables. These decision variable are those quantities whose values are to be determined. Identify the variables and denote them by $x_1, x_2, x_3...$
Step-2 Identify the objective function and express it as a linear function of the variables introduced in step 1.
Step-3 In a L.P.P the objective function may be in the form of maximizing profits or minimizing costs, so after expressing the objective function as a linear function of the decision variables, we must find the type of optimization i.e. maximization or minimization identify the type of objective function.
Step-4 Identify the set of constraints, stated in terms of decision variables and express them as linear inequations or equations as the case may be.

**8**

Solution of the Linear Programming Problems

(i) First of all formulate the given problem in terms of mathematical constraints and an objective function.
(ii) The constraints would be inequations which shall be plotted and relevant area shall be shaded and check that feasible region is bounded or unbounded.
(iii) The corner points of common shaded area shall be identified and the coordinates corresponding to these points shall be substituted in the objective function.
(iv) The coordinates of one corner point which maximize or minimize the objective function shall be optimal solution of the given problem.
Note that if feasible region is unbounded, then a maximum or a minimum value of the objective function may not exist. However, if it exists, it must occur at a corner point of feasible region.

Conditional Probability

If E and F are two events associated with the sample space of a random experiment, the conditional probability of the event E given that F has occured is given as:

$$P(E/F) = \frac{P(E \cap F)}{P(F)} = \frac{n(E \cap F)}{n(F)}, P(F) \neq 0$$

Properties of Conditional Probability

1. Let E & F be events of sample space S of an experiment, then we have
   $P(S/F) = P(F/F) = 1$.
2. If A and B are any two events of a sample space S & F is an event of S such that $P(F) \neq 0$, then
   $P((A \cup B)/F) = P(A/F) + P(B/F) - P((A \cap B)/F)$
   In particular if A and B are disjoint events, then
   $P((A \cup B)/F) = P(A/F) + P(B/F)$
3. $P(E'/F) = 1 - P(E/F)$

Multiplication Theorem on Probability

For two events E & F associated with a sample space S, we have
$$P(E \cap F) = P(E)\,P(F/E)$$
$$= P(F)\,P(E/F)$$
$$\text{provided } P(E) \neq 0 \ \& \ P(F) \neq 0$$
The above result is known as Multiplication Rule of Probability.

Independent Events

Two or more events are said to be independent if occurrence or non-occurrence of any of them does not affect the probability of occurrence or non-occurrence of other events. For example, when two cards are drawn from a pack of 52 playing cards with replacement (the first card drawn is put back in the pack & then the second card is drawn).

(i) If E & F are independent, then
$$P(E \cap F) = P(E)\,P(F)$$
$$P(E/F) = P(E), P(F) \neq 0$$
$$P(F/E) = P(F), P(E) \neq 0$$

(ii) Three events A, B & C are said to be mutually independent, if
$$P(A \cap B) = P(A)\,P(B)$$
$$P(A \cap C) = P(A)\,P(C)$$
$$P(B \cap C) = P(B)\,P(C)$$
$$\& \ P(A \cap B \cap C) = P(A)\,P(B)\,P(C)$$

If at least one of the above is not true for three given events, we say that the events are not independent.

PROBABILITY

Baye's Theorem

- **Partition of a Sample Space**
  A set of events $E_1, E_2, \ldots, E_n$ is said to represent a partition of the sample space S if
  (a) $E_i \cap E_j = \phi, i \neq j, i, j = 1, 2, 3, \ldots n$
  (b) $E_1 \cup E_2 \cup \ldots \cup E_n = S$
  (c) $P(E_i) > 0$ for all $i = 1, 2, \ldots n$

- **Theorem of Total Probability**
  Let $\{E_1, E_2, \ldots, E_n\}$ be a partition of the sample space S, and suppose that each of the events $E_1, E_2, \ldots, E_n$ has nonzero probability of occurence. Let A be any event associated with S, then
  $$P(A) = \sum_{j=1}^{n} P(E_j)P(A/E_j)$$

- **Baye's Theorem:** If $E_1, E_2, \ldots, E_n$ are non-empty events which constitute a partition of sample space S & A is any event of non-zero probability.
  $$P(E_i/A) = \frac{P(E_i)P(A/E_i)}{\sum\limits_{j=1}^{n} P(E_j)P(A/E_j)} \qquad \text{for any } i = 1, 2, 3, \ldots, n$$

Map-13

Random Variable & its Probability Distributions

A random variable is a real valued function whose domain is the sample space of a random experiment.

The probability distribution of a random variable X is the system of numbers.

$$X \quad : \quad x_1 \quad x_2 \quad \dots \quad x_n$$
$$P(X): \quad p_1 \quad p_2 \quad \dots \quad p_n$$

where, $p_i > 0$, $\displaystyle\sum_{i=1}^{n} p_i = 1, i = 1, 2, \dots, n$

The real numbers $x_1, x_2, \dots, x_n$ are the possible values of the random variable X and p_i $(i = 1, 2, \dots, n)$ is the probability of the random variable X taking the value x_i i.e., $P(X = x_i) = p_i$

Mean of a Random Variable

The mean (μ) of a random variable X is also called the expectation of X, denoted by E(X)

$$E(X) = \mu = \sum_{i=1}^{n} x_i p_i$$

Here $x_1, x_2, \dots, x_n$ are possible values of random variable X, occuring with probabilities $p_1, p_2, \dots, p_n$ respectively.

Variance of a Random Variable

Let X be a random variable whose possible values $x_1, x_2, \dots, x_n$ occur with probabilities $p(x_1), p(x_2), \dots, p(x_n)$ respectively. Also let $\mu = E(X)$ be the mean of X, then the variance of X is given as:

$$\text{Var}(X) \text{ or } \sigma_x^2 = \sum_{i=1}^{n} (x_i - \mu)^2 p(x_i) = E(X - \mu)^2 = E(X^2) - [E(X)]^2$$

The non-negative number, $\sigma_x = \sqrt{\text{Var}(X)}$ is called the Standard Deviation of random variable X.

Bernoulli Trials & Binomial Distribution

Bernoulli Trials :

Trials of a random experiment are called Bernoulli trials, if they satisfy the following conditions:

(i)   There should be a finite number of trials.

(ii) The trials should be independent.

(iii) Each trial has exactly two outcomes: success or failure.

(iv) The probability of success remains same in each trial.

Binomial Distribution :

The probability distribution of number of successes in an experiment consisting of n Bernoulli trials may be obtained by the binomial expansion $(q + p)^n$, where p is probability of success in each trial and $p + q = 1$. Hence, this distribution (also called Binomial distribution B(n, p)) of number of successes X can be written as:

X	0	1	2	---	x	n
P(x)	$^nC_0 q^n$	$^nC_1 q^{n-1} p^1$	$^nC_2 q^{n-2} p^2$		$^nC_x q^{n-x} p^x$	$^nC_n p^n$

The probability of x successes $P(X = x)$ is also denoted by $P(x)$ is given as:

$$P(x) = {}^nC_x q^{n-x} p^x, \quad x = 0, 1, \dots, n \qquad (q = 1 - p).$$

This $P(x)$ is called the probability function of the binomial distribution.

CHAPTERWISE
MIND MAPS
& RTCs ENGLISH

FLAMINGO: PROSE   MIND MAP

SUMMARY OF THE STORY

"The Last Lesson" is the tender story of a young Alsatian boy and his last French lesson. The setting is an unnamed town in Alsace. The French districts of Alsace and Lorraine went into Prussian hands. The new Prussian rulers discontinued the teaching of French in the schools of these two districts. The French teachers were asked to leave. Now M. Hamel could no longer stay in his school.

One such student of M. Hamel, Franz who dreaded French class and M. Hamel's iron ruler, came to the school that day thinking he would be punished as he had not learnt his lesson on participles. But on reaching school, he found Hamel dressed in his fine Sunday clothes and the old people of the village sitting quietly on the back benches. Franz was unable to figure anything out as everything about the day was unusual. He sat down there wondering what was going on when M. Hamel announced that today was the last French lesson that he was going to give as an order had come from Berlin to teach only German in the schools of Alsace and Lorraine. Even though Franz feared his master and had no idea about French participles, this news came as a shock to him. That was the first day when he realized that how important French was for him, but it was his last lesson in French.

When M. Hamel asked Franz to recite the rules of participles, he wanted to get it right but he was too nervous and mixed everything up. M. Hamel did not scold him for not being able to answer correctly. Instead he said that it is because the students have often postponed their learning till tomorrow. They always feel that there is time to learn. He further adds that Franz's identity as a Frenchman did not have any weightage as he could neither speak nor write his own language. M. Hamel does not only blame the students for this situation. He feels that the parents are not very interested in their children's education. Hamel goes on to describe the French language as the clearest and the most logical language in the world. He felt that people should always cling to their own language as he believes that when people are enslaved, it is through their language that they can find the key to their prison. He further said about the French language that it was the most beautiful, clearest and most logical language of the world. Finally with a very heavy heart, M. Hamel stood up; he was very sad as he walked to the blackboard, took a chalk and wrote on it "Vive La France" which means "Long Live France" and declared the class dismissed.

1. THE LAST LESSON

by Alphonse Daudet

CHARACTER SKETCH: M. Hamel

M. Hamel is an experienced teacher who has been teaching in school for forty years. He imparts primary education in all subjects. He is a hard task master and students like Franz, who are not good learners, are in great dread of being scolded by him. The latest order of the Prussian rulers upsets him. He has to leave the place for ever and feels heartbroken. He feels sad but exercises self-control. His performance during the last lesson is exemplary. He is kind even to a late comer like Franz. He uses a solemn and gentle tone while addressing the students. He has a logical mind and can analyze problems and deduce the reasons responsible for it. He knows the emotional hold of a language over its users. He is a good communicator and explains everything patiently. Partings are painful and being human, M. Hamel too is no exception. He fails to say goodbye as his throat is choked. On the whole, he is a patriotic gentleman.

CHARACTER SKETCH: Franz

Franz was a student in one of the schools in the districts of Alsace. His schoolmaster was M. Hamel and he was much scared of him. Franz enjoyed spending much of his time outside. He liked the warm and bright day and loved to listen to the chirping of the birds and to watch the drilling of the Prussian soldiers.

In addition to this, the boy had an acute sense of understanding, feeling, recognition and respect. At first, he did not show any interest in M. Hamel's teaching. He didn't even prepare his lesson on participles. However, Franz was forced to change his opinion about M. Hamel. When he got to know that M. Hamel would not able to take any French lessons after the order from Berlin pronouncing that only German language would be taught in the schools of French districts of Alsace and Lorraine, he felt sad. He started respecting the man who had spent forty years in the same school.

Reference to Context

Read the extracts given below and answer the questions that follow.

I.   I started for school very late that morning and was in great dread of a scolding, especially because M. Hamel had said that he would question us on participles, and I did not know the first word about them.

  (a)   Name the title of the story.

  (b)   Name the author.

  (c)   On what would M. Hamel question the class?

  (d)   Did Franz know anything about it?

II.   When I passed the town hall there was a crowd in front of the bulletin-board. For the last two years all our bad news had come from there — the lost battles, the draft, the orders of the commanding officer — and I thought to myself, without stopping, "What can be the matter now?" Then, as I hurried by as fast as I could go, the blacksmith, Wachter, who was there, with his apprentice, reading the bulletin, called after me, "Don't go so fast, bub; you'll get to your school in plenty of time!"

  (a)   Why was Franz late for school that day?

  (b)   What attracted Franz on his way to school?

  (c)   "Don't go so fast, bub; you'll get to your school in plenty of time!" Who said these lines?

  (d)   Describe the atmosphere of the school on usual days.

III.   While I was wondering about it all, M. Hamel mounted his chair, and, in the same grave and gentle tone which he had used to me, said, "My children, this is the last lesson I shall give you. The order has come from Berlin to teach only German in the schools of Alsace and Lorraine. The new master comes tomorrow. This is your last French lesson. I want you to be very attentive."

  (a)   How did the classroom look different that last day?

  (b)   Why did M. Hamel say that it was going to be his last lesson?

  (c)   How did Franz react to the declaration that it was their last French lesson?

  (d)   Who occupied the back benches in the classroom on the day of the last lesson?

IV.   I heard M. Hamel say to me, "I won't scold you, little Franz; you must feel bad enough. See how it is! Every day we have said to ourselves, 'Bah! I've plenty of time. I'll learn it tomorrow.' And now you see where we've come out. Ah, that's the great trouble with Alsace; she puts off learning till tomorrow. Now those fellows out there will have the right to say to you, 'How is it; you pretend to be Frenchmen, and yet you can neither speak nor write your own language?' But you are not the worst, poor little Franz. We've all a great deal to reproach ourselves with."

  (a)   What was unusual about M. Hamel's dress and behaviour on the day of his last French lesson?

  (b)   How did Franz perform when his turn came to recite?

  (c)   "We've all a great deal to reproach ourselves with." Comment.

  (d)   How did M. Hamel praise the French language?

V.   Then he turned to the blackboard, took a piece of chalk, and, bearing on with all his might, he wrote as large as he could — "Vive La France!"

  (a)   What did M. Hamel teach the class in his 'last lesson'?

  (b)   Franz was able to understand everything that day. Why?

  (c)   Why words did M. Hamel write on the blackboard before dismissing the last class?

  (d)   What did the words mean?

ANSWER KEY

I. (a) The Last Lesson

(b) Alphonse Daudet

(c) M. Hamel would question the class on participles.

(d) No, Franz did not know even the first word about them.

II. (a) He was allured by the attractions on the way to school, and hence, was late for the school.

(b) Franz was attracted by the warm weather outside. The birds that chirped at the edge of the forest and the Prussian soldiers who were drilling also slowed down his interest to go to school.

(c) Watcher, the blacksmith, said these lines.

(d) On usual days, the school no longer looked like a school. The noises inside the school could be heard out in the street. Children used to be in a playful mood, opening and closing their desks and shouting their lessons in chorus. The teacher had to use his ruler to silence the class.

III. (a) On the last day, M. Hamel's classroom looked like an ideal classroom. There was a deep silence in the class. No one spoke a word. All were sad.

(b) Alsace was conquered by the Prussians and as a result a new order came from Berlin to ban teaching of French in the schools of Alsace. The order further said that all the French teachers like M. Hamel had to leave the territory within a day, and therefore, that class was to be his last lesson.

(c) Franz was shocked to hear that M. Hamel was leaving and that it was his last lesson. He realised that he would not be able to read and speak is own mother tongue and regretted his lack of interest and carelessness.

(d) The back benches were occupied by the people of the village—Old Hansar, who had on his three cornered hat, the former Mayor, the former postmaster and several other elders.

IV. (a) On the day of his last French lesson, Franz was astounded when he was welcomed by a kind and polite M. Hamel which was contrary to his nature. Moreover, he was dressed in his best clothes, a beautiful green coat, frilled shirt and an embroidered black silk cap, which he wore only on inspection and prize days.

(b) When it was Franz's turn to recite, he got mixed up on the first words and stood at his place, ashamed. He did not have the courage to look up and face his teacher.

(c) M. Hamel reproaches himself for his students' unsatisfactory progress in studies. He held himself responsible because he used to give his own personal work during school time instead of learning their lessons.

(d) M. Hamel called French the most beautiful language in the world. According to him, it was the clearest and the most logical language. He wanted the people of France to guard it amongst themselves and never forget it.

V. (a) In his 'last lesson', M. Hamel taught the class about grammar, then about writing and finally a lesson in history. More than this, he made his students realise the importance of their mother tongue, and taught them to take a pride their language.

(b) Franz thought that probably he had never paid so much attention in the class, and that M. Hamel had never explained everything with so much patience. Perhaps, these were the reasons that he was able to understand everything that day.

(c) M. Hamel wrote the words 'Vive La France!' in big letters on the blackboard before dismissing the last class.

(d) These words meant, Long Live France!'

MIND MAP

The story, "Lost Spring" deals with the deplorable condition of poor children who get forced to miss the simple joyful moments of childhood because of their socio-economic conditions. These children are not given the opportunity of schooling and are compelled to start working early in life. The author Anees Jung strives hard to advocate elimination of child labour through her book.

I – Sometimes I find a rupee in the garbage.
The first part talks about the writer's impressions about the life of the unfortunate rag pickers. The rag pickers migrate from Dhaka and find a settlement in Seemapuri.
The story is of Saheb – a rag picker. The author meets him and asks why he does not go to school. On getting a reply that there was no school in his locality, she makes a false promise that she would open a school for him. She talks to the boy and gets to know that his parents came to the city in search of better life and he ended up living on the streets. Saheb is the son of parents who migrated from Bangladesh. They came to Delhi in 1971 as their house and fields were destroyed by storms. Then they began to live in Seemapuri, a slum near Delhi. The author explores the life in the slums of Seemapuri – the place where Saheb lives. They live without any identity like the ration card, or voter card – after all filling the stomach is more important than having an identity. It is a very sad thing that the garbage that others throw away is like gold to them and they look for food and livelihood in that. The story explores the problems Saheb faces – getting exposed to hazardous waste in the garbage dumps, walking about barefoot, no nourishment or clothes on his body.
The author then comments on the discrepancy between Saheb's desire and the reality. He yearns to be comfortably off, enjoy pleasures of life, play tennis and wear shoes but ends up working in a tea-stall. He no longer remains a free bird nor a master of his own.

II – I want to drive a car.
In the second part, the author meets a boy called Mukesh. Mukesh stays in Firozabad and belongs to a family of bangle makers. Firozabad is popular for its glass-blowing industry. The working environment and the living conditions are pathetic there. Children work in dingy cells and around hot furnaces that make them blind early in adulthood. Since they are weighed down by debt, they cannot think or find any way to escape this trap.
Mukesh wanted to be a driver and a motor-mechanic, and was not at all eager to continue bangle making. But the people thought that it was their karma that they were born into the caste of bangle-makers. So they were destined to make bangles and they could not do anything else. Thousands of children were engaged in bangle making and many of them lost their eyesight before becoming adults. aevery family. Mukesh took the writer to his house where the writer came to know that his grandfather had become blind working in the factory. Similarly in another family, the author came to know how the husband was happy that he had been able to make a house for his own family to live in but the wife complained that she did not get a full meal in her whole life. Hundreds of years of slavery had killed the initiative of people to think of a better life. They carried on their miserable life as they did not have the courage to rebel against tradition. They did not have money to start their own new kind of enterprise. If someone dared to start a new line, there were police, middle-men, sahukars and politicians to persecute them.
But Mukesh is different from rest of the folks there. He dreams to become a motor mechanic aand the author is happy to know about that.

2. LOST SPRING

by **Anees Jung**

Shaeb-e-Alam was a rag-picker who lived in Seemapuri. His family had migrated from Dhaka to India with the hope of finding better life conditions. Every morning, he roamed about streets collecting garbage. Many other boys also accompanied him. His family lived in miserable conditions. He used to search valuable things in garbage to earn his livelihood but despite being poor, he was full of hope. Later, he was employed in a teastall. He now became a labourer and lost his carefree life. He was burdened with responsibility of the job. He lost his childhood due to his poverty which made him work as a child labour.

Mukesh lived in Firozabad and was born in the family of bangle makers. He aspired to become a motor mechanic. Unlike others in Firozabad who were burdened in the stigma of caste in which they were born, Mukesh did not want to follow the traditional profession. In this way, he was a path breaker and had a determination to change his circumstances. Mukesh was born in a very poor family. To increase the income of the family, he also worked with his father in glass furnaces, making bangles. There was a spark of rebellion in him. He was confident and determined to become a motor mechanic. His dreams and aspirations were practical. He dreamt only of what he could achieve or what was within his reach.

Reference to Context

Read the extracts given below and answer the questions that follow.

SOMETIMES I FIND A RUPEE IN THE GARBAGE

I. "If at the end of the day we can feed our families and go to bed without an aching stomach, we would rather live here than in the fields that gave us no grain," say a group of women in tattered saris when I ask them why they left their beautiful land of green fields and rivers.

(a) To which country did Saheb's parents originally belong?

(b) Why did they come to India?

(c) What does the reference to chappals in 'Lost Spring' signify?

(d) 'Garbage to them is gold'. Why does the author say so about the ragpickers?

II. "I sometimes find a rupee, even a ten-rupee note," Saheb says, his eyes lighting up. When you can find a silver coin in a heap of garbage, you don't stop scrounging, for there is hope of finding more. It seems that for children, garbage has a meaning different from what it means to their parents. For the children it is wrapped in wonder, for the elders it is a means of survival.

(a) What does Saheb look for in the garbage dumps?

(b) What job did Saheb take up?

(c) Was he happy?

(d) What does the writer mean when she says, 'Saheb is no longer his own master'?

III. "I am paid 800 rupees and all my meals."

(a) Name the title of the prose.

(b) Name the author of the story.

(c) Who is the speaker of the above lines?

(d) How much money did he use to earn by working at the tea stall?

I WANT TO DRIVE A CAR

IV. "It is his karam, his destiny," says Mukesh's grandmother, who has watched her own husband go blind with the dust from polishing the glass of bangles. "Can a god-given lineage ever be broken?" she implies.

(a) Who was Mukesh? What was his dream?

(b) What is Firozabad famous for?

(c) How does the author narrate the child labour prevailing in Firozabad?

(d) 'It is his karam, his destiny.' Explain.

V. "Why not organise yourselves into a cooperative?" I ask a group of young men who have fallen into the vicious circle of middlemen who trapped their fathers and forefathers.

(a) Why does the author say that the bangle-makers are caught in a vicious web?

(b) Why could the bangle-makers not organise themselves into a cooperative?

(c) What forces conspire to keep the workers in the bangle industry of Firozabad in poverty?

(d) Why was Mukesh's dream of learning to drive a car a mirage?

ANSWER KEY

I.   (a) Saheb's parents originally belonged to Bangladesh.

    (b) They left their village in Dhaka in 1971 due to extreme poverty and migrated to Delhi and started living at Seemapuri.

    (c) The rag pickers were extremely poor. They did not have any money to buy chappals. The author argues that the children are so poor that they could not have any shoes.

    (d) Garbage means 'gold' to the poor ragpickers. It is a means of their survival.

II.   (a) Saheb looks for some silver coin or currency notes in the garbage dumps. It is as valuable as gold for him.

    (b) Saheb took up the job of performing odd jobs at a tea stall

    (c) No, he was unhappy because he was tied down by the work he had to do, thus losing his own independence.

    (d) The writer meant that till Saheb was a ragpicker, he was a carefree boy, who would work, have time for himself and enjoy the work he was doing. But from the time he started working in a tea stall, he changed. He had to become responsible and could not be free like earlier. He was no longer his own master.

III.   (a) Lost Spring

    (b) Anees Jung is the author of the story.

    (c) Saheb said the above lines.

    (d) He used to get 800 rupees.

IV.   (a) Mukesh was the son of a poor bangle maker of Firozabad. He dreamt of becoming a motor mechanic and a car driver. He even insisted on becoming his own master.

    (b) Firozabad is the centre of India's glass-blowing industry. It is famous for its bangles.

    (c) Around 20,000 children work in glass furnaces with high temperatures, in dingy cells without air and light. There they slog their daylight hours, often losing the brightness of their eyes. Many of them lose their eyesight before they become adults.

    (d) Mukesh's grandmother believes in destiny. She believes that they cannot escape from the God-given lineage. It is their destiny to suffer like this and had stopped taking any initiative to change their fate.

V.   (a) The author says that bangle makers are caught in a vicious web because they are not able to form cooperative societies for their betterment and are forced to follow and obey sahukars and policemen.

    (b) The bangle-makers could not organise themselves into a cooperative because they were trapped in the vicious circle of sahukars, middlemen, policemen, bureaucrats and politicians, who exploited them. If they tried to organise themselves, they would be beaten by the police and put in jail.

    (c) They include sahukars, middlemen, policemen, bureaucrats and politicians, who exploited them.

    (d) Mukesh belonged to the bangle-makers of Firozabad where each family was engaged in bangle-making. He wanted to be a motor mechanic and learn how to drive a car. However, because he was caught up in the vicious cycle created by others, he would not be able to fulfil his dream.

MIND MAP

SUMMARY OF THE STORY

"Deep Water" is an extract taken from the book, 'Of Men and Mountains' written by William Douglas. In this extract, the author talks about his fear of water and thereafter, how he finally overcame it.

The writer begins the story by informing us that he had decided to learn swimming at the Y.M.C.A in Yakima when he was ten or eleven years old. The Y.M.C.A pool was not dangerous as it was only two or three feet deep at the shallow end and nine feet deep at the other. The author reveals his first fearful experience in the water when he was barely three or four years old and his father took him to the beach in California. He hung on to his father but still the powerful waves knocked him down and swept over him, leaving him breathless. Terror of the overpowering force of waves was inflicted in his heart.

The second incident happened when he was 11 years old. He was at YMCA pool sitting by the pool side. A big bully boy threw him into the deep end of the pool. The narrator nearly drowned.

These two incidents developed fear of water in the narrator's mind. He had to work very hard to overcome his deeply ingrained fear of water that he had got infected with at the YMCA pool after the tragic incident. The fear spoilt all his excursions with his friends. Whenever he accompanied his friends to Cascades, Tieton, Warm lake, the fear of water seized him, his legs paralysed and icy horror clutched his heart.

Finally, one October, he decided to learn swimming from an instructor. He practised in a pool five days a week, an hour each day. The instructor put a belt around him and attached a rope to it. He held on to the end of the rope as the author swam across the pool. The terror returned to the author every time his instructor relaxed his hold on the rope.

Gradually, he learnt to exhale under water and then raise his nose and inhale. Eventually, the fear of putting his head under water left him and then the instructor taught him to kick with his legs. At first, his legs didn't work properly, but then bit by bit he could command them. Finally, in April, the instructor was convinced that he could swim the length of the pool. He had created a swimmer.

Despite the approval of his instructor, the author was dubious whether he would still be traumatised when he was alone in the pool. The fear did come back when he tried swimming alone but he fought it by swimming longer. He was still not fully satisfied and decided to go to Wentworth in New Hampshire. He dived off a dock and Triggs island and swam two miles across the lake to Stamp Act Island. Only once he felt the terror return when he was in the middle of the lake. But he paid no heed to it. At his first opportunity, he went up the Tieton to Comrad Meadows, up the Conrad Creek Trail to Medade Glacier and camped in the high meadow by the side of Warm Lake. The next morning, he swam across to the other shore and back. For the first time, he was sure that he had conquered his fear.

This experience gave Douglas great perspectives. He felt that only those who have known terror and conquered it can understand how he felt. He realized that there is peace in death and that the terror is only in the fear of death. He experienced both the feeling of dying and the terror that the fear of death can produce. Now that he had conquered his fear, he felt absolutely free and released.

3. DEEP WATER

by William Orville Douglas

CHARACTER SKETCH: William Douglas

William Douglas had great passion for water. Since childhood he had a mind for swimming but had for aversion for water when a wave swept over and buried him. On the second occasion, at the age of ten or eleven, a big boy tossed him up and threw deep in the pool that created stark fear in his mind.

The terror of water followed him everywhere he went. But he was determined to get rid of his fear and was able to do so through his continuous efforts.

To get rid of it, he made a strong resolve. He decided to overcome his fear through his will. He engaged an instructor who perfected him in swimming. The instructor gave him hundreds of exercises and taught him to inhale and exhale. Then after three months or so, he was able to dive, swim back and across the lake and recede his terror.

Thus, through his efforts, Douglas was able to overcome it. Getting terrible fear and having conquered it, his will to live became intense. He started enjoying every minute of living. His experience and ultimate conquest of his far is a lesson for all the readers.

CHARACTER SKETCH: Instructor

The instructor has no name in the account "Deep water", but comes across as a man of strong will and determination who plays an instrumenal role in making Douglas a confident swimmer. It was due to his efforts that William Douglas was able to overcome his fear. The instructor built a swimmer out of Douglas piece by piece. For three months he held him high on a rope attached to his belt so that he could go back and forth. He also taught him the technique of inhaling and exhaling in water.

Reference to Context

Read the extracts given below and answer the questions that follow.

I.   It had happened when I was ten or eleven years old. I had decided to learn to swim. There was a pool at the Y.M.C.A. in Yakima that offered exactly the opportunity.

    (a)   Name the title of the story.

    (b)   Name the author.

    (c)   How old was Douglas when he decided to learn swimming?

    (d)   Where did he decide to learn swimming?

II. From the beginning, however, I had an aversion to the water when I was in it. This started when I was three or four years old and father took me to the beach in California.

    (a)   How old was Douglas when his father took him to the beach in California?

    (b)   How did Douglas' introduction to the YMCA pool revive his childhood fear of water?

    (c)   What factors made Douglas decide in favour of the YMCA pool?

    (d)   What was the author's early childhood fear of the water? How did it affect him the rest of his life?

III. I landed in a sitting position, swallowed water, and went at once to the bottom. I was frightened, but not yet frightened out of my wits. On the way down I planned: When my feet hit the bottom, I would make a big jump, come to the surface, lie flat on it, and paddle to the edge of the pool.

    (a)   What misadventure happened while William Douglas was making an attempt to learn swimming in the YMCA pool?

    (b)   When Douglas realised that he was sinking, how did he plan to save himself?

    (c)   What did Douglas experience when he went down to the bottom of the pool for the first time?

    (d)   *'I was frightened, but not yet frightened out of my wits.'* Explain.

IV. Several hours later, I walked home. I was weak and trembling. I shook and cried when I lay on my bed. I couldn't eat that night. For days a haunting fear was in my heart. The slightest exertion upset me, making me wobbly in the knees and sick to my stomach.

    (a)   What sort of terror seized Douglas as he went down in the water with a yellow glow?

    (b)   Mention any two long term consequences of the drowning incident on Douglas.

    (c)   'This handicap stayed with me as the years rolled by'. Which handicap does the author refer to?

    (d)   Why did Douglas fail to come to the surface of the pool as he hoped to?

V.   Thus, piece by piece, he built a swimmer. And when he had perfected each piece, he put them together into an integrated whole. In April he said, "Now you can swim. Dive off and swim the length of the pool, crawl stroke."

    (a)   How did Douglas decide to overcome his fear of water?

    (b)   How did the instructor turn Douglas into a swimmer?

    (c)   'But I was not finished'. What was unfinished for Douglas?

    (d)   How did Douglas remove his residual doubts about his fear of water?

ANSWER KEY

I. (a) Deep Water   (b) William Douglas

(c) Douglas was about ten or eleven years old when he had decided to learn swimming.

(d) He decided to learn swimming in the pool the Y.M.C.A. in Yakima.

II. (a) Douglas was three or four years old when his father took him to the beach in California.

(b) Douglas' introduction to the YMCA pool revived his childhood fear of water as, when he had not yet learnt swimming; he was thrown into the pool's deep end by a bully and sank to the bottom despite his best efforts.

(c) Douglas' mother recommended that he should learn swimming at the YMCA swimming pool because it was much safer and was only 2-3 feet at the shallow end and 9 feet deep at the other end.

(d) The author and his father once went to the beach of California when the former was three or four. While playing in the surf of the sea, the author was knocked down by the water and was buried under it. He lost his breath and a deep fear developed in his mind.

III. (a) Douglas was sitting on the side of the pool waiting for other boys to come when unexpectedly, a fat boy arrived there. Seeing Douglas sitting timidly, the boy grabbed him and threw him into the deepest part of the pool and left him to drown.

(b) When Douglas realised that he was sinking, he thought that when his feet would hit the bottom, he would make a big jump, come to the surface and lie flat on it. Then he would easily paddle to the edge of the pool.

(c) As Douglas went down to the bottom of the pool for the first time, he felt the way down the pool to be very long and his lungs were ready to burst. He summoned all his strength and jumped up, but could not reach the surface and began to sink again.

(d) When Douglas was thrown into the deepest part of the YMCA pool, he didn't know swimming which increased the risk of drowning. But, he did not get frightened by the fear of sinking. On the contrary, he strengthened his mind and applied his wit to overcome the situation.

IV. (a) When Douglas went down in the water with a yellow glow for the second time, a sheer, stark terror seized him. It was beyond control or understanding. Douglas was paralysed with fear and could not move his limbs.

(b) After the drowning incident, Douglas always felt terrified near water. He was deprived of enjoying water activities like canoeing, boating, swimming, fishing, etc. Fear gripped him when he came near water.

(c) Here, the word 'handicap' refers to the fear of water that possessed Douglas first on the California Beach and later at the YMCA Pool.

(d) When Douglas was drowning in the swimming pool, he tried to come to the surface of the pool but failed because he was overcome with fear and could not move his limbs. He felt that he would die.

V. (a) After the misadventure at the YMCA Pool, Douglas found his fears for water assuming an alarming height. He decided to overcome this fear by getting effective training from a professional trainer.

(b) The instructor built a good swimmer out of Douglas piece by piece. He taught him all the strokes of swimming and how to exhale and inhale when out of water and inside water.

(c) At the end of his rigorous training to swim, Douglas' trainer informed him that his job was completed. Yet Douglas was not entirely satisfied. He had his own fears and anxieties regarding his swimming skills. He wanted to overcome the last bit of fear from his mind.

(d) Douglas removed his residual doubts by swimming across Warm Lake to the opposite shore and back. He says, "I shouted with joy, and Gilbert Peak returned the echo. I had conquered my fear of water"

MIND MAP

SUMMARY OF THE STORY

"The Rattrap" is a short story about an old disheartened peddler and thief who is taken in and shown generosity by a young woman whose kindness changes his bitter attitude to life. The peddler is a man who has fallen upon misfortune and now resorts to selling rattraps, begging, and thievery.

The story begins like a fairytale. The central character is a beggar and petty thief who goes about selling rattraps of wire to make a small living. The peddler led a lonely life. One day while he was thinking about his rattraps, an idea struck him. He thought that the world itself was a rattrap. As soon as anybody touched it, the trap closed on them. He was amused to think of some people who were already trapped, and some others who were trying to reach the bait in the trap. The story unfolds gradually with the various baits being offered to the beggar. One evening, the rattrap peddler took shelter in an old man's cottage who had been a crofter at Ramsjö Ironworks. The amiable and generous man offered him dinner and tobacco. He even showed him the thirty kronor bills, earned by selling his cow's milk, kept in a leather pouch that hung near the window. However, the next morning, the rattrap peddler stole the money and made his escape through the forest. But as he got lost in the woods, he realised that the thirty kronor bills had been a bait to trap him in the huge rattrap that the world is.

Next at the Ramsjö ironworks, while seeking shelter for the night, the tramp bites the bait offered to him by the owner (though he initially refuses it), the ironmaster. Edla, the ironmaster's daughter offers yet another bait for the tramp by asking him to stay over Christmas even after his truth dawns on the hosts. At the church, the ironmaster and Edla were shocked to know that a certain rattrap seller had robbed one of their old crofters. As they returned, the father wondered what the rattrap peddler would have robbed them of. The daughter, however, felt dejected.

On returning home, they were informed, by the valet, that the man had left empty-handed. On the contrary, he had left a package, as a Christmas present, for Edla.The peddler left a package containing a small rattrap with the three ten kronor bills that he had stolen from the crofter. Along with that he left a letter thanking Edla for her generosity and asking her to return the bills to the crofter. He wrote, "The rattrap is a Christmas present from a rat that would have been caught in this world's rattrap if he had not been raised to captain, because in that way he got power to clear himself." It was signed as "Caption von Stahle".

Thus, 'The Rattrap' is a story that gives us a psychological insight into human nature. The author highlights how greed for material things entrap human beings. The story upholds the belief that the essential goodness of a human being can be awakened through love and understanding. It brings into focus the idea that the world is a rattrap.

4. THE RATTRAP

by Selma Lagerlöf

CHARACTER SKETCH: The Peddler

Selma Lagerlöf draws the character of the peddler with all sympathy and understanding. The rattrap peddler was a tall man who had his own imagination and meditation. He lived by making and selling rattraps from scrap materials he got by begging. His life was sad and monotonous. Since the world had never been kind to him, he was full of bitterness and malice against it. The peddler experienced unwanted joy at everyone else's discomfort, pain at being ensnared by the devilish ways of the world. He was also philosophical and thoughtful. While plodding along the road, left to his own meditations, the peddler was struck by the idea that this world around him with its lands and cities is a big rattrap. It had never existed for any other purpose than to set baits for its people. On the other hand, begging and petty thievery occasionally were his means of livelihood.

He is not morally upright. He does not even spare his host, the old crofter and steals his 30 kronors. He is an opportunist; takes advantage of situations. But the essential goodness in him is awakened through love and understanding of Miss Elda Willmansson.

CHARACTER SKETCH: The Crofter

The crofter was an old man without a wife or a child. He was lonely but trusting. He was hospitable and gullible. He was a man of liberal beliefs, so he gladly allowed the peddler to stay in his cottage for the night. Not only that, he served him with supper and tobacco for his pipe and amused him with the game of cards also. He showed him the thirty kronor from his pouch which he received as a payment. He was happy to get someone to talk to in his loneliness. He valued the presence of the peddler so much that he shared his confidences generously with him.

Reference to Context

Read the extracts given below and answer the questions that follow.

I.   **But one day this man had fallen into a line of thought, which really seemed to him entertaining. He had naturally been thinking of his rattraps when suddenly he was struck by the idea that the whole world about him — the whole world with its lands and seas, its cities and villages — was nothing but a big rattrap. It had never existed for any other purpose than to set baits for people.**

     (a)   Why had the peddler to resort to petty thievery?

     (b)   Why was the peddler amused at the idea of the world being a rattrap?

     (c)   Why did the peddler knock on the cottage by the roadside?

     (d)   What hospitality did the peddler receive from the crofter?

II.   **The stranger must have seemed incredulous, for the old man got up and went to the window, took down a leather pouch which hung on a nail in the very window frame, and picked out three wrinkled ten-kronor bills. These he held up before the eyes of his guest, nodding knowingly, and then stuffed them back into the pouch.**

     (a)   'The old man was just as generous with his confidences as with his porridge and tobacco.' Explain.

     (b)   Why did the Crofter show the thirty kronor to the peddler?

     (c)   What do we learn about the crofter's nature from the story?

     (d)   Who was the owner of Ramsjö iron mills? Why did he visit the mills at night?

III.   **But half an hour later the rattrap peddler stood again before the door. He did not try to get in, however. He only went up to the window, smashed a pane, stuck in his hand, and got hold of the pouch with the thirty kronor. He took the money and thrust it into his own pocket. Then he hung the leather pouch very carefully back in its place and went away.**

     (a)   Why did the peddler return to the Crofter's house after half an hour?

     (b)   What made the peddler take the woodland road to his destination?

     (c)   Having taken the Crofter's money as bait, the peddler got trapped into a rattrap. Comment.

     (d)   Why did the Ironmaster invite the peddler to his home?

IV.   **"My name is Edla Willmansson," said the young girl. "My father came home and said that you wanted to sleep here in the forge tonight, and then I asked permission to come and bring you home to us. I am so sorry, Captain, that you are having such a hard time."**

     (a)   Why did the peddler agree to go with Edla?

     (b)   How did the peddler celebrate his Christmas at the manor house?

     (c)   "Edla sat and hung her head even more dejectedly than usual." Why did she behave in that manner?

     (d)   What were the contents of the package left by the peddler as a Christmas gift fort Edla?

V.   **"The rattrap is a Christmas present from a rat who would have been caught in this world's rattrap if he had not been raised to captain, because in that way he got power to clear himself. "Written with friendship and high regard, "Captain von Stahle."**

     (a)   Name the title of the story.

     (b)   Name the author.

     (c)   Who wrote the letter?

     (d)   To whom was the letter written?

ANSWER KEY

I. (a) The rattrap seller lived mostly by selling rattraps that he himself made. At times, when his business did not go well, he had to resort to petty thievery for survival.

(b) The peddler believed that the world with all its riches and joys, food and shelter appears as a rattrap to tempt people. He was amused to think of many other people he knew, who were already caught in the trap, and some others who were circling around the bait.

(c) The peddler knocked on the cottage by the roadside to seek shelter for the night.

(d) The peddler was surprised as he was not only welcomed at the night time but was also provided food and shelter. The crofter gave him a roll of tobacco for his pipe. He also played a game of cards with him.

II. (a) The way the peddler was welcomed by the crofter was unusual. The crofter generously served him food and tobacco and let him stay with him. He also showed him his great treasure of an amount of thirty kronors.

(b) The Crofter to shared his joy of earning thirty kronors from the creamery as the payment of previous month's supply. However, he felt that the peddler did not believe him. Thus, he showed the money to convince him.

(c) The Crofter was lonely and trusting but he was hospitable and gullible. Without any doubt on the peddler, he invites the peddler inside his house at night and shares not only his food but also the whereabouts of his earned money. He was friendly and talkative also.

(d) The owner of the Ramsjö iron mills was an ambitious and prominent ironmaster. He visited the mills at night to make sure that good iron was shipped out from his mills to the market.

III. (a) Even though the peddler had been generously treated by the Crofter, the former was tempted to steal his thirty kronor, and therefore, he returned to the Crofter's house when he was away.

(b) After stealing the crofter's money, the peddler began to feel insecure going the main road where he could be easily arrested by the police. To avoid any risk he took the woodland road.

(c) The peddler believed his own philosophy that the whole world is a rattrap and the attractions here are baits attracting people into its deadly doors. But by taking the Crofter's money, the peddler had forgotten his philosophy and took the bait and allowed himself to be caught.

(d) Ironmaster knew that Von Stahle had too retired from the force. The peddler had the similar looks of Von Stahle and the Ironmaster took him for his lost friend; therefore, wanted him to come to him home.

IV. (a) When Edla Willmansson, the Ironmaster's daughter, came and asked the peddler to come home, he agreed and went with her because she seemed friendly and that boosted up the peddler's confidence.

(b) It was the first Christmas that peddler ever celebrated in his whole life so peacefully. The whole day and throughout the Christmas night, he was sleeping that was interrupted only by the calls to eat at intervals.

(c) Edla was sad and upset as she had heard that peddler was actually a thief who had recently robbed a crofter. She felt that she had done wrong in offering shelter to a thief.

(d) The package left by the peddler as a Christmas gift for Edla contained a rattrap, thirty kronor in crumpled notes (robbed from the crofter) and a brief note for her explaining his conduct.

V. (a) The Rattrap

(b) Selma Lagerlof

(c) Peddler wrote the letter as Captain von Stahle.

(d) The letter was written to Edla.

MIND MAP

SUMMARY OF THE STORY

The story 'Indigo', written by Louis Fischer narrates Gandhiji's struggle for justice to the poor peasants of Champaran. In those days, most of the arable land in the Champaran district was divided into large estates owned by Englishmen and worked by Indian tenants. The chief commercial crop was Indigo. The landlords compelled all tenants to plant Indigo on 15% of their land and surrender the entire Indigo harvest as rent. This was done by a long term contract. The British didn't need the Indigo crop any more when Germany developed synthetic Indigo. But to release the peasants from the 15% agreement, they demanded compensation. Some illiterate peasants agreed but the others refused.

When Louis Fischer first met Gandhi in 1942 at his ashram in Sevagram, he told him how and why he decided to disobey the British in 1917. Gandhi had gone to the December 1916 annual convention of the Indian National Congress in Lucknow where he met a poor peasant named Rajkumar Shukla who pleaded Gandhi to visit Champaran. Rajkumar Shukla was one of the sharecroppers who was determined enough to accompany Gandhi everywhere till he fixed a date to visit his district. Impressed by the resoluteness of the peasant, Gandhi agreed to meet him in Calcutta and go with him to Champaran from there. After a few months when Gandhi went to Calcutta, the two of them boarded a train for the city of Patna in Bihar. From there Shukla led him to the house of a lawyer named Rajendra Prasad. Mahatma Gandhi's humble and simple attire made the servants mistake him for another poor peasant. However, Gandhi was not allowed to draw water from the well as they thought that he might turn out to be an untouchable.

Then, Gandhi decided to go to Muzzafarpur to gather more information about the condition of the peasants in Champaran. The news of Gandhi's advent and his mission spread rapidly through Muzzafarpur and Champaran. Many lawyers and peasant groups came in large numbers to support him. Gandhi came to know that the lawyers were charging a fee from the peasants. The lawyers accepted the fact that their charges were high and for a poor peasant it was irksome. Gandhiji rebuked them. He advised them against taking the farmers' cases to the law court as he felt that all that was needed was to make them feel liberated from fear. He stressed on counselling as this would give the peasants enough confidence to fight their fear. He looked into the matter, stood by the side of the poor peasants and fought a long battle of one year, managing to get justice for them. This made the peasants courageous and made them aware of their fundamental rights.

Gandhi's work at Champaram didn't just confine to political or economic struggle. He also worked on social issues like arrangements for education, health and hygiene for the families of the poor peasants. He taught them the lessons of self-reliance and self-dependence. This was one of the first struggles that paved the way for India's independence.

5. INDIGO

by Louis Fischer

CHARACTER SKETCH: Rajkumar Shukla

Rajkumar Shukla was a poor peasant from Champaran. He was a sharecropper under the British landlords there. Under an old agreement, the peasants were compelled by the British to grow indigo on 15% of their land and part with it as rent. Later, to free them from Indigo cultivation, they collected compensation. This became a big trouble for all the peasants in Champaran and there was no one to help them. For this, Rajkumar Shukla had been advised to speak to Gandhiji who he was told, would be able to do something about their problem.

Rajkumar Shukla was resolute and tenacious to take Gandhi with him. It was because of his determination that Gandhiji, went on to initiate one of the most powerful movements in the history of our national struggle.

Reference to Context

Read the extracts given below and answer the questions that follow.

I. When I first visited Gandhi in 1942 at his ashram in Sevagram, in central India, he said, "I will tell you how it happened that I decided to urge the departure of the British. It was in 1917."

   (a)   Name the title of the prose.

   (b)   Name the author.

   (c)   When did the author first visit Gandhi?

   (d)   Where was the ashram located?

II. Gandhi told Shukla he had an appointment in Cawnpore and was also committed to go to other parts of India. Shukla accompanied him everywhere. Then Gandhi returned to his ashram near Ahmedabad. Shukla followed him to the ashram. For weeks he never left Gandhi's side. "Fix a date," he begged. Impressed by the sharecropper's tenacity and story Gandhi said, "I have to be in Calcutta on such-and-such a date. Come and meet me and take me from there."

   (a)   Who was Raj Kumar Shukla?

   (b)   Why did Rajkumar Shukla want to take Gandhiji to Champaran?

   (c)   What made Gandhiji accompany Raj Kumar Shukla to Champaran?

   (d)   How were Gandhiji and Raj Kumar Shukla treated by Rajendra Prasad's servants? Why?

III. He said, "I have come to the conclusion that we should stop going to law courts Taking such cases to the courts does little good. Where the peasants are so crushed and fear-stricken, law courts are useless. The real relief for them is to be free from fear."

   (a)   Who is 'he' in the above lines?

   (b)   Why did Gandhiji decide to go to Muzaffarpur before going to Champaran?

   (c)   What was extraordinary about Professor Malkani's accommodating Gandhiji in his home?

   (d)   Why did Gandhiji feel that taking the Champaran case to the court was useless?

IV. Gandhi did not leave. Instead he proceeded to Motihari, the capital of Champaran. Several lawyers accompanied him. At the railway station, a vast multitude greeted Gandhi. He went to a house and, using it as headquarters, continued his investigations.

   (a)   Why was Gandhiji stopped on his way to the village where a peasant was maltreated?

   (b)   What did the landlords compel the peasants to do as per the terms of a long-term contract?

   (c)   What happened when the British planters asked the peasants for compensation for releasing them from the 15 per cent agreement?

   (d)   What did Gandhiji learn from the voluntary support of the villagers in Champaran?

V. They accordingly went back to Gandhi and told him they were ready to follow him into jail. "The battle of Champaran is won," he exclaimed. Then he took a piece of paper and divided the group into pairs and put down the order in which each pair was to court arrest.

   (a)   How did Gandhiji make the judge release him without bail?

   (b)   Why was Gandhiji opposed to Charles Freer Andrews helping him in Champaran?

   (c)   "The battle of Champaran is won!" What led Gandhiji to make this remark?

   (d)   'Civil disobedience had triumphed, the first time in modern India.' Comment.

ANSWER KEY

I. (a) Indigo

(b) Louis Fischer

(c) The author first visited Gandhi in 1942.

(d) The ashram was located in Sevagram in central India.

II. (a) Raj Kumar Shukla was a peasant from Champaran. He was a sharecropper under the British landlords there.

(b) The sharecropping system had become a big trouble for all the peasants in Champaran and there was no one to help them. Shukla heard from someone that Gandhiji could solve their problems, and therefore, wanted to take Gandhiji in Champaran.

(c) Gandhiji had no plan to involve himself in any mass movements. But when he heard about the miseries of the Champaran peasants under the British landlords and that the Indian lawyers there didn't do anything honestly for the peasants, he decided to accompany Shukla to Champaran.

(d) When Gandhiji and Raj Kumar Shukla reached Rajendra Prasad's home, he was not at home. His servants thought that Gandhiji was also an 'untouchable' and asked them to stay on the ground and refused to drink water from the well.

III. (a) Gandhiji is referred to as 'he' in the above lines.

(b) Muzaffarpur was en route to Champaran. Gandhiji decided to first go to Muzaffarpur because he wanted to gather all the facts regarding the sharecroppers' problems beyond what Shukla had imparted to him.

(c) Professor Malkani was a British Government professor at Muzzafarpur. Since Gandhiji was fighting against the same government for freedom and home-rule, no one except him harboured Gandhiji for fear of the British, and therefore, Professor Malkani's act was extraordinary.

(d) When Gandhiji saw that the illiterate peasants still relied on the Indian lawyers who promised justice for them, he knew how foolish that was. Gandhiji saw that the poor Indians would not get justice as long as the law, prosecutors, courts, judge and the accused being British.

IV. (a) Gandhiji was stopped on his way to the village where a peasant was maltreated because the police feared that his presence along with many furious people and the sight of the ill-treated peasant would cause a mutiny in Champaran.

(b) The landlords forced peasants to plant indigo on 15 per cent of their land. All the indigo produce had to be surrendered as rent.

(c) The sharecropping agreement seemed irksome to the peasants. Therefore, many of them signed it willingly. However, others engaged lawyers to fight their cases. So the landlords hired thugs.

(d) When Gandhiji saw the voluntary support the uneducated peasants gave him, he learned that what India wanted was a strong leader and that he could certainly win the battle of Champaran.

V. (a) The crafty British judge wanted to postpone the trial so as to get Gandhiji without the cover and support of the peasants to put him behind the bars. Sensing this, Gandhiji declared that he was guilty and requested the court to grand him his punishment. At this point, the judge was forced to announce the verdict and released Gandhiji without bail.

(b) Gandhiji was opposed to Charles Freer Andrews helping him in Champaran because he was a foreigner. He felt that a foreigner's help should not be sought to free India of foreigners. According to him self-reliance was of utmost importance.

(c) Gandhiji said these words when he was able to win the lawyers' trust. Earlier, these lawyers had certain misconceptions about Gandhiji but as they saw his determination towards the peasants' liberation, they came in his full support.

(d) Gandhiji began his Civil Disobedient Movement in Champaran by refusing to leave the place as ordered by the police authorities. His arrest and trial followed. But finally the judiciary had to release Gandhiji and drop his case due to pressure from the peasants and thus his Civil Disobedient Movement became successful in Champaran.

MIND MAP

SUMMARY OF THE STORY

Poets and Pancakes is an excerpt from the book My Years with Boss in which the author Asokamitran recounts his days in Gemini Studios working under the founder S.S. Vasan; cutting out and filing newspaper clippings. The excerpt is a humorous description of the day to day affairs of the studio, and the influence of movies on every aspect of life in India.

Pancake was the brand name of the makeup material that Gemini Studios bought in truck-loads; and the studio was the favourite haunt of poets. The author describes these two in humorous detail, hence the title.

The make-up room dazzled with incandescent lights at all angles around half a dozen large mirrors. It caused a 'fiery misery' to the artists as they ended up scorched bearing their heat for extensive hours under the heavy layers of pancake on their faces. The studio had men from different regions of the country; and these 'nationally integrated make-up men' used truck-loads of pancake and other locally made potions and lotions to 'turn any decent-looking person into a hideous crimson hued monster'; perhaps because the blazing lights required them to look 'ugly' like that to appear good in the movie. They worked in a strict hierarchy, with the chief make-up man 'making chief actors ugly', his senior assistant, the second level actors, and so on, down to the middle-aged 'office boy' who slapped make up on the extras. The office boy had joined many years ago with the aspiration of becoming an actor, writer, etc., and was a bit of a poet, too. He kept pounding the author with his poetry as well as complaints against Subbu, the No.2 at Gemini, who he thought had risen so high only because of favourable circumstances, being born a Brahmin.

Subbu, in fact, was the favourite of The Boss because he was loyal, inspired and full of prompt solutions to every problem. Apart from this, he was an accomplished man of letters, a poet capable of higher forms who chose to write for the masses. Working in the story department, he had composed many original story poems and authored a vast novel with deftly etched characters. He was regarded as a fine actor. He loved everyone and happily provided for the numerous acquaintances and relations who had made his home their own. Among the khadi-clad, Gandhi worshipping crowd of dreamers, the story department had the legal adviser as the lone oddity— a man of cold logic clad in pant, tie and coat.

Gemini Studios was a favourite haunt of poets, who leisured over coffee and swore hatred for the godless communist. The Studios welcomed the Moral Rearmament Army—a kind of countermovement to international Communism— and watched their plays 'Jotham Valley' and 'The Forgotten Factor' over and over again. It hosted the English poet Stephen Spender, who spoke of freedom and democracy; and was later discovered by the author as one of six eminent men of letters who had described 'their journeys into Communism and their disillusioned return' in essays compiled in 'The God That Failed'.

6. POETS AND PANCAKES

by **Ashokamitran**

CHARACTER SKETCH: Kothamangalam Subbu

Kothamangalam Subbu, the No. 2 at Gemini Studios, has been portrayed by the author as a multi faceted man 'tailor-made for films'. He had struggled through difficult times to reach this position, though he may have had exposure to affluent circumstances and people. He had a calm demeanour and stayed cheerful even after a flop film. He loved everybody and involved everybody in his work. The Boss loved him for he could be inspired when commanded. He was immensely creative and resourceful and could readily offer multiple alternatives for any requirement of filming a scene. He was a poet capable of composing high and complex forms but he chose to cater to the masses for the sake of films. He created many original 'story poems' and authored a novel with finely delineated characters. He was acclaimed as a better actor than the main ones, yet was content playing small roles. He was charitable and improvident and didn't even appear conscious of the fact that he was supporting many relations and acquaintances that had made his home their permanent residence. Despite being so good and loved, he had an enemy in the 'office boy' who hated him and held him responsible for his own miserable and insignificant existence.

CHARACTER SKETCH: Office Boy

The make-up department of the Gemini Studios had an 'office boy' in his early forties who was responsible for applying make- up on the extras who would stand in the crowd. He had joined the studios years ago in the hope of becoming a star actor or a top screen writer, director or lyrics writer, and was a bit of a poet, too. So, whenever there was no crowd shooting, he would annoy the author with epic sessions of complaining how his great literary talent was being allowed to go waste in the make-up department. As it usually happens in such cases, all his frustration was directed towards a single person Kothamangalam Subbu, whom he held solely responsible for all his woes, ignominy and neglect. Though Subbu must have struggled more than him as no firmly established film producing companies or studios existed when he began his career, the 'office boy' believed resentfully that being a Brahmin he must have had all good fortune and advantage.

Reference to Context

Read the extracts given below and answer the questions that follow.

I. **All this shows that there was a great deal of national integration long before A.I.R. and Doordarshan began broadcasting programmes on national integration.**

   (a)   Explain how 'all this' in the above extract shows 'national integration'?

   (b)   What kind of makeup was used in the studio?

   (c)   How was the makeup of the actors done?

   (d)   How did it change the appearance of the person on whom it was applied?

II. **On the days when there was a crowd shooting, you could see him mixing his paint in a giant vessel and slapping it on the crowd players.**

   (a)   Who is 'him' in the above extract?

   (b)   What was 'the idea' behind his method of applying makeup on the crowd?

   (c)   How did he trouble the author when there was no crowd shooting?

   (d)   Where was all his anger directed?

III. **On the contrary, he must have had to face more uncertain and difficult times, for when he began his career, there were no firmly established film producing companies or studios.**

   (a)   Who is 'he' in the given extract? Who is he being compared with?

   (b)   In what context does the author describe this person 'he'?

   (c)   What qualities of this person does the author enumerate?

   (d)   This virtuous person was hated by one man. Who and why?

IV. **Then one day, The Boss closed down the Story Department and this was perhaps the only instance in all human history where a lawyer lost his job because the poets were asked to go home.**

   (a)   Explain how a lawyer lost his job because the poets were fired?

   (b)   What was distinctive about the lawyer?

   (c)   How did he end someone's brilliant acting career?

   (d)   Name 'The Boss'.

V. **Their 'Jotham Valley' and 'The Forgotten Factor' ran several shows in Madras and along with the other citizens of the city, the Gemini family of six hundred saw the plays over and over again.**

   (a)   Which group presented these two plays?

   (b)   In what manner did it inspire Tamil theatre?

   (c)   What was the real purpose of the group's visit?

   (d)   A famous English poet's visit to Gemini Studios for a similar purpose was a mystery then. How was it later revealed to the author?

ANSWER KEY

I. (a) The makeup Department of Gemini Studios had people from different regions of the country—a Bengali head succeeded by a Maharashtrian who was assisted by a Dharwar Kannadiga, an Andhra, a Madras Indian Christian, an Anglo-Burmese and the usual local Tamils.

   (b) The studio used truck-loads of pancake brand of makeup and a number of other locally made potions and lotions.

   (c) The makeup of the actors was done in a strict hierarchy. The chief makeup man applied makeup on the lead actors, his senior assistant, on the second leads and so on, down to the 'office boy' who applied paint on the crowd players.

   (d) The makeup turned any decent-looking person into a hideous crimson hued monster.

II. (a) 'Him' refers to the 'office boy' of the makeup department who was responsible for applying makeup on the crowd players.

   (b) The idea was to close every pore on the surface of the face in the process of applying make-up.

   (c) When there was no crowd shooting, the 'office boy' inundated the author with his frustration about his literary talents going waste in the makeup department; and complaints about Subbu.

   (d) All his anger was directed at Kothamangalam Subbu, the no. 2. in Gemini Studios.

III. (a) 'He' refers to Kothamangalam Subbu, the No. 2 in Gemini Studios. He is being compared with 'the office boy' who held him responsible for all his misery.

   (b) The office boy resented that Subbu was the Boss's favourite. He thought Subbu had had a favourable life being a Brahmin; and held him responsible for his own ignominy and neglect. In this context, the author describes the virtues of Subbu to show how wrong the office boy was.

   (c) The author describes that Subbu was an excellent poet and actor; was always cheerful and helpful even in failure; and supported many relations and acquaintances. He was loyal, and so inspired and resourceful that The Boss depended on his multiple solutions for every problem.

   (d) He was hated by the office boy who considered himself no less worthy and believed Subbu had reached his position only by virtue of his birth as a Brahmin.

IV. (a) The lawyer worked in the Story Department where everybody else was a poet or a writer. So, when The Boss closed the department down, he too lost his job as did those poets.

   (b) The lawyer was a man of cold logic amidst the dreamers, the writers and poets. While all the others were Gandhians and wore khadi, he was neutral and wore pant, coat and tie.

   (c) The legal adviser recorded and replayed the angry outburst of a brilliant actress against the producer of the film which terrorised her so much that she could not recover and her career ended.

   (d) The Boss at Gemini Studios was S.S. Vasan.

V. (a) The Moral Rearmament Army of Frank Buchman.

   (b) Almost all Tamil plays had a scene of sunrise and sunset in the manner of 'Jotham Valley' with a bare stage, a white background curtain and a tune played on the flute.

   (c) The MRA was a kind of countermovement to international Communism and it convinced S.S. Vasan to host a reception of its views.

   (d) The English poet Stephen Spender also visited to share his aversion to Communist ideals. His visit as well as his language baffled everyone and it remained a mystery until the author discovered him among six eminent essayists who had described 'their journeys into Communism and their disillusioned return' in 'The God That Failed'

MIND MAP

SUMMARY OF THE STORY

The Interview is an excerpt taken from the author Christopher Silvester's introduction to the Penguin Book of Interviews, An Anthology from 1859 to the Present Day.

Interview has become a commonplace of journalism with every literate person having read an interview and several thousand celebrities having been interviewed. So, opinions on interview vary considerably. While some regard it as a source of truth in its highest form and, as an art in its practice; others despise it as an unwarranted intrusion into their lives, and feel it diminishes them just like photographing, as believed in some primitive societies, steals the soul.

For VS Naipaul, interviews wound and eat away a part of you; while Lewis Carrol is horrified at how they lionize you. Rudyard Kipling's wife wrote in her diary how their day in Boston was ruined by two reporters. Kipling considers interviewing immoral, an assault on one's person, a cowardly and vile act and a crime that warrants punishment. He believes that a respectable man would never ask or give an interview; though he himself had earlier perpetrated this assault on Mark Twain. Similarly, H.G. Wells, despite being a frequent interviewee, called interview an ordeal; and later, himself interviewed Joseph Stalin.

Notwithstanding the drawbacks pointed out by famous interviewees, interview is a supremely serviceable medium of communication. The excerpt from the interview of Umberto Eco, a professor at the University of Bologna in Italy renowned for his staggeringly large and wide-ranging literary output is a case in point. The interviewer, Mukund Padmanabhan from The Hindu newspaper, engages the professor, whose novel The Name of the Rose sold more than ten million copies, in an interesting communication interspersed with clever questions that goad him to unravel facts; and air his opinions and responses. Mukund asks Umberto how he manages to do so many different things. He replies that, on the contrary, he is actually always doing the same thing! He pursues his philosophical interests through his academic work and his novels; and portrays it in his books for children by talking about peace and non-violence. He says that his professor's appreciation of the story telling style of his doctoral thesis encouraged him to adopt the narrative style for all his academic writings, and later, to write novels, too. He wrote novels in the 'interstices' or empty spaces or spare time he got in his full time occupation as an academic. Being branded a novelist despite having 40 scholarly works against a mere 5 novels bothers him because he considers himself 'a university professor who writes on Sundays'; but it is okay since no scholarly work can reach the millions his narrative work does. He says, the immense popularity of his serious novel The Name of the Rose which has a detective thread and delves into metaphysics, theology and medieval history proves that readers like difficult reading experience. He says, the reason for his novel's success remains a mystery; for he believes what clicks for a novel in a certain period or age is unpredictable.

7. THE INTERVIEW
by Christopher Silvester

CHARACTER SKETCH: Mukund Padmanabhan

Mukund is a journalist employed with the daily newspaper The Hindu. He was assigned the job of interviewing professor and novelist Umberto Eco on the super success of his latest novel. Mukund shows his skills as a good interviewer. It is clear from his questions that he has done his homework before the interview— collected all information about the professor's education, body of work and other writers' comments on him. His questions succeed in eliciting the desired responses.

Mukund converses effectively to prepare the groundwork before coming to the super success of his new novel. He starts impressively by quoting a contemporary author who wondered how Eco managed to do the wide variety of things he did. He prods Eco to elaborate on his responses with connector questions like, 'Which is?' He is appreciative and encouraging with his own comments on Eco's work— 'your scholarly work has a certain playful and personal quality about it.' It enables him to enquire whether this 'marked departure' from the regular depersonalised, often boring academic style was adopted by him or it came naturally to him. Once he gets Eco engrossed in fondly recounting how he came to write novels, Mukund poses his main question about his latest novel that sold more than 10 million copies. He solicits Eco's self assessment whether he considered himself a novelist or an academic. He asks intelligent questions about the reason behind the novel's super success—How did it appeal to readers despite dealing with difficult subjects and weaving a detective yarn? He presents his own assessments—Did the novel's period of medieval history fascinate readers? Mukund emerges as a skilful interviewer who frames productive queries and conducts the session in a cordial and mutually satisfying experience.

CHARACTER SKETCH: Umberto Eco (5 January 1932 – 19 February 2016)

Umberto Eco is a professor at the University of Bologna in Italy. He had acquired a formidable reputation as a scholar for his ideas on semiotics (the study of signs), literary interpretation, and medieval aesthetics before he turned to writing fiction. His staggeringly large and wide-ranging body of work includes literary fiction, academic texts, essays, children's books and newspaper articles. He gained intellectual superstardom with his novel The Name of the Rose which sold more than 10 million copies.

Eco emerges as a genial intellectual who converses frankly with his interviewer and communicates his ideas and opinions well. He offers intelligent and analytical response to every query and does not evade any. He says, though others get the impression that he does a variety of things, he actually pursues the same bunch of ethical, philosophical interests whether he writes academic or children's books, or novels. He calls himself 'a professor who writes on Sundays' since he works as an academic and writes fiction only in the interstices, i.e., empty spaces or spare time squeezed in between; and, attends academic conferences rather than writers' clubs. He makes a smart analysis of how his serious novel sold 10 to 15 million copies, saying this many readers do not always want easy experiences. At the same time, he admits that the reason is a mystery because it is unpredictable exactly what appeals to the readers at the precise time of publication of a particular novel.

Reference to Context

Read the extracts given below and answer the questions that follow.

I. **"I can't understand how one man can do all the things he does."**

(a)   Who said these words?

(b)   Name the 'one man' being referred to in this sentence?

(c)   How does this person respond to this statement?

(d)   How does he identify himself?

II. **I have some philosophical interests and I pursue them through my academic work and my novels.**

(a)   Who said these words and to whom?

(b)   What was the occasion when these words were spoken?

(c)   What was the question to which these words formed a response?

(d)   How does he explain what he says here?

III. **Say, you are coming over to my place. You are in an elevator and while you are coming up, I am waiting for you.**

(a)   In response to which question does the speaker say these lines?

(b)   What specific term does the speaker give to such time periods?

(c)   How does he relate them to matter in the universe?

(d)   How does he utilise these time periods?

IV. **Because I consider myself a university professor who writes novels on Sundays.**

(a)   Who is the speaker of these lines?

(b)   To what does he respond with these words?

(c)   What reason does he give to justify this claim?

(d)   How does he manage a variety of work?

V. **Mukund: Not everyone can do that of course. Your non-fictional writing, your scholarly work has a certain playful and personal quality about it.**

(a)   What does Mukund refer to with 'that'?

(b)   How does Mukund compare Eco's 'playful and personal quality' of scholarly work with the work of other writers?

(c)   How does Mukund describe the 'regular academic style'?

(d)   What made Eco depart from the 'regular academic style'?

ANSWER KEY

I.   (a) These are the words of English academic and novelist David Lodge quoted by Mukund Padmanabhan while he interviewed Umberto Eco.

      (b) The 'one man' mentioned here is Umberto Eco, a professor at the University of Bologna in Italy, renowned for his academic and fiction writing.

      (c) Eco says that he is actually doing the same thing always though it appears as a variety of work to others.

      (d) He identifies himself as an academic who writes on Sundays.

II.   (a) Umberto Eco said these words to Mukund Padmanabhan, the journalist from The Hindu.

      (b) These words were spoken while Eco was being interviewed by Mukund Padmanabhan.

      (c) He was responding to the wonderment of a fellow writer about how he managed to do all the different things he did.

      (d) Eco explains that he does the same thing all the time; as he pursues the same bunch of ethical, philosophical interests through his academic work, novels and even children's books, wherein he wrote only about peace, non-violence, etc.

III. (a) Eco says this in response to the question about how he manages to do a wide variety of things. He had a secret behind his ability to manage. This was an example of that.

      (b) Eco calls these time periods 'interstices' or empty spaces.

      (c) He says these empty spaces in life were like the empty spaces in atoms which if eliminated will shrink the universe to the size of a fist.

      (d) He utilises these time periods in conceiving and writing articles, etc.

IV. (a) Umberto Eco, a professor at the University of Bologna in Italy, renowned for his academic and fiction writing, is the speaker.

      (b) He says this in affirmation to the query whether being called a novelist bothered him.

      (c) He justifies his claim by saying that he works as a professor, identifies himself with the academic community, and attends academic conferences rather than writers' clubs.

      (d) He utilises the 'interstices' or 'empty spaces' in his life for ideating and writing novels, articles, etc.

V.   (a) Umberto Eco says that he works in empty spaces, e.g. while waiting for his visitor who is in the elevator to reach his third floor from the first, he utilises this empty space to write an article. Mukund refers to this unusual capability as 'that'.

      (b) Mukund says Eco's style is informal in a marked departure from regular academic style.

      (c) He says the regular academic style of other scholars is invariably depersonalised and often dry and boring.

      (d) When Eco's first Doctoral dissertation written in narrative style was appreciated and published as a book by his professor, he was encouraged to adopt it for good and depart from the regular academic style.

MIND MAP

SUMMARY OF THE STORY

'Going Places' is the story of an adolescent girl called Sophie, who, like many of her age, is filled with fantasies and desires. She comes from a poor family. She wishes to own her own boutique after school. If not that, she is very certain that she can become an actress or a fashion designer. Her friend, Jansie, tells her that dreams come true if you have money or experience.

Sophie lives in a house, which is very small for the number of people in her family. Her family does not believe her, as she is known to make up stories and scenarios in her head that are far from reality. Her elder brother Geoff, who does not let anyone enter his life, fascinates her. He is strong, handsome and tall. She is jealous of his silence and wants him to take her on bike rides. Sophie fantasises about Danny Casey, an Irish football player, whom she had seen playing in innumerable matches. Sophie imagined that Danny was in love with her and loved her. She thought that she too loved him. She was very excited and shared the treasured secret with her brother Geoff. He was skeptical of his sister's claim but she convinced him eventually. Sophie told him that she was looking at the clothes in Royce's window when Danny he came and stood beside her. She described his appearance to convince her brother. When her father entered the room, Geoff told him about Sophie's encounter with Danny Casey. Her father responds that if Danny remains focussed then he might be a better player. Sophie said in favour of Danny that his ability is not to be questioned. When the father is informed that Sophie said that Danny was going to buy a shop, he dismisses them by calling it another of Sophie's wild stories and states that she is going to get herself in trouble one day.

The next Saturday, Sophie went to watch the customary United match with her family. United won two-nil and Casey drove in the second goal. Sophie's face glowed with pride at the exemplary genius of Danny Casey. The next week Jansie interrogated about her encounter with Casey. She told her that Geoff had told her brother, Frank, who let Jansie know. Sophie wished that Geoff had kept it a secret between them but then she convinced Jansie that it was indeed the truth and made her promise to keep it a secret. Sophie was relieved to know that Geoff hadn't told Frank about her meeting with Casey the next week.

After dark, Sophie walked by the canal and sat down on a wooden bench under a solitary elm tree where lovers sometimes came. While waiting, Sophie imagined Danny coming. She imagined her own excitement at the prospect of his arrival. Not until sometime had elapsed, she began to think that Danny wasn't coming at all. Her worries were not emotional but about the failure of her love. She rose to go back. Yet she hoped against hope that Danny would meet her in the arcade in front of the Royce's Store. But Danny never turned up. Sophie's fantasy came to an end. However, Sophie still fantasises about her hero, unperturbed.

8. GOING PLACES

by A.R. Barton

CHARACTER SKETCH: Sophie

Sophie has been portrayed as the central character in the story 'Going Places'. She perfectly represents the girls of her age in poor families. Sophie always lives in a dream world, dreaming impossible things. The opening scene of the story clearly tells what sort of girl she is. She is not ready to accept the reality of her family's condition and dreams of having a boutique of her own.

She makes up the story of meeting Danny Casey, a charming and upcoming footballer. Nobody believes her but she refuses to accept that it is only her fantasy. Rather, she starts believing that she has met him and to prove that she is telling the truth and makes up another story that she has fixed a date with him. She is so lost in her dreams that she actually goes to the canal and waits for him but he does not show up. She knows that he will not come, but still she becomes sad. On the whole, we can say that she was adamant who did not listen to anybody except her heart which always created problems for her.

CHARACTER SKETCH: Jansie

Even though Sophie and Jansie were of the same age, their characters were poles apart. Jansie unlike her friend Sophie was a very practical and down-to-earth person. She belonged to a middle class family. She knew they were all going to work in the biscuit factory after leaving school and hence, did not entertain Sophie's absurd ideas and imaginations. She did not have high ambitions in life like Sophie.

Though she was sensible and practical, she was nosey and she loved to gossip.

Reference to Context

Read the extracts given below and answer the questions that follow.

I.   "When I leave," Sophie said, coming home from school, "I'm going to have a boutique." Jansie, linking arms with her along the street; looked doubtful.

    (a)   Name the title of the story.

    (b)   Name the author.

    (c)   What did Sophie want to open?

    (d)   Who was Jansie?

II. He was kneeling on the floor in the next room tinkering with a part of his motorcycle over some newspaper spread on the carpet. He was three years out of school, an apprentice mechanic, travelling to his work each day to the far side of the city. He was almost grown up now, and she suspected areas of his life about which she knew nothing, about which he never spoke. He said little at all, ever, voluntarily. Words had to be prized out of him like stones out of the ground. And she was jealous of his silence. When he wasn't speaking it was as though he was away somewhere, out there in the world in those places she had never been.

    (a)   Why did Sophie wish to become an actress?

    (b)   What was the special fascination of the teenager Sophie?

    (c)   Explain the character of Geoff.

    (d)   Why was Sophie jealous of Geoff's silence??

III. The table lamp cast an amber glow across her brother's bedroom wall, and across the large poster of United's first team squad and the row of coloured photographs beneath, three of them of the young Irish prodigy, Casey.

    (a)   Why did Sophie long for her brother's affection?

    (b)   What was Sophie's latest lie?

    (c)   Why did Sophie like Danny Casey?

    (d)   What did Sophie tell Geoff about Danny Casey?

IV. Sophie glared at the ground. Damn that Geoff, this was a Geoff thing not a Jansie thing. It was meant to be something special just between them. Something secret.

    (a)   '*Damn that Geoff*, this was a Geoff thing not a Jansie thing.' Who said these lines and to whom?

    (b)   Why did Sophie say so?

    (c)   Write a character sketch of Jansie.

    (d)   Did Geoff keep up his promise?

V.   And afterwards you wait there alone in the arcade for a long while, standing where he stood, remembering the soft melodious voice, the shimmer of green eyes. No taller than you. No bolder than you. The prodigy. The innocent genius. The great Danny Casey.

    (a)   'It was a perfect place, she had always thought so'. Which is the place described?

    (b)   What were Sophie's expectations when she walked to the park?

    (c)   '*I can see the future and how I will have to live with this burden.*' What burden is Sophie talking about?

    (d)   What thoughts came to Sophie's mind as she sat by the canal?

ANSWER KEY

I.   (a)   Going Places

     (b)   A. R. Barton

     (c)   Sophie wanted to have a boutique of her own.

     (d)   Jansie was Sophie's friend.

II.   (a)   Sophie was interested in opening a boutique. For this, she needed money. So, she thought that she should become an actress and have the boutique on the side.

     (b)   The unknown outlying districts of her city, unknown places beyond her country, and the world of places where she had never been were great fascination for Sophie.

     (c)   Geoff was Sophie's elder brother. He had been out of school for three years and was almost grown up. He dreamed to become a motor mechanic and worked hard for it and became one.

     (d)   Sophie was a nonstop speaker, but on the other side Geoff was a silent young man. His world remained a fascination for her. She felt that when he was not speaking, his mind was way at some unknown place, and so she felt jealous of him.

III. (a)   Sophie found in her brother, Geoff a patient listener to all her fantasies and also the one she could confide in. This made her quite fond of Geoff and long for his affection.

     (b)   The latest of her lies was that she had an unexpected meeting with Danny Casey, the Irish football player. She further told that the great hero was in love with her and that he had promised an evening with her in a park.

     (c)   The young Irish Danny Casey was a sports icon. He was tall and handsome with a strong dark face. Naturally, she was attracted to him and imagined him to be fit for her love.

     (d)   Sophie told Geoff that she met Danny Casey at Royce's window and he had gentle green eyes. Sophie also told him that she had a talk with Danny and asked for an autograph but they both neither had pen nor paper.

IV.   (a)   Sophie said the above lines to Jansie.

     (b)   Sophie knew Jansie was a rumour-monger. She feared that Jansie would spread the story about this meeting with Danny. That was why she was annoyed with her brother Geoff for telling others the information she had shared with him.

     (c)   Jansie belonged to a middle class family. Though she was sensible and practical, she was nosey. She loved to gossip and did not have high ambitions like Sophie.

     (d)   Sophie told Geoff about her meeting with Danny Casey and asked Geoff not to disclose it. However, Geoff didn't keep his promise to Sophie. He told the story to Frank who further told his sister, Jansie about it.

V.   (a)   For the fancy date, Sophie walked by the canal in the evening. She used to play there in her childhood.

     (b)   Sophie expected that she would meet Danny Casey in the park. She was happy that she would get an autograph from Danny Casey and that she would be able to convince everyone that she had not been a liar.

     (c)   Sophie is talking about her habit of telling lies and her helplessness in keeping this burden down for ever.

     (d)   Sophie was waiting for Danny Casey, sitting by the canal, imagining him coming. However, after some time, when he did not turn up, reality hit her hard and she became sad. She thought that her family would never believe her and her brother Geoff would be disappointed.

FLAMINGO: POETRY   MIND MAP

SUMMARY OF THE POEM

The poem, "My Mother at Sixty Six" by Kamala Das explores the feelings of melancholy and pain that a daughter experiences while leaving her mother, all by herself, at a ripe old age.

In the first stanza, the poet begins with telling that the last Friday morning, she was driving to Cochin. She saw her mother who was sitting beside her. The use of the phrase "Last Friday Morning" is not just to depict a day but also to show that it is past now. In other words, the poet uses this phrase in order to tell that time never stops. Everything in the world moves into the past.

The poet probably tries to compare her mother with "Last Friday Morning" as both had their springtime (mother was young and the day had its morning) but now they are in the past (the day has gone and her mother's youth has also gone). She found that her mother was dozing with her mouth open. Her face was as pale as that of a corpse. The poet painfully realized that her mother is not going to live long. This painful thought haunted her. Here, the poet shows the typical love and affection which is present in a mother-daughter relation. Thus in the very first lines, the central theme of the poem is revealed.

The poet is pained and shifts her attention outside the car in order to drive out the negative feelings. She changes her sad mood. The scene outside the window is of growing life and energy. The rapidly sprinting trees alongside the merrily playing children symbolize life, youth and vitality. The poet here is reminded of her own childhood when her mother had been young, whereas now she is encircled with the fear of losing her and that has made her insecure.

She is at the airport to take a flight. It indicates departure and separation which creates melancholy. As she bids goodbye to her mother, the image of the old, worn out mother in the twilight of years strikes her again. Here again a simile is used to compare her mother with a late winter's moon whose light is obstacled by fog and mist. She looks old as, her personality is dimmed by age. The poet is feeling the pain of separation, leaving her mother and going. Also, her childhood fear of losing her mother which she feels that earlier was temporary but now, could be forever as she could die of old age, is haunting her. She is so pained that it is natural for her to cry but keeping a brave front she hides her tears and smiles. She bids farewell to her mother and keeping her hope of seeing her again alive, says "see you soon, Amma". She hides her sorrow as she does not want to create a painful environment for her mother and conveys to her that as she is enjoying her life similarly her mother should also be happy and enjoy her life.

1. MY MOTHER AT SIXTY-SIX

ABOUT THE POET

The poet, Kamala Das also wrote by her pen-name 'Madhavikutty'. She was born in Kerala and is one of India's first poets. Her writings reflect exploration of a wide range of relationships from a woman's point of view—as a daughter, a wife and a mother. Her works are filled with a woman's desire for self-expression and freedom. External factors do not reflect in her writings, her writings bring out her true inner feelings.

Her five poetry books Summer in Calcutta, The Descendants, The Old Playhouse and other Poems, The Anamalai Poems, and Only the Soul Knows How to Sing are some of her well-known works. Her novel, *Alphabet of Lust* and her collection of short stories called *Padmavati the Harlot and Other Stories* are also some of her well-known works.

In the poem 'My Mother at Sixty-Six', she talks about her mother. This poem is based on mother-daughter relation and the poet shares her feelings for her mother.

POETIC DEVICES/FIGURES OF SPEECH IN THE POEM

1. Simile: This rhetorical device is used when an overt comparison is made between two different things with the use of 'as' or 'like'. In this poem, the poet uses the device of simile on two instances. In lines 5 – 7, she compares her mother's face with that of a corpse and uses the word "like" while making that comparison. In lines 15 – 16, she again compares her mother with the moon in wintertime and uses the word "as" while making this comparison.

Example:

- Her face ashen like that of a corpse.
- Wan, pale as a late winter's moon.

2. Personification: This rhetorical device is used to bestow human qualities on something that is not human. In this poem, the poet uses the device of personification in line 12 with respect to trees. She imagines the trees to be young figures that are running alongside her car.

Reference to Context

Read the extracts given below and answer the questions that follow.

I. "Driving from my parent's home to Cochin last Friday
    morning, I saw my mother, beside me, doze,
    open mouthed, her face ashen like that
    of a corpse and realized with pain
    That she was old as she looked but soon
    put that thought away…"
    (a) Where was the poet coming from? Where was she driving to?
    (b) How does the poet describe her mother and what did she notice about her?
    (c) Why was her mother's face looking like that of a corpse?
    (d) Why was the realisation painful?

II. "and looked out at young
    trees sprinting, the merry children spilling
    out of their homes…"
    (a) What was the poet 'looking' at? What did she notice?
    (b) Why did the poet start 'looking out'?
    (c) What did the poet see when she looked out the moving car?
    (d) What does the phrase 'trees sprinting' signify?

III. "and looked out at young
     trees sprinting, the merry children spilling
     out of their homes, but after the airport's
     security check, standing a few yards
     away, I looked again at her, wan,
     pale as a late winter's moon and felt that
     old familiar ache…"
     (a) Why did the poet look at her mother again? What did she observe?
     (b) What did the images of 'young trees' and 'merry children' symbolize?
     (c) How can the trees sprint?
     (d) Identify the figure of speech used in these lines.

IV. " but after the airport's
    security check, standing a few yards
    away, I looked again at her, wan, pale
    as a late winter's moon…"
    (a) Where was the poet standing?
    (b) Who does 'her' here refer to?
    (c) What does the poet compare her mother's face to and why?
    (d) Explain 'wan, pale as a late winter's moon'.

V. " and felt that old
    familiar ache, my childhood's fear,
    but all I said was, see you soon, Amma,
    all I did was smile and smile and smile."
    (a) What is the poet's old, familiar ache? How did that ache return at the airport?
    (b) What was the poet's parting words?
    (c) Did the poet share her thoughts with her mother? Why do you think so?
    (d) Why did the poet only 'smile'?

ANSWER KEY

I. (a) The poet had gone to her parents' home to visit them. She was now going to Cochin airport on a Friday morning.

(b) The poet describes her mother as old, pale, cold and senile. She noticed that her mother was sleeping with her mouth open and her face was the colour of ash, just like that of a dead body.

(c) The poet's mother had lost all its glow due to ageing. As she dozed off beside her, the mother looked almost like a corpse, for her face looked pale, colourless and seemed to have lost the fervor of life.

(d) The realisation that her mother had grown very old was painful because it brought with it the distressing thought that she was nearing her death, whose cruel hands would separate the poet from her mother and she would not be able to see her again.

II. (a) The poet was looking at her mother. She noticed the mother's ashen and almost lifeless face distraught with pain.

(b) The poet started looking out of the window because she wanted to drive away the pain and agony she experienced on seeing her aged mother. She wanted to drive away her helplessness in the wake of her mother's ageing and approaching death.

(c) The poet saw young trees running past her moving car and also the children rushing out of their homes to play. Both the trees and children were full of life in comparison to her pale and lifeless mother.

(d) Here, the phrase 'tress sprinting' signifies time, which has passed at a fast pace.

III. (a) The narrator looked at her mother once again for the last time before she left to reassure herself about the well-being of her mother. She had tried to drive away the pain she had felt on seeing her weak and aged mother. One last time she looked at her to wish her goodbye. She observed that her mother looked lifeless and dull like a late winter's moon.

(b) Trees and children symbolize the spring of life, its strength, vigour and happiness which contrasts with the lifelessness and helplessness that sets in with age.

(c) he car was moving when the poet looked out, so the tress appeared to be running in the opposite direction. Thus, the trees have been described as 'sprinting'.

(d) The figure of speech used in these lines is simile; her mother's pale appearance is compared to that of a late winter's moon.

IV. (a) The poet was at the Cochin airport waiting to board the plane after the security check.

(b) 'Her' here refers to the poet's mother.

(c) The poet compares her mother's face to a late winter's moon. Just as a 'late winter's moon' looks colourless and dull because of mist and fog, the poet's mother's face looks pale and lacks brightness due to old age.

(d) 'Late winter's moon' refers to the moon during the late winter season, which appears pale and lusterless because of mist and fog. In this simile, the poet compares the mother's pale and withered face with the winter's moon. The mother's face also seemed to have lost its radiance which was now misted by age. Winter symbolizes death and the waning moon symbolizes decay which is also reflected on the mother's face.

V. (a) The poet used to separate from her mother in her childhood. Those separations were painful to her. After so many separations this pain and separations were familiar to the poet. It was an ache of helplessness. At the airport she faced another separation from her mother and it reminded her of the number of separations in the past. It was also the fear of separation of mother's death.

(b) The poet's parting words were, "See you soon, Amma', suggesting hope to herself and her mother that they will meet again.

(c) The poet did not share her fears and agony with her mother. She only bid goodbye to her with the hope of seeing her soon. I think the poet did not share her thoughts with her aged mother because it would have unnecessarily disturbed her frail old mother. Moreover, her thoughts were caused by the fear of the unknown.

(d) The poet only smiled to hide her guilt, anxiety and fear of the unknown. Also, she wanted to bid a cheerful farewell to her mother before boarding the flight.

MIND MAP

SUMMARY OF THE POEM

In the first stanza, Spender describes the miserable condition of the children. The faces of the children are unlike the usual children of schools. Instead of being exuberant and energetic, they are like rootless weeds, unwanted and cast out. A particular tall girl is described by the poet as having a bowed down head which shows the burden of the stressed life she leads. Another boy who is as thin as a paper also has the same undernourished look on his face. He has a scared expression in his eyes. The poet says there is one particular boy who is a little younger than the rest but still has his hopes and dreams with him. He waits for the time when he can go out in the open to play. The environment of gloom has not yet engulfed his dreams and hopes.

In the second stanza, the poet describes the classroom which is also dirty and neglected like its inhabitants. The classroom too exhibits an atmosphere of depression and gloom. The walls are cream in colour and on them the names of the donors are engraved. The walls have pictures of the great poet Shakespeare, a cloudless city skyline and the splendid Tyrolese valley which are in sharp contrast to the dark atmosphere of the classroom. There is a world maps on the wall which is their window to the outside world; their classroom windows show their dark future in the dirty alleys only.

In the third stanza, the pensive poet suddenly turns belligerent and feels that Shakespeare is 'wicked' as he is misleading those naïve children through his words which is not only unreal for them, but has a negative impact on their minds. He feels that this would instigate them to steal or take unfair means as they desperately make attempts to escape from their cramped holes. Their existence is indeed, very sad. These deprived children are so skinny that it appears that they are 'wearing' skins. The spectacles they are wearing have glass which has been broken and mended. Their entire appearance reflects their misery and deprivation. The maps displayed in their classroom are no reality for them. Their world is slum; their doom is in the slum.

In the final stanza, the poet uses a pacifying tone and appeals to the governor, inspector and the visitors to do something about the condition of these slum schools. The map showing the beautiful world can be their reality too if a little will and effort are put together. The poet hopes for a better future of these children and wants the authorities to realize their responsibilities and free the children from such grave-like confinements. The children must break away from the school boundaries and enjoy the world beyond.

2. AN ELEMENTARY SCHOOL CLASSROOM IN A SLUM

ABOUT THE POET

Stephen Spender was born on February 28, 1909, in London. The son of a journalist, he grew up steeped in the art of writing. His life as a poet and writer began in the 1920s while he was at Oxford, where he surrounded himself with respected writers, such as W. H. Auden, Christopher Isherwood, Cecil Day Lewis, and Louis MacNeice. He was a prolific writer, authoring and editing many books. Besides poetry, he published several plays, novels, and short stories and many nonfiction works. His books of poetry include *Poems of Dedication* (1946), *The Edge of Being* (1949), *The Generous Days* (1969), *and Dolphins* (1994). His non-fiction works include *The Creative Element* (1953), *The Struggle of the Modern* (1963), *and Love-Hate Relationships* (1974).

Spender's poem "An Elementary School Classroom in a Slum" first appeared in 1964 in his Selected Poems.

POETIC DEVICES/FIGURES OF SPEECH IN THE POEM

1. **Simile**
   Example:
   * like rootless weeds
     This expression is used to describe the health of children, how much malnutrition affected them.
   * Like catacombs
     These children live in cramped lines of houses where only darkness is there, same are the catacombs where dead bodies are buried. Their life is also in darkness, their aim, their ambition all are in darkness.
   * slums as big as doom
     Living in slum is like living in hell.
2. **Metaphor:**
   Example:
   * rats eyes
     Boys anxiety and timidity is like that of a rat.
   * reciting a father's gnarled disease
     The boy's body speaks of gnarled disease inherited from father.
   * tree room abode in a tree
   * future's painted with a fog
     Just as fog limits our visibility during winters, the children future is always blocked by hopelessness.
   * spectacles of steel
     This suggests that they are wearing spectacles made of steel, and this suggests that they see only darkness; their future is dark.
3. **Alliteration**
   * far far from gusty waves   * surely Shakespeare   * bottle bits

Reference to Context

Read the extracts given below and answer the questions that follow.

I.   **Far far from gusty waves these children's faces.**
     Like rootless weeds, the hair torn around their pallor:
     The tall girl with her weighed-down head. The paperseeming boy,
     with rat's eyes.
     (a)   What are the children compared to?
     (b)   Why do you think does the poet mention only the faces of the children?
     (c)   Why do you think the tall girl is sitting with a weighed-down head?
     (d)   Give two phrases which tell us that the children are undernourished.

II. **The stunted, unlucky heir**
     of twisted bones, reciting a father's gnarled disease,
     His lesson, from his desk. At the back of the dim class
     One unnoted, sweet and young. His eyes live in a dream,
     Of squirrel's game, in tree room, other than this.
     (a)   Who is the 'unlucky heir' and what has he inherited?
     (b)   Who is sitting at the back of the dim class?
     (c)   What is the stunted boy reciting?
     (d)   Explain, 'in tree room, other than this'?

III. **Surely, Shakespeare is wicked, the map a bad example,**
     With ships and sun and love tempting them to steal—
     For lives that slyly turn in their cramped holes
     From fog to endless night? On their slag heap, these children
     Wear skins peeped through by bones and spectacles of steel
     With mended glass, like bottle bits on stones.
     (a)   Why is Shakespeare described as wicked?
     (b)   How do the slum children look like?
     (c)   Why is ship a tempting reality in the lives of the slum children? What else tempts the children?
     (d)   Explain: 'from fog to endless night'.

IV. **And yet, for these**
     Children, these windows, not this map, their world,
     Where all their future's painted with a fog,
     A narrow street sealed in with a lead sky
     Far far from rivers, capes, and stars of words.
     (a)   Which map is the poet talking about in the above lines?
     (b)   Who are 'these children'? What do 'these windows' refer to?
     (c)   What kind of future does the poet foresee for them?
     (d)   Why does the poet say that the narrow street is sealed?

V.   **Unless governor, inspector, visitor,**
     This map becomes their window and these windows
     That shut upon their lives like catacombs,
     Break O break open till they break the town
     And show the children to green fields, and make their world
     Run azure on gold sands, and let their tongues
     Run naked into books, the white and green leaves open
     History theirs whose language is the sun.
     (a)   Who can improve the lot of the poor slum children?
     (b)   What does the poet want his readers break?
     (c)   What does the poet want for the children?
     (d)   Explain: "History is theirs whose language is the sun".

ANSWER KEY

I.   (a)   The children have pale faces and torn and scattered hair all over their faces and hence, they are compared to rootless weeds.

(b)   The poet mentions only the faces of the children in the classroom to bring out the pain they suffer. Their existence is entirely based on sufferings, poverty and want, darkness and death. As one's pain is expressed only on his/her face; therefore, the poet mentions only 'faces' in the poem.

(c)   The girl is sitting with a weighed-down head probably because she is depressed due to abject poverty or family tussles. She also feels humiliated and embarrassed because of the lack of education.

(d)   i. rootless weeds

ii. rat's eyes

II.   (a)   The boy with stunted growth and twisted bones, sitting at the desk, is referred to as 'unlucky heir'. He has inherited the deformity of gnarled disease that makes him a living example of his father's sufferings.

(b)   An unnoted, sweet young boy is sitting at the back of the dim class. He is dreaming of squirrels playing games on trees. He is also dreaming of his future that will be free of sarrow.

(c)   The stunted boy is reciting his lessons, but due to his disease, his voice is weak and sick and thus he recites his diseased inheritance instead.

(d)   The unnoted boy desires to play in the hollows of the tree rather than attending to the lessons in the classroom. He likes the hollows inside the tree. For him, the classroom is very boring.

III. (a)   Shakespearean stories are full of fortunate, beautiful, happy, romantic characters and magical places and palaces. When these stories are told in the classroom, the children are attracted to these stories and try to imitate these heroic characters but in reality they are troubled by disease and despair. Their literary training is a far cry. That is why Shakespeare has been described as wicked.

(b)   The slum children are extremely starved and malnourished. The poet compares their bodies to the large pile of waste metal remains. They are like skeletons wearing broken glasses as spectacles.

(c)   Far away from seas and oceans, the children have not seen a real ship or real sea. They are also tempted by the brightness of the sky and the love in the stories they have heard.

(d)   With reference to the passage, the expression 'from fog to endless night' describes the miserable and pathetic lives of the slum children from start to finish. From foggy mornings till late nights, these children make desperate attempts to live their life, sustaining it despite all odds. Their life is full of misery, hopelessness and suffering.

IV.   (a)   The poet is talking about the map which depicts only the world of the privileged and the important, the world that comprises civilised domes, bells, flowers and the scenic beauty of nature.

(b)   These are the children of the Elementary school classroom in a slum. 'These windows' are the windows of the classroom where the children are now sitting and which shows only narrow streets and dark sky symbolising their dark future.

(c)   The future of these children is quite dim. It has been painted with fog. It means the poor children have no bright hopes about their future. As we can't see things in the fog, in the same way the future of these children stares at darkness. There is no one to guide them and hence, it is bleak.

(d)   The poet says that the narrow street is sealed as these provide no opportunity to make an access to the vast outer world of wisdom.

V.   (a)   The ruler, the educationists, the teachers and the general public by their efforts can improve the lives of the slum children.

(b)   The poet wants his readers to break the windows of the classroom that shut out their freedom in the classroom. The windows always remain closed and restrict light from entering the classroom making it a catacomb for the children.

(c)   The poet wants that these children should be properly educated, so that they get the energy and warmth of the sun which is symbolic of light and knowledge.

(d)   According to the poet, history is made by those people who speak the language of the Sun. It means those who are given access to the world of opportunities are the ones who accomplish feats.

MIND MAP

SUMMARY OF THE POEM

Originally written in Spanish, 'Keeping Quiet' by Pablo Neruda is based on introspection and retrospection. It is a deceptively simple poem about the need for a little bit of soul-searching which tells us how a moment of silent introspection will make us realise the utter futility of our aggressive endeavours.

The poem opens in an arresting and dramatic way. By asking the reader to count to twelve, the poet calls for a time to be tranquil and unmoving. His use of the number twelve could be associated to the clock hours or possibly, even the number of months in a year. Both attributions however, effectively depict how our hours and months pass by before us, as we continue to chase after them.

He requests everyone not to speak because languages create barriers between people. The moment when everyone stops moving and speaking would bring everyone together and lead us to introspection. In this view, symbolism may also be seen in the use of the phrase, "move our arms so much" which in this context, if taken lightly can be considered as merely brisk walking, but could also be signifying violence or our selfish pursuits. It is to be noted as well how the poet mentions "once" and "one second" in this stanza. The appeal is set on the premise that humans are constantly speaking and constantly moving- again, a reinforcement of his earlier idea about on the lack of time to be still and introspective.

In stanza 3, the poet introduces the impact of such behavior. The poet then proceeds to ask the reader to ponder, consider and bask on the glory of this rare occurrence where the usual flurry of diverse human activity is now silenced to a standstill and in surprising unity. As humans are perceived to be unique in their own ways and possess free will, a complied deliberate silence of all shall create this mysterious yet wonderfully unusual unanimity.

The poem develops by providing what ensues through this quietness. The poet shows how because of this, humans would now have more time to think about their actions and how they would have the time to notice the details that surround their daily lives. The poet says that everyone is working continuously, to achieve one's goals. People are threatened by death and the fear forces them to work endlessly so that they can achieve everything quickly. In this mad rush, they do not realize the repercussions of their acts. He wants us to pause and come out of the mad rush. He wants us to be happy about our achievements and celebrate them. He wants us to overcome the fear of death and to relax for a while. We should know the results of our deeds and celebrate our achievements. Also, the poet asks us to learn from earth which seems to be still when seen from far away but is bustling with life with all the flora and fauna within.

Having presented the dilemma, the poet effectively passes the baton to the reader and gives him the power and the choice to be still and begin his own introspection and retrospection. As with the central idea of his poem, the call to pause and be mindful of one's own self and ways, resonates to the very conclusion of the poem.

3. KEEPING QUIET

ABOUT THE POET

Pablo Neruda, the pseudonym of Neftali Ricardo Reyes Basoalto, was a Nobel Prize-winning Chilean poet. He was a famous poet and politician and regarded as one of the prominent writers of the 20th century. Neruda wrote in a variety of styles such as love poems as in his collection *Twenty Poems of Love and a Song of Despair*, surrealist poems, historical epics, and overtly political manifestoes. His poetry bears an impact on his political activities and expresses his experiences in repression during his exile. He wrote in green ink which was his personal symbol for desire and hope. His writings are simple, wherein lies their beauty. The Colombian novelist Gabriel García Márquez once called Neruda "the greatest poet of the 20th century in any language."

POETIC DEVICES/FIGURES OF SPEECH IN THE POEM

1. **Alliteration**

   Example:

• sudden strangeness	• hurt hands	• clean clothes
• we will	• we would	• wars with

Reference to Context

Read the extracts given below and answer the questions that follow.

I.   Now we will count to twelve

and we will all keep still.

For once on the face of the Earth

Let's not speak in any language,

Let's stop for one second,

and not move our arms so much.

    (a)   Name the poem and the poet.

    (b)   Why does the poet want us to keep quiet?

    (c)   Why does the poet ask everyone to stop using any language?

    (d)   What does the poet mean by 'not move our arms'?

II.   Fisherman in the cold sea

would not harm whales

and the man gathering salt

would look at his hurt hands.

    (a)   What does 'fisherman' symbolize?

    (b)   What does the poet ask fishermen not to do?

    (c)   What do the 'hurt hands' imply?

    (d)   What message does the poet seem to give in these lines?

III.   Those who prepare green wars,

wars with gas, wars with fire,

victory with no survivors,

would put on clean clothes

and walk about with their brothers

in the shade, doing nothing.

    (a)   What does the poet mean by 'Green Wars'?

    (b)   Who are 'those' who prepare green wars?

    (c)   What does 'put on clean clothes' signify?

    (d)   What poetic device is used in the third line of the extract?

IV.   What I want should not be

confused with total inactivity.

Life is what it is about;

I want no truck with death.

If we were not single-minded

about keeping our lives moving,

and for once could do nothing, perhaps

a huge silence might interrupt this sadness

of never understanding ourselves and

of threatening ourselves with death.

    (a)   What does Neruda imply by 'total inactivity'?

    (b)   What is the 'sadness' that the poet refers to in the poem?

    (c)   What is man 'single-minded' about?

    (d)   What does "truck with death" mean? Why does the poet not want a truck with death?

V.   **Perhaps the Earth can teach us**
   as when everything seems dead
   and later proves to be alive.
   Now I'll count upto twelve
   and you keep quiet and I will go.

    (a)   What and how can the Earth teach us?
    (b)   What is the significance of 'keeping quiet'?
    (c)   Why does the poet count upto twelve?
    (d)   Explain, 'you keep quiet and I will go.'

ANSWER KEY

I.   (a)   The name of the poem is Keeping Quiet and the poet is Pablo Neruda.

    (b)   The poet wants us to keep quiet in the hope that the moment of tranquility might help us in finding the answers to our problems.

    (c)   Language helps us to communicate with other people. The poet wants us to be silent and motionless for one second. He wants this time of silence for talking to oneself, not for talking to other people, so he doesn't want us to use any language.

    (d)   The poet wants us not to move our arms because any kind of physical activity will restrain us to introspect. Not moving our arms suggest no activity and no harm. There would be no wars and no violence.

II.   (a)   Fisherman is a symbol to represent the mighty/rich/influential people of the world. Those people who have been indiscriminately exploring nature and Mother Earth for their own vested interests.

    (b)   The poet asks fishermen not to hurt or injure the whales in the seas.

    (c)   'Hurt hands' means that human beings are oblivious of the pain they are causing to themselves in the pursuit of amassing more and more comforts. They have no time for themselves.

    (d)   In these lines Neruda conveys that the desire of man for more and more progress and advancement has done more destruction than development. Man seems to have no concern and care for his brethren.

III.   (a)   Green wars, i.e., wars with gas, wars with fire are deadly weapons to kill the mother earth. These are the nuclear and chemical weapons created by man and used in waging wars against countries. In short, it is the war against the environment.

    (b)   The word 'those' in the above stanza is used for the politicians, statesmen and those overambitious powers who in their zeal for dominance are involved in initiating and aggravating wars.

    (c)   'Put on clean clothes' signifies the feelings of their mutual understanding.

    (d)   Paradox is used in the third line of the extract as opposite ideas are explained by this phrase.

IV.   (a)   'Total inactivity' would imply that mankind should channelize his activities towards construction and he should put an end to his destructive activities. It certainly does not mean "no action" because life is an ongoing process.

    (b)   The poet refers to the 'sadness' which arises due to the fact that people fail to understand themselves. They have no time to introspect about their actions and their consequences.

    (c)   Man is single-minded about his own progress and advancement. He is so focused on his own development that he forgets to visualize the pros and cons of reckless development. The consequences and impact of materialistic progress should be taken into consideration.

    (d)   Truck with death means an association with death. The poet says that by "stillness" he doesn't mean total inactivity which is akin to death; what he means has nothing to do with death for he knows that life is a process of activities.

V.   (a)   The Earth teaches us the art of preserving and resurrecting life on Earth. It teaches us to remain calm on the surface. At times, the Earth seems to be dead but under this dormant surface; there is an amazing life, which goes on to prove that there can be life under apparent stillness.

    (b)   It is important to keep quiet because it will enable us to look within ourselves and understand what we are really looking for. We can then find solutions to our problems.

    (c)   The poet wants to achieve peace by counting upto twelve. He wants us to introspect in a moment of silence.

    (d)   Pablo Neruda implores mankind to keep quiet and experience the ecstatic moments of silence. This meditation will help to create a new trend of thoughts and bring changes in thought process. After having achieved his intentions, the poet quietly departs leaving man to meditate, introspect and revel in that very exotic moment.

MIND MAP

SUMMARY OF THE POEM

In this poem, John Keats praises all the beautiful things present around us and the world. According to him, beautiful things get treasured in our mind and grow more beautiful with the passage of time. They provide eternal happiness, everlasting joy to us and leave their imprints on the mind of all human beings who hold a strong bonding with the earth. According to the poet, this earth has abundance of pessimistic people; hatred among the people and sadness that lurks everywhere in human's life. He holds humans responsible for every negative thing on this earth. According to him, only beautiful things can make our soul pure and thoughts alive.

The closing paragraph tells us of some of the beautiful things on Earth. The examples cited by the poet are the sun, the moon, trees, flowers, streams, musk-rose blooms, architectural sepulchers, even fairy tales or heroic legends Keats sees beauty in the 'simple sheep; innocent humans seeking solace in nature, and Mother Nature in its own way sprouts a shady abode of relief and consolation. The expression 'Lily of the Valley' is quite well-known and rouses images of a delicate lone white flower holding up its head amidst a setting of thorns and barbs and everything contrary in nature to delicateness.

The poet also sees beauty in the death of martyrs and legends. 'The mighty dead' are those martyrs who have died bravely for a cause. We honour them by erecting magnificent, grand sepulchers in which beauty is seen. If one looks around, there are innumerable beautiful things to notice – they seem to flow immortally as a fountain, from the gods above to help the pitiable human beings to cope with the harshness of life.

4. A THING OF BEAUTY

ABOUT THE POET

John Keats, one of the supreme English poets and a major figure in the Romantic Movement, was born in 1795 in Moorfields, London. He was one of the main figures of the second generation of Romantic poets along with Lord Byron and P.B. Shelly despite his work having been in publication for only four years before his death.

Although his poems were not generally well received by critics during his life, his reputation grew after his death, so that by the end of the 19th century, he had become one of the most beloved of all English poets. He had significant influence on a diverse range of poets and writers. The poetry of Keats is characterized by sensual imagery, most notably in the series of odes. Today, his poems and letters are some of the most popular and most analysed in English literature. His notable works are: *To autumn*; *Ode to Nightingale*; *On first looking into Chapman's Homer*; *Ode on a Grecian Urn*.

'A Thing of Beauty' is an excerpt from his poem, 'Endymion: A poetic Romance' (1818), considered to be an epic poem.

POETIC DEVICES/FIGURES OF SPEECH IN THE POEM

1. **Alliteration**: There are three pairs of alliteration – N-sound in "Noble" and "Natures" the C sounds in "Cooling" and "Covert" and B-sound in the words "Band" and "Bind".

2. **Metaphor**: Metaphor is evidently used in "bower quiet", "sweet dreams", "wreathing a flowery band". "pall" and "endless fountain of immortal drink".

3. **Imagery**: The immense use of imagery can be found in the phrase "flowery bands" which visualizes a bunch of flowers like a band. The use of the phrase "shady boon" also pictures the blessing to be shady. The words "daffodils in green world", "clear rills", grandeur of dooms", etc., are instances of use of imagery. "Cooling covert" and "endless fountain of eternal drink" are one of the notable examples of imagery used in this poem.

Reference to Context

Read the extracts given below and answer the questions that follow.

I.   **A thing of beauty is a joy forever**
     Its loveliness increases, it will never
     Pass into nothingness; but will keep
     A bower quiet for us and a sleep
     Full of sweet dreams and health and quiet breathing

     (a)   How is a thing of beauty a joy forever?
     (b)   Describe the kind of joy a beautiful thing provides.
     c)   Explain: "never pass into nothingness."
     (d)   What do you understand by a 'bower'?

II. **Therefore, on every morrow, are we wreathing**
     A flowery band to bind us to the Earth,
     Spite of despondence, of the inhuman dearth
     Of noble natures, of the gloomy days,
     Of all the unhealthy and o'er-darkened ways
     Made for our searching.

     (a)   What are the flowery bands that bind us to the Earth?
     (b)   Why is there an 'inhuman dearth of noble natures'?
     (c)   What message do the above lines convey?
     (d)   Explain 'spite of despondence'. Why are we despondent?

III. **…yes, in spite of all,**
     Some shape of beauty moves away the pall
     From our dark spirits.

     (a)   Why are our spirits referred to as 'dark'?
     (b)   Explain: "Some shape of beauty."
     (c)   How does beauty help us when we are burdened with grief?
     (d)   Identify the figure of speech in the second line.

IV. **…Such the sun, the moon,**
     Trees old, and young, sprouting a shady boon
     For simple sheep; and such are daffodils
     With the green world they live in; and clear rills
     That for themselves a cooling covert make
     'Gainst the hot season; the mid forest brake,
     Rich with a sprinkling of fair musk-rose blooms;

     (a)   What does 'simple sheep' symbolise'?
     (b)   What images of beauty has the poet refereed to?
     (c)   How do 'daffodils' and 'rills' enrich the environment?
     (d)   Explain: 'the green world they live in.'

V.   **And such too is the grandeur of the dooms**
     We have imagined for the mighty dead;
     All lovely tales that we have heard or read;
     An endless fountain of immortal drink,
     Pouring unto us from heaven's brink.

     (a)   Who are the 'mighty dead'? How do we know about them?
     (b)   Which evil things do we possess and suffer from?
     (c)   What is the thing of beauty mentioned in these lines?
     (d)   What does Keats mean by 'an endless fountain of immortal drink'?

ANSWER KEY

I.   (a)   A thing of beauty is the source of constant joy. Its beauty goes on increasing. It will never pass into nothingness.

   (b)   Anything that is beautiful provides us an unending, everlasting and eternal joy. It leaves an indelible imprint on our heart and soul.

   (c)   The joy that a thing of beauty give us is eternal. It never loses its importance and it only increases with time. It does not fade away or die out because it leaves an indelible imprint on our heart and soul.

   (d)   A bower is a pleasant place in the shade under a tree. It protects persons/animals from the hot rays of the sun.

II.   (a)   Here beautiful and pleasant things have been referred to as flowery bands. It is only those things which have beauty of some or the other kind that bind us to this Earth, or in a way, keep us going. The memory of our beautiful experiences helps us strengthen our bond with the Earth.

   (b)   Nowadays, there are only few people who are noble in character and are generous. There is a dearth of such noble souls on our earth; as these days people are mostly selfish and do not think about others.

   (c)   The above lines convey that life is full of sadness and hopelessness. People have become selfish, and there is a scarcity of noble people.

   (d)   It means despite the existence of gloom and darkness around, things of beauty make life on earth worth living. We possess the evil qualities of malice and suffer from the lack of noble qualities. That is why, we feel despondent.

III.   (a)   Our spirits are dejected due to extreme sadness and disappointment which may be the result of our own evil actions. So, the poet refers to them as dark.

   (b)   Beauty is an abstract idea and has no specific shape. The poet here means beauty in some form or some beautiful object which provides us eternal joy.

   (c)   Whenever we look at a beautiful object, we are filled with comfort and joy. When we are burdened with grief, a thing of beauty comes as a ray of hope, and makes us forget our sorrow and suffering at least for some time.

   (d)   The word 'pall' in the second line is an example of metaphor. Our souls are covered in sadness and disappointment which are compared to a pall or shroud covering the dead.

IV.   (a)   Sheep and lamb are envisioned as symbols of innocence and serene beauty. Jesus Christ was a shepherd and was surrounded by his flock of sheep, his followers. Keats has made special reference to the sheep as symbols of divine beauty.

   (b)   The poet appreciates the simplicity and serenity of beauty through an image of the sun, the moon, the trees, the sheep, the daffodils, the green pastures, the livid streams, and a fair bloom of musk-roses.

   (c)   Daffodils bloom among the green surroundings. The clear water rills or small streams offer a cooling shelter in the hot season.

   (d)   Beauty of nature is at its best in the green surroundings of meadows and pastures which provide support to all human beings. It is in the green world that all living creatures find true happiness and joy and feel relaxed.

V.   (a)   Our ancestors, who were great in their own ways, and the dead emperors have been referred to as the mighty dead. We come to know about them by reading or hearing valorous tales, which speak of their gallantry and exalted sacrifices. They are a source of motivation and inspiration for us through their sagas of their noble deeds.

   (b)   Jealousy and hatred fill our lives with sadness and take away our carefreeness. These are the evils which make us suffer in life.

   (c)   The thing of beauty mentioned in these lines is the multitude of stories celebrating the glory of our powerful ancestors, which we have read or heard.

   (d)   Beauty, according to Keats, is a perennial source of motivation and inspiration. He considers it an endless fountain from which mankind can drink the elixir of life.

MIND MAP

SUMMARY OF THE POEM

'A Roadside Stand' depicts the impoverished lives of the rural folk and compares and contrasts their life of scarcity with the affluence of the cities. The poem highlights the disparity between the cities and the villages in terms of progress and development that lead to distress and unhappiness among the dwellers of the latter.

Putting up a roadside shed, a few villagers wait yearningly for wealthy city dwellers whizzing past in their shiny cars, to stop and give them some of the cash flow that makes cities flourish.

To their disappointment, if any pacing car ever slowed down, it was to due to their annoyance with the shed showing botched directions and blotting the landscape. The villagers don't care if they are hurting the scenery. Their concern is the empty promises of the government authorities to uplift them.

There is news that the rural poor would be relocated near the theatre and the shops and well provided for so that they would have no worries. But this scheme of enforcing benefits on them is only a calculated scheme to rob them of their land, suppress their voices and disable their thinking. They force them to sleep rather than work which ultimately destroys their sleep for ever.

The villagers wait endlessly for some city money to come their way, but the city people are far removed from their life in the village. A car stops to buy a gallon of gas which the roadside stand doesn't have while there are no takers for the farmers' produce that they have in plenty. The poet highlights the disconnect between the rural and urban lives.

5. A ROADSIDE STAND

ABOUT THE POET

Robert Frost (1874-1963) is a highly acclaimed American poet of the twentieth century. He is known for his realistic depictions of rural life in New England in the early twentieth century through which he examined complex social and philosophical themes. His poetry exhibits his command of American colloquial speech and familiarity with landscapes. His lively portrayal of characters shows his concern with human tragedies and fears; and depicts man's endless strife and final reconciliation with the complexities and burdens of life.

Frost won four Pulitzer Prizes for Poetry and was awarded the Congressional Gold Medal in 1960 for his poetic works. On July 22, 1961, he was named poet laureate of Vermont. In the poem A Roadside Stand, Frost portrays the lives of the rural poor who live a life of deprivation. He highlights their plight as they yearn to earn from a good commerce with the city folk; but the latter have no interest in their humble goods, and they are forced to be entrapped in government schemes.

POETIC DEVICES/FIGURES OF SPEECH IN THE POEM

1.	Transferred epithet:	'polished traffic'; 'selfish cars' (people are polished and selfish)
2.	Personification:	'the sadness that lurks behind the window'; 'the roadside stand that too pathetically pled' (sadness and roadside stand given human quality)
3.	Alliteration :	'greedy good doers'(successive g and d sounds); 'beneficent beasts of prey' (b sounds); 'pathetically pled'(p sounds)
4.	Oxymoron:	'greedy good doers'; 'beneficent beasts of prey'(opposite ideas used together)
5.	Metaphor:	the flower of cities; swarm over their lives (symbolic of bees)

Reference to Context

Read the extracts given below and answer the questions that follow.

I. A roadside stand that too pathetically pled,
It would not be fair to say for a dole of bread,
But for some of the money, the cash, whose flow supports
The flower of cities from sinking and withering faint.
(a) Where was the roadside stand located?
(b) What did the roadside stand plead for?
(c) What figure of speech has been used in the words, "flower of cities"?
(d) What supports the flower of cities from withering?

II. The hurt to the scenery wouldn't be my complaint
So much as the trusting sorrow of what is unsaid:
Here far from the city we make our roadside stand
And ask for some city money to feel in hand
To try if it will not make our being expand,
And give us the life of the moving-pictures' promise
That the party in power is said to be keeping from us.
(a) What is the poet' complaint?
(b) Explain how the expression, "trusting sorrow" is an antithesis? What does it highlight?
(c) Explain, "make our being expand".
(d) What is "the moving-pictures' promise"? Explain "keeping from us"?

III. Sometimes I feel myself I can hardly bear
The thought of so much childish longing in vain,
The sadness that lurks near the open window there,
That waits all day in almost open prayer
For the squeal of brakes, the sound of a stopping car,
Of all the thousand selfish cars that pass,
Just one to inquire what a farmer's prices are.
(a) What "childish longing in vain" does the poet refer to?
(b) Which figure of speech has the poet used in the line, "The sadness that lurks near the open window"?
(c) What is the farmers' "open prayer" for?
(d) Why are the cars that pass by said to be "selfish"?

IV. It is in the news that all these pitiful kin
Are to be bought out and mercifully gathered in
To live in villages, next to the theatre and the store,
Where they won't have to think for themselves anymore
While greedy good-doers, beneficent beasts of prey,
Swarm over their lives enforcing benefits
That are calculated to soothe them out of their wits
(a) What is the irony in the expression "mercifully gathered"?
(b) Why will "they won't have to think for themselves anymore"?
(c) Explain, "enforcing benefits".
(d) What does the phrase, "calculated to soothe them out of their wits" mean?

V. No, in country money, the country scale of gain,
The requisite lift of spirit has never been found,
Or so the voice of the country seems to complain,
I can't help owning the great relief it would be
To put these people at one stroke out of their pain.
And then next day as I come back into the sane,
I wonder how I should like you to come to me
And offer to put me gently out of my pain.

(a)   Explain the lines "No, in country money, the country scale of gain, the requisite lift of spirit has never been found"?

(b)   What is the "great relief" the poet talks about?

(c)   Could he realize his wish? Give reasons.

(d)   What does the poet want from the society?

ANSWER KEY

I.   (a)   The little new shed was located in front at the edge of the road where the traffic sped.

        (b)   It pled for some of the money, the cash flow that made the cities bloom.

        (c)   The expression 'flower of cities' is a metaphor where the thriving cities are symbolic of a blooming flower.

        (d)   The cash flow or the trade and commerce involving big money supports the flower of cities from withering.

II.   (a)   The poet's complaint regards the sorrow that befalls the poor villagers because they trust the promise of better life, but they are denied even a small share of the city money.

        (b)   'Trusting sorrow' is antithetical because the poor people trust the authorities to deliver on their promise of uplifting their lot and give them happiness, but what they get is only sorrow as the promise is not kept.

        (c)   'Make our being expand' refers to robust health and high spirits that the poor villagers will get to have if they have the money which city people thrive on.

        (d)   Moving pictures usually depict life of comfort and style. The villagers are promised that life but the political party in power which has the wherewithal to make that possible refrains from doing so.

III.   (a)   The poet refers to the longing or endless wait of the farmers at the roadside stand for city folk to buy their farm produce and give them some of the money that makes cities flourish. He calls the farmers' longing childish because like children, the farmers fail to perceive the reality (about callous cityfolk) and choose to live in a world of make believe.

        (b)   It is personification as the abstract idea or emotion 'sadness' has been given a human action of 'lurking'.

        (c)   The open prayer is for at least one car among the thousand speeding by the roadside stand to halt and buy some of the farm produce on sale there.

        (d)   'The cars' represent the city folk who are selfish because despite having a lot of money, they do not want to spend even a little with for buying the poor farmers' goods.

IV.   (a)   The irony is that the government claims to show mercy by relocating the poor farmers but in reality, this is a cruel move to rob them of their lands as well as minds.

        (b)   The government assures them that all their needs will be taken care of so that they will not have to 'think' or worry for their livelihood anymore.

        (c)   The self-proclaimed greedy do-gooders are actually forcing down the announced benefits to them, because the farmers want not these benefits but rather good trade of their farm produce to better their condition.

        (d)   The benefits are forced on the poor farmers so that they would not have to think about working for their livelihood which would dull their minds and make them the puppets of the 'greedy do-gooders'.

V.   (a)   It means that the flow of money in the villages (country) has never been profitable enough to lift the condition and spirit of the countryfolk unlike the cities where the cash flow makes lives blossom like a flower.

        (b)   The poet is so aggrieved by the plight of the countryfolk that he says it would be a great relief if he could wipe out their misery in one stroke.

        (c)   He could not realize his wish. He admits that it is not possible to do so. He instead calls upon everyone to help.

        (d)   The poet calls upon everyone to relieve him of the pain he feels for the poor farmers, which means he wants everyone to join hands to uplift their lot slowly maybe but steadily.'

MIND MAP

SUMMARY OF THE POEM

In this feminist poem, which is critical of the male world, Aunt Jennifer creates an alternate world of freedom in her tigers. The tigers of Aunt Jennifer's stitchings are representative of her desire of a free spirit.

The first stanza opens with Aunt Jennifer's tapestry of tigers who are fearless of their environment. "Bright topaz denizens of a world of green" – evokes an image that these regal tigers are unafraid of other beings in the jungle. Bright here signifies their powerful and radiant persona. The Tigers stride in sleek chivalric certainty. The pacing of the Tigers may characterize fluid and controlled motion, as compared to the rhythmic movement of the first line. Nevertheless, the Tigers may be marching back and forth, because their movement is constrained to their tree top since there are men present there. There is a sense of certainty and confidence in the way these tigers move as can be seen in the line – "They pace in sleek chivalric certainty".

In the second stanza, the reality of Aunt Jennifer is revealed as she is feeble, weak and enslaved, very much the opposite of the tigers she was creating. Her fingers are fluttering through her wool as she sews. This fluttering may be the nervous movement of her fingers as she works. Her physical and mental trauma is depicted in the line – "find even the ivory needle hard to pull". Even though a wedding ring doesn't weigh much, "the massive weight of uncle's wedding band, sits heavily upon Aunt Jennifer's hand" signifying the amount of dominance her husband exercised over her. This also means that her inner free spirit has been shackled by the patriarchal society.

The last stanza starts on a creepy note about Aunt Jennifer's death. Even her death couldn't free her from the ordeals she went through which can be seen in "When Aunt is dead, her terrified hands will lie still ringed with ordeals she was mastered by". But her art work which was her escape route or in a way, her inner sense of freedom, will stay forever, proud and unafraid.

6. AUNT JENNIFER'S TIGERS

ABOUT THE POET

One of America's leading public philosophers, Adrienne Rich, was a poet, essayist, and feminist. She was called "one of the most extensively read and powerful poets of the second half of the 20th century" and was credited with bringing "the oppression of women to the forefront of poetic discourse". She published twenty-five volumes of poetry, three collections of essays and more than half a dozen other writings. Rich's prose collections are widely-acclaimed for their erudite, lucid, and poetic treatment of politics, feminism, history, racism and many other topics.

"Aunt Jennifer's Tigers" was an early attempt by Rich to define male and female relationships. She eloquently voices the poem in a third-person narrative which sets herself apart from Aunt Jennifer. The prevailing theme of "Aunt Jennifer's Tigers" is Aunt Jennifer's oppression through marriage, and her utilization of embroidery as her only form of self-expression.

POETIC DEVICES/FIGURES OF SPEECH IN THE POEM

1. **Irony**
   - Chivalric certainty, weight of wedding band, prancing proud.
   It is ironical that Aunt Jennifer's creations will continue to prance freely, when she continues to be chained by the woes of life.
2. **Alliteration**
   - "Fingers fluttering."
   The repeated "f" sounds in her "fingers fluttering" make the poem enjoyable to read aloud as the repeated consonant sounds allow the words to appear perhaps, playful, continuing the 'mood' from the first stanza.
3. **Repetition**
   - tigers prance across a screen; will go on prancing.
   It creates a horrifying ambience of the oppressor and the oppressed. The theme of male chauvinism runs throughout the poem creating a fearsome atmosphere of fierce and fearless tigers on the prowl.
4. **Metaphor**
   - Ringed ordeals – Aunt's woes surrounded her so that even death would not fall her.
   - Bright to paz denizens – The poet compares the yellow stripes of the tigers to a precious stone, topaz.
5. **Transferred epithet**
   - "terrified fingers" – Aunt Jennifer is terrified; so, her fingers flutter.
6. **Personification**
   - "They pace in sleek chivalric certainty."
   In this line, Adrienne Rich has given the tigers a chivalric characteristic through personification. As much as fairytales and stories disagree, tigers in real life, are not noble or gentlemanly, they are wild animals.
   - "The tigers in the panel that she made/Will go on prancing, proud and unafraid."
   Here, Adrienne Rich uses pride, a humanly attribute, to offer a way for the reader to really understand how important these tigers are, and how they have the courage and pride that Aunt Jennifer never had.

Reference to Context

Read the extract given below and answer the questions that follow.

I.   Aunt Jennifer's tigers prance across a screen,

Bright topaz denizens of a world of green.

They do not fear the men beneath the tree;

They pace in sleek chivalric certainty.

    (a)   How are Aunt Jennifer's tigers described?

    (b)   What are her tigers symbolic of?

    (c)   Why are they described as 'denizens of a world of green'?

    (d)   Which poetic device is used in the last line here?

II   Aunt Jennifer's fingers fluttering through her wool

Find even the ivory needle hard to pull.

The massive weight of Uncle's wedding band

Sits heavily upon Aunt Jennifer's hand.

    (a)   Why are Aunt Jennifer's fingers fluttering?

    (b)   Explain: 'massive weight of uncle's wedding band'?

    (c)   Why does she find it hard to pull the ivory needle?

    (d)   How is Aunt Jennifer affected by the 'weight of matrimony'?

III.   When Aunt is dead, her terrified hands will lie

Still ringed with ordeals she was mastered by.

The tigers in the panel that she made

Will go on prancing, proud and unafraid.

    (a)   Why has Aunt Jennifer created the tigers so different from her own character?

    (b)   Why is she "ringed with ordeals"?

    (c)   Why are Aunt Jennifer's hands 'terrified'?

    (d)   What is Aunt Jennifer's death symbolic of?

IV.   They do not fear the men beneath the tree;

They pace in sleek chivalric certainty.

    (a)   Name the poem and the poet of these lines.

    (b)   Who are 'they' in the above lines and where do you find them?

    (c)   Why are 'they' not afraid of the men?

    (d)   What does the word 'sleek' mean?

V.   The tigers in the panel that she made

Will go on prancing, proud and unafraid.

    (a)   Who terrified the Aunt?

    (b)   What did she do to face the terror?

    (c)   Why did Aunt Jennifer make the tigers?

    (d)   What will happen to her tigers after her death?

ANSWER KEY

I. (a) Aunt Jennifer's tigers have been described golden yellow in colour. They are chivalric, bold and fearless as they prance across the screen with confidence.

   (b) Her tigers are symbolic of Aunt Jennifer's desire for freedom. They are also symbols of great strength and self-confidence.

   (c) They have been called 'denizens of a world of green' because they are the natives of dense green forests where they are known for their strength and valour.

   (d) In the above lines, 'chivalric certainty' is an example of alliteration.

II. (a) Aunt Jennifer lives in constant fear of her husband. Her fluttering fingers are a sign of nervousness as she is traumatized and terrorized by the constraints of her married life.

   (b) The expression is symbolic of male authority and power. Marriage seems to bind the woman mentally as well as physically. In the poem, Aunt Jennifer is trapped in gender oppression and does not get enough freedom to express herself. She is burdened by the domestic responsibilities and the authority of her husband.

   (c) Aunt Jennifer finds it very hard to pull through the ivory needle because she is enslaved and enfeebled. She finds it hard to pull more because of mental suppression rather than physical weakness.

   (d) Aunt Jennifer cannot do things freely. In trying to meet the expectations of her husband, she seems to lose her identity. The freedom that she dreams of through her art, is itself symbolic of her oppressed self.

III. (a) Aunt Jennifer is weak and submissive, whereas the tigers are strong, bold and powerful. The tigers of Aunt Jennifer's tapestry are representative of her desire of a free spirit, emphasising the fact that she pines for freedom from her burdensome wedlock. She is bound by the constraints of her married life, while the tigers are free to move about in the green woods.

   (b) The 'ring' here refers to her wedding band or ring, which has brought with it a host of family responsibilities. She feels so surrounded (i.e., ringed) by her marital constraints that it seems like an ordeal to her. This also means that her free spirit has been jailed by the patriarchal society. There is no escape for her even after death.

   (c) Aunt Jennifer has been enslaved by the wedding ring. After undergoing the harsh and bitter experiences of her married life, she feels weak and shaken. Even in death her hands will continue to be afraid and continue to be surrounded, or "ringed", by the ordeals of her life.

   (d) Aunt Jennifer's death is symbolic of her complete submission to her suppression.

IV. (a) The poem is 'Aunt Jennifer's Tigers'. The poet is Adrienne Rich.

   (b) They are Aunt Jennifer's tigers. We find them in the forests and also in the panel being embroidered by Aunt Jennifer.

   (c) They are not afraid of the men because they are brave and confident.

   (d) The word 'sleek' means 'elegant' or 'glossy'.

V. (a) Her husband (Uncle) and the immense pressure of conforming to the stereotype laid down by patriarchal society terrified the Aunt.

   (b) She embroidered tigers on the panel to face the terror. It served as a vent to her burdened spirit and an escape to freedom.

   (c) Aunt Jennifer crated the tigers which are symbols of confidence and fearlessness because she wants to be like them. She wants to break free from the marital responsibilities that have tethered her all her life.

   (d) The tigers are eternal. They will keep on prancing even after her death.

MIND MAP

SUMMARY OF THE STORY

Charley was quite an ordinary man from New York. One evening he reached the Grand Central Railway Station, New York, after a long day's work in the office. While waiting for a train on the second level, Charley found a door and tunnel down.

Curious as he always was, Charley suspected it was a mysterious tunnel.

Following the tunnel, he took steps down and reached the third level of the station. Grand Central Station, New York, has only two levels. In the third level, Charley saw dim gas lamps, string-watches brass spittoons, people in old styled costumes, men with sideburns, handlebar moustaches and beards, and so on, a hundred year old world and people. When he saw the June 11, 1894 edition of the popular newspaper The World which stopped its publication before 1994, he knew had travelled back in time. He went to buy two rail tickets to Galesburg where he had spent his childhood; but the booking clerk took his modern day currency to be fake (that age had different currency) and threatened to call the Police.

Charley met his psychiatrist friend Sam Weiner and told him about this experience. The psychiatrist interpreted it as a mental disorder; and called his experience 'waking dream wish fulfilment'. Charley's friends related his experience with his hobby of stamp collection which they said gave him a 'temporary refuge from reality' or an escape from the struggles of life by fantasizing about a happy world. Charley disagrees because his grandfather was a stamp collector and so was President Roosevelt and neither escaped from reality! Stamp collecting was Charley's favourite pastime; and his collection had been started by his grandfather himself.

Stamps make the central theme of the story. They connect the old world and the new; they are one thing that exists in both worlds; so, they enable the escape into the third level and a nostalgic bygone era.

Charley imagines not only the third level, an elaborate 1894 railway station and his quaint experience there; but also that his psychiatrist friend himself believed and experienced all of it and actually lived his fantasy! To substantiate this, he even imagines finding a first day cover mailed by Sam to his grandfather's address in Galesberg; so that his wife too believes that Sam has found the third level and retreated to Galesberg, and starts searching for the third level with him.

1. THE THIRD LEVEL

by Jack Finney

CHARACTER SKETCH: Charley

Charley is representative of a typical young urban man bogged down by the complexities and worries of fast paced life in the modern cities. He yearns to break free of the modern world which is 'full of insecurity, fear, war, worry and all the rest of it'.

He knew that the Grand Central station had a hierarchical system of two levels: trains to urban destinations in the first level and, to suburban, in the second. He must have stood wondering whether there could be a third level which would lead to country destinations; and must often have reminisced about the peaceful world of his childhood. He shows his vivid imagination and sharp memory of his childhood as he visualises the elaborate details of the bygone era; and betrays his nostalgia about his happy and peaceful childhood in Galesberg. He longs for some train in the third level to take him there because the existing levels cannot lead to that old world charm.

His creative genius comes to the fore when he thinks the Grand Central is growing like a tree, pushing out new corridors and staircases like roots'. The Grand Central had always been an exit, a way of escape for everyone, in Charley's opinion; and maybe that's how he had imagined escaping through a tunnel.

He has the conviction to imagine that Sam the psychiatrist too would fall for his fascinating experience, would actually buy tickets and escape to the wonderful old world. He is intelligent enough to device the method of 'first day cover' sent by Sam addressed to his (Charley's) grandfather and found by him (Charley, the grandson) in his stamp collection.

CHARACTER SKETCH: Sam, the psychiatrist

Sam is representative of a psychiatrist in a city who is flooded with unhappy patients burdened and stressed by the complexities of the modern world. He understands that the fast life in cities is full of 'insecurity, fear, war, worry and all the rest of it' and everyone squirms to escape all this. He shows insight as he explains Charley's weird experience of the third Level as a waking dream wish fulfilment. That he expresses the same disenchantment himself and yearns to retreat to the old world where people had no psychiatric issues is evident in Charley imagining his escape to Galesberg in 1894; as he always said he liked the sound of the place when Charley shared his schooldays experience with him.

Reference to Context

Read the extracts given below and answer the questions that follow.

I. The presidents of the New York Central and the New York, New Haven and Hartford railroads will swear on a stack of timetables that there are only two.

(a) What does 'two' in the above extract refer to?

(b) What is the author's contradiction or argument against it?

(c) How does he justify his claim?

(d) How do his friends react to his justification?

II. Well, maybe, but my grandfather didn't need any refuge from reality; things were pretty nice and peaceful in his day, from all I hear, and he started my collection.

(a) In what context does the narrator mention 'refuge from reality'?

(b) What collection does he speak of here?

(c) What does the narrator find in his collection that proved the existence of the third level?

(d) What does this convey about the narrator?

III. Then I walked down another flight to the second level, where the suburban trains leave from, ducked into an arched doorway heading for the subway — and got lost.

(a) What kind of trains left from the first level?

(b) How did Charley get lost in the Grand Central Station despite having been in and out of it hundreds of times?

(c) Where did Charley come out after he 'got lost'?

(d) What did he see there to his amazement?

IV. There were brass spittoons on the floor, and across the station a glint of light caught my eye; a man was pulling a gold watch from his vest pocket.

(a) What was the place described in the above extract?

(b) How did Charley reach there?

(c) What did he see there? How did he confirm his conjecture about it?

(d) What knowledge dawned on him as he looked at the ticket window?

V. That night, among my oldest first-day covers, I found one that shouldn't have been there. But there it was. It was there because someone had mailed it to my grandfather at his home in Galesburg; that's what the address on the envelope said.

(a) What is a first-day cover?

(b) Which first-day cover does the narrator talk of in the above extract?

(c) What did it contain?

(d) How did it reach Charley?

ANSWER KEY

I.   (a)   It refers to two levels of the Grand Central Station.

   (b)   When others swear the station had only two levels, the author contradicts, saying it has three.

   (c)   He justifies his claim by saying he had been on the third level the night he was late from office.

   (d)   His psychiatrist friend Sam calls his experience of the third level a waking dream wish fulfilment and the other friends agree saying it was his 'temporary refuge from reality' just as his stamp collecting hobby was.

II.   (a)   When the narrator insists he had been on the third level when the Grand Central actually had only two, his friends say it showed he was seeking 'refuge from reality' which his hobby of stamp collecting also pointed to.

   (b)   He speaks of his prized collection of stamps which had been started by his grandfather.

   (c)   He finds a first- day cover sent from Galesberg on July 18, 1894 by Sam to his grandfather's address in Galesberg.

   (d)   It conveys the ingenuity and creative imagination of the narrator. He weaves a clever sequence of events to tell his story of intersection of time and space.

III.   (a)   Trains like the Twentieth Century left from the third level.

   (b)   Charlie thought the Grand Central was growing like a tree, pushing out new corridors and staircases like roots because he would always lose his way and bump into new doorways and stairs and corridors.

   (c)   Charley came out on the third level of the Grand Central Station.

   (d)   He noticed open-flame gaslights, brass spittoons, string watches, women in leg-of-mutton sleeves and skirts to the top of high-buttoned shoes, and men sporting sideburns, beards and handlebar moustaches like the age of eighteen-ninety-something.

IV.   (a)   It was the third level of the Grand Central Station.

   (b)   Charley lost his way as he ducked into an archway on the second level and found himself in an unfamiliar deserted corridor. After a long walk through it, he came out on the third level.

   (c)   The things and people on the third level appeared to be like they were in eighteen- ninety something. To make sure, he walked over to the newsboy and found a stack of The World daily dated June 11, 1894 with him.

   (d)   He knew that he could buy tickets that would take Louisa and him anywhere in the United States in the year 1894. And he wanted two tickets to Galesburg, Illinois, where he had spent his childhood.

V.   (a)   Stamp collectors mail envelopes carrying newly issued stamps to themselves on the very first day of sale; and the postmark proves the date. These envelopes are called first-day covers. They're never opened for they contain only a blank paper.

   (b)   The narrator talks of the first day cover sent by his psychiatrist friend Sam from Galesberg to his grandfather's address in Galesberg.

   (c)   It contained a letter from Sam that he had found the third level and was in Galesberg for two weeks. He had advised Charley and Louisa that they must keep looking for the third level and join him because life there was indeed worth it.

   (d)   Charley imagined that Sam took a train from the third level to Galesburg from where he sent the first day cover to substantiate his claim that the third level of Grand Central existed and even Sam believed in it. Since it contained the century old date July 18, 1894, it is not possible that it was actually sent on that date. It was all part of Charley's fantasy.

MIND MAP

SUMMARY OF THE STORY

The story revolves around the Maharaja of Pratibandapuram, Jilani Jung Jung Bahadur, whose death at the hands of a tiger had been foretold by astrologers when he was born. The story is a satire on the pride and stubbornness of those in power.

Soon after he was born, the astrologers predicted that one day the Tiger King would grow up to be a great warrior but he would have to meet his death. As the astrologers uttered these words, a miracle took place. The ten-day old child said that all those who are born are meant to die someday. He wished to know the cause of his death. The Chief astrologer said that he was born in the hour of the bull. The bull and the tiger are enemies; therefore, his death would come from a tiger.

The crown prince grew taller and stronger with each passing day. He was brought up like an Englishman, under the influence of western culture. At the age of twenty, the State came into his hands.

Soon the Maharaja searched and killed his first tiger to show his superiority and rebellion against fate. Considering this to be his victory over his destined future, he called upon the state astrologer. The latter informed him that he had no life threat from the first ninety-nine of his hunted tigers but it was the hundredth one that he needed to protect himself from. Nevertheless, the Maharaja decided to kill at least hundred tigers as a challenge against this foretold destiny.

The State banned tiger hunting by anyone except the Maharaja. A proclamation was issued stating that if anyone dared to even hurt a tiger, all his property would be confiscated by the State. In keeping with this vow, the Maharaja outrightly denied even a British official, "durai," who desired to hunt down a tiger.

Within ten years, the Maharaja managed to kill seventy tigers. The tiger population became extinct in the forests of Pratibandapuram. The Maharaja called the dewan and expressed his desire to get married to a girl from a royal family belonging to a State with a large tiger population. The dewan followed his orders and the Maharaja got married to such a girl. Jung Jung Bahadur killed five or six tigers each time he visited his father-in-law. In this way, he was able to kill ninety-nine tigers. Now that he had killed ninety-nine tigers, he was more anxious to kill the last one. By this time, the tigers had become extinct even in his father-in-law's kingdom. The Maharaja was eager to kill the hundredth tiger and then he could give up tiger hunting altogether. He was sunk in gloom as the hundredth tiger could not be found. However, one day when he heard that the sheep began to disappear in his own state, hope returned to him. He was so thrilled that he even announced a three-year exemption from all taxes for that village and set out on the hunt. But the hundredth tiger was not easily found. The Maharaja got so furious that many officers lost their jobs. One day, he was so enraged that he ordered the dewan to double the land tax. The dewan figured that if the Maharaja did not find the tiger soon then it would have a bad impact on the kingdom. He was relieved to see the tiger which had been brought from the People's park in Madras and was kept hidden in his house. At midnight, the dewan and his aged wife dragged the tiger to the car and drove it straight to the forest where the Maharaja was hunting. The tiger wandered into the Maharaja's presence and he shot the beast with boundless joy. The tiger fell on the ground. The Maharaja was so ecstatic that he ordered the tiger to be brought to the capital in grand procession.

After the Maharaja left, the hunters found out that the tiger was not dead at all. The Maharaja had missed the target. The tiger had just fainted from the shock of the bullet that was fired at it. However, out of the fear of losing their jobs, everyone decided not to tell the Maharaja about this. Finally one of the hunters shot the tiger dead and they took it in a procession through the town and buried it. A tomb was erected over it.

Maharaja quit hunting forever after this hundredth 'kill'. A few days later, he decided for a grand celebration of his son's third birthday. As a gift, he decided to buy a toy tiger for his son which, unknown to him, was of poor craftsmanship.

While playing with his son one day, a tiny sliver of the rough wooden surface pierced his right hand and he died of infection. Thus, ironically the fateful hundredth tiger, though a wooden one, was the cause of the Maharaja's death and proved the prediction of the astrologers correct.

2. THE TIGER KING

by Ramaswamy Aiyer Krishnamurthy

CHARACTER SKETCH: The King

The Maharaja of Pratibandapuram was called the Tiger King. At his birth, astrologers predicted his death because of a tiger. But the baby had something miraculous about him. He was only of ten days when he challenged the prediction of the astrologers and asked them the manner of death.

The Crown Prince was brought up in an English environment. He grew up tall, sturdy, brave and deserved to be called a Maharaja in every case. He became the king of his state at the age of twenty and was determined to fulfill his pledge. He was strong enough to kill the wild tigers with his bare hands. Being a man of firm determination and self-respect, he stood against a British officer by refusing him permission to hunt in his forest. He was cunning to arrange his marriage with a princess whose father's forest had the maximum number of tigers. Yet he appears to be powerless before fate because this powerful king was finally killed by a sliver from a worthless wooden tiger! His death brought him great shame. His boldness, cunning, strength and bravery failed miserably at the hands of an insignificant wooden tiger. He can also be laughed at for believing the astrologers blindly, for the dereliction of duty as a king, for imposing tax on the villagers out of rage, for forgetting the sanctity and meaning of marriage and for dismissing his officers for no official reason. Thus, it can be said that the king was highly conceited and lacked worldly wisdom.

Reference to Context

Read the extracts given below and answer the questions that follow.

I. The Maharaja of Pratibandapuram is the hero of this story. He may be identified as His Highness Jamedar-General, Khiledar-Major, Sata Vyaghra Samhari, Maharajadhiraja Visva Bhuvana Samrat, Sir Jilani Jung Jung Bahadur, M.A.D., A.C.T.C., or C.R.C.K. But this name is often shortened to the Tiger King.

    (a)   Name the title of the story

    (b)   Name the author.

    (c)   Who is the hero of the story?

    (d)   By what other names the Maharaja was identified?

II. The chief astrologer placed his finger on his nose in wonder. A baby barely ten days old opens its lips in speech! Not only that, it also raises intelligent questions! Incredible! Rather like the bulletins issued by the war office, than facts. The chief astrologer took his finger off his nose and fixed his eyes upon the little prince. "The prince was born in the hour of the Bull. The Bull and the Tiger are enemies, therefore, death comes from the Tiger," he explained.

    (a)   Who was the Tiger King?

    (b)   What made the chief astrologer place his finger on his nose?

    (c)   Why were the astrologers surprised while they were studying the horoscope of the ten-day old prince?

    (d)   What was the prophecy made by the chief astrologer?

III. There were innumerable forests in the Pratibandapuram State. They had tigers in them. The Maharaja knew the old saying, 'You may kill even a cow in self-defence'. There could certainly be no objection to killing tigers in self-defence. The Maharaja started out on a tiger hunt.

    (a)   What kind of life was enjoyed by crown prince Jung Bahadur till he reached the age of twenty?

    (b)   What led the Maharaja to start out on a tiger hunt?

    (c)   What was the astrologer's reaction when the Maharaja told him that he had killed his first tiger?

    (d)   *"What if the hundredth tiger were also killed?"* What did the astrologer reply to this?

IV. At another time he was in danger of losing his throne. A high-ranking British officer visited Pratibandapuram. He was very fond of hunting tigers. And fonder of being photographed with the tigers he had shot. As usual, he wished to hunt tigers in Pratibandapuram. But the Maharaja was firm in his resolve. He refused permission. "I can organise any other hunt. You may go on a boar hunt. You may conduct a mouse hunt. We are ready for a mosquito hunt. But tiger hunt! That's impossible!"

    (a)   Why was it a celebration time for all the tigers inhabiting Pratibandapuram?

    (b)   Why did the Maharaja ban tiger hunting in the state?

    (c)   What sort of hunt did the Maharaja offer to organise for the high-ranking British officer?

    (d)   *"At another time he was in danger of losing his throne"*. How?

V. But he had to be extremely careful with that last tiger. What had the late chief astrologer said? "Even after killing ninety-nine tigers the Maharaja should beware of the hundredth..." True enough. The tiger was a savage beast after all. One had to be wary of it. But where was that hundredth tiger to be found? It seemed easier to find tiger's milk than a live tiger.

    (a)   Why did the Tiger King decide to get married?

    (b)   Why was the Maharaja so anxious to kill the hundredth tiger?

    (c)   How did the dewan manage to arrange the hundredth tiger for the Maharaja?

    (d)   How did the Tiger King celebrate his victory over the killing of the hundredth tiger?

ANSWER KEY

I.   (a) The Tiger King

(b) Kalki

(c) The Maharaja of Pratibandapuram is the hero of this story.

(d) The Maharaja of Pratibandapuram was identified as His Highness Jamedar-General, Khiledar-Major, Sata Vyaghra Samhari, Maharajadhiraja Visva Bhuvana Samrat, Sir Jilani Jung Jung Bahadur, M.A.D., A.C.T.C., or C.R.C.K.

II. (a) Jilani Jung Jung Bahadur, the king of Pratibandapuram, was known as the Tiger King.

(b) When the baby Maharaja was only ten days old, he not only spoke but also raised intelligent questions to the chief astrologer. He asked him about the manner of his death. This made the chief astrologer place his finger on his nose in wonder.

(c) When the astrologers were studying the horoscope of the prince, the infant prince suddenly began to speak clearly and wisely. This surprised the astrologers.

(d) The astrologer told that the prince was born in the hour of the bull. The Bull and the Tiger are enemies; therefore, the prince would be killed by a tiger.

III. (a) The prince enjoyed a luxurious life. He drank the milk of an English cow, was brought up by an English nanny, tutored in English by an Englishman and saw nothing but English films. When he reached the age of twenty, the State came into his hands.

(b) When the Maharaja of Pratibandapuram was born, an astrologer had predicted that his death would be caused by a tiger. The Maharaja wanted to prove the prediction wrong. So, he started out on a tiger hunt to save his life.

(c) On being told that the Maharaja had killed his first tiger, the astrologer announced that he could kill ninety-nine tigers but he must be very careful with the hundredth tiger.

(d) The astrologer said that if the hundredth tiger were also killed, then he would tear up all his books on astrology, set fire to them, and shall cut off his tuft, crop his hair short and become an insurance agent.

IV. (a) It was a celebration time for all the tigers inhabiting Pratibandapuram because the Maharaja had banned tiger hunting in the state. Except the Maharaja, no one was allowed to hunt tigers.

(b) The Maharaja banned tiger hunting in the state so that only he could kill the required number of tigers and escape the prophecy.

(c) For the high-ranking British officer, the Maharaja was prepared to organise any other hunt, but a tiger hunt was impossible.

(d) Since the Maharaja denied permission to the British officer to hunt tigers, he stood in danger of losing his throne and kingdom.

V.   (a) Few days after his hunting expedition, the tiger population in Majaraja's country became extinct. So, he decided to get married in the royal family of a state that had a large number of tigers.

(b) The Maharaja was so anxious to kill the hundredth tiger because killing the last tiger would mean that he has proved the prophecy wrong and thus save his life.

(c) The dewan's tiger was poor and weak. He had brought him from the People's Park, Madras, to protect it from the Maharaja's gun. At midnight, the dewan and his wife took him to the forest where the Maharaja was hunting and left it there.

(d) When he thought that he had killed the hundredth tiger, the king returned to his capital and ordered his staff to bring the dead tiger in a grand procession. The tiger was buried and a tomb was erected over it.

MIND MAP

SUMMARY OF THE STORY

Journey to the end of the earth is a travelogue in which the author recounts her journey to the coldest, driest, windiest continent in the world, Antarctica, under the Students on Ice programme led by Geogg Green in a Russian research vessel — the Akademik Shokalskiy.

She is filled with profound wonder that the immense white landscape with uninterrupted blue horizon and India were part of the same landmass, Gondwana, when dinosaurs walked the earth. Gondwana thrived for 500 million years, before the age of the mammals got under way, and the landmass disintegrated into countries as we know today. India was pushed northwards, jamming against Asia to buckle its crust and form the Himalayas; and South America drifted away opening up the Drake Passage to create a cold circumpolar current that keeps Antarctica frigid, desolate, and at the bottom of the world.

Antarctica stores 90 per cent of the earth's total volume of ice. Life here ranges from the microscopic midges and mites to the mighty blue whales and icebergs as big as countries. The silence in the expansive white landscape bathed in 24-hour austral summer light forces one to ponder how human civilisations in a paltry 12,000 years — barely a few seconds on the geological clock—managed to create a ruckus forcing dominance over Nature. The burgeoning human populations jostle for limited resources, and the unmitigated burning of fossil fuels has covered the earth with a blanket of carbon dioxide increasing the average global temperature.

Antarctica remains pristine without human habitation, and holds in its ice-cores half-million-year-old carbon records that will help to study and examine the Earth's past, present and future. Students on Ice programme provides students with such inspiring educational opportunities to help them foster a new understanding and respect for our planet. Witnessing glaciers retreating and ice shelves collapsing, one knows the threat of global warming is very real. The simple ecosystem and lack of biodiversity make it the perfect place to study how little changes in the environment can have big repercussions. Phytoplankton, the microscopic grasses of the sea that nourish and sustain the entire Southern Ocean's food chain, assimilate carbon and synthesise organic compounds during photosynthesis. Scientists warn that a further depletion in the ozone layer will affect the activities of phytoplankton, which in turn will affect the lives of all the marine animals and birds of the region, and the global carbon cycle. The phytoplankton is a great metaphor for the rule of existence: Take care of the small things and the big things will fall into place. Walking on the icesheet above living sea water, the author realises that everything does indeed connect.

3. JOURNEY TO THE END OF THE EARTH

by **Tishani Doshi**

CHARACTER SKETCH: The author/narrator

The author is a teenager among others in a research visit to Antarctica. She comes across as an ardent nature lover, noticing the life, the lack of biodiversity and the pristine silence on the white landscape. Being at the landmass which was one with her country India fascinates her. She feels strongly for the threat of global warming. The white continent gives her epiphanies or revelations like the ruckus humans have created in a naturally peaceful world how taking care of small things will go a long way in solving big problems of Climate Change.

Reference to Context

Read the extracts given below and answer the questions that follow.

I.   To visit Antarctica now is to be a part of that history; to get a grasp of where we've come from and where we could possibly be heading.

(a)   What was 'that history' which the author mentions here?

(b)   How did the present day Indian landscape form?

(c)   What understanding about 'where we could possibly be heading' dawns on her in Antarctica?

(d)   What is very mind boggling in the author's view?

II. It's an immersion that will force you to place yourself in the context of the earth's geological history. And for humans, the prognosis isn't good.

(a)   What is the 'immersion' referred to in the above extract?

(b)   What is the earth's geological history?

(c)   What fact about India infused the author with wonder when she set foot on Antarctica?

(d)   Why is the prognosis not good for humans?

III. Climate change is one of the most hotly contested environmental debates of our time. Will the West Antarctic ice sheet melt entirely? Will the Gulf Stream ocean current be disrupted? Will it be the end of the world as we know it? Maybe. Maybe not.

(a)   What stark contrast with the other parts of the world does Antarctica present?

(b)   For what other reason is Antarctica a crucial element in this hot debate?

(c)   Under which programme did the author visit Antarctica?

(d)   How did she reach the frigid continent?

IV. The reason the programme has been so successful is because it's impossible to go anywhere near the South Pole and not be affected by it.

(a)   Which programme is being referred to in the above extract? Who heads the programme?

(b)   What does the programme aim for?

(c)   What was the purpose of this particular visit?

(d)   Why was this particular batch of visitors chosen over others?

V.   Antarctica, because of her simple ecosystem and lack of biodiversity, is the perfect place to study how little changes in the environment can have big repercussions.

(a)   Which living organism does the author name to show little changes having big repercussions?

(b)   What is the ecological significance of this organism?

(c)   How can this little thing have big repercussions?

(d)   What metaphor for existence does the author give in this context?

ANSWER KEY

I.   (a)   'That history' refers to the fact that millions of years ago both India and Antarctica were part of the same landmass Gondwana.

     (b)   India broke away from Gondwana and pushed northwards, jamming against Asia to buckle its crust and form the Himalayas.

     (c)   She understands the significance of Cordilleran folds and pre-Cambrian granite shields; ozone and carbon; evolution and extinction.

     (d)   Thinking about all that can happen in a million years is very mind-boggling in her view.

II.   (a)   The 'immersion' refers to the author's deep engrossment in the ubiquitous, consecrating silence in Antarctica's expanse of white ice which was interrupted only by the occasional avalanche or calving ice sheet.

     (b)   The earth's geological history is the evolution of the present day continents, oceans and biosphere, the evidence of which is contained in the layers of rock and ice on the earth's surface.

     (c)   The fact that India and the immense, white, frigid Antarctica before her eyes were part of the same southern supercontinent Gondwana at the age when dinosaurs roamed and humans were yet to arrive infused the author with profound wonder.

     (d)   The prognosis (i.e., forecast of a likely outcome) is not good because human civilisations have being around for a paltry 12,000 years — barely a few seconds on the geological clock; and within that short span, have wreaked havoc on Nature with a burgeoning population straining limited resources, unbridled construction wiping out forests; and unmitigated burning of fossil fuels blanketing the earth in Carbon dioxide, increasing the average global temperature.

III.   (a)   Antarctica is the only place in the world, which has never sustained a human population and therefore remains relatively 'pristine' in this respect.

     (b)   It holds half-million-year-old carbon records trapped in its layers of ice which are valuable to study and examine the Earth's past, present and future.

     (c)   The author visited Antarctica under the Students on Ice programme which gave inspiring educational opportunities to students to foster new understanding of our planet.

     (d)   Her journey began 13.09 degrees north of the Equator in Madras, and involved crossing nine time zones, six checkpoints, three bodies of water, and at least as many ecospheres to reach the frigid continent.

IV.   (a)   The programme is Students on Ice headed by Canadian Geoff Green.

     (b)   It aims to take high school students to the ends of the world and provide them with inspiring educational opportunities which will help them foster a new understanding and respect for our planet.

     (c)   The visit to Antarctica was undertaken to study and examine the Earth's past, present and future trapped in its layers of ice. It holds in its ice-cores half-million-year-old carbon records.

     (d)   Geoff Green got tired of carting celebrities and retired, rich, curiosity-seekers who could only 'give' back in a limited way. With Students on Ice, he offers the future generation of policy-makers a life-changing experience at an age when they're ready to absorb, learn, and most importantly, act.

V.   (a)   The author gives the example of the microscopic sea-grasses phytoplankton, which nourish and sustain the entire Southern Ocean's food chain.

     (b)   Phytoplankton assimilate carbon and synthesise organic compounds during photosynthesis.

     (c)   Depletion in the ozone layer will affect the activities of phytoplankton, which in turn will affect the lives of all the marine animals and birds of the region, and the global carbon cycle.

     (d)   The author remarks that in the parable of the phytoplankton, there is a great metaphor for existence: take care of the small things and the big things will fall into place.

MIND MAP

SUMMARY OF THE STORY

Dr. Sadao Hoki was a Japanese surgeon. He studied in America and returned with Hana, a Japanese girl whom he met there and married in Japan. While most of the doctors were sent to serve the Japanese army in the World War II, Sadao was allowed to stay home for two reasons: he was perfecting a discovery on cleaning wounds and the old General might need him for an operation.

He lived with his wife Hana and two children on the Japanese sea-coast. His house was located on the sea-coast where he had spent his childhood. Once while the couple was enjoying the mist at dusk on their porch, they noticed some movement near the sea. A man 'flung' out of the ocean, walked few steps and then fell unconscious. He was badly injured. They discovered that the white man was an escaped prisoner of war, a sailor from an American warship. He had lost a lot of blood due to a gun wound and a rock injury.

The couple knew that they would be termed treacherous if they did not inform the police or the army about it, who would eventually kill the man. But, they could not bring themselves to do what seemed the best course of action at that point, i.e., to throw the man back into the sea. After a lot of speculation, the doctor thought of treating the dying man on humanitarian grounds before deciding his fate.

Though unwilling to help his enemy, Dr. Sadao took the young soldier into his house and provided him with medical aid. Sadao performed a difficult operation and removed the bullet efficiently. Hana helped her husband in whatever way she could. She herself took every possible care of the American, even fed him with her own hands.

Under Hana's care and the expert medical administration of Dr. Sadao, the young American recuperated. Soon his scared servants left him. Dr. Sadao saw that the soldier was getting well and looked absolutely alright. Once his patient was no more in need of him, the doctor turned into a patriot, conspiring to kill him in his sleep. He informed the General of the American and the General promised that he would send his private men to kill the American. Sadao awaited the American's death every morning but to his gloom the man was still alive, healthier and posing danger to him. He decided to get rid of the stranger and the inconvenience his presence caused. He packed him off on a boat with the basic necessities like food, bottled water and two blankets to a nearby isolated island from where he was to board a Korean ship to freedom and safety. He even gave the young man his own flashlight, to be used in time of need as well as to signal Dr. Sadao about his well-being. Thus, Tom departed secretly.

Sadao became the real man, a true human being who realized the essential worth of human life and universal brotherhood. He thought beyond countries and continents and races and wars. He found no reason to believe that the American was his enemy. Thus, Sadao rose above narrow prejudices and acted in a truly humanitarian way.

4. THE ENEMY

by Pearl Sydenstricker Buck

CHARACTER SKETCH: Dr. Sadao Hoki

Dr. Sadao Hoki was a famous Japanese surgeon and a scientist. He was perfecting a discovery which would render wounds entirely clean. He is a perfect role model for all the doctors of the world who really upholds the values of his profession. His father had taken great care of his upbringing and instilled in his mind that he had to be a great doctor and surgeon. He sent him to America at the age of 22 to learn medicine. He stayed there for 8 years and observed strict self-discipline. He met Hana, another Japanese girl and fell in love with her. However, he waited until his father's approval and married her only after the approval.

The best trait of his personality comes to light when he risked his own life and the entire family and dared to save an enemy. Japan and America were at war in the World War II. During this an American POW, Tom is washed ashore near his home. Sadao saves him. He faces opposition from his servants but he knows his responsibilities as a doctor. He is a man of clear conscience.

Not only is he a good human being, he is a perfect and skilled doctor also. General Takima also had great faith in him.

CHARACTER SKETCH: Hana

Hana is the embodiment of a loving, dedicated and caring wife. She loves her family. She always has love and affection in her heart for Sadao. In spite of being married for so many years, she is still the same loving wife. She often assists Sadao in his medical operations as she helped him with anesthetics while he operated on Tom. She gets scared when a man in uniform appears at the gate. She is full of human consideration. Though she does not have good feelings for the enemy soldier; she does not turn him over for fear of disturbing his wounds. She assists her husband in performing the operation on the wounded soldier. She is quite hardworking. When Yumi, the nurse refuses to wash Tom, she does it herself. When the servants leave Sadao's home in protest, she does all the chores herself. However, she is not as courageous as Sadao.

Reference to Context

Read the extracts given below and answer the questions that follow.

I.   **Sadao knew that his education was his father's chief concern. For this reason he had been sent at twenty-two to America to learn all that could be learned of surgery and medicine. He had come back at thirty, and before his father died he had seen Sadao become famous not only as a surgeon but as a scientist.**

(a)   Who was Dr. Sadao?

(b)   What was his father's chief concern about Dr. Sadao?

(c)   Why was Dr. Sadao kept in Japan and not sent abroad with the troops?

(d)   Where, when and how did Dr. Sadao meet Hana?

II.   **Sadao hesitated again. "The strange thing is," he said, "that if the man were whole I could turn him over to the police without difficulty. I care nothing for him. He is my enemy. All Americans are my enemy. And he is only a common fellow. You see how foolish his face is. But since he is wounded…"**

(a)   In what condition did Dr. Sadao find the American soldier at the seashore?

(b)   What did Dr. Sadao and Hana learn about the man?

(c)   Why didn't Dr Sadao put the wounded man back in the sea even though he was his enemy?

(d)   How did Dr. Sadao and Hana take the man inside their house?

III. **"It will be better for her to empty her stomach," he thought. He had forgotten that of course she had never seen an operation. But her distress and his inability to go to her at once made him impatient and irritable with this man who lay like dead under his knife.**

(a)   Why did Hana wash the wounded soldier herself?

(b)   What help did Dr. Sadao seek from Hana while operating on the wounded white man?

(c)   What made a cool surgeon like Sadao speak sharply to his wife? What was her reaction?

(d)   What forced Dr. Sadao to be impatient and irritable with his patient?

IV.   **"What will be their fate if their father is condemned as a traitor?"**

(a)   Identify the title.

(b)   Name the author.

(c)   Who said the above line?

(d)   Why did she say so?

V.   **"Well, well!" the old man said in a tone of amazement, "so I did! But you see, I was suffering a good deal. The truth is, I thought of nothing but myself. In short, I forgot my promise to you."**

(a)   Who said the above lines and to whom?

(b)   How did Hana react when she saw a messenger at the door in official uniform?

(c)   Why did the General spare the American soldier?

(d)   What plan did Dr. Sadao devise to get rid of the man?

ANSWER KEY

I. (a) Dr. Sadao Hoki was a famous Japanese surgeon and scientist.

(b) Sadao's education was his father's chief concern.

(c) The General considered Dr. Sadao indispensable. He felt that his life could be saved only by him as he was very skilled. He also did not trust anyone except Dr. Sadao. So, Dr. Sadao was not sent with troops.

(d) Dr. Sadao met Hana in America at a party hosted by his professor Harley.

II. (a) While standing outside their house, Dr. Sadao and his wife saw something crawl out of the sea. They rushed and found that he was a wounded prisoner of war. He was motionless with his face in the sand. He had suffered a gun wound on the right side of his lower back and was bleeding very badly.

(b) As Dr. Sadao and Hana turned the man's head, they saw that he was a white man with yellow long hair. From his battered cap, they learnt that he was a sailor from an American warship.

(c) Dr Sadao could not put the wounded man back in the sea even though he was an enemy because he was a Doctor and the foremost duty of a doctor is to save life. He knew the man would die if not tended medically. So, he rescued him to give medical treatment.

(d) Dr. Sadao and Hana lifted the man inside their house. They carried him up the steps and into the side door of the house. The door opened into a passage, and down the passage they carried the man towards an empty bedroom.

III. (a) Hana washed the wounds of the American soldier herself because the domestic servants refused to do it as he was from an enemy country.

(b) Dr. Sadao asked Hana to fetch towels. He asked her to help him turn the wounded soldier. Sadao asked Hana to administer an anaesthetic to the wounded white man, if required. He also asked her to soak cotton with the anaesthetic and hold it near his nostrils.

(c) Hana choked at the moment when Dr. Sadao started operating. Sadao sharply told her not to faint because he couldn't stop at the moment. After listening this, Hana clapped her hands to her mouth and ran out.

(d) Sadao heard Hana retching in the garden and said it would be better for her to empty her stomach. But her distress and his inability to go her at once made him impatient and irritable with his patient.

IV. (a) The Enemy

(b) Pearl S. Buck

(c) Yumi said the above line.

(d) She said so because Dr. Sadao was treating an American soldier.

V. (a) The General said the above lines to Dr. Sadao.

(b) When Hana saw the messenger in official uniform, she felt helpless and afraid. She thought the servants must have already told the Japanese army about the enemy sheltered in their house.

(c) The General was in great pain and had to be operated on. In his own pain, he forgot all about the soldier. Hence, he didn't spare the soldier, he had only forgotten about him.

(d) Dr. Sadao devised the plan of letting the man escape to the nearest uninhabited island. He put his boat on the shore with food and clothing and advised the man to row to the little island.

MIND MAP

SUMMARY OF THE STORY

"Should Wizard Hit Mommy?" by John Updike revolves around the conflicting views of a child and a parent.

Jack was the father of two little kids – Jo and Bobby. His wife Clare was carrying their third child. When it came to telling Jo a bedtime story, you could always see Jack in the bed with the little girl of four telling stories.

But the problem was, Jack's stories were the ditto copies of his one and only story – story of Roger, a creature that suffered loneliness in a forest because it suffered from certain disabilities. Every new story that Jack told Jo was a variation of the base story and mostly the difference in the story was Roger's being a cat, chipmunk, mouse, fish, etc., and the deformity or illness it suffered. In telling the stories, Jack was able to indulge his gift for creating suspense and his love of language, even when the references would go over Jo's head. Jack crafts Roger Skunk in his own image: a skunk who is isolated from other animals much like Jack was as a young boy. Roger is lonely because of his smell. One Saturday Jack asked Jo about whom the story should be today. Roger Skunk, she said firmly. Jack started the story of the tiny creature Skunk, who lived in the dark deep woods. He smelled so bad that other animals of the jungle would not play with him. They would run away and Roger Skunk would stand there all alone. Though Jo is unaware, Jack is channeling his frustration in his marriage into the story, and becomes increasingly upset when Jo contradicts him, as it reminds him of Clare.

Roger Skunk went to the wise old owl and told his problem. The owl asked Skunk why he did not see the Wizard. Then he went to the Wizard and told that he smelled very bad and all the little animals used to run away from him. The wise owl had told wizard that he could help in that manner. The Wizard took his magic wand and asked Roger Skunk what he wanted to smell like. Roger Skunk told him that he would like to smell like roses. The Wizard chanted and Roger Skunk started smelling like roses. The Wizard asked Roger Skunk to pay seven pennies. Roger Skunk said that he had four pennies only and he began to cry. The Wizard directed Roger to go to the nearby magic well and he would find three pennies there. Roger Skunk took out three pennies from the well and gave them to the Wizard. Now all the other animals gathered around him because he smelled so good. They played various games and laughed. It began to get dark so they all ran home to their mummies.

But as the story is about to reach its climax, Jo grows all the more fussy and distracted and Jack changes the structure of his story in hopes of re-capturing his daughter's interest. He tells her that when Roger came home from the wizard's house, his mother was furious. Instead of being happy that he had changed his smell, she is angry. She demands that they return to the wizard so he can change Roger back and his mother can hit the wizard over the head. But Jo demands Jack to change the story: she wants the wizard to refuse to change Roger back, and to hit Roger's "stupid mommy" over the head with his wand. Unprepared for his daughter's intensity and violent wish, Jack attempts to explain that Roger was better off with his old smell because it was what his mother wanted and he loved his mother more than he cared what the other animals thought about him.

Thoroughly tired, Jack brings story time to an end and urges Jo to go to sleep. Jo, in turn, demands that, in tomorrow's story, the wizard must hit Roger Skunk's mother over the head instead. Jack does not answer her, and instead goes downstairs to finally help his wife. When he gets downstairs however, Jack is too weary to help, and instead sits in a chair and watches his wife repaint their living room. He sees the molding in their house as a cage surrounding him and his wife. He has no desire to work with her or even talk to her or touch her.

5. Should Wizard Hit Mommy

by **John Updike**

CHARACTER SKETCH: Jack

Jack is the protagonist of the story 'Should Wizard Hit Mommy?' and lives with his pregnant wife Clare, their four-year-old daughter Jo, and their two-year-old son, Bobby. Jack is conscious of his duties as a father and husband. Uninspired by and disillusioned with the responsibilities of family life, Jack uses the stale ritual of telling his daughter a bedtime story to avoid helping his wife re-paint their living room to prepare for the arrival of their third child. A talented storyteller, Jack takes pride in creating engrossing stories for Jo even though he is quickly running out of fresh ideas. He has the typical parental attitude and opinion that parents know what is best for their children. Jack feels caught in an ugly middle position physically, emotionally and mentally. He did not like women to take anything for granted, to the extent that he extends the story, changing the ending, giving it the face that he wants to. Jack is someone who is not used to his authority being questioned. Though a loving parent, he finds it hard to accept the fact now Jo has a mind of her own. His insensitivity and impatience comes across his dealings with his daughter, and the facts that an adult's viewpoint is different from a child's perspective.

CHARACTER SKETCH: Jo

Jack and Clare's four-year-old daughter, Jo is a growing girl. She is growing taller by the day, has begun to contradict things her parents tell her, and no longer falls asleep at nap time. All of these traits worry and upset Jack because he realizes he will soon have another woman in his life contradicting him the way his wife Clare does. Indeed, Jo is intent on exercising her opinions and having her ideas heard, even at a young age. With respect to the story of Roger Skunk, Jo does not agree with the ending that her father proposes. As a young child, Jo relates to Roger's desire to be accepted by his peers, and she does not understand why Roger's mother would force him to return to his original smell when it made the other little animals run away. Jo is too young to understand the concept of sacrifice, and therefore, believes Roger's mother to be the villain of the story who deserves punishment.

Reference to Context

Read the extracts given below and answer the questions that follow.

I.   A new animal; they must talk about skunks at nursery school. Having a fresh hero momentarily stirred Jack to creative enthusiasm. "All right," he said. "Once upon a time, in the deep dark woods, there was a tiny little creature by the name of Roger Skunk. And he smelled very bad."

   (a)   Who was Jo?

   (b)   What custom did Jack follow in the evenings and for Saturday naps?

   (c)   What was the basic plot of each story told by Jack?

   (d)   Which animal did Jo suggest for the story that day?

II.   "Mr Owl," Roger Skunk said, "all the other little animals run away from me because I smell so bad." "So you do," the owl said. "Very, very bad." "What can I do?" Roger Skunk said, and he cried very hard.

   (a)   Why was Roger sad?

   (b)   Why did Roger Skunk go the owl?

   (c)   What did the wise owl advise Roger to do?

   (d)   How did the wizard manage to help the Skunk?

III.   "All right. He said, 'But Mommy, all the other little animals run away,' and she said, 'I don't care. You smelled the way a little skunk should have and I'm going to take you right back to that wizard,' and she took an umbrella and went back with Roger Skunk and hit that wizard right over the head."

   (a)   How did Roger Skunk pay the wizard?

   (b)   Why was Roger Skunk's mom angry with him?

   (c)   What did she finally tell him?

   (d)   How did the Skunk's mother get Roger Skunk's old smell back?

IV.   "Tomorrow, I want you to tell me the story that that wizard took that magic wand and hit that mommy" — her plump arms chopped forcefully — "right over the head."

   (a)   Why did Jo think Roger Skunk was better off with the new smell?

   (b)   What did Jo want Roger Skunk's mother to be punished for?

   (c)   Why did Jo insist that her father should tell her the story with a different ending?

   (d)   How did Jo want the Wizard to behave when mommy Skunk approached him?

V.   "That was a long story," Clare said.

   (a)   Name the title of the story.

   (b)   Name the author.

   (c)   Who was Clare?

   (d)   What was she doing?

ANSWER KEY

I. (a) Joanne or Jo was a four-year girl, who loved listening to her father's stories. She was very curious about everything.

(b) On Saturdays, Jo didn't feel sleepy. Jack would tell her a story out of head in the evenings and for Saturday naps. This custom had begun when she was two years old.

(c) The stories that Jack used to tell Joe were about a small creature, Roger. Roger would go to the wise owl whenever in trouble. The wise owl would ask him to go to the wizard who would finally solve Roger's problem.

(d) Jo suggested 'skunk' for the story that day. It was a new animal for her.

II. (a) Roger was sad because he was not like his friends. He was either blind, deaf or numb. Due to his disability, his friends didn't allow him to play with them. He was bored of his mother's company all the time.

(b) Roger Skunk went to the owl because he wanted his smell to be removed so that he could have friends with whom he could play.

(c) The wise owl advised Roger to go to the wizard who lived alone in a small house. The wizard could cure Roger's deformity.

(d) The wizard took out his magic wand and asked Roger Skunk what he wanted to smell like. When Roger said that he wanted to smell like roses, the wizard chanted some magic words and fulfilled Roger Skunk's wish.

III. (a) The wizard wanted seven shillings but Roger Skunk only had four shillings to pay him. On seeing Roger Skunk's sad face, the wizard took pity on him and directed him for the remaining three shillings. Roger Skunk went in search of them and eventually paid the money to the wizard.

(b) Roger Skunk's mother was angry with him since he no longer smelled the way all skunks smelled.

(c) Roger Skunk's mother finally asked him to go along with her to the wizard to revoke the spell.

(d) Roger Skunk's mother went to the wizard and hit him on the head and asked him to give back Roger Skunk's smell. The wizard obliged and gave the baby skunk's smell back.

IV. (a) Jo thought about Roger Skunk and his wish to smell better in order to play with his friends from a child's perspective. For her, it was important that wishes are fulfilled, and a wish of being able to play was the foremost.

(b) Jo believed that Roger Skunk's mother was insensitive, cruel and unfair. She didn't let him retain smell of roses which he had got from the wizard. It would have helped him make friends.

(c) According to Jo, Roger Skunk was happy with the smell of roses. She did not want him to smell bad. That is why; she insisted that her father should re-tell the story with a different ending.

(d) Jo wanted the Wizard to hit mommy Skunk back on her head and refuse to change Roger Skunk's smell when she approached him.

V. (a) Should Wizard Hit Mommy

(b) John Updike

(c) Clare was Jack's wife.

(d) She was painting the woodwork alone because Jack was busy narrating the story to Jo.

MIND MAP

The play entitled "On the Face of It" written by Susan Hill depicts beautifully yet grimly the sad world of the physically impaired. It is a socio-psychological story of two invalids who live with two different views. Derry is a young boy who lived a miserable life since a bottle of acid deformed his face and Mr. Lamb, a lame old man who lived a cheerful life even after he had lost one of his legs in a blast.

It is a fine day and Mr. Lamb is in his garden. He is an old man with a tin leg. He leads a lonely life and is always ready to accept any visitor who comes in his garden. One day, Derry, a young boy of fourteen sneaks into Mr. Lamb's garden. He slowly enters Mr. Lamb's garden without having any knowledge of his presence. Mr. Lamb figures out that someone is in his garden and cautions Derry about the apples lying on the ground for he could trip on them. Startled by this, Derry confesses that he entered the garden only because he thought that nobody lived there. Mr. Lamb welcomes him to his garden and assures him that the door is always open for people who want to come in.

Derek has low self-esteem and thinks people are afraid of him for because of his burnt face. He has bitterness for the world. People stay away and refuse to accept him in the mainstream of life. So he feels alienated from the society and wants to live in seclusion. When Derry asked him if he was interested in knowing more about him, he answered that there is nothing God made that doesn't interest him. He even loves the weed garden that others condemn as rubbish. He finds no difference between Derry and him. Just as Derry had a burned face, Mr. Lamb had a tin leg in place of the real one that got blown off in the war. Kids call him names but it doesn't bother him. Derry feels that he could cover his tin leg with his trousers and no one could notice them. On the other hand, Mr. Lamb tells him that people get tired of seeing it. There are a lot of other things in the world to stare at. Mr. Lamb's concept of beauty is relative and it reminds Derry of the story of the Beauty and the Beast. The Beauty loved the dreadful Beast for what he was inside and when she kissed him he transformed into a handsome prince. But Derry feels that no matter what, nobody would ever kiss him and he will always remain the same. Only his mother kissed him that too on the other side of the face. He felt that she does so just because she has to. He did not care if anybody ever kissed him. He knew that he is always going to have half a face. Mr. Lamb assures him that the world had a whole face to be looked at. Derry asks him if he feels that the old garden is the whole world. Mr. Lamb replies that the world has been the same for him anywhere else.

He advises Derek to think of the beautiful objects of the world, and avoid people's comments and love all mankind because hatred corrodes us and hurts more than acids. He considers Derek to be his friend.

Mr. Lamb tells a story to inspire Derek. Once there was a timid man who refused to come out in fear of fatal accident. In his room a picture fell of the wall on his head and he died. This changes Derek's attitude and he takes interest in Mr. Lamb's talking and likes to listen more to Mr. Lamb and wants to help Mr. Lamb in his work.

Derek wants to go home and inform his mother that he would be late. He promises to come back. His mother stops him but he is adamant saying if he does not go there he would never be able to go anywhere. When he comes back he sees lamb lying on the ground. It is ironical that he finds Mr. Lamb dead. In this way, the play depicts the heart rendering life of physically disabled people with their loneliness, aloofness and alienation.

6. ON THE FACE OF IT

by Susan Hill

Mr. Lamb is an old man. Probably he had served in the army where one of his legs was blown off in the war. Now he has a tin leg. He stays in a big house and a decent garden full of flowers, weeds and crab apples. He spends most of his time in reading books or sitting in the garden. He is gentle and kind. He keeps the gate of his garden open. Everyone is welcome in his garden. When Derry strays into his garden, he warmly welcomes him.

Mr. Lamb had adjusted himself with his physical impairment, and had rather got over it with the passage of time. He has learnt how to keep himself steady on the ladder while plucking apples from the branches. Children call him 'Lamey-Lamb' when he goes down the street but he is undisturbed and take it as fun and thus, they are not afraid of him. They come into garden for apples and pears. On his part, Mr. Derek enjoys their company.

Derry is a 14 year old young lad whose face is half burnt because of acid spill on it. His ugly looks have made him a pessimist and a loner with various negative complexes. Derry is a introvert kid, always frustrated, angry, and withdrawn. Moreover, he is low in confidence and dwells in self-pity. He hates when people stare or pity him.

Reference to Context

Read the extracts given below and answer the questions that follow.

I.   **DERRY:** I thought it was empty....an empty house.

MR LAMB: So it is. Since I'm out here in the garden. It is empty. Until I go back inside. In the meantime, I'm out here and likely to stop. A day like this. Beautiful day. Not a day to be indoors.

DERRY: [Panic] I've got to go.

MR LAMB: Not on my account. I don't mind who comes into the garden. The gate's always open. Only you climbed the garden wall.

(a)   Who was Derry?

(b)   What kind of garden did Mr. Lamb have?

(c)   Why did Derry wish to get out of Mr. Lamb's garden immediately after getting into?

(d)   Why did Mr Lamb leave his gate always open?

II.   **MR LAMB:** Later on, when it's a bit cooler, I'll get the ladder and a stick, and pull down those crab apples. They're ripe for it. I make jelly. It's a good time of year, September. Look at them....orange and golden. That's magic fruit. I often say. But it's best picked and made into jelly. You could give me a hand.

DERRY: What have you changed the subject for? People always do that. Why don't you ask me? Why do you do what they all do and pretend it isn't true and isn't there? In case I see you looking and mind and get upset? I'll tell....you don't ask me because you're afraid to.

(a)   How did Mr. Lamb keep himself busy when it was a bit cool?

(b)   *"But I'm not....I'm not afraid. People are afraid of me."* Why did Derry say so?

(c)   Why, according to Derry, had the old man changed the subject?

(d)   *"You got burned in a fire,"* said Mr Lamb. What do you think had happened to Derry's face?

III. **MR LAMB:** Some call them weeds. If you like, then....a weed garden, that. There's fruit and there are flowers, and trees and herbs. All sorts. But over there....weeds. I grow weeds there. Why is one green, growing plant called a weed and another 'flower'? Where's the difference. It's all life.... growing. Same as you and me.

DERRY: We're not the same.

MR LAMB: I'm old. You're young. You've got a burned face, I've got a tin leg. Not important. You're standing there.... I'm sitting here. Where's the difference?

(a)   "It ate my face up. It ate me up." When did Derry say these words? Why?

(b)   What did Mr Lamb try to explain Derry through the example of a weed and a flower?

(c)   How did Mr Lamb react to Derry's query: 'Aren't you interested'?

(d)   Mr. Lamb said to Derry: 'It's all relative. Beauty and Beast'. What did he mean by that?

IV.   **MR LAMB:** You could lock yourself up in a room and never leave it. There was a man who did that. He was afraid, you see. Of everything. Everything in this world. A bus might run him over, or a man might breathe deadly germs onto him, or a donkey might kick him to death, or lightning might strike him down, or he might love a girl and the girl would leave him, and he might slip on a banana skin and fall and people who saw him would laugh their heads off. So he went into this room, and locked the door, and got into his bed, and stayed there.

DERRY: For ever?

MR LAMB: For a while.

DERRY: Then what?

MR LAMB: A picture fell off the wall on to his head and killed him.

[Derry laughs a lot]

(a)   Name the title.

(b)   Name the author.

(c)   Mr Lamb told Derry the story of a man who hid himself in his room. Why did the man do so?

(d)   What was the result in the end?

V.   MOTHER: You think I don't know about him, you think. I haven't heard things?

DERRY: You shouldn't believe all you hear.

MOTHER: Been told. Warned. We've not lived here three months, but I know what there is to know and you're not to go back there.

DERRY: What are you afraid of? What do you think he is? An old man with a tin leg and he lives in a huge house without curtains and has a garden. And I want to be there, and sit and....listen to things. Listen and look.

(a)   How, according to Derry, did the tin leg not trouble Mr Lamb?

(b)   What did Derry's mother think of Mr Lamb?

(c)   What argument did Derry give to convince his mother to go to the old man's garden?

(d)   What made Derry resolve to go to the old man?

ANSWER KEY

I.   (a) Derek, also called Derry, was a young boy of 14. He was a quiet, shy and defiant boy.

(b)   Mr Lamb's garden had flowers, birds, fruit trees as well as a place for rearing bees.

(c)   Derry went into Lamb's garden because he thought it was empty. However, when he saw Mr. Lamb there and that he had been being watched by Mr. Lamb, he felt ashamed and wished to get out of the garden.

(d)   Mr Lamb always kept his gate open because he did not mind strangers entering his house. He liked to talk to them and learn different things from them.

II.   (a) When it's a bit cooler, Mr. Lamb got a ladder and a stick to pull down the crab apples. He called them magic-fruit and liked to make jelly out of them.

(b)   Derry said so because on looking at his face people found it bad and frightful. They thought it was the ugliest thing they had ever seen.

(c)   Derry thought that the old man had changed the subject because he was afraid to ask him about his burnt face.

(d)   Derry's face did not burn in a fire. He got acid all down that side of his face and it burned it all away.

III.   (a) Derry said these words to Mr Lamb when he narrated the horrific incident when his face got burned by acid. He said this because the burning of the face destroyed all the happiness in his life.

(b)   Through the example of a weed and a flower, Mr. Lamb talked against discrimination and the futility of appearance. He told Derry that people should have a broader perception and positive attitude towards life.

(c)   Mr Lamb told Derry that he was interested in anybody and anything. There's nothing God made that did not interest him.

(d)   Mr. Lamb believed in the relativity theory of beauty. He said that everyone has beauty inside but people hardly recognize that. The beautiful ones are not always good at heart and the ugly ones can have a beautiful heart.

IV.   (a) On The Face Of It

(b)   Susan Hill

(c)   The man was afraid of everything. He felt that he would die if he went out and so he hid himself in a room.

(d)   In the end, a picture fell off the wall on his head and killed him.

V.   (a) Derry thought that the old man can wear trousers and cover up his tin leg. So, people don't have to notice and stare at, as they do at his face.

(b)   Derry's mother was quite sceptical of Mr. Lamb. She thought he was not a good man. She claimed that she has heard many things about Mr Lamb and some have also warned her against him. That is why; she did not want Derry to associate with him in any way.

(c)   Derry said that he wanted to go to the old man's house because he wanted to spend time with him and listen to the things that matter. Things nobody else has ever said. Things he wanted to think about.

(d)   Derry no longer cared about his face and looks. He was more concerned what he thinks and feels what he wanted to see and hear. He knew that if he did not go back there, he will never be able to go anywhere.

MIND MAP

SUMMARY OF THE STORY

The story "Evans Tries An O-Level", written by Colin Dexter is an interesting story depicting how a prisoner called James Evans fools all the officers of the prison to escape under a well-laid out plan.

Evans a kleptomaniac was imprisoned thrice and was able to escape every time, therefore he was nicknamed 'Evans the Break'. Now he was in the prison for the fourth time and all of a sudden expressed the wish to appear in the O-Level German Examination which was actually an effort to break the prison. Thinking that Evans may have a genuine interest in O-level German, the Governor wanted to give him a chance. For this, a German teacher would come to teach him for ten months in the prison. But he doesn't want Evans to disgrace him by escaping his premises and so he gets involved in the security arrangements himself.

Evans was placed in the heavily guarded Recreational Block, just across D wing. There were two locked doors between his cell and the yard which boasted of a high wall. Moreover, all the prison officers were also on the alert. The Governor got a microphone installed in Evans' cell while Stephens kept a hawk's eye on Evans.

Two prison officers, Mr. Jackson and Mr. Stephens, thoroughly checked his cell for any sign of a possible escape. Even his razor, nail-file and nail scissors were taken away. But hitting on a tiny emotional cord hidden in the stern looking Jackson, Evans managed to retain his filthy bobble hat by claiming it to be his "lucky charm."

Evans cell was bugged so that the Governor could himself listen to each and every conversation in the cell. The invigilator Rev. S. McLeery left his house at 8:45 am as the exam was to begin at 9:15 am. McLerry came with a brown suitcase, having semi-inflated rubber ring, needed for hemorrhoids. Stephen sitting outside the cell every now and then peeped into the cell.

The exam went on smoothly. Stephen escorted the invigilator to the main gate and looked into Evan's cell and found the invigilator McLeery (actually Evans) wounded and informed the Governor. The latter informed that he was alright and asked them to let him to follow Evans. Who had left Thus he escaped the prison. When the invigilator was not found in the hospital they went to the residence of Rev. S. Mc Leery only to find him 'bound and gagged in his study in Broad Street'. He had been there, since 8.15 a.m. Now everything was clear to the Governor. Evan escaped the prison the fourth time. But by taking the hint from the correction slip the Governor reached the hotel where Evans was staying. He captured him and came to know how he planned his escape. The Governor said that his game was over. Evans surrendered himself to the Governor. Evans was handcuffed and sent away with a prison officer in the prison van. But here again he befooled the Governor. Both the prison officer and the prison van were part of the plan devised by Evan's friends.

Once again he was a free bird.

7. EVANS TRIES AN O-LEVEL

by **Colin Dexter**

CHARACTER SKETCH: James Roderick Evans

James Roderick Evans was a very cunning, smart and a deceitful prisoner. He was imprisoned in H.M. Oxford prison under the careful vigil of the Governor and other prison officials. Originally a non-violent kleptomaniac, he was arrested multiple times which made him a thief in the end. However, he was shrewd enough to be able to escape from the prison as many as three times. Therefore, he was famous by the name of "Evans the Break".

He was very amusing and good at making friends. Though he did not have an attractive appearance, he had a cheerful smile. He had the ability to get people to do whatever he wanted. He also had a way with deception. He took special care while disguising himself as others, especially in the case where he disguised himself as the invigilator. We never see him losing his cool which tells us that he is supremely confident of himself and always has a backup plan at hand. With his charm and his expertise, he is almost like a negative hero.

CHARACTER SKETCH: The Governor

The Governor of the H.M. prison, Oxford appears to be considerate and kind-hearted fellow at the start as he arranges for an O-Level examination for a prisoner notorious for his ability to escape from the prison. However, he is quite skeptical of Evans and makes every arrangement to make sure that Evans doesn't escape.

He is the primary antagonist of the main character Evans. He has been characterised as an intelligent and able prison officer but in the end, he turns out to be 'good-for-a-giggle-Governor'. The Governor tries to exert all caution but Evans eventually manages to escape. This was mainly due to the lapse in communication and flawless execution of work.

Reference to Context

Read the extracts given below and answer the questions that follow.

I.   **"Evans the Break" as the prison officers called him. Thrice he'd escaped from prison, and but for the recent wave of unrest in the maximum-security establishments up north, he wouldn't now be gracing the Governor's premises in Oxford; and the Governor was going to make absolutely certain that he wouldn't be disgracing them.**

   (a)   Why was Evans called 'Evans the Break'?

   (b)   How did the Governor, Oxford Prison describe Evans to the Secretary Examination Board?

   (c)   What facts about Evans did the Governor of Oxford Prison not reveal to the Secretary of the Examination Board?

   (d)   Why was Evans put in the Oxford Prison?

II. **Jackson was the senior prison officer on D Wing, and he and Evans had already become warm enemies. At Jackson's side stood Officer Stephens, a burly, surly-looking man, only recently recruited to the profession.**

   (a)   Name the title.

   (b)   Name the author.

   (c)   Who were the two visitors that came to Evans's cell in the morning?

   (d)   What did they want to do?

III. **"Me 'at? Huh!" Evans put his right hand lovingly on top of the filthy woollen, and smiled sadly. "D'you know, Mr Jackson, it's the only thing that's ever brought me any sort o' luck in life. Kind o' lucky charm, if you know what I mean. And today I thought — well, with me exam and all that..."**

   (a)   How do we know that Evans had no chance of getting through the O-level German examination?

   (b)   Why did he take the test?

   (c)   What reason did Evans give to keep his hat on his head?

   (d)   What was the actual reason?

IV. **McLeery's hitherto amiable demeanour was slightly ruffled by this tasteless little pleasantry, and he answered Jackson somewhat sourly. "If ye must know, I suffer from haemorrhoids, and when I'm sitting down for any length o' time —"**

   (a)   Who was McLeery?

   (b)   What were the contents of the small brown suitcase that McLeery carried?

   (c)   Jackson found a puzzling thing in McLeery's suitcase. What was it?

   (d)   How did McLeery explain it?

V.   **"Elsfield Way", McLeery had said; and there it was staring up at the Governor from the last few lines of the German text: "From Elsfield Way drive to the Headington roundabout, where..." Yes, of course. The Examinations Board was in Elsfield Way, and someone from the Board must have been involved in the escape plan from the very beginning: the question paper itself, the correction slip...**

   (a)   Who was Carter? What did the Governor ask him to do?

   (b)   What did the Detective Superintendent inform the Governor about Evans?

   (c)   What clues did the answer sheet of Evans provide to the Governor?

   (d)   Why did the Governor send one of his teams to Newbury?

ANSWER KEY

I.

(a) Evans was called 'Evans the Break' because he had escaped from the prison thrice. Seeing his ability to deceive the prison officers, everybody called him by that name.

(b) The Governor described Evans to be a pleasant sort of a chap. He called him one of the stars at Christmas concert. The Governor further said that Evans is not a violent person and his only vice is that he is a congenital kleptomaniac.

(c) The Governor of Oxford Prison did not reveal to the Secretary of the Examination Board that Evans was called 'Evans the Break' by the prison officers. He had already escaped from the prison three times.

(d) James Roderick Evans was a kleptomaniac. Due to his tendency to attempt another jailbreak, he was put in the Oxford Prison at Carfax.

II.

(a) Evans Tries An O-Level

(b) Colin Dexter

(c) The two visitors that came to Evans's cell were Jackson and Stephens. Jackson was a senior officer while Stephens was newly recruited to the profession.

(d) They wanted to take all the sharp objects out of Evans's cell because he could blackmail or injure anyone during exam.

III.

(a) Evans did not have any chance of getting through the O-level German examination because he was not able to understand even a simple German expression like "Guten Glück."

(b) Evans took the test in an attempt to plan his escape from prison.

(c) Evans wore a bobble hat at the time of his examination. When he was asked to remove that, Evans pleaded to let stay it because he believed it was his lucky charm.

(d) Since Evans had clipped his hair short to pass off as Mcleery later, he needed to keep his hat on to avoid being detected.

IV.

(a) Rev. Stuart McLeery was a parson at St. Mary Mags, a monastery. He was supposed to invigilate Evan's examination at the Oxford Prison.

(b) The contents of the small brown suitcase that McLeery carried were a sealed question paper envelope, a yellow invigilation form, a special 'authentication' card from the Examination Board, a paper knife, a Bible, a copy of 'The Church Times' and a smallish semi-inflated rubber ring.

(c) A small semi-inflated rubber ring in McLeery's suitcase puzzled Jackson. It was about twelve inches in diameter.

(d) McLeery explained that he suffered from haemorrhoids. He needed the rubber ring when he was sitting down for some length of time.

V.

(a) Carter was a detective superintendent. The Governor told him to take McLeery along with him as he was the only one who could help in locating Evans.

(b) McLeery informed the Governor that he had spotted Evans drive off along Elsfield Way. They chased the car but had lost the track. So, they assumed that Evans must have come back into the city.

(c) The clues left on the question paper were part of a well-laid out plan. It helped the Governor to locate the place where Evans was hiding.

(d) The Governor sent one of his teams to Newbury on the instructions given in the correction slip. He thought that the best place to search for Evans was Newbury.

MIND MAP

SUMMARY OF THE STORY

The "Memories of Childhood", written by Zitkala-Sa and Bama has extracts from the writings of two different female writers from the marginalized communities.

The Cutting of My Long Hair—Zitkala-Sa

The first part deals with the account of Simmons, An American Indian, who fought against the prejudices of the society against American Indians. She describes her experiences on her first day at the Carlisle Indian School. Zitkala-Sa's first day at school is unpleasant. The noise made by the breakfast bell, the clatter of the shoes and the constant murmuring voices of foreign tongue annoyed her. She was forced to wear clothes that were considered undignified in her culture. At the breakfast table, she does not understand the rules and makes several mistakes.

More atrocities were to follow for the new girl. Zitkala-Sa's friend overhears a talk about cutting the long hair of the new girls. For Ziatkala-Sa this was absolutely atrocious. Zitkala-Sa learned from her mother that hair would be shingled only for the unskilled warrior, cowards and mourners. She decided to fight back and got herself hidden in a dim room under the bed. Everybody looked for her and called her name but eventually she was caught. Her voluble protests bear no fruit and her hair is also shingled forcibly on the very first day. This extract describes the narrator's agony. She lost her beautiful long hair. Nobody provided comfort to her. So she felt herself as one of the many animals by a herder.

We too are Human Beings—Bama

The second part is an excerpt from the autobiography 'Karukku' by Bama – a Tamil Dalit.

Bama was an innocent child living in a village. She had never heard of the word untouchability during her childhood. Certain small incidents of her life made her feel that she was born in the marginalized caste. She was a peppy girl. She used to walk back home from school and covered ten minutes of walk in half an hour to one hour as she watched all the fun games such as street play, puppet show, snake charmer, performing monkey, the Maariyaata temple and the pongal offerings being cooked in front of the temple. The plethora of beauty that she experienced on the way back from school made her very happy.

Once when she was in the class 3, while going home, she saw her people working hard work, the landlords humiliated them. Bama further narrates how an elder of their street was humiliated just because he belonged to the Dalit community. The village landlord sent the elderly man to get some vadai for him. The man held the packet by its string. He was not supposed to touch the packet as his touch would pollute the vadai. That is why; he had to carry the packet by its string. At first, she was amused but her brother told her that they belonged to a low caste. So people from upper caste believed that the food packet would be polluted, if it was touched by them. When Bama's elder brother told her all the reasons behind this, her mind filled with revolt. Not only this, her brother was once asked about the street he lived in to determine the caste he belonged to. She was enraged thinking why her elders worked so hard for those people who despised them so much. She wanted her people to stop paying undue respect and reverence to the upper caste people. Her brother told her that if they studied hard and made progress in their lives, it would help them in throwing away the indignities. Education, he said was their weapon with which they could fight back the society. Bama did the same and got many friends in her life. Education gave her double-sided sword to fight very sharply against the unjustified caste system.

8. MEMORIES OF CHILDHOOD

by **Zitkala-Sa and Bama**

CHARACTER SKETCH: Zitkala-Sa

Zitkala-Sa's real name was Gertrude Simmons. She was a native American who was sent to the Carlisle Indian school at a young age. On the first day, she felt like she had lost her freedom. She faced indignity, indiscrimination and exploitation. She was forced to get her hair shingled against which she protested to the best of her capability. She ran away, hid under her bed but finally had to surrender. She was treated like a wooden toy. She represents all the native American women who were exploited at the hands of their masters. She suffered extreme humiliation and was treated like an animal. She had to speak a new language, wear short skirts and shoes. But despite all of this barbarism, Zitkala-Sa showed her resistance. She didn't give up meekly and protested till the end, though she didn't succeed.

CHARACTER SKETCH: Bama

Bama was a small innocent school girl from a Dalit community in south India. She was unaware of the discrimination on the basis of caste. She was upset to experience the distinction based on class and caste. They could not touch food and other items of the upper caste people. They had to work for them and bow their heads before them. When she was told by her brother, about the reality, she was angry. Her spirit revolted against this injustice. She felt terribly sad and agitated. She could not understand this inhuman treatment since all are human beings. She wanted honour for all. Her brother Annan told her that she could do away with these indignities if she worked hard. When she realized that only education could bring the change, she resolved to choose a constructive path and studied hard and topped in the class. In this way, she won everyone's respect and became a role model for all the Dalit women.

Reference to Context

Read the extracts given below and answer the questions that follow.

THE CUTTING OF MY LONG HAIR (ZITKALA-SA)

I. **The first day in the land of apples was a bitter-cold one; for the snow still covered the ground, and the trees were bare. A large bell rang for breakfast, its loud metallic voice crashing through the belfry overhead and into our sensitive ears. The annoying clatter of shoes on bare floors gave us no peace.**

    (a)   What did Zitkala-Sa remember about her 'first day in the land of apples'?

    (b)   How did Zitkala-Sa react to the various sounds that came when the large bell rang for breakfast?

    (c)   "*I felt like sinking to the floor,*" says Zitkala-Sa. When did she feel so and why?

    (d)   How were the Indian girls dressed?

II. **"No, I will not submit! I will struggle first!" I answered. I watched my chance, and when no one noticed, I disappeared. I crept up the stairs as quietly as I could in my squeaking shoes, — my moccasins had been exchanged for shoes. Along the hall I passed, without knowing whither I was going.**

    (a)   What did Judewin tell Zitkala-Sa?

    (b)   How did she react to it?

    (c)   Why did Zitkala-Sa not want her hair to be cut short?

    (d)   How did Zitkala-Sa try to prevent the shingling of her hair?

WE TOO ARE HUMAN BEINGS (BAMA)

III. **At times, people from various political parties would arrive, put up a stage and harangue us through their mikes. Then there might be a street play, or a puppet show, or a "no magic, no miracle" stunt performance. All these would happen from time to time. But almost certainly there would be some entertainment or other going on.**

    (a)   How long it would take Bama to walk home from her school and why?

    (b)   What were the articles in stalls and shops that fascinated Bama on her way back from school?

    (c)   What sort of shows or entertainment in the streets attracted Bama?

    (d)   What actions of the people would Bama watch keenly in the bazaar?

IV. **Annan told me all these things. And he added, "Because we are born into this community, we are never given any honour or dignity or respect; we are stripped of all that. But if we study and make progress, we can throw away these indignities. So study with care, learn all you can. If you are always ahead in your lessons, people will come to you of their own accord and attach themselves to you. Work hard and learn."**

    (a)   What was going on at the opposite corner when Bama came to her street one day?

    (b)   How did Bama come to know about untouchability?

    (c)   Why did the landlord's man ask Bama's brother on which street he lived?

    (d)   What advice did Annan offer Bama?

V. **And I studied hard, with all my breath and being, in a frenzy almost. As Annan had urged, I stood first in my class. And because of that, many people became my friends.**

    (a)   Identify the prose.

    (b)   Name the author.

    (c)   Who is 'I' in the above lines?

    (d)   Do you think Bama followed the advice that Annan gave to her?

ANSWER KEY

I. (a) Zitkala-Sa remembered the beginning of the first day in the land of apples as a bitterly cold one. The trees were bare. A large bell rang for breakfast. Its loud metallic sound crashed through the belfry overhead and into their sensitive ears.

(b) The annoying clatter of shoes on bare floors gave her no peace. She received a cultural shock because of the unknown language. Her spirit tore itself in struggling for its lost freedom.

(c) Zitkala-Sa felt sinking to the floor when the blanket she had donned over her immodest-looking dress was stripped from her shoulders. She felt uncomfortable and ashamed in her tight-fitting clothes.

(d) The Indian girls were in stiff shoes and tightly sticking dresses. The small girls wore sleeved aprons and shingled hair.

II. (a) Judewin warned Zitkala-Sa that she had overheard the white woman saying that Zitkala-Sa's long and heavy hair would be cut. Judewin also advised her to submit and resign to her fate.

(b) Zitkala-Sa reacted strongly and said that she would not give up without struggling. She decided to resist and stand-up against it.

(c) Zitkala-Sa belonged to a Native American warrior tribe. Their tradition was to keep long and heavy hair. Only those warriors captured by the enemy had their hair shingled. Therefore for her, this was absolutely atrocious.

(d) When no one was noticing, Zitkala-Sa crept up the stairs and found a large dark room to hide in. She hid under the bed farthest from the door.

III. (a) Though it was possible to cover the distance in ten minutes, it took Bama half an hour to walk home from her school. This was because; many attractions on the way slowed her down.

(b) Bama witnessed a variety of interesting things which fascinated her. She saw the dried fish stall, the sweet stall and the stall selling fried snacks. Then there were wild lemurs, needles being sold, clay beads and tools for cleaning out the ears on sale.

(c) The snake charmer, street plays, puppet shows and stunt performances were a few interesting things that attracted Bama. She also noticed the pongal offerings being cooked in front of the temple.

(d) She watched the way each waiter would cool the coffee in the various coffee clubs. She would also watch how people, chopping up onion, would turn their eyes elsewhere to avoid irritation in their eyes.

IV. (a) The elder was carrying a small packet by its string. He was holding it out so as not to touch it. There seemed to be Vadais in the packet because it was stained with oil. Bama wanted to laugh because that way the packet could get undone and the Vadais could fall out.

(b) When Bama saw an elder of her community carrying a packet of Vadais by its string, she narrated the incident to her brother. Her brother told her that they were not supposed to touch the upper caste people. Their touch could pollute them. It was only then that Bama knew of the social discrimination faced by their community.

(c) When Annan was returning home from the library, the landlord's man asked him his name. He asked this to ascertain Annan's caste, because all the lower caste people lived in one area of the town.

(d) Annan asked Bama to study hard and top all exams. He also told her that if she was successful in life, people would come to her of their own accord.

V. (a) Memories Of Childhood

(b) Zitkala-Sa and Bama

(c) In the above lines the author 'Bama' is referred to as 'I'.

(d) Yes, Bama did follow Annan's advice. She studied hard and stood first in her class.

www.ingramcontent.com/pod-product-compliance
Lightning Source LLC
LaVergne TN
LVHW081045210726
843510LV00014B/1038